500 Quick Bread Recipes

(500 Quick Bread Recipes - Volume 1)

Valeria Tyler

Content

CHAPTER 1: QUICK BREAD BREAKFAST RECIPES..10

1. Almond Flour Berry Muffins....................10
2. Amazing Apple Nut Muffins....................10
3. Applesauce Raisin Muffins....................11
4. Aunt Emy's Baking Powder Biscuits.........11
5. Banana Cream Cheese Stuffed French Toast 12
6. Bananas Foster Muffins..............................12
7. Bazlamaca (Croatian Cornbread)...............13
8. Better Bran Muffins....................................13
9. Biscuits And Country Sausage Gravy (Diabetic Friendly)..14
10. Blueberry Banana Bread.............................14
11. Blueberry Oat/Yogurt Muffins.................15
12. Bob's Red Mill Wheat Biscuits...................15
13. Breakfast Biscuits (Pampered Chef).........16
14. Buttermilk Cathead Biscuits.......................16
15. Buttermilk And Sour Cherry Scones For Afternoon Tea And Picnics.................................17
16. Buttery Farm Biscuits.................................17
17. Cheesy Bacon Egg Muffins........................18
18. Chocolate And Roasted Cherry "Scones".18
19. Cranberry Oat Bran Muffins......................19
20. Cranberry Orange Pecan Quick Bread......20
21. Cranberry Apricot Flax Seed Muffins.......20
22. Delicious Blueberry Muffins With Crumb Topping..21
23. Diabetic Blueberry Muffins........................21
24. Easy Moist Banana Blueberry Muffins......22
25. Feather Light Bran Muffins........................22
26. Ginger Scones The Inn At Little Washington..23
27. Gourmet 1, 2, 3 Biscuit...............................23
28. Healthy Heart Muffins................................24
29. Healthy Pumpkin Pomegranate Muffins...24
30. Irish Soda Bread Scones..............................25
31. Jillian Michael's Blueberry Banana Muffins 25
32. Low Fat Strawberry Banana Bread............26
33. Marvelous! Mocha Muffins........................27
34. Oat Bran And Banana Muffins..................27
35. Ohhhhh So Good Monkey Bread Muffins 28
36. Orange Nut Muffins....................................28
37. Orange And Poppy Seed Quick Bread......29
38. Orange Cranberry Muffins.........................29
39. Pb J Muffins..30
40. Poppy Seed Crumble Muffins....................30
41. Protein Muffins...31
42. Raisin Walnut Muffins (Gift Mix In A Jar) 31
43. Raspberry Poppy Seed Muffins..................32
44. Red River Date Muffins..............................33
45. Ricotta Cheese Scones.................................33
46. Scones With Leftover Cranberry Sauce.....34
47. Sesame Crunch Banana Muffins................34
48. Sour Cream Berry Muffins..........................35
49. Strawberry Shortcake Muffins....................36
50. Sunshine Blueberry Muffins........................36
51. Texas Sized Lemon Muffins........................37
52. The Everything Muffins..............................37
53. The Ultimate Coconut Scones....................38
54. Whole Wheat Carrot Muffins.....................38
55. Yule Oatcakes...39

CHAPTER 2: QUICK BREAD DESSERT RECIPES..40

56. Apple Muffins (Nova Scotia Style)............40
57. Banana Bundt Bread....................................40
58. Banana Caramel Biscuit For One...............41
59. Berry Citrus Mini Muffins..........................41
60. Choc A Mocha Muffins...............................42
61. Chocolate Crispy Biscuits............................42
62. Cinnamon Nut Flatbread............................43
63. Cornbread (Low Fat)...................................43
64. Cranberry Nut Muffins................................44
65. Crumbly, Sweet And Buttery Cornbread ..44
66. Dulce De Leche And Praline (Nougat) Muffins..45
67. Easy And Quick Corn Dog Muffins..........45
68. Gingerbread Scone.......................................46
69. Gluten Free Yorkshire Pudding.................46
70. Gorgeous Chocolate Muffins.....................47
71. Healthy Apple Carrot Zucchini Muffins...47
72. Honey Biscuits (Cookies)............................48
73. Hugh Yorkshire Puddings...........................49
74. Italian Wine Biscuits....................................49
75. Kristie's Shortbread Biscuits.......................49
76. Lemon Currant Biscuits..............................50

77. Lemon Yoghurt Muffins! 50
78. Lemonberry Muffins 51
79. Light Chocolate Chip Scones 52
80. Low Fat Pumpkin Pie Muffins 52
81. Low Fat Apple Oatmeal Muffins With Walnuts 53
82. Macadamia Burnt Butter Biscuits 53
83. Maida Heatter's Blueberry Muffins 54
84. Maple/Bran Dog Biscuits 55
85. Meemaw's Sweet Cornbread 55
86. Mickey's Quick Sticky Buns 56
87. Nutella And Banana Bread 56
88. Peanut Butter And Chocolate Chip Muffins 57
89. Pistachio Banana Bread 57
90. Pistachio Muffins 58
91. Pumpkin Raspberry Muffins 58
92. Sweet Coffee House Scones II 59
93. Sweet Molasses Bran Muffins 59
94. Sweet Potato Nut Bread 60
95. Sweet And Moist Banana Muffins 60
96. Traditional Scottish Pure Butter Shortbread Cookies Biscuits 61
97. Triple Chocolate Zucchini Loaf, Or Muffins 61
98. Valentine Biscuits 62
99. Viennese Biscuits 63
100. Viennese Shortbread Biscuits 63
101. Wheat Banana Walnut Chocolate Chip Bread 64
102. Yorkshire Pudding With Blue Cheese 64
103. Yorkshire Puddings I 65
104. Yummy And Easy Raisin Muffins 65
105. Zesty Blueberry Muffins 66

CHAPTER 3: QUICK BREAD PICNIC RECIPES 66

106. All Bran Pineapple And Fruit Muffins 66
107. Almond, Orange, And Blueberry Muffins 67
108. Applesauce Banana Bread 68
109. Banana Muffins With Chocolate Hazelnut Crunchies 68
110. Chocolate Chip It Snackin Muffins 69
111. Cosmic Chocolate Chip Banana Muffins 69
112. Cream Cheese Muffins 70
113. Flax Morning Glory Muffins 70
114. Flying Biscuit Cafe Low Fat Banana Muffins 71
115. Good For You Banana Bread 71
116. Grannies Cheese Scone Recipe 72
117. High Fiber Bran Muffins 72
118. Honey Graham Muffins 73
119. Honey Mustard And Cheddar Muffins 73
120. Hungarian Biscuits 74
121. Jalapeño Cornbread 74
122. Jana's Grandmother's Cornbread 75
123. Lemon Verbena Blueberry Scones 75
124. Lemonade Muffins 76
125. Lincolnshire Poacher Cheese Scones Strictly For Grown Ups! 77
126. Low Fat (But You Wouldn't Know It) Banana Bread 77
127. Low Fat Peachy Oatmeal Muffins 78
128. Moist Apple Muffins With Pecan Topping 78
129. Moist Jumbo Banana Wheat/Oat Bran Muffins 79
130. Muffins A Vegetable Medley 80
131. Oaty Banana Mini Muffins (Oamc) 80
132. Onion And Red Pepper Corn Muffins 81
133. Popcorn Muffins 81
134. Raisin Pumpkin Muffins 82
135. Raisinet Banana Muffins 82
136. Raspberry Vanilla Nut Muffins 83
137. Red Pepper Corn Muffins 83
138. Rosemary Scones 84
139. Round Up Valley Muffins #RSC 84
140. Soaked Grain Muffins Or Quick Bread 85
141. Southern Cheesy Date Biscuits 86
142. Spice Oat Muffins Weight Watchers Point Value 3 86
143. Sugar And Spice! Glazed Lemon Tea Scones 87
144. Tahini Sunflower Seed Scones 88
145. Toblerone Cream Cheese Muffins 88
146. Tortilla Chip Cornbread 89
147. Very Tasty Cheesy Cheddar And Oat Scones 90
148. Whole Grain Spelt Biscuits 90
149. Yeo Valley Lemon Drizzle Cake/Muffins 91
150. Yogurt Bran Muffins 91

CHAPTER 4: QUICK BREAD CHOCOLATE RECIPES 92

151. Awesome Chocolate Chocolate Chip Muffins 92
152. Banana Bran Muffins With Lindt Chocolate Inside 93
153. Banana Bran Muffins With A Hint Of Chocolate 93
154. Banana Carob Chocolate Muffins 94
155. Banana Chocolate Muffins 94
156. Banana Muffins With Chocolate Peanut Frosting 95
157. CHOCOLATE RASPBERRY MUFFINS 95
158. COLOSSAL Chocolate Chunk Muffins ... 96
159. Cappuccino Chocolate Chunk Muffins 96
160. Chocolate Almond Scones 97
161. Chocolate Anzac Biscuits 98
162. Chocolate Banana Muffin 98
163. Chocolate Banana Nut Muffins 99
164. Chocolate Breakfast Muffins 99
165. Chocolate Brownie Muffins 100
166. Chocolate Carrot Squash Muffins 100
167. Chocolate Cherry Nut Muffins 101
168. Chocolate Chocolate Banana Bread 102
169. Chocolate Cinnamon Scones 102
170. Chocolate Cornbread 103
171. Chocolate Fruit Muffins 103
172. Chocolate Hazelnut Crinkle Biscuits 104
173. Chocolate Lava Muffins 105
174. Chocolate Lovers Wheat Bran Muffins ... 105
175. Chocolate Nut Wafers 106
176. Chocolate Oatmeal Biscuits 106
177. Chocolate Pudding Zucchini Muffins 107
178. Chocolate Pumpkin Muffins 107
179. Chocolate Streusel Pecan Muffins 108
180. Chocolate Viennese Biscuits 108
181. Dee's Chocolate Banana Bread 109
182. Dee's Chocolate Muffins 109
183. Double Chocolate Banana Oatmeal Muffins (Fiber) 110
184. Double Chocolate Muffins 110
185. Eggless, Milkless Chocolate Muffins 111
186. English Scones With Chocolate Chunks. 112
187. Fat Free Chocolate Banana Muffins 112
188. Fat Free Chocolate Muffins 113
189. Ginger Chocolate Chewy Biscuits 113
190. Gluten Free Chocolate Peanut Butter Banana Bread 114
191. Gluten Free, Protein And Fiber Rich Chocolate Strawberry Muffin 114
192. Healthy Low Fat Blueberry (Or Chocolate) Oatmeal Muffins 115
193. High Fiber Chocolate Zucchini Muffins 116
194. Hurricane Chocolate Muffins 116
195. I Want To Keep This A Secret ? Chocolate Muffins 117
196. Low Fat Chocolate Banana Muffins 117
197. Low Fat Double Chocolate Muffins 118
198. Magic Microwave Muffin Sinless Chocolate Banana (Gluten Free) 118
199. Mexican Chocolate Oatmeal Pepita Mini Muffins 120
200. No Fat Chocolate Zucchini Muffins 121
201. Orange And Chocolate Muffins 121
202. Peanut Butter Chocolate Drops Muffins 122
203. Peanutty Chocolate Banana Bread 122
204. Pomegranate And Chocolate Chunk Scones 123
205. Pumpkin Chocolate Muffins 123
206. Quick Chocolate Drop Scones 124
207. Simple Chocolate Biscuits 125
208. Sour Cream Banana Bread With Chocolate Glaze 125
209. Sour Cream Chocolate Chocolate Chip Banana Bread 126
210. Triple Chocolate Quick Bread 127
211. Triple Chocolate Zucchini Muffins 127
212. Vegan Chocolate Chunk Muffins 128
213. Vegan Chocolate Nut Butter Muffins 129
214. Whole Wheat Vegan Chocolate Zucchini Mini Muffins 129
215. Yummy Chocolate Biscuits 130

CHAPTER 5: QUICK BREAD FRUIT RECIPES 130

216. 5 Ingriedient Banana And Brown Butter Muffins 130
217. Any Fruit Muffins 131
218. Apple Hazelnut Muffins (Gf, Vegan) 131
219. Apple And Cheddar Cheese Muffins 132
220. Apple And Cheddar Scones 133
221. Apple And Cinnamon Breakfast Muffins (Nigella) 134
222. Apple And Orange Muffins 134
223. Apple, Apricot And Raisin Muffins 135

224. Apricot And Cheese Danish Muffins 135
225. Avocado And Bacon Muffins 136
226. Banana Applesauce Blueberry And Walnut Fat Free Quick Bread 137
227. Banana Yogurt Protein Muffins 137
228. Banana And Maple Muffins 138
229. Blueberries And Cream Mall Muffins 138
230. Blueberry (or Raisin) Bran Muffins 139
231. Blueberry And Pecan Scones 140
232. Cranberry And White Chocolate Scones 140
233. Date And Raisin Muffins 141
234. Date And Spice Muffins 141
235. English Fruit Muffins (Bread Machine) .. 142
236. Fresh Fruit Muffins 142
237. Fresh Lemon And Ginger Muffins 143
238. Fruit Nut Brown Bread 143
239. Fruit Compote Muffins 144
240. Fruit N Nut Muffins 145
241. Fruit Nut Harvest Muffins 145
242. Fruit Upside Down Muffin 146
243. Gluten Free Apple And Cinnamon Muffins 146
244. Gourmet Scones Add Any Fruit! 147
245. Healthy Fruit Muffins 148
246. Holiday Fruit And Nut Gems 148
247. Incredible Oat Bran Muffins, Plain, Blueberry Or Banana 149
248. Jimmy Griffin's Perfect Raspberry And Raisin Irish Scone 149
249. Kaak Lebi Hilw (Orange And Cumin Biscuits) 150
250. Kittencal's Muffin Shop Jumbo Blueberry Or Strawberry Muffins 151
251. Lemon And Chia Seed Muffins 152
252. Low Fat Fruit Muffins 152
253. Low Fat Fruit And Nut Banana Bread.... 153
254. Mimi's Raspberry And Lemon Muffins With Streusel Topping 154
255. Orange, Banana And Oat Bran Breakfast Muffins 154
256. Overnight Banana Sticky Buns With Pecans 155
257. Papaya Or Mango Oat Muffins 156
258. Passion Fruit Raspberry Muffins 157
259. Peach And Brown Sugar Muffins 158
260. Peach And Tomato Muffins 158
261. Pear And Ginger Muffins 159
262. Pear And Pumpkin Muffins 159
263. Pineapple Coconut Muffins 160
264. Pineapple And Sour Cream Muffins 160
265. Pumpkin Fruit Bread/muffins 161
266. Pumpkin Fruit And Nut Muffins 162
267. Quick And Easy English Date And Nut Bread 162
268. Raisin Or Date Bran Muffins 164
269. Raisins And/or Cranberry Scones 164
270. Rosemary, Pear, And Asiago Scones 165
271. Scrumptious Bran Muffins With Fruit.... 165
272. Spicy Apple And Sultana Muffins 166
273. Strawberry And Cream Scones 167
274. Tea And Fruit Muffins 168
275. The Blueberry And Straw Berry Muffins Ever 168
276. Tomato And Parmesan Breakfast Muffins 169
277. Tropical Fruit Muffins 169
278. White Chocolate Fruit Scones 170
279. White Chocolate, Coconut And Banana Muffins 170
280. Whole Fruit Orange Bran Muffins 171
281. Wholemeal Fruit Muffins 171

CHAPTER 6: QUICK BREAD NUT RECIPES 172

282. Aidan's Banana Nut Bread 172
283. Almond Chocolate Biscuits 173
284. Anne's Banana Nut Bread 173
285. Anzac Biscuits (Cookies) 174
286. Atwood Inn Breakfast Scones 174
287. Aunt Cora's Nut Bread 175
288. Banana Bread With Coconut Rum 175
289. Banana Crunch Muffins (w/grape Nuts) 176
290. Banana Macadamia Nut Bread (Abm) 177
291. Banana Macadamia Nut Muffins 177
292. Banana Nut Cake/Bread 178
293. Banana Nut Chocolate Chip Bread 178
294. Banana Nut Crunch Muffins 179
295. Banana Nut French Toast 179
296. Banana Nut Scones 180
297. Banana Nut Snack Muffins For Bill 180
298. Banana Snack Muffins 181
299. Banana, Coconut Lime Bread 181
300. Banana, Orange Pecan Muffins 182
301. Banana Nut Muffins 183

302. Blueberry Pecan Muffins 183
303. Braided Banana Date Nut Bread (ABM) 184
304. Buttery Cinnamon Nut Bread With Almond Glaze 184
305. Cheddar Apple Nut Bread..........................185
306. Chocolatey Delight Pumpkin Oat Muffins 185
307. Cinnamon Coffee Scones 186
308. Coconut Choc Chip Muffins..........................187
309. Coconut Banana Muffins..........................187
310. Cranberry Nut Scones 188
311. Cranberry Walnut Scones 188
312. Dorothy's Banana Nut Bread..........................189
313. Double Chocolate Macadamia Nut Muffins 189
314. Easy Banana Bread Chocolate Nut..........190
315. Easy Low Carb Lemon Blueberry Nut Butter Muffins..........................191
316. Every Which Way Quick Bread...............191
317. Fiber One Banana Nut Muffins 192
318. Fig, Date, And Walnut Quick Bread........192
319. Gluten Free Moist Mango And Nut Bread 193
320. Golden Harvest Muffins II 194
321. Grain Free Blueberry Muffins..................194
322. Great Aunt Marie's Banana Nut Bread ...195
323. Greek Muffins..........................195
324. Hartson's Moist Banana Strawberry Nut Bread..........................196
325. Hawaiian Nut Bread 197
326. Healthy Delicious Muffins 197
327. Healthy Apple Spice Muffins 198
328. Healthy Good Morning Muffins 199
329. Holiday Banana Bread 199
330. Holiday Raisin Nut Pumpkin Bread 200
331. Judy's Date Muffins 200
332. Lemon Nut Bread 201
333. Lower Fat Banana Nut Chip Muffins......201
334. Mama's Banana Bread 202
335. Maple Nut Muffins 203
336. Maple Pecan Biscuits 203
337. Merry Cherry Nut Yeast Scones 204
338. Mini Pecan Muffins..........................204
339. Mr. Food's Date Nut Bread......................205
340. Noe Valley Bakery Blueberry Pecan Scones 205
341. North Carolina Applesauce Muffins........206
342. Nut Butter Gems 206
343. Nut Muffins 208
344. Oatmeal Banana Raisin Nut Muffins 208
345. Orange Cranberry Nut Bread.................. 209
346. Orange Date Nut Bran Muffins.............. 209
347. Orange Date Pumpkin Bread 210
348. Orange Pecan Bran Muffins 211
349. Peach And Coconut Muffins 211
350. Pecan Cinnamon Muffins 212
351. Pecan Pie Surprise Muffins 212
352. Pennsylvania Grange Banana Nut Bread Grange # 1751 213
353. Perfect Pumpkin Mini Muffins 213
354. Pineapple Muffins With Coconut And Brown Sugar Topping.......................... 214
355. Polenta Quick Bread With Lemon And Thyme 215
356. Pumpkin Banana Nut Muffins 215
357. Sarah's Zucchini Nut Bread 216
358. Scd Gluten Free Cinnamon Apple Scones 217
359. Slovak Nut Bread.......................... 217
360. Sourdough Nut Batter Bread................... 218
361. Spiced Peach Nut Bread.......................... 218
362. Strawberry Pecan Scones.......................... 219
363. Strawberry Macadamia Nut Muffins....... 219
364. Sun Nut Bread (Bread Machine)............. 220
365. Sunburst Quick Bread.............................. 220
366. Super Almond Banana Bread (Gluten/Grain Free!).......................... 221
367. Super Quick Banana Nana Nut Muffins 221
368. Sweet Potato Pecan Biscuits 222
369. Sweet Potato Raisin Muffins 222
370. Terry's Banana Nut Bread........................ 223
371. Ultimate Banana Nut Bread (Cake?) 223
372. Vanilla Glazed And Pecan Streuseled Date Bread 224
373. White Chocolate Banana Muffins........... 225
374. Whole Grain Blueberry Muffins (Health Nut!) 225
375. Whole Wheat Healthy Banana Nut Bread 226
376. Yogurt Cranberry Nut Muffins 227
377. Zucchini Nut Bread By Sheila................. 227

CHAPTER 7: AWESOME QUICK BREAD RECIPES..........................228

378. Almond And Blueberry Muffins 228
379. Amazing Cinnamon Chip Scones 228
380. Apple Cinnamon Streusel Muffins Sugar Free 229
381. Apple Oatmeal Muffins 229
382. Apricot Orange Yogurt Muffins..............230
383. Aunt Annie's Bran Muffins 231
384. Bacon Cheese Biscuits..............................231
385. Baked Creamy Chicken And Cornbread.231
386. Banana Almond Muffins...........................232
387. Banana Bran Oat Muffins.........................233
388. Banana Muffins By Jenny 233
389. Banana Nut Muffins, Healthy..................234
390. Bananaumpkin Muffins............................234
391. Bisquick Cheese Bread Or Biscuits (Like Red Lobster!)..235
392. Boosted Banana Muffins...........................236
393. Bread Pudding Muffins 236
394. Caramelized Butternut Squash Gems......237
395. Carrot Cake Muffins (Good For You!) ...237
396. Cheddar Green Onion Biscuits 238
397. Cheddar Applesauce Muffins...................238
398. Cheddar Scones With Dill 239
399. Cheese Scones With Gomashio...............239
400. Cheesy Buttermilk Drop Biscuits............240
401. Chicken Chile Cheese Muffins.................240
402. Chocolate Fudge Muffins 241
403. Chocolate Hazelnut Swirled Banana Bread (Or Muffins) 242
404. Cornmeal Cheddar Scones 242
405. Cranberry Harvest Muffins 243
406. Curry Spiced Carrot And Date Muffins..244
407. Date And Cheddar Good Day Muffins ..244
408. Daughter's Banana Bread..........................245
409. Delicious Pumpkin Muffins 245
410. Delicious Whole Grain Muffins 246
411. Diabetic Cinnamon Bun Scones..............246
412. Double Chocolate Buckwheat Muffins...247
413. Double Pear Muffins 248
414. Drought Buns (Currant Scones)..............248
415. Easiest Banana Muffins Ever...................249
416. Easy Cheese Scones..................................249
417. Easy Dog Biscuits 250
418. Easy Low Fat Whole Wheat Irish Soda Bread..250
419. Elf Biscuits 250
420. English Muffins With Eggs, Cheese And Ham 251
421. English Royalty Scones............................ 251
422. Fat Free, Sugar Free Whole Wheat Blueberry Muffins... 252
423. Flavorful Sausage Gravy And Biscuits For A Cold Morning.. 253
424. Gelt Biscuits... 253
425. Gluten Free Irish Soda Bread.................. 254
426. Gluten Free Cheddar Bay Biscuits 254
427. Golden Muffins 255
428. Grandma's Scones 255
429. Grandma's Blueberry Banana Applesauce Bread For The Bread Machin............................ 256
430. Green Chilies Corn Muffins 256
431. Green Pistachio Muffins 257
432. Harvest Morning Muffins 258
433. Healthy Butternut Squash Muffins.......... 258
434. Healthy Muffins 259
435. High Fiber Cholesterol Free Oat Bran Muffins 259
436. Honey Vanilla Bran Muffins.................... 260
437. Hot Biscuits 260
438. Jalapeno And Bacon Cornbread Muffins261
439. Kahlua Muffins 261
440. Khanom Puto (A Steamed Sweet Savory Coconut Muffin) 262
441. Kingsbys' No Yeast Biscuits.................... 263
442. Lemon Chocolate Chip Muffins 263
443. Lemon Poppy Seed Surprise Snack Muffins 264
444. Lemon Thyme Biscuits............................. 264
445. Low Fat Sugar Free Zucchini Bread/Muffins... 265
446. Maple Oat Nut Scones Starbucks............ 265
447. Mayonnaise Biscuits (Cookies)................ 266
448. Melissa's Drop Biscuits With Green Onions 266
449. Mile High Biscuits 267
450. Mini Italian Biscuits.................................. 267
451. Mom's Bran Muffins 268
452. Mom's Refrigerator Bran Muffins 268
453. Muesli Muffins (21 Day Wonder Diet: Day 20) 269
454. Oatmeal Walnut Muffins.......................... 269
455. Oatmeal Muffins.. 270
456. Orange Blueberry Scones......................... 270
457. Orange Cranberry Cream Scones 271

458. Orange Marmalade Muffins 272
459. Paleo Apple Cinnamon Muffins 272
460. Parsley And Chive Scones 273
461. Pat's Orange Pecan Muffins 273
462. Peanut Butter Cream Cheese Banana Nut Bread (Healthier Verison) 274
463. Peanut Butter Oatcakes...........................275
464. Pecan Cheese Biscuits 275
465. Pineapple Carrot Muffins 276
466. Pumpkin Bread / Muffins 276
467. Pumpkin Muffins [vegan] 277
468. Quick Gluten Free Scones.........................277
469. Quick Mix Muffins....................................277
470. Ree's Herbed Cornbread...........................278
471. Sage Cornbread..279
472. Scottish Scones 279
473. Snitch Biscuits..280
474. Sour Cream Peach Muffins 280
475. Southern Sausage Onion Cornbread 281
476. Spicy Corn Muffins With Irish Cheddar Cheese..281
477. Spinach Cornbread....................................282
478. Stevia Whole Wheat Banana Bread..........282
479. Stove Top Biscuits 283
480. Strawberry Oat Mini Muffins...................283
481. Sugar Free, Gluten Free, Low Fat Peanut Butter Banana Bread..284
482. Swedish Scones..284
483. Sweet Potato Muffins (Great For After Turkey Day)...285
484. Sweet Squash (Mini) Muffins 285
485. T's Chocolate Chip Scones........................286
486. The Very Best Blueberry Bran Muffins...286
487. Thyme Biscuits 287
488. Vegan Choco Low Fat Muffins 288
489. White Chocolate Chip Cranberry Banana Bread With Coconut Flour 288
490. White Chocolate Macadamia Nut Muffins 289
491. Whole Wheat Banana Muffins.................289
492. Whole Wheat Banana Nut Muffins 290
493. Whole Wheat Pumpkin Muffins...............290
494. Winter Squash Oatmeal Muffins 291
495. Ww Crumb Topped Jumbo Bran Muffins 291
496. Ww Vanilla Biscuits (Cookies).................292
497. Yogurt Honey Health Mini Muffins 292
498. Yorkshire Pudding With Herbs 293
499. Yummy Banana Nut Bread...................... 294
500. Yummy Pumpkin And Cream Cheese Muffins 294

INDEX 296

CONCLUSION 301

Chapter 1: Quick Bread Breakfast Recipes

***

1. Almond Flour Berry Muffins

Serving: 12 muffins, 12 serving(s) | Prep: 15mins | Ready in:

Ingredients

- 2 cups blueberries (frozen or fresh)
- 1/2 cup water
- 2 1/2 cups almond meal
- 1/2 teaspoon baking soda
- 1 teaspoon ground cinnamon
- 1/2 teaspoon pure vanilla extract
- 1/2 cup honey
- 3 eggs

Direction

- Heat oven to 325°F
- In a small saucepan, simmer the berries with the water until the berries release their juice and the mixture has thickened slightly. Let cool.
- Combine the dry ingredients.
- Combine the wet ingredients (berries too) in a separate bowl.
- Add dry ingredients to wet and mix well.
- Evenly fill each baking cup with the batter.
- Bake for 25 to 30 minutes.

Nutrition Information

- Calories: 189.7
- Total Fat: 11.1
- Sodium: 71.5
- Fiber: 3.1
- Saturated Fat: 1.1
- Sugar: 14.9
- Total Carbohydrate: 19.8
- Cholesterol: 46.5
- Protein: 6

2. Amazing Apple Nut Muffins

Serving: 12 muffins, 12 serving(s) | Prep: 15mins | Ready in:

Ingredients

- 1 egg
- 2/3 cup apple juice or 2/3 cup milk
- 1/2 cup vegetable oil
- 1 teaspoon vanilla
- 1/4 cup sugar
- 2 cups flour
- 1/4 cup brown sugar
- 1 tablespoon baking powder
- 1/2 teaspoon salt
- 1/2 cup pecans or 1/2 cup walnuts, chopped
- 1 apple, chopped and peeled
- 1 tablespoon sugar
- 1/2 teaspoon cinnamon

Direction

- Preheat oven to 400.
- In a large bowl, beat egg with juice/milk, oil and vanilla.
- Stir in flour, sugars, baking powder, and salt until moistened.
- Stir in nuts and apple.
- Fill large, paper-lined muffin cups with batter.
- Mix the last amount of sugar and cinnamon and sprinkle on muffins.
- Bake for 20 minutes.

Nutrition Information

- Calories: 245.4
- Total Carbohydrate: 29.8
- Cholesterol: 17.6
- Protein: 3.1
- Sugar: 12.6
- Sodium: 196.3
- Fiber: 1.3
- Total Fat: 13
- Saturated Fat: 1.6

3. Applesauce Raisin Muffins

Serving: 12 serving(s) | Prep: 10mins | Ready in:

Ingredients

- 3 cups flour
- 2 teaspoons baking powder
- 1 teaspoon ground cinnamon
- 1/2 teaspoon ground allspice
- 1/2 teaspoon baking soda
- 1/2 teaspoon salt
- 2/3 cup sugar
- 1 1/3 cups unsweetened applesauce
- 1/3 cup vegetable oil
- 1 teaspoon vanilla extract
- 1/2 cup raisins

Direction

- In large bowl, combine dry ingredients.
- In medium bowl, whisk together the sugar, applesauce, oil and vanilla until well blended.
- Add the applesauce mixture to the flour mixture and stir until just blended. Fold in the raisins.
- Divide batter into muffin tins. Bake 25-28 minutes at 400.

Nutrition Information

- Calories: 241.8
- Cholesterol: 0
- Sugar: 17.4
- Total Carbohydrate: 43.3
- Fiber: 1.5
- Protein: 3.5
- Total Fat: 6.4
- Saturated Fat: 0.8
- Sodium: 211.9

4. Aunt Emy's Baking Powder Biscuits

Serving: 12 serving(s) | Prep: 20mins | Ready in:

Ingredients

- 3 cups flour
- 1/2 cup Crisco
- 3 teaspoons baking powder
- 1 teaspoon salt
- 1 cup milk

Direction

- Stir above dry ingredients together until well blended.
- Add milk slowly and mix well.
- Turn our thickened dough onto hard even surface and knead several times.
- Roll out dough to approximately 1/2 inch thickness.
- Fold dough over to form double thickness.
- Cut out in cylinder shapes.
- Bake at 400 degrees in ungreased pans for 10-15 minutes.

Nutrition Information

- Calories: 202.9
- Protein: 3.9
- Total Fat: 9.6
- Sugar: 0.1
- Total Carbohydrate: 25.1
- Cholesterol: 2.9

- Saturated Fat: 3.1
- Sodium: 295.1
- Fiber: 0.8

5. Banana Cream Cheese Stuffed French Toast

Serving: 12 pieces, 6 serving(s) | Prep: 10mins | Ready in:

Ingredients

- 12 slices of good quality bread
- 4 eggs
- 2 cups milk
- 1 pinch salt
- 8 ounces cream cheese (softened)
- 1 teaspoon confectioners' sugar
- 1 teaspoon vanilla
- 1 ripe banana (mashed in a dash of lemon juice to prevent browning)
- Garnish with
- 1 dash confectioners' sugar
- 1 cup raspberries
- Cool Whip

Direction

- To make the filling: Mash cream cheese, banana, sugar, and vanilla.
- Slice bread in half and make little "half sandwiches" with the filling inside.
- Next, beat the eggs, milk, and salt in a separate bowl.
- Heat butter in a skillet over medium heat.
- Dip the little half-sandwiches in the egg/milk mixture and place in the skillet.
- I cook 4 little half-sandwiches at a time for 3 minutes on the first side and 2 on the second until they are golden brown on each side.
- Sprinkle with confectioner's sugar and top with raspberries and whipped cream!
- Note: To keep them warm while I cook the rest, I keep them in a warm oven as they get done. Also, be sure to add more butter each time you put new sandwiches in the pan.

Nutrition Information

- Calories: 398.9
- Total Carbohydrate: 38.1
- Cholesterol: 194
- Protein: 14
- Sodium: 565.2
- Fiber: 3
- Sugar: 6.6
- Total Fat: 21.3
- Saturated Fat: 11.6

6. Bananas Foster Muffins

Serving: 34-36 muffins | Prep: 15mins | Ready in:

Ingredients

- 1 1/2 cups flour
- 1 1/2 teaspoons baking soda
- 1/4 teaspoon salt
- 1/2 teaspoon cinnamon, plus
- 1/4 teaspoon cinnamon
- 1 1/4 cups mashed ripe bananas (about 3 large bananas)
- 1/4 cup firmly packed dark brown sugar
- 1/2 cup sugar, plus
- 2 tablespoons sugar
- 1/2 cup unsalted butter, melted
- 1/4 cup milk
- 8 tablespoons dark rum (divided use)
- 1 large egg

Direction

- Preheat oven to 350°F.
- Sift flour, baking soda, salt, and 1/2 teaspoons cinnamon into a large bowl. Combine bananas, brown sugar, 1/2 cup sugar, butter, milk, 2 tablespoons rum, and egg in medium bowl. Mix into dry ingredients.

- Fill greased mini-muffin pans 3/4 full.
- Bake until muffins are golden brown and tester inserted into center comes out clean, about 15 minutes. While muffins are baking, dissolve the remaining 2 tablespoons sugar and 1/4 cinnamon into the remaining 6 tablespoons rum. Brush the glaze onto the muffins while still warm in the pan. Cool the muffins on a rack.
- Store tightly covered at room temperature for up to 3 days, or freeze for longer storage.

Nutrition Information

- Calories: 80.3
- Sodium: 76.8
- Sugar: 5.9
- Total Carbohydrate: 10.9
- Cholesterol: 13.7
- Protein: 0.9
- Total Fat: 3
- Saturated Fat: 1.8
- Fiber: 0.3

7. Bazlamaca (Croatian Cornbread)

Serving: 4-6 serving(s) | Prep: 5mins | Ready in:

Ingredients

- 1 lb cream-style cottage cheese
- 1/2 cup brown sugar
- 2 large eggs
- 1/2 teaspoon salt
- 4 tablespoons unsalted butter, melted
- 1/2 cup cornmeal
- 1/2 cup unbleached all-purpose flour
- 1/4 teaspoon baking soda
- 1 cup sour cream

Direction

- Grease a 9 x 9 inch baking pan.
- Preheat the oven to 425 degrees F.
- Mix the first four ingredients together.
- Add the remaining ingredients and mix well.
- Pour the batter into the pan and bake until the top is nice and brown.
- Slice and serve warm with sliced fruit, berries, cream, or syrup.

Nutrition Information

- Calories: 594.3
- Sugar: 27.2
- Total Carbohydrate: 56.1
- Cholesterol: 178.6
- Protein: 22.1
- Total Fat: 31.9
- Sodium: 912.4
- Fiber: 1.5
- Saturated Fat: 18.9

8. Better Bran Muffins

Serving: 12 Muffins | Prep: 20mins | Ready in:

Ingredients

- 1 cup all-purpose flour
- 1/2 cup white sugar
- 2 1/2 teaspoons baking powder
- 1/2 teaspoon baking soda
- 1/2 teaspoon salt
- 1 1/4 cups post 100% bran, all-bran cereal
- 1 cup milk
- 1 egg
- 1/4 cup vegetable oil

Direction

- Stir together Bran cereal and milk. Let stand 5 minutes.
- In a separate bowl, combine flour, sugar, baking powder, baking soda and salt - set aside.

- To the bran cereal and milk, add egg and oil mixing until blended.
- Add flour mixture stirring just until combined. Do not overmix.
- Fill muffin cups and bake for about 20 minutes or until done at 325°F.

Nutrition Information

- Calories: 146.2
- Saturated Fat: 1.2
- Sodium: 256.1
- Fiber: 2.1
- Sugar: 9.4
- Protein: 3.1
- Total Fat: 6.1
- Total Carbohydrate: 22.1
- Cholesterol: 20.5

9. Biscuits And Country Sausage Gravy (Diabetic Friendly)

Serving: 4 serving(s) | Prep: 0S | Ready in:

Ingredients

- 4 ounces uncooked bulk turkey breakfast sausage
- 1 tablespoon butter
- 2 tablespoons all-purpose flour
- 1/4 teaspoon black pepper
- 1/8 teaspoon salt
- 1 1/2 cups nonfat milk
- 4 cheddar biscuits (Cheddar Biscuits from Diabetic Living)
- fresh sage leaf (optional)

Direction

- In a medium saucepan cook sausage over medium heat until browned, using a wooden spoon to break up meat as it cooks. Add butter to saucepan. Stir until butter is melted. Stir in flour, 1/4 teaspoon black pepper and 1/8 teaspoon salt. Cook and stir 1 minute. Whisk in milk. Cook and stir until thickened. Cook and stir 1 minute more.
- Split each Cheddar Biscuit. Serve sausage mixture over split biscuits. If desired, garnish with fresh sage.
- 4 Servings: 1/2 cup gravy and 1 biscuit each.

Nutrition Information

- Calories: 349.1
- Total Carbohydrate: 34.7
- Cholesterol: 56.6
- Total Fat: 17.9
- Sodium: 650.5
- Fiber: 1
- Sugar: 6
- Protein: 12.1
- Saturated Fat: 5.6

10. Blueberry Banana Bread

Serving: 1 Loaf, 4-6 serving(s) | Prep: 5mins | Ready in:

Ingredients

- 2 cups Bisquick baking mix
- 3/4 cup quick-cooking oats
- 2/3 cup sugar
- 1 cup mashed ripe banana (2 medium)
- 1/4 cup milk
- 2 eggs
- 1 cup frozen blueberries (thawed or use fresh)

Direction

- Stir Bisquick, oats, sugar, bananas, milk and eggs in bowl until moistened.
- Beat vigorously 30 seconds.
- Gently stir in blueberries.
- Heat oven to 350°F and pour ingredients into a greased loaf pan.
- Bake 45 to 55 minutes or until toothpick inserted in center comes out clean.

- Cool for about 10 minutes and remove from pan.

Nutrition Information

- Calories: 571.2
- Saturated Fat: 3.7
- Total Carbohydrate: 103.7
- Cholesterol: 109.1
- Total Fat: 13.4
- Sodium: 809.6
- Fiber: 5
- Sugar: 56.8
- Protein: 11.5

11. Blueberry Oat/Yogurt Muffins

Serving: 10 muffins, 10 serving(s) | Prep: 10mins | Ready in:

Ingredients

- 1 cup dry oats
- 1 cup flour
- 1 teaspoon baking powder
- 1/2 teaspoon baking soda
- 3/4 cup brown sugar
- 1 egg
- 1/4 cup melted butter
- 1 (6 ounce) container low-fat vanilla yogurt
- 1/2 cup low fat cottage cheese
- 1 1/2 cups blueberries

Direction

- Mix oats with yogurt and cottage cheese.
- Mix flour, baking powder and soda.
- Add beaten egg, sugar and butter to oat mixture.
- Add flour and mix well.
- Fold in berries.
- Bake 400 degrees for 18 minutes.

Nutrition Information

- Calories: 245.6
- Total Fat: 6.7
- Saturated Fat: 3.5
- Cholesterol: 34.6
- Protein: 6.7
- Sodium: 197
- Fiber: 2.5
- Sugar: 19.2
- Total Carbohydrate: 40.7

12. Bob's Red Mill Wheat Biscuits

Serving: 18 biscuits | Prep: 8mins | Ready in:

Ingredients

- 2 cups unbleached white flour
- 1 cup whole wheat flour
- 3 tablespoons sugar
- 3 teaspoons baking powder
- 1 teaspoon baking soda
- 1 teaspoon salt
- 12 tablespoons cold unsalted butter, diced
- 1 cup buttermilk

Direction

- Preheat oven to 425°F.
- Sift together flours, sugar, baking powder, baking soda, and salt.
- Using your fingers, rub cubes of cold butter into the flour until it resembles coarse crumbs.
- Add buttermilk and stir until moistened, then knead a few times, just enough to make the dough come together.
- Drop about 1/4 cup dough onto parchment paper and flatten slightly, or you may choose to roll about half inch thick and cut them, placing them on a parchment paper lined baking sheet.
- Bake for about 12 minutes, or until tops are golden brown and a toothpick comes out clean.

Nutrition Information

- Calories: 155
- Sugar: 2.8
- Cholesterol: 20.9
- Protein: 2.9
- Total Fat: 8.1
- Saturated Fat: 5
- Sodium: 275.6
- Fiber: 1.2
- Total Carbohydrate: 18.4

13. Breakfast Biscuits (Pampered Chef)

Serving: 12-18 biscuits | Prep: 20mins | Ready in:

Ingredients

- Biscuit Dough
- 2 cups flour
- 1 teaspoon sugar
- 1/4 teaspoon salt
- 1 tablespoon baking powder
- 1/3 cup butter or 1/3 cup margarine, chilled
- 2/3 cup milk
- Filling 1
- 1/4 cup crumbled sausage, cooked
- 1/4 cup grated sharp cheddar cheese
- Filling 2
- 1/2 cup chopped canned peaches
- 3 tablespoons red raspberry preserves
- Filling 3
- 1/2 cup ricotta cheese or 1/2 cup soft cream cheese
- 3 tablespoons orange marmalade

Direction

- Preheat oven to 450 degrees. Mix together flour, sugar, salt and baking powder.
- Cut in butter with Pastry Blender until mix is size of small peas.
- Add milk all at once. Stir until dough sticks together. (Food processor may be used. Use frozen butter cut into pieces) with floured hands, knead dough a little on lightly floured pastry cloth or board.
- Roll out half of dough to about 1/4" thick.
- Place about a scant teaspoons of your choice of filling on dough near the edge.
- Fold dough over filling. Cut and seal into crescent with 3" Cut `n Seal.
- Cut a slash or two in the top.
- Place on Baking Stone. Repeat using remainder of dough. Bake at 350 degrees for 10 minutes.
- Breakfast Biscuits may be frozen. Defrost and warm in the oven (wrapped in foil) before serving.

Nutrition Information

- Calories: 190.8
- Fiber: 0.8
- Total Carbohydrate: 25.8
- Protein: 4.5
- Sodium: 210.7
- Saturated Fat: 4.9
- Sugar: 7.3
- Cholesterol: 23.1
- Total Fat: 7.9

14. Buttermilk Cathead Biscuits

Serving: 6 biscuits | Prep: 45mins | Ready in:

Ingredients

- 2 1/2 cups all-purpose flour
- 1/2 teaspoon salt
- 1/4 teaspoon baking soda
- 1 tablespoon baking powder
- 1 -1 1/2 cup buttermilk
- 6 tablespoons shortening
- butter, melted, for brushing over biscuits

Direction

- Preheat the oven to 450°.
- In a mixing bowl, combine the flour, salt, baking soda, and baking powder.
- Cut in the shortening, using your fingers or a pastry cutter, until the flour mixture has the consistency of course-ground cornmeal.
- Make a well in the center of the dry mixture and add the buttermilk.
- Stir the mixture until the buttermilk is fully incorporated.
- Turn the dough out onto a lightly floured surface and knead carefully a couple of times.
- To make the biscuits, pinch off a 3-inch ball of dough and mold a slightly rounded ball.
- Place the biscuits onto an ungreased baking pan.
- Bake for 15-18 minutes, or until the tops of the biscuits turn a light golden brown.
- Remove from the oven and brush with melted butter.

Nutrition Information

- Calories: 320.2
- Total Fat: 13.7
- Sodium: 471.7
- Fiber: 1.4
- Total Carbohydrate: 42.3
- Protein: 6.7
- Saturated Fat: 3.5
- Sugar: 2.1
- Cholesterol: 1.6

15. Buttermilk And Sour Cherry Scones For Afternoon Tea And Picnics

Serving: 1 large scone, 4-6 serving(s) | Prep: 10mins | Ready in:

Ingredients

- 250 g plain flour
- salt
- 2 tablespoons golden granulated sugar
- 1 teaspoon bicarbonate of soda
- 150 ml buttermilk
- 50 ml milk
- 75 g dried sour cherries

Direction

- Preheat the oven to 200 C/190 C fan/Gas Mark 5. Dust a baking sheet with flour.
- Sieve together the flour, salt, sugar and bicarbonate of soda. Mix together the buttermilk and milk. Make a well in the centre and pour on the buttermilk mixture. Mix well until the dough is even, and stir in the sour cherries.
- To shape for cooking, set the dough on a floured surface and turn around in your hands, until you have a neat round shape. Use a floured knife to score the surface into 4 or 6 sections.
- Transfer to the floured baking sheet and bake for 20 - 25 minutes. Set aside on a rack to cool. Best eaten straight away, but can be stored for up to 3 days in an airtight container.

Nutrition Information

- Calories: 331.9
- Total Fat: 1.6
- Sodium: 362.4
- Fiber: 2.1
- Cholesterol: 3.2
- Saturated Fat: 0.6
- Sugar: 8.3
- Total Carbohydrate: 68.3
- Protein: 9.7

16. Buttery Farm Biscuits

Serving: 12 Biscuits | Prep: 10mins | Ready in:

Ingredients

- 2 cups flour
- 1 tablespoon baking powder
- 1/4 teaspoon salt
- 1/4 cup cold unsalted butter, cut into small pieces (or use salted and leave out the salt)
- 3/4 cup skim milk

Direction

- Combine flour, baking powder salt.
- Cut the butter into the flour using 2 knives or a pastry blender, keep cutting until the mixture looks like coarse crumbs.
- With a fork stir in the milk, very gently, until a soft dough forms.
- Don't over mix.
- Place the dough on a baking sheet (jelly roll pan) and with floured hands press it into a 9" x 9" square.
- Use a spatula or the dull side of a knife and cut the dough into 12 biscuits without actually cutting them apart.
- Bake in 400F oven for about 15-20 minutes or until they are golden.
- Transfer to a wire rack cool for about 10 minutes.
- Serve with homemade fruit jam or anything else that takes your fancy.

Nutrition Information

- Calories: 116.6
- Cholesterol: 10.5
- Total Carbohydrate: 17
- Sodium: 149.2
- Fiber: 0.6
- Sugar: 0.1
- Protein: 2.8
- Total Fat: 4.1
- Saturated Fat: 2.5

17. Cheesy Bacon Egg Muffins

Serving: 6 muffins, 3 serving(s) | Prep: 5mins | Ready in:

Ingredients

- 12 large egg yolks
- 4 slices cooked bacon
- 1/4 cup shredded cheddar cheese
- 4 slices deli turkey (optional)

Direction

- Spray a 6-muffin tin with cooking spray or use foil muffin cups and preheat oven to 350 degrees. Chop bacon and turkey. Mix all ingredients and pour into muffin tins about 3/4 full. Bake for 10-15 minutes at 350 degrees. Optional: you can cut biscuits in two and roll out for a crust if you want them to be more filling.

Nutrition Information

- Calories: 276.7
- Sugar: 0.4
- Total Carbohydrate: 2.6
- Protein: 14.7
- Total Fat: 22.5
- Saturated Fat: 8
- Sodium: 279
- Fiber: 0
- Cholesterol: 850.9

18. Chocolate And Roasted Cherry "Scones"

Serving: 8 small scones, 8 serving(s) | Prep: 1hours | Ready in:

Ingredients

- 3/4 cup fresh pitted cherries or 3/4 cup thawed frozen pitted.cherries, halved
- 1/3 cup miniature chocolate chip

- 1 cup ground almonds
- 1/2 cup ground pumpkin seeds
- 2 tablespoons flax seeds, ground
- 1/2 cup arrowroot or 1/2 cup tapioca starch
- 1/2 teaspoon baking soda
- 1/2 teaspoon kosher salt
- 1/4 cup Earth Balance buttery sticks
- 1/4 cup non-hydrogenated shortening
- 2 large eggs
- 1 teaspoon vanilla
- 1/3 cup jaggery or 1/3 cup fine-grind raw sugar
- 3/4 teaspoon apple cider vinegar

Direction

- Heat oven to 450F and line a rimmed baking sheet with parchment.
- Spread the cherries out in one layer on the sheet.
- Roast for 15 minutes, stirring halfway through. Set aside and let cool.
- Reduce the oven to 350F and line a baking sheet with parchment.
- In a large bowl, whisk the almond and pumpkin seed flours, chia seed, arrowroot starch, baking soda and salt.
- Cut in the Earth Balance Buttery Sticks and shortening until the mixture consists of pea-sized lumps.
- In a small bowl, beat the eggs with the vanilla, jaggery and vinegar. Pour into the flour mixture and mix just until the dough comes together.
- Stir in the chocolate chips and cooled cherry-chocolate mixture.
- Spread in a lined 6" springform pan and bake 20 minutes.
- Score into 8 scones with a bench scraper or sharp knife (do not separate the pieces).
- Return to the oven and bake for 25 minutes longer.
- Remove the springform ring and bake a final 15 minutes.
- Cool 30 minutes, then cut along the score lines and separate the pieces.

Nutrition Information

- Calories: 307.6
- Saturated Fat: 4.5
- Sodium: 244.3
- Sugar: 14.8
- Total Carbohydrate: 26.6
- Total Fat: 20.7
- Fiber: 3.6
- Cholesterol: 46.5
- Protein: 7.5

19. Cranberry Oat Bran Muffins

Serving: 12 muffins | Prep: 15mins | Ready in:

Ingredients

- 1 1/2 cups flour
- 1/2 cup oat bran
- 3/4 teaspoon salt
- 1/3 cup sugar
- 3 teaspoons baking powder
- 2 eggs
- 1/4 cup vegetable oil
- 1 cup milk
- 1 cup cranberries, chopped
- 1 cup walnuts, chopped
- 1 teaspoon orange peel, grated

Direction

- Preheat oven to 400 degrees F.
- In a bowl combine dry ingredients (flour - baking powder) and set aside.
- In another bowl beat together eggs, vegetable oil and milk and stir into dry ingredients.
- Stir in cranberries, walnuts and orange peel.
- Pour into muffin tins and bake for 20 minutes or until muffins are done.

Nutrition Information

- Calories: 221.4

- Total Fat: 12.9
- Fiber: 2.1
- Sugar: 6.3
- Cholesterol: 33.9
- Protein: 5.5
- Saturated Fat: 2
- Sodium: 258.8
- Total Carbohydrate: 23.7

20. Cranberry Orange Pecan Quick Bread

Serving: 1 loaf, 15 serving(s) | Prep: 10mins | Ready in:

Ingredients

- 2 eggs, beaten
- 1/2 cup vegetable oil
- 1 1/2 cups flour
- 1/2 teaspoon salt
- 1 cup sugar
- 1 teaspoon baking soda
- 1 cup cranberries, chopped
- 3 tablespoons orange juice concentrate
- 1/2 cup pecans, ground fine

Direction

- Preheat oven to 325°F.
- Combine eggs and oil. Sift in dry ingredients, and blend with an electric mixer. Don't overmix.
- Stir in the last three ingredients with a spoon. Pour into a greased and floured loaf tin.
- Bake at 325°F for 30-40 minutes, until a toothpick inserted in comes out with only a few crumbs clinging to it.

Nutrition Information

- Calories: 204.6
- Protein: 2.6
- Total Fat: 10.7
- Saturated Fat: 1.4
- Sodium: 171.2
- Fiber: 1
- Total Carbohydrate: 25.5
- Cholesterol: 28.2
- Sugar: 15.1

21. Cranberry Apricot Flax Seed Muffins

Serving: 12 Muffins, 12 serving(s) | Prep: 15mins | Ready in:

Ingredients

- 1 cup Hodgson Mill multi-grain hot cereal
- 1 cup flour
- 1 tablespoon baking powder
- 1/2 teaspoon baking soda
- 1/2 teaspoon salt
- 1/2 cup sugar
- 1 cup carrot, shredded
- 1 cup apple, peeled and finely chopped
- 1/2 cup skim milk
- 2 eggs
- 1/4 cup applesauce
- 1 teaspoon vanilla extract
- 1/2 cup walnuts, chopped (optional)
- 1/2 cup dried cranberries
- 3/4 cup dried apricot

Direction

- Preheat oven to 400°F
- Line 12 muffin cups with liners, or grease them with nonstick spray.
- Blend dry ingredients together, then add remaining ingredients and mix until well-blended- the batter will be thick and lumpy.
- Spoon batter into muffin cups, and bake 20-25 minutes or until golden brown.

Nutrition Information

- Calories: 122.8

- Sodium: 266.9
- Fiber: 1.6
- Sugar: 14.5
- Cholesterol: 35.5
- Protein: 2.9
- Total Fat: 1.1
- Saturated Fat: 0.3
- Total Carbohydrate: 26.2

22. Delicious Blueberry Muffins With Crumb Topping

Serving: 8 serving(s) | Prep: 15mins | Ready in:

Ingredients

- 1 1/2 cups all-purpose flour
- 3/4 cup white sugar
- 1/2 teaspoon salt
- 2 teaspoons baking powder
- 1/3 cup vegetable oil
- 1 egg
- 1/3 cup milk
- 1 cup fresh blueberries
- 1/2 cup white sugar
- 1/3 cup all-purpose flour
- 1/4 cup butter, cubed
- 1 1/2 teaspoons ground cinnamon

Direction

- Preheat oven to 400 degrees F.
- Grease muffin cups or line with muffin liners.
- Combine 1 1/2 cups flour, 3/4 cup sugar, salt and baking powder.
- Place vegetable oil into a 1 cup measuring cup; add the egg and enough milk to fill the cup.
- Mix this with the flour mixture.
- Fold in the blueberries.
- Fill muffin cups right to the top, and sprinkle with crumb topping mixture.
- To Make Crumb Topping: Mix together 1/2 cup sugar, 1/3 cup flour, 1/4 cup butter, and 1 1/2 teaspoons cinnamon.
- Mix with fork, and sprinkle over muffins before baking.
- Bake for 20 to 25 minutes in the preheated oven, or until done.

Nutrition Information

- Calories: 384.1
- Sugar: 33.1
- Total Fat: 16.1
- Sodium: 301.7
- Fiber: 1.5
- Saturated Fat: 5.3
- Total Carbohydrate: 57
- Cholesterol: 39.9
- Protein: 4.3

23. Diabetic Blueberry Muffins

Serving: 10 serving(s) | Prep: 15mins | Ready in:

Ingredients

- 2 cups all-purpose flour
- 2 teaspoons baking powder
- 3/4 teaspoon salt
- 1/2 stick cup light margarine, softened
- 1 cup Splenda sugar substitute (or other measure-for-measure sugar substitute)
- 1/4 cup honey
- 2 large eggs
- 1 teaspoon vanilla
- 1/2 cup skim milk
- 1 cup fresh blueberries or 1 cup frozen blueberries

Direction

- Preheat oven to 350° F.
- Line 10 muffin cups with paper liners.
- Sift together flour, baking powder, and salt, set aside.
- Beat together margarine, Splenda, and honey with an electric mixer until light and fluffy.

- Add eggs one at a time beating well after each addition.
- Stir in vanilla.
- Alternately stir in flour mixture and milk, beginning and ending with flour mixture.
- Fold in berries.
- Spoon batter into paper lined muffin cups, and bake until golden brown and a toothpick inserted comes out clean, about 25-30 minutes.
- Cool in pan 10 minutes on a wire rack.
- Remove from pan.
- Cool completely on wire rack.

Nutrition Information

- Calories: 165.6
- Protein: 4.5
- Sodium: 269.5
- Fiber: 1.1
- Total Carbohydrate: 34.5
- Cholesterol: 37.5
- Total Fat: 1.3
- Saturated Fat: 0.4
- Sugar: 13.2

24. Easy Moist Banana Blueberry Muffins

Serving: 12 serving(s) | Prep: 10mins | Ready in:

Ingredients

- 3 large ripe bananas
- 3/4 cup sugar
- 1 egg, slightly beaten
- 1/3 cup melted butter
- 1 cup blueberries
- 1 teaspoon baking soda
- 1 teaspoon baking powder
- 1/2 teaspoon salt
- 1 1/2 cups flour

Direction

- Mash bananas in a large mixing bowl.
- Add sugar and egg.
- Add butter and blueberries.
- Combine dry ingredients and gently stir into banana mixture.
- Pour into 12 well-greased muffin cups.
- Bake at 375 degrees for 20 minutes.

Nutrition Information

- Calories: 193.9
- Fiber: 1.6
- Total Fat: 5.8
- Saturated Fat: 3.4
- Sodium: 283.8
- Protein: 2.6
- Sugar: 17.9
- Total Carbohydrate: 34.1
- Cholesterol: 29

25. Feather Light Bran Muffins

Serving: 30 muffins | Prep: 15mins | Ready in:

Ingredients

- 1 cup 100% bran (Nabisco)
- 1 cup boiling water
- 1/2 cup Crisco
- 1 1/2 cups white sugar
- 2 eggs, beaten
- 1 pint buttermilk
- 2 1/2 cups flour
- 2 1/2 teaspoons baking soda
- 1/2 teaspoon salt
- 2 cups all-bran cereal (Kelloggs)

Direction

- Preheat oven to 400 degrees.
- Combine Nabisco 100% Bran and boiling water and let cool.
- Cream Crisco and sugar.
- Add eggs, buttermilk, flour, soda, and salt.

- Fold in Kellogg's All Bran.
- Fill muffin tins half full and bake 15 minutes.

Nutrition Information

- Calories: 133.8
- Cholesterol: 14.8
- Protein: 2.8
- Total Fat: 4.3
- Saturated Fat: 1.3
- Fiber: 2
- Sodium: 180.2
- Sugar: 11.8
- Total Carbohydrate: 23.2

26. Ginger Scones The Inn At Little Washington

Serving: 20 scones, 20 serving(s) | Prep: 20mins | Ready in:

Ingredients

- 2 1/2 cups all-purpose flour
- 5 teaspoons baking powder
- 5 tablespoons sugar
- 3 tablespoons cold butter, diced
- 1/2 cup milk
- 1/2 cup cream, divided
- 1 egg yolk
- 1/2 cup minced candied ginger

Direction

- Preheat oven to 375°F.
- Line two baking sheets with waxed paper.
- In a large bowl, combine the flour, baking powder, sugar and butter with an electric mixer.
- Add the milk, 1/4 cup of the cream, the egg yolk, and the candied ginger. Mix until just incorporated (do not overmix.).
- Turn the dough out onto a lightly floured service and roll out to 3/4" thickness.
- Use a heart-shaped or round cutter to cut out the scones. Place the scones on the baking sheets.
- Brush the tops of the scones with the remaining 1/4 cup cream. Bake for 4 minutes, rotate, and bake for 5 minutes more.
- Remove from the sheets with a spatula and cool on a wire rack.
- Serve with strawberry jam (and clotted cream, if you like.).

Nutrition Information

- Calories: 108.7
- Cholesterol: 21.5
- Saturated Fat: 2.5
- Sodium: 108.7
- Fiber: 0.4
- Sugar: 3.2
- Total Carbohydrate: 15.8
- Total Fat: 4.2
- Protein: 2.1

27. Gourmet 1, 2, 3 Biscuit

Serving: 8-10 biscuits, 4-6 serving(s) | Prep: 5mins | Ready in:

Ingredients

- 2 1/4 cups Bisquick baking mix
- 2/3 cup water, less 1 Tbl
- 1 tablespoon dry white wine

Direction

- Follow the recipe on the Bisquick box making the following changes. Although milk can be used, try this: replace with water then take out 1 Tbsp. of water (or milk if used) and add 1 Tbsp. wine.
- The wine makes it like homemade, yeast bread! It has become a must in many of my recipes.

- If you have another recipe you've been used to making, try it substituting 1 Tbsp. wine for 1 Tbsp. other liquid.
- *NOTE: I prefer Black Tower wine for cooking but in a pinch have used another dry white wine; always promising myself next time to keep BT in supply!

Nutrition Information

- Calories: 291.9
- Fiber: 1.4
- Cholesterol: 1.4
- Protein: 5.4
- Total Fat: 10.4
- Sugar: 7.9
- Total Carbohydrate: 42.8
- Saturated Fat: 2.7
- Sodium: 862.3

28. Healthy Heart Muffins

Serving: 12 muffins | Prep: 10mins | Ready in:

Ingredients

- 3 egg whites
- 3/4 cup skim milk
- 1 cup low-fat yogurt
- 3/4 cup applesauce
- 2 cups wholemeal flour
- 1/2 cup rolled oats
- 1/2 cup oat bran
- 3 teaspoons baking powder
- 2 teaspoons cinnamon
- 3/4 cup raisins
- 3/4 cup dried apricot, diced

Direction

- Beat egg whites lightly.
- Add milk, yoghurt and apple sauce.
- In a separate bowl combine dry ingredients and dried fruit.
- Add liquid to dry ingredients, combine with care.
- Spoon into muffin tins.
- Bake 180 C for 20 minutes.

Nutrition Information

- Calories: 182.2
- Protein: 6.5
- Total Fat: 1.2
- Fiber: 2.8
- Sugar: 11.4
- Total Carbohydrate: 39.1
- Saturated Fat: 0.4
- Sodium: 134.9
- Cholesterol: 1.5

29. Healthy Pumpkin Pomegranate Muffins

Serving: 12 muffins | Prep: 10mins | Ready in:

Ingredients

- 1 cup all-purpose flour
- 3/4 cup whole wheat flour
- 1/4 cup Grape-nuts cereal (or similar cereal)
- 1/2 cup sugar or 1/2 cup Splenda granular
- 1 1/2 teaspoons baking powder
- 1/2 teaspoon baking soda
- 1 teaspoon cinnamon
- 1 cup canned pumpkin
- 1 cup fat-free buttermilk or 1 cup soured milk
- 1 egg, beaten
- 3/4-1 cup pomegranate seeds

Direction

- Preheat oven to 350. Coat 12 muffin cups with cooking spray.
- Mix dry ingredients in a large bowl.
- In a second bowl, combine wet ingredients.
- Toss pomegranate seeds in the flour mix to coat.

- Add wet ingredients to flour mix. Stir until just combined.
- Pour into muffin cups. Bake for 20-30 minutes. Let cool before unmolding.

Nutrition Information

- Calories: 127
- Total Fat: 0.9
- Total Carbohydrate: 27.6
- Protein: 3.3
- Sugar: 10.9
- Cholesterol: 15.5
- Saturated Fat: 0.2
- Sodium: 165.7
- Fiber: 2.4

30. Irish Soda Bread Scones

Serving: 8 scones | Prep: 30mins | Ready in:

Ingredients

- 2 cups all-purpose flour
- 3 tablespoons firmly packed light brown sugar
- 1 1/2 teaspoons baking powder
- 1/2 teaspoon baking soda
- 1/2 teaspoon caraway seed
- 1/2 teaspoon salt
- 1/3 cup unsalted butter, chilled
- 1/2 cup buttermilk
- 1 large egg
- 1/2 cup coarsely chopped walnuts
- 1/4 cup raisins
- 1/4 cup golden raisin
- 1 egg yolk, mixed with
- 1/2 teaspoon water, for glaze

Direction

- Preheat oven to 375°; butter a 10-inch diameter circle in the center of a baking sheet.
- In a big bowl, stir the flour, brown sugar, baking powder, baking soda, caraway seeds, and salt.
- Cut the butter into ½ inch cubes and distribute them over the flour mixture.
- Using a pastry blender, cut in the butter until it resembles coarse crumbs.
- In a small bowl, stir the buttermilk and egg together; add the buttermilk mixture to the flour mixture and stir to combine.
- The dough will be sticky; with lightly floured hands, knead in the nuts and raisins until evenly distributed.
- With lightly floured hands, pat the dough into a 9-inch diameter circle in the center of the prepared baking sheet.
- Brush the egg yolk mixture over the top and sides of the dough.
- With a serrated knife, cut into 8 wedges.
- Bake for 20-25 minutes, or until a pick comes out clean.

Nutrition Information

- Calories: 298.3
- Fiber: 1.7
- Cholesterol: 64.9
- Saturated Fat: 5.8
- Sodium: 322.3
- Sugar: 11.4
- Total Carbohydrate: 38.2
- Protein: 6.3
- Total Fat: 14

31. Jillian Michael's Blueberry Banana Muffins

Serving: 12 muffins | Prep: 15mins | Ready in:

Ingredients

- 3/4 cup very ripe mashed banana (about 2)
- 3/4 cup nonfat plain yogurt
- 1/2 cup honey

- 1/3 cup olive oil
- 2 teaspoons vanilla extract
- 2 1/2 cups white whole wheat flour
- 2 teaspoons aluminum-free baking powder
- 1/2 teaspoon baking soda
- 1/2 teaspoon salt
- 1 cup blueberries (fresh or frozen)
- 1/2 cup chopped walnuts, toasted (optional)

Direction

- Place oven rack in centre of oven.
- Preheat oven to 425 degrees.
- Lightly spray a 12-cup muffin tin with olive oil or line with paper liners.
- Place the bananas, yogurt, honey, olive oil and vanilla in a large bowl. Stir together until well mixed.
- In a separate bowl sift together the flour, baking powder, baking soda and salt. Add the dry ingredients to the banana mixture and stir until just combined.
- Fold in the blueberries and nuts (if using).
- Spoon the batter into the prepared muffin tin. Place the tin in the oven and reduce the heat to 400 degrees.
- Bake for 35 to 40 minutes or until tops spring back when lightly touched.
- Let cool in the tin for 10 to 15 minutes before transferring to a cooling rack. Serve warm.
- For longer storage, let cool completely and store in an airtight container for up to three days or in the freezer for up to 2 months.

Nutrition Information

- Calories: 211.4
- Saturated Fat: 1
- Sodium: 223.2
- Sugar: 15.9
- Total Carbohydrate: 36.1
- Cholesterol: 0.3
- Total Fat: 6.7
- Fiber: 3.4
- Protein: 4.5

32. Low Fat Strawberry Banana Bread

Serving: 2 regular-sized loaves, 24 serving(s) | Prep: 20mins | Ready in:

Ingredients

- 4 bananas, very ripe
- 2 cups fresh strawberries
- 2 cups flour
- 1 cup whole wheat flour
- 1/2 cup sugar
- 2 teaspoons baking soda
- 1 teaspoon baking powder
- 1 teaspoon salt
- 2 large eggs
- 1/2 cup unsweetened applesauce
- 2 tablespoons canola oil
- 2 teaspoons vanilla extract
- 1/2 cup walnuts, chopped

Direction

- Mash bananas in large bowl. Add hulled strawberries and mash as well.
- Combine with eggs, applesauce, oil, vanilla and sugar. Combine dry ingredients in a separate bowl, add to banana strawberry mixture. Mix in chopped walnuts last.
- Spoon batter into 2 standard sized loaf pans, or three medium-sized pans which have been lightly sprayed with non-stick cooking spray.
- Bake in 350 degree oven for 50-60 minutes or until toothpick stuck in center of pans comes out clean.

Nutrition Information

- Calories: 127.8
- Total Fat: 3.5
- Saturated Fat: 0.4
- Sodium: 223.7
- Total Carbohydrate: 22.1
- Cholesterol: 15.5

- Protein: 2.9
- Fiber: 1.8
- Sugar: 7.8

33. Marvelous! Mocha Muffins

Serving: 12-15 muffins, 12 serving(s) | Prep: 10mins | Ready in:

Ingredients

- 2 cups all-purpose flour
- 2 tablespoons unsweetened baking cocoa
- 2 1/2 teaspoons baking powder
- 1/2 teaspoon salt
- 1/3 cup brown sugar
- 1 cup milk
- 1/3 cup vegetable oil
- 1 tablespoon instant coffee granules
- 1 large egg
- 1 cup semi-sweet chocolate chips

Direction

- Heat oven to 400°F Grease bottoms only of 12 regular-size muffins cups with shortening or cooking spray, or line muffin cups with paper baking cups.
- In a medium bowl, Mix flour, cocoa, baking powder, and salt; set aside. In large bowl, beat brown sugar, milk, oil, coffee and egg with fork or wire whisk. Stir in flour mixture just until flour is moistened. Fold in chocolate chips. Divide batter evenly among cups.
- Bake 18 to 20 minutes or until toothpick inserted in the center comes out clean. When done, immediately move muffins from pan to cooling rack.

Nutrition Information

- Calories: 242.2
- Total Fat: 11.7
- Saturated Fat: 4
- Cholesterol: 20.5
- Sodium: 193
- Fiber: 1.7
- Sugar: 13.6
- Total Carbohydrate: 32.6
- Protein: 4.2

34. Oat Bran And Banana Muffins

Serving: 6 large muffins, 6 serving(s) | Prep: 10mins | Ready in:

Ingredients

- 2 1/4 cups oat bran
- 1/4 cup walnuts, chopped
- 2 bananas, ripe mashed
- 1 teaspoon baking powder
- 2 egg whites
- 1/4 cup raw sugar
- 1 1/4 cups skim milk or 1 1/4 cups evaporated milk
- 2 tablespoons vegetable oil

Direction

- In a bowl, combine oat bran, baking powder and raw sugar.
- Gradually stir in the walnuts banana, egg whites, milk and oil.
- Spoon mixture into a non-stick muffin tray and bake for 20-25 minutes or until golden brown.

Nutrition Information

- Calories: 253.1
- Fiber: 6.8
- Sugar: 13.8
- Protein: 10.5
- Total Fat: 10.5
- Saturated Fat: 1.5
- Sodium: 111
- Total Carbohydrate: 44.4

- Cholesterol: 1

35. Ohhhhh So Good Monkey Bread Muffins

Serving: 12 serving(s) | Prep: 20mins | Ready in:

Ingredients

- 1 (16 ounce) packagejumbo flakey biscuit dough
- 1/2 cup packed brown sugar
- 1 (3 1/2 ounce) package instant butterscotch pudding mix
- 1/2 cup granulated sugar
- 1 teaspoon ground cinnamon
- 1/2 cup butter, melted

Direction

- Preheat oven to 350 degrees and grease and prepare muffin tin.
- Separate tube of dough into 8 biscuits. Cut each into quarters.
- In a medium bowl, combine brown sugar, pudding mix, granulated sugar and cinnamon. Mix well.
- Coat each quarter in melted butter. Roll each quarter in the brown sugar mixture.
- Divide pieces evenly among 12 greased muffin cups. Pour remaining brown sugar mixture over each filled muffin cup.
- Bake 15 to 18 minutes. Using a spoon, carefully remove each muffin from muffin pan.
- Serve warm.

Nutrition Information

- Calories: 257.4
- Sodium: 448.5
- Sugar: 20
- Protein: 2.6
- Total Fat: 12.8
- Saturated Fat: 6.2
- Fiber: 0.4
- Total Carbohydrate: 33.9
- Cholesterol: 20.7

36. Orange Nut Muffins

Serving: 12 Muffins | Prep: 10mins | Ready in:

Ingredients

- 2 cups flour
- 1/3 cup sugar
- 1 teaspoon baking powder
- 1/4 teaspoon salt
- 1/2 teaspoon baking soda
- 1 cup Grape-nuts cereal
- 2 eggs, slightly beaten
- 1 cup orange juice
- 1 tablespoon orange rind
- 1/3 cup salad oil

Direction

- Preheat oven to 400°F.
- Sift together the flour, sugar, baking powder, salt and soda.
- Stir in Grape Nuts.
- Combine eggs, orange juice, orange peel and oil.
- Add to dry ingredients all at once.
- Stir just until moistened.
- Fill greased muffin pans 2/3 full.
- Bake at 400°F for 20 to 25 minutes.

Nutrition Information

- Calories: 207.2
- Total Fat: 7.2
- Saturated Fat: 1.2
- Sodium: 202.5
- Sugar: 8.6
- Total Carbohydrate: 31.7
- Fiber: 1.5

- Cholesterol: 35.2
- Protein: 4.4

37. Orange And Poppy Seed Quick Bread

Serving: 1 loaf, 10 serving(s) | Prep: 20mins | Ready in:

Ingredients

- 1 1/2 cups unbleached all-purpose flour
- 1 teaspoon baking powder
- 1/4 teaspoon salt
- 1/4 cup milk
- 1/3 cup freshly squeezed orange juice
- 1 orange, zest of
- 6 tablespoons butter, softened
- 2/3 cup sugar
- 2 eggs, room temperature and lightly beaten
- 3 tablespoons poppy seeds

Direction

- Preheat oven to 350 degrees and grease a 6 cup loaf pan.
- In a small bowl, whisk together flour, baking powder and salt. In another small bowl, combine milk, juice, and zest. In a large bowl, with a handheld electric mixer, cream together the butter and sugar until light and fluffy (about 3 min.).
- Add eggs, one at a time, beating on low speed.
- Add the flour mixture and the juice mixture alternately, beginning and ending with the flour mixture, scraping and stirring with a rubber spatula until just combined, being careful not to overmix the batter.
- Gently fold in the poppy seeds and pour the batter into the prepared pan. Bake for about 45 minutes, or until the cake begins to pull away from the sides of the pan and a tester inserted into the middle of the cake comes out clean.
- Cool in pan for 10 minutes before removing.

Nutrition Information

- Calories: 217.6
- Protein: 4
- Saturated Fat: 5
- Sugar: 14.5
- Sodium: 161.5
- Fiber: 0.8
- Total Carbohydrate: 29.6
- Cholesterol: 61.5
- Total Fat: 9.5

38. Orange Cranberry Muffins

Serving: 12 serving(s) | Prep: 10mins | Ready in:

Ingredients

- 1 whole large orange, peel, pith and flesh included
- 1/2 cup orange juice
- 1 egg
- 1/4 cup oil
- 1 1/2 cups flour
- 1 teaspoon baking powder
- 1 teaspoon baking soda
- 1/2 cup sugar
- 1/2 cup dried cranberries

Direction

- Cut up orange into 8 sections and blend in blender with juice, egg, and oil until smooth.
- Mix remaining dry ingredients.
- Pour blended wet into dry and mix until just moistened.
- Distribute in greased muffin pan and bake at 375F for 15-20 minutes.

Nutrition Information

- Calories: 147.2
- Saturated Fat: 0.8
- Sodium: 141.5

- Fiber: 0.9
- Sugar: 10.4
- Cholesterol: 17.6
- Total Fat: 5.2
- Total Carbohydrate: 23.2
- Protein: 2.3

39. Pb J Muffins

Serving: 12 muffins | Prep: 15mins | Ready in:

Ingredients

- 1 cup whole wheat flour
- 1 1/2 cups unbleached all-purpose flour
- 1 1/2 teaspoons baking powder
- 1/4 teaspoon baking soda
- 1/2 teaspoon salt
- 3/4 cup natural creamy peanut butter
- 3/4 cup 1% low-fat milk
- 1/2-3/4 cup honey
- 1/2 cup finely grated carrot
- 1/2 cup finely grated zucchini
- 2 eggs, beaten
- 1/4 cup canola oil
- 1/4 cup all-fruit strawberry preserves or 1/4 cup raspberry preserves

Direction

- Preheat oven to 400°.
- Spray paper muffin cups with nonstick cooking spray.
- In a large bowl, combine flours, baking powder, baking soda, and salt.
- With two knives or a pastry blender, cut in peanut butter until coarse crumbs form and mixture is no longer powdery.
- Add milk, honey, carrot, zucchini, eggs, and oil; stir until well moistened.
- Spoon about 2 tablespoons batter into each muffin cup.
- Top each with about 1 teaspoon fruit preserves.
- Cover with remaining batter.
- Bake 15-20 minutes, until toothpick inserted in center comes out clean.

Nutrition Information

- Calories: 308.9
- Total Fat: 14
- Saturated Fat: 2.4
- Sugar: 17.6
- Protein: 8.8
- Sodium: 268.1
- Fiber: 2.9
- Total Carbohydrate: 40.1
- Cholesterol: 36

40. Poppy Seed Crumble Muffins

Serving: 18 muffins | Prep: 15mins | Ready in:

Ingredients

- 200 g flour
- 3 teaspoons baking powder
- 100 g sugar
- 1 teaspoon vanilla
- 2 eggs
- 150 g butter, melted and slightly cooled again
- 50 g poppy seeds
- 150 g creme fraiche
- Crumbs
- 75 -100 g flour

Direction

- In a big bowl combine flour and baking powder. Add sugar, vanilla, eggs, butter, poppy seeds and crème fraiche. Using a mixer work into a smooth dough (will take about 2 minutes).
- Take 3-4 heaped tbsp. of the dough and place in a second bowl. Add as much of the additional flour as needed to make coarse crumbs (they shall be rather soft).

- Fill dough into prepared muffin pans and top with crumbles.
- Bake in the preheated oven at 180°C for about 25 minutes.

Nutrition Information

- Calories: 189.3
- Saturated Fat: 6.5
- Total Carbohydrate: 18.4
- Cholesterol: 52.7
- Protein: 3
- Total Fat: 11.8
- Sodium: 120.1
- Fiber: 0.7
- Sugar: 6.1

41. Protein Muffins

Serving: 18 muffins, 18 serving(s) | Prep: 10mins | Ready in:

Ingredients

- 1 cup whole wheat flour
- 1/2 cup ground oatmeal
- 1/2 cup ground quinoa
- 1/2 cup ground chia seeds
- 1/2 cup ground roasted soybeans
- 1/2 cup ground flax seeds
- 1 tablespoon baking soda
- 1 teaspoon salt
- 1/2 cup sugar
- 2 1/2 cups fine shredded carrots
- 1 3/4 cups skim milk
- 1/2 tablespoon vanilla
- 1 egg

Direction

- Mix dry ingredients.
- Mix wet ingredients in separate bowl, then add to dry.
- Bake for 16-18 @ 400 F depending on the size of your muffin tins.

Nutrition Information

- Calories: 108.8
- Fiber: 2.6
- Total Carbohydrate: 18.9
- Protein: 3.9
- Total Fat: 2.3
- Saturated Fat: 0.3
- Sodium: 369.8
- Sugar: 6.5
- Cholesterol: 10.8

42. Raisin Walnut Muffins (Gift Mix In A Jar)

Serving: 18 muffins, 18 serving(s) | Prep: 10mins | Ready in:

Ingredients

- JAR Ingredients
- 1 1/4 cups sugar
- 1/2 teaspoon salt
- 2 teaspoons cinnamon
- 1/4 teaspoon baking soda
- 1 tablespoon baking powder
- 2 cups flour
- 1/2 cup walnuts, chopped
- 1/2 cup dark raisin
- ADDITIONAL INGREDIENTS (to be added by the recipient)
- 1 cup butter, melted
- 2 eggs
- 2 teaspoons vanilla extract

Direction

- Creating the Gift in a Jar:
- Wash and thoroughly dry a 1-quart wide-mouth canning jar.

- Layer the ingredients in the jar as listed above starting with the sugar, salt, cinnamon, baking soda, powder, flour, walnuts and then raisins - make sure to press firmly with a flat bottomed object after each addition; make the layers as level as possible.
- Secure the lid and decorate as desired; attach the instructions for making these cookies found below.
- RAISIN WALNUT MUFFINS GIFT TAG:
- Additional ingredients to be added by the recipient: 1 cup melted butter, 2 eggs and 2 tsp vanilla extract.
- RAISIN WALNUT MUFFIN INSTRUCTIONS:
- Preheat oven to 400.
- In a large bowl, combine the butter, eggs and extract.
- Add the contents of the jar, and stir until just mixed; do not overstir.
- Spoon the batter into greased or papered muffin tins, filling each cup two-thirds full.
- Bake for 20 minutes, or until a toothpick inserted in the center comes out clean.
- Cool for 10 minutes in the tin, then transfer to a wire rack and cool completely.
- Serve immediately or store in an airtight container for up to 1 week.

Nutrition Information

- Calories: 238.6
- Total Fat: 13.1
- Saturated Fat: 6.9
- Fiber: 0.9
- Total Carbohydrate: 28.6
- Protein: 2.9
- Sodium: 223.9
- Sugar: 16.5
- Cholesterol: 50.6

43. Raspberry Poppy Seed Muffins

Serving: 12-18 muffins | Prep: 35mins | Ready in:

Ingredients

- 1 cup sugar
- 1/2 cup butter
- 4 egg yolks
- 1 vanilla beans, split or 1 teaspoon vanilla extract
- 1 cup sour cream
- 1/4 cup poppy seed
- 8 1/2 ounces cake flour
- 1/2 teaspoon baking powder
- 1 teaspoon baking soda
- 6 egg whites
- 1/4 teaspoon cream of tartar
- 1 -2 pint raspberries

Direction

- Preheat oven to 350 F. Grease and flour muffin tins.
- Mix together butter and sugar in a mixer on second speed.
- Add split vanilla bean (or 1 tsp. vanilla extract) into egg yolks.
- Slowly add yolks, one at a time, to butter/sugar mixture. Beat until mixture is a soft lemon color.
- Stir in sour cream and poppy seeds.
- Sift the dry ingredients together and add into egg yolk mixture.
- In a separate bowl, beat egg whites, sugar and cream of tartar until stiff.
- Fold into egg yolk mixture. Gently stir in 1-2 pints of fresh raspberries.
- Bake in greased muffin tins for 20-25 minutes.

Nutrition Information

- Calories: 305
- Total Fat: 14.7
- Sodium: 215.8
- Sugar: 18.4
- Total Carbohydrate: 38.3
- Cholesterol: 91.7
- Saturated Fat: 8
- Fiber: 2.4

- Protein: 5.9

44. Red River Date Muffins

Serving: 12 serving(s) | Prep: 50mins | Ready in:

Ingredients

- 3⁄4 cup old fashioned oats or 3⁄4 cup quick oats
- 1⁄2 cup red river cereal, uncooked
- 1 cup buttermilk (or 1T lemon juice, fill cup with milk)
- 1 cup flour
- 3⁄4 cup packed brown sugar
- 1 teaspoon baking powder
- 3⁄4 teaspoon baking soda
- 1⁄2 teaspoon salt
- 1 egg
- 1⁄3 cup butter, melted
- 1 cup chopped dates

Direction

- Combine oats, Red River and milk in large bowl, let stand 40 minutes.
- Combine remaining dry ingredients.
- Add butter and egg to cereal mixture.
- Add dry ingredients mix well.
- Stir in dates.
- Spoon into 12 greased muffin tins.
- Bake at 375 degrees for 20-25 minutes or until set.
- Turn out to cool and store in airtight container, if there are any to store.
- Prep time includes letting cereal soak for 40 minutes.

Nutrition Information

- Calories: 210.7
- Sugar: 23.7
- Protein: 3.5
- Total Fat: 6.2
- Sodium: 275.4
- Cholesterol: 32
- Saturated Fat: 3.5
- Fiber: 2
- Total Carbohydrate: 37

45. Ricotta Cheese Scones

Serving: 6 scones | Prep: 15mins | Ready in:

Ingredients

- 1⁄2 cup light ricotta cheese (or regular)
- 1 egg
- 1 tablespoon nonfat milk (or regular, cream .. etc)
- 2 teaspoons cinnamon
- 2 cups all-purpose flour
- 1⁄2 cup white sugar
- 2 teaspoons baking powder
- 1⁄2 teaspoon baking soda
- 1⁄2 teaspoon salt
- 1⁄2 cup shortening
- For dusting
- sugar
- cinnamon

Direction

- Preheat oven to 350F degrees, and spray a baking sheet with non-stick cooking spray.
- In a small bowl, combine ricotta cheese, egg, milk and cinnamon.
- Mix well with a fork until well combined and not very lumpy.
- (Do not mix until all lumps disappear).
- In a large bowl, combine flour, sugar, baking powder, baking soda and salt.
- Cut in shortening until mixture resembles coarse cornmeal.
- Stir in cheese mixture lightly, then combine quickly.
- Be careful not to overmix, knead no more than 10 times.

- You may need to add another tablespoon of milk depending on your flour, dough should be slightly sticky and shiny.
- Place on the baking sheet, and pat into 3/4 inch thickness.
- Cut round into 6 wedge-shaped pieces.
- Move scones so they are not touching, and dust with sugar and cinnamon.
- Back 15-20 minutes, or until browned.

Nutrition Information

- Calories: 411.2
- Saturated Fat: 5.6
- Total Fat: 19.9
- Sodium: 459.3
- Fiber: 1.6
- Sugar: 17
- Total Carbohydrate: 50.8
- Cholesterol: 37.4
- Protein: 7.8

46. Scones With Leftover Cranberry Sauce

Serving: 8 scones, 6-8 serving(s) | Prep: 25mins | Ready in:

Ingredients

- 2 cups all-purpose flour, plus more for work surface
- 8 tablespoons chilled unsalted butter, cut into small pieces
- 5 tablespoons sugar, plus 1 tablespoon sugar (for topping)
- 1 tablespoon baking powder
- 1/2 teaspoon salt
- 1 teaspoon vanilla extract
- 1/2 teaspoon ground nutmeg (optional)
- 2 teaspoons sour cream
- 2/3 cup half-and-half, plus one tablespoon for brushing
- 1/2 cup left over cranberry sauce
- melted white chocolate or ganache, for drizzling

Direction

- Preheat oven 425 degrees. In a bowl, whisk together flour, 5 tablespoons sugar, baking powder, nutmeg (optional) and salt. Cut in butter with a pastry blender or two forks until mixture resembles coarse crumbs. Gently fold in cranberry sauce. In a small bowl, (with one or two stirs) mix the half and half, vanilla extract, and sour cream together. Make a hole in the middle of the flour mixture and pour the liquid mixture in, and start to gently incorporate liquid mixture into flour mixture. On a lightly floured surface, knead dough gently, about 5 times. Pat into a 1-inch this round. Cut into 8 wedges; place in a lightly greased baking sheet 2 inches apart. Brush tops with remaining tablespoon half and half; sprinkle with remaining tablespoon sugar. Bake until golden brown. 15 minutes (know your oven some ovens may need a few more minutes). Let cool on a wire rack. You can also eat warm.
- You may drizzle with white chocolate sauce or white chocolate sauce.

Nutrition Information

- Calories: 403.6
- Saturated Fat: 11.9
- Fiber: 1.4
- Sugar: 19.5
- Total Carbohydrate: 53.1
- Protein: 5.3
- Total Fat: 19.1
- Sodium: 397.2
- Cholesterol: 51.4

47. Sesame Crunch Banana Muffins

Serving: 16 serving(s) | Prep: 30mins | Ready in:

Ingredients

- 2 ripe medium bananas, mashed
- 1 cup skim milk
- 2 egg whites
- 2 tablespoons vegetable oil
- 1 teaspoon vanilla extract
- 1 1/2 cups rolled oats, uncooked
- 1/2 cup all-purpose flour
- 1/2 cup whole wheat flour
- 2 tablespoons sugar
- 1 tablespoon baking powder
- 1/2 teaspoon salt
- 4 tablespoons packed brown sugar
- 2 tablespoons chopped walnuts
- 2 tablespoons whole wheat flour
- 1 tablespoon sesame seeds
- 1 tablespoon margarine
- 3/4 teaspoon nutmeg
- 3/4 teaspoon cinnamon

Direction

- Prepare Sesame Crunch Topping by combining last 7 ingredients, set aside. Prep muffin cups.
- Combine bananas, milk, egg whites, oil and vanilla in large bowl. Combine oats, flours, sugar, baking powder and salt in medium bowl; stir into banana mixture until just moistened. Fill prepared muffin cups about 3/4 full. Sprinkle topping evenly over batter in each cup. Bake 20 to 25 minutes until golden on top and wooden toothpick inserted into center comes out clean. Cool slightly in pan before transferring to wire.

Nutrition Information

- Calories: 132.5
- Protein: 3.7
- Saturated Fat: 0.6
- Sodium: 167.2
- Total Carbohydrate: 21.3
- Cholesterol: 0.3
- Total Fat: 4
- Fiber: 2
- Sugar: 7

48. Sour Cream Berry Muffins

Serving: 12 muffins | Prep: 20mins | Ready in:

Ingredients

- 2 cups all-purpose flour
- 1 cup sugar
- 1 teaspoon baking powder
- 1/2 teaspoon baking soda
- 1/2 teaspoon salt
- 2 eggs
- 1 cup sour cream
- 1/2 cup vegetable oil
- 1 teaspoon vanilla extract
- 1 1/2 cups raspberries or 1 1/2 cups blueberries or 1 1/2 cups blackberries

Direction

- Preheat oven to 400°; line 12-cup muffin pan with paper liners.
- In a big bowl, whisk together flour, sugar, baking powder, baking soda, and salt.
- In another bowl, whisk together eggs, sour cream, oil, and vanilla until well blended.
- Add egg mixture to the flour mixture and stir until just blended; gently fold in berries.
- Divide batter evenly among prepared muffin cups.
- Bake for 20-25 minutes or until a pick comes out clean.
- Let cool in pan on a wire rack for 3 minutes, then transfer to the rack to cool.

Nutrition Information

- Calories: 278.7
- Fiber: 1.6
- Total Carbohydrate: 35.1
- Cholesterol: 41
- Total Fat: 14

- Saturated Fat: 3.7
- Sodium: 207.5
- Sugar: 18.1
- Protein: 3.8

49. Strawberry Shortcake Muffins

Serving: 12 muffins | Prep: 20mins | Ready in:

Ingredients

- 2 cups flour
- 1/2 cup sugar, divided
- 2 teaspoons baking powder
- 1/2 teaspoon salt
- 1 cup milk
- 1 egg, slightly beaten
- 1/4 cup butter, melted
- 12 strawberries, sliced

Direction

- Heat oven to 425°; grease 12 muffin cups.
- Combine flour, 1/4 cup of the sugar, baking powder and salt in a large bowl; stir in the milk, egg and butter, stirring only enough to dampen all the flour, the batter should not be smooth.
- Spoon into prepared muffin cups, filling each about 2/3 full.
- Press strawberry slices into the batter, pointed side up; sprinkle each muffin with 1 teaspoon sugar.
- Bake until golden, 15-18 minutes.

Nutrition Information

- Calories: 165.2
- Sodium: 207.7
- Fiber: 0.8
- Sugar: 9
- Protein: 3.5
- Total Fat: 5.2
- Saturated Fat: 3.1
- Cholesterol: 28.5
- Total Carbohydrate: 26.3

50. Sunshine Blueberry Muffins

Serving: 12 muffins, 12 serving(s) | Prep: 15mins | Ready in:

Ingredients

- Batter
- 2 cups flour
- 1/3 cup sugar
- 2 teaspoons baking powder
- 1 teaspoon baking soda
- 1/2 teaspoon salt
- 1 cup fresh blueberries or 1 cup frozen blueberries
- 2 eggs
- 1/3 cup oil
- 1 (8 ounce) carton lemon yogurt
- 1 lemon, zest of
- Glaze
- 3/4 cup powdered sugar
- 4 -5 teaspoons milk

Direction

- Preheat oven to 400*.
- Line medium muffin pans with paper liners or grease bottoms only.
- For batter, combine flour, sugar, baking powder, baking soda and salt in large bowl.
- Add blueberries; toss to coat well.
- In small bowl, whisk egg and oil; blend in yogurt and 1 teaspoon of the lemon zest.
- Add egg mixture to dry ingredients and stir just until moistened. Batter will be lumpy.
- Spoon batter into prepared muffin pans, filling each cup 3/4 full.
- Bake 12-14 minutes or until golden brown.
- Cool slightly.
- For glaze, combine the remaining lemon zest, powdered sugar and milk in small bowl and mix well.

- Drizzle glaze over muffins.

Nutrition Information

- Calories: 220
- Saturated Fat: 1.4
- Sodium: 286.4
- Fiber: 0.8
- Total Carbohydrate: 34.6
- Cholesterol: 36.2
- Total Fat: 7.4
- Sugar: 17.8
- Protein: 4.2

51. Texas Sized Lemon Muffins

Serving: 6 serving(s) | Prep: 15mins | Ready in:

Ingredients

- 1 3/4 cups all-purpose flour
- 3/4 teaspoon baking soda
- 1 teaspoon baking powder
- 1/4 teaspoon salt
- 1 1/2 cups granulated sugar
- 4 tablespoons lemon zest
- 1 large egg
- 8 ounces sour cream
- 1 large lemon, juice of
- 1/4 cup butter, melted

Direction

- Combine flour, baking soda, b. powder, salt and one cup of sugar in a large bowl. Make a well in the center. Set aside.
- Mix together 2 tbsp. of lemon zest, egg, sour cream, half the lemon juice and butter.
- Add the center of dry mixture, blend well and spoon into large greased muffins pans.
- Bake at 350 for 20 minutes.
- Blend together remaining sugar, lemon juice and zest.
- Drizzle glaze over tops of warm muffins.
- Makes 6 Texas sized muffins.

Nutrition Information

- Calories: 486.9
- Sodium: 427.5
- Fiber: 1.4
- Sugar: 51.8
- Total Carbohydrate: 80.4
- Cholesterol: 72.1
- Total Fat: 16.7
- Saturated Fat: 9.8
- Protein: 5.8

52. The Everything Muffins

Serving: 18 muffins, 18 serving(s) | Prep: 25mins | Ready in:

Ingredients

- 2 cups all-purpose flour
- 4 teaspoons baking powder
- 1 teaspoon salt
- 1 cup granulated sugar
- 1/2 cup sweet butter, melted
- 2 eggs (extra large)
- 1 cup milk
- 1 cup macadamia nuts, coarsely chopped
- 8 ounces white chocolate chips or 8 ounces white chocolate pieces
- 1/4 cup light raisins (optional)
- 1/4 cup dark raisin (optional)
- 2 ounces chopped walnuts (optional)
- 2 ounces chopped raw cashews (optional)
- 2 ounces chopped pecans (optional)
- 2 ounces semi-sweet chocolate chips (optional)
- 2 ounces milk chocolate chips (optional)
- 2 ounces peanut butter chips (optional)
- 2 ounces butterscotch chips (optional)

Direction

- Preheat oven to 375 degrees.

- Prepare your muffin pan by lightly brushing on a layer of melted butter.
- Let firm in refrigerator while preparing recipe.
- Or, you may choose to just line pan with paper liners.
- In a bowl, mix the flour, baking powder, salt, and sugar.
- Add melted butter, beaten eggs, and milk to the dry ingredients, and stir only enough to moisten.
- Mix in macadamia nuts, white chocolate chips, raisins, walnuts, raw cashews, pecans, chocolate chips, peanut butter chips and butterscotch chips.
- Spoon batter muffin pan about 3/4 full.
- Bake in 375 degree oven for approximately 18-20 minutes or until a toothpick inserted into the center comes out clean and dry.
- Remove from oven and cool for 10 minutes before turning out of pan.
- ENJOY!

Nutrition Information

- Calories: 277.5
- Protein: 4
- Total Fat: 16
- Saturated Fat: 7.1
- Sodium: 237
- Fiber: 1
- Sugar: 19
- Total Carbohydrate: 31.1
- Cholesterol: 40.7

53. The Ultimate Coconut Scones

Serving: 8 serving(s) | Prep: 10mins | Ready in:

Ingredients

- 2 cups all-purpose flour
- 1 tablespoon baking powder
- 1/4 cup sugar
- 1/2 teaspoon sea salt
- 5 tablespoons butter, cut into cubes and very cold
- 1 cup full-fat coconut milk (you can use the coconut milk chunks, you really should use full-fat if you want full flavor!)
- 1/2 cup shredded unsweetened coconut

Direction

- Preheat your oven to 450°F. Line a baking sheet with parchment paper or a Silpat.
- In a food processor pulse together the flour, sugar, baking powder, and salt. Add in the butter and pulse a few times until the mixture is crumbly. Add the shredded coconut and pulse 2-3 times, just to mix.
- Pour into a large bowl and add the coconut milk; using a spoon mix together until the dry ingredients are incorporated.
- Press into a 9-inch circle and cut into eighths. Place on baking sheet and bake 12-15 minutes or until the bottoms are just slightly browned. Serve hot with a simple glaze of powdered sugar and milk, with a pat of butter, or just plain!

Nutrition Information

- Calories: 428.3
- Protein: 4.7
- Saturated Fat: 18.5
- Fiber: 3.2
- Sugar: 26.4
- Cholesterol: 19.1
- Total Fat: 22.7
- Sodium: 364.1
- Total Carbohydrate: 53.6

54. Whole Wheat Carrot Muffins

Serving: 12 muffins | Prep: 30mins | Ready in:

Ingredients

- 1 cup plain flour
- 1 cup whole wheat flour
- 1 cup brown sugar
- 1 teaspoon baking soda
- 2 teaspoons baking powder
- 3⁄4 teaspoon salt
- 1⁄2 teaspoon allspice
- 1⁄2 teaspoon ginger
- 6 ounces non-fat vanilla yogurt
- 1⁄2 cup nonfat milk
- 1 egg
- 2 tablespoons sunflower oil (or canola oil)
- 1 teaspoon vanilla
- 1 medium carrot
- 1 tablespoon lemon zest
- 1 cup powdered sugar

Direction

- Preheat the oven to 350°F.
- Mix all the dry ingredients (plain flour, whole-wheat flour, brown sugar, baking soda, baking powder, salt, allspice and ginger) in a bowl.
- In another bowl, beat the egg lightly and mix with oil, milk, vanilla and yogurt.
- Pour the wet mix into the dry mix and stir.
- Grate the carrot and add it to the mix.
- Fill the muffin tins up to 3/4 of their height because they will grow in the oven.
- Bake for about 15 minutes. To make sure that they are ready, you can insert a toothpick in the center of the muffins and see if it comes out clean. Do not overcook because they will lose moistness.
- For the icing, put the lemon zest in a small bowl and slowly add the powdered sugar. Mix until all the sugar dissolves (if the mixture is too dry, add a little more lemon zest).
- Place the mixture on top of the muffins with a spoon or pastry bag and let it dry until it hardens.

Nutrition Information

- Calories: 220.2
- Saturated Fat: 0.5
- Sodium: 338.7
- Sugar: 29.5
- Total Carbohydrate: 45.6
- Cholesterol: 16
- Protein: 3.9
- Total Fat: 3.1
- Fiber: 1.6

55. Yule Oatcakes

Serving: 12 16 | Prep: 30mins | Ready in:

Ingredients

- 3 1⁄2 cups old fashioned oats
- 1 teaspoon salt
- 2 tablespoons flour
- 1⁄2 cup vegetable shortening
- 1⁄2 cup water (up to, probably less)
- 1⁄2 cup sugar (you can use up to 1 cup of sugar, or leave it out entirely for a plain oatcake. Personally I think t)

Direction

- Combine all ingredients except the water in a bowl. Add water JUST TO DAMPEN until you can roll it into a ball. Let the ball alone on the counter for about 10 minutes. Now take a handful and roll it out about 1/8 - 1/4 inch thick. Cut into circles with cutter or top of a drinking glass. Place on ungreased baking sheets and bake 350 for 30 minutes or until lightly browned. Transfer to wire rack to cool.

Nutrition Information

- Calories: 203.2
- Cholesterol: 0
- Sugar: 8.7
- Total Carbohydrate: 25.1
- Fiber: 2.4
- Protein: 3.9
- Total Fat: 10

- Saturated Fat: 2.7
- Sodium: 195

Chapter 2: Quick Bread Dessert Recipes

***

56. Apple Muffins (Nova Scotia Style)

Serving: 12-14 muffins | Prep: 10mins | Ready in:

Ingredients

- 2 cups flour
- 4 teaspoons baking powder
- 3 tablespoons sugar
- 1/2 teaspoon salt
- 2 teaspoons cinnamon and brown sugar
- 2 tablespoons melted butter
- 1 egg, beaten
- 1 cup milk
- 1 cup diced apple (I prefer Granny Smith)

Direction

- Sift dry ingredients together 3 times.
- Add combined liquids and then add apples.
- Fill greased muffin pan 2/3 full and sprinkle with Cinnamon and B. Sugar mixture. Bake in hot oven at 400 degrees for 20-25 mins (sometimes less, keep an eye on them).

Nutrition Information

- Calories: 133.2
- Fiber: 0.8
- Total Carbohydrate: 22.6
- Cholesterol: 25.6
- Protein: 3.4
- Total Fat: 3.3
- Saturated Fat: 1.8
- Sodium: 248.2
- Sugar: 5.1

57. Banana Bundt Bread

Serving: 1 cake, 16 serving(s) | Prep: 10mins | Ready in:

Ingredients

- 2 cups bananas (overripe)
- 1 cup sugar
- 1 cup vegetable oil
- 3 large eggs
- 3 cups all-purpose flour
- 1 teaspoon baking soda
- 1 teaspoon salt

Direction

- Preheat oven to 350°F.
- Lightly grease and flour Bundt pan and set aside.
- Whisk flour, baking soda and salt together and set aside.
- Combine banana, sugar, eggs and oil in a large bowl.
- Stir flour mixture into banana mixture in thirds.
- Pour batter into Bundt pan.
- Bake at 350 F for 1 hour or until toothpick comes out clean.

Nutrition Information

- Calories: 284.6
- Saturated Fat: 2.1
- Sugar: 14.9
- Total Carbohydrate: 34.7
- Cholesterol: 39.7

- Total Fat: 14.8
- Sodium: 237.8
- Fiber: 1.1
- Protein: 3.8

58. Banana Caramel Biscuit For One

Serving: 1 serving(s) | Prep: 5mins | Ready in:

Ingredients

- 2 tablespoons caramel ice cream topping
- 5 slices bananas
- 1 frozen buttermilk biscuit

Direction

- Generously butter 1 disposable aluminum pot pie pan.
- Spread ice cream topping over bottom of pan.
- Place banana slices over topping, making sure to place one slice in the center, then overlapping as necessary.
- Place biscuit over bananas.
- Bake at 375°F for 22 to 25 minutes or until top of biscuit is golden brown.
- Invert onto serving plate.

Nutrition Information

- Calories: 295.9
- Cholesterol: 0.4
- Protein: 4.8
- Sodium: 745.4
- Sugar: 0
- Total Carbohydrate: 51.6
- Fiber: 0.4
- Total Fat: 8.7
- Saturated Fat: 2.4

59. Berry Citrus Mini Muffins

Serving: 24 mini- muffins, 12 serving(s) | Prep: 10mins | Ready in:

Ingredients

- 1 cup flour
- 1/4 cup wheat bran
- 1 teaspoon baking powder
- 1/8 teaspoon salt
- 2 tablespoons unsalted butter, softened
- 1/2 cup sugar
- 1/2 cup egg substitute
- 2 teaspoons lemon zest
- 1/2 cup orange juice
- 1 cup blueberries
- 1 cup strawberry

Direction

- Preheat oven to 325°F.
- Prepare a mini muffin tray by either placing lining in the cups or greasing.
- Combine the first 4 ingredients together and set aside.
- Cream together butter and sugar, then gradually incorporate egg substitute.
- Add lemon zest and orange juice to the sugar mixture.
- Gradually incorporate dry mixture into wet.
- Fold in blueberries and strawberries. I cut the blueberries in half and the strawberries in 4 to 6 pieces depending on their size. If you are using frozen fruits, make sure that the fruit are defrosted and drained of their excess liquid to prevent from watering down the muffins.
- Bake for 15 to 20 minutes, until lightly colored on the top.

Nutrition Information

- Calories: 110.4
- Cholesterol: 5.1
- Protein: 2.5
- Saturated Fat: 1.2
- Sodium: 75.3

- Fiber: 1.4
- Sugar: 11.2
- Total Carbohydrate: 21.2
- Total Fat: 2.2

60. Choc A Mocha Muffins

Serving: 6 Mufins | Prep: 15mins | Ready in:

Ingredients

- 75 g unsalted butter
- 75 g milk chocolate, broken into pieces
- 75 g granulated sugar
- 2 medium eggs, lightly beaten
- 75 g self raising flour, sifted
- 125 g milk chocolate, broken into pieces
- 50 ml double cream
- 1 tablespoon instant coffee granules

Direction

- Preheat the oven to 180c/fan160c/gas4. Lie a deep 6 hole muffin tin with muffin cases. Place the butter and 75g chocolate in a heatproof bowl place over a pan of simmering water until melted- do not allow the bowl to touch the water.
- Remove the bowl from the heat stir in the sugar. Using a wooden spoon, gradely beat in the eggs. Fold in the flour until smoothly combined. Spoon the mixture into the muffin cases until each is half full.
- To make the ganache, place the remaining chocolate, cream coffee in a heatproof bowl place over simmering water - again do not allow the bowl to touch the water. Once the chocolate has melted, remove from heat, stir thoroughly allow to cool slightly.
- Spoon a teaspoon of the ganache into each muffin case the top with the remaining muffin mixture. Bake for 20-25 mins, or until the muffins are springy to the touch.
- Transfer the muffins to a wire rack, while hot, top each with the remaining ganache, smoothing it with a round bladed knife.
- Serve warm or cold. The muffins will keep for up to 2 days in the fridge.

Nutrition Information

- Calories: 378.6
- Sodium: 52.1
- Total Carbohydrate: 32.6
- Saturated Fat: 13.6
- Fiber: 1.6
- Sugar: 17.5
- Cholesterol: 108.2
- Protein: 6.4
- Total Fat: 24.8

61. Chocolate Crispy Biscuits

Serving: 15-18 cookies, 15 serving(s) | Prep: 15mins | Ready in:

Ingredients

- 125 g butter or 125 g margarine
- 1 cup sugar
- 1 egg
- 1 teaspoon vanilla extract
- 2 cups rice bubbles or 2 cups Rice Krispies
- 1 cup self raising flour
- 1 cup chocolate chips

Direction

- Preheat oven to 180 degrees Celsius.
- Line a baking tray with baking paper.
- Cream butter and sugar together till pale and creamy.
- Add egg and vanilla and beat till smooth.
- Add remaining ingredients.
- Stir till well combined.
- Place heaped tablespoons of mixture on trays.
- Allow room for spreading.

- Bake 15 - 17 minutes, then cool for 5 minutes.
- Transfer to wire rack.

Nutrition Information

- Calories: 214.3
- Sodium: 85.2
- Fiber: 0.9
- Total Carbohydrate: 29.9
- Total Fat: 10.5
- Saturated Fat: 6.4
- Sugar: 19.8
- Cholesterol: 30.2
- Protein: 2.1

62. Cinnamon Nut Flatbread

Serving: 12 serving(s) | Prep: 15mins | Ready in:

Ingredients

- 12 rhodes dinner rolls, thawed to room temperature
- 3 tablespoons butter, softened
- 1/2 cup sugar
- 1/2 cup chopped walnuts
- 1 teaspoon cinnamon
- Glaze
- 1 cup powdered sugar
- 1 -2 tablespoon milk

Direction

- Spray counter lightly with non-stick cooking spray. Combine rolls and roll into a 10x15-inch rectangle. Place dough on a sprayed baking sheet. Poke with a fork several times to prevent bubbles from forming and spread with softened butter.
- Combine sugar, nuts and cinnamon and sprinkle over the buttered dough. Bake at 375°F 12-15 minutes or until golden brown on the edges. Combine glaze ingredients and drizzle over warm flat bread.

Nutrition Information

- Calories: 207.3
- Protein: 3.5
- Total Fat: 7.7
- Saturated Fat: 2.5
- Sodium: 160.4
- Fiber: 0.9
- Total Carbohydrate: 32.2
- Cholesterol: 8.8
- Sugar: 19.6

63. Cornbread (Low Fat)

Serving: 12 serving(s) | Prep: 20mins | Ready in:

Ingredients

- 1 cup flour
- 1 cup cornmeal
- 1/4 cup sugar
- 1 teaspoon baking soda
- 1/2 teaspoon salt
- 1 cup plain nonfat yogurt
- 2 egg whites

Direction

- Preheat oven to 400 degrees.
- Beat egg whites until soft peaks form.
- Mix dry ingredients together in bowl.
- Stir in yogurt.
- Fold in the egg whites.
- Mix well.
- Bake at 400 degrees in 8" square or round pan. (I used a cast iron skillet sprayed with cooking spray) for about 20 minutes.

Nutrition Information

- Calories: 105.1
- Saturated Fat: 0.1
- Fiber: 1

- Sugar: 5.9
- Total Carbohydrate: 21.5
- Total Fat: 0.5
- Sodium: 230.4
- Cholesterol: 0.4
- Protein: 3.7

64. Cranberry Nut Muffins

Serving: 12 muffins | Prep: 0S | Ready in:

Ingredients

- 3⁄4 cup Miracle Whip
- 1 1⁄4 cups orange juice concentrate, undiluted
- 2 eggs, beaten
- 2 cups fresh cranberries or 2 cups frozen cranberries
- 2 cups flour
- 3⁄4 cup sugar
- 1⁄2 cup chopped nuts
- 2 teaspoons orange rind
- 1 teaspoon baking powder
- 1 teaspoon baking soda

Direction

- Combine Miracle Whip, orange juice, eggs and cranberries.
- In a separate bowl, combine remaining ingredients.
- Stir wet mixture into dry ingredients. Fill greased muffin cups. Bake at 350F for 20-25 minutes. Let stand for 10 minutes. Remove from pan.

Nutrition Information

- Calories: 225.2
- Total Carbohydrate: 43.3
- Cholesterol: 35.2
- Protein: 5
- Total Fat: 4
- Saturated Fat: 0.7
- Sodium: 186.6
- Fiber: 2.1
- Sugar: 24.6

65. Crumbly, Sweet And Buttery Cornbread

Serving: 8 pieces, 8 serving(s) | Prep: 10mins | Ready in:

Ingredients

- 5 tablespoons unsalted butter, divided, melted
- 3⁄4 teaspoon salt
- 1 1⁄4 cups cornmeal
- 1 cup flour
- 1⁄4 cup whole wheat flour
- 1 cup buttermilk
- 1 tablespoon baking powder
- 1⁄2 teaspoon baking soda
- 1 large egg
- 1⁄2 cup sugar
- 1⁄2 cup corn oil, for baking

Direction

- Preheat oven to 424, in a medium sized cast iron skillet put corn oil and let it heat in the oven while it preheats.
- Mix all dry ingredients together in a medium sized bowl.
- Mix all wet ingredients together, except the corn oil that's used above and reserve 1 TBL of the melted butter.
- Make a well in the center of the dry ingredients, put the wet and stir as little as possible until combined. The batter may be lumpy.
- Pour into cast iron skillet and bake until set around 25 to 30 minutes. After 15 minutes reduce oven heat to 400. Top with remaining 1 TBL melted butter and enjoy.

Nutrition Information

- Calories: 393.1
- Protein: 5.5
- Total Fat: 22.6
- Saturated Fat: 6.8
- Fiber: 2.2
- Sugar: 14.2
- Total Carbohydrate: 43.7
- Cholesterol: 43.6
- Sodium: 482

66. Dulce De Leche And Praline (Nougat) Muffins

Serving: 18 muffins, 1 serving(s) | Prep: 15mins | Ready in:

Ingredients

- 300 g flour
- 150 g brown sugar
- 2 large eggs
- 80 g butter
- 120 ml oil (canola)
- 200 g Greek yogurt
- 200 g dulce de leche (caramel cream)
- 100 g pralines (hazelnut or almond nougat)
- 20 ml milk
- 3 tablespoons unsweetened cocoa
- 50 g hazelnuts (ground)
- 2 teaspoons baking powder
- 1 pinch salt
- vanilla extract (optional)

Direction

- Beat butter, oil and sugar in a bowl until fluffy.
- Add 2 whole eggs and keep on beating.
- Mix flour with baking powder and a pinch of salt and add to dough.
- Add yoghurt and incorporate.
- If using add vanilla extract.
- Transfer half of dough to a separate bowl.
- Melt nougat in 20ml of milk (I use the microwave on 700Watt for about 45 seconds).
- Caramel/Dulce de Leche dough:
- Add dulce de leche to one half of dough and incorporate.
- Nougat dough:
- Add cocoa, hazelnuts and melted nougat and incorporate.
- Preheat oven at 175°C.
- Spoon dark dough into muffin tin or muffin molds.
- Add light, caramelly dough on top (or vice versa).
- Bake at 175°C for about 25 minutes. If muffins get too dark, cover with aluminum foil.
- Enjoy!

Nutrition Information

- Calories: 3767
- Protein: 56.7
- Total Fat: 225.4
- Saturated Fat: 63.1
- Cholesterol: 545.7
- Sodium: 1651.9
- Fiber: 19
- Sugar: 149.5
- Total Carbohydrate: 398.8

67. Easy And Quick Corn Dog Muffins

Serving: 6 muffins, 3-6 serving(s) | Prep: 5mins | Ready in:

Ingredients

- 8 1/2 ounces corn muffin mix
- 1 egg
- 1/3 cup milk
- 3 hot dogs, cooked
- ketchup (optional)

Direction

- Prepare the corn muffin batter as directed on the box.
- Chop the hot dogs into bite-size pieces.
- Mix in the hot dog pieces into the batter.
- Pour batter into a greased muffin tin.
- Bake for 15-20 minutes or until a toothpick inserted into the center of a muffin comes out clean.
- Eat plain or with ketchup.
- Enjoy!
- Note: You can add more of less hot dog, depending on your own tastes.

Nutrition Information

- Calories: 526
- Saturated Fat: 8.9
- Sugar: 17.9
- Total Carbohydrate: 59.1
- Cholesterol: 91.2
- Protein: 13.7
- Total Fat: 25.7
- Sodium: 1207.3
- Fiber: 5.2

68. Gingerbread Scone

Serving: 8 scones, 8 serving(s) | Prep: 15mins | Ready in:

Ingredients

- 2 cups all-purpose flour
- 3 tablespoons brown sugar
- 2 teaspoons baking powder
- 1 teaspoon ginger
- 1/2 teaspoon baking soda
- 1 teaspoon cinnamon (ground)
- 1/4 cup butter
- 1 egg (seperated, beaten)
- 1/3 cup molasses
- 1/4 cup milk
- sugar
- nutmeg whipped cream (Nutmeg Whipped Cream)

Direction

- Preheat oven to 400.
- Combine flour, brown sugar, baking powder, ginger, baking soda, salt, and cinnamon.
- Cut in butter until mixture is crumbly.
- Stir together egg yolk, molasses, and milk, add to flour mixture, stir until combined (mixture may seem dry).
- Place on lightly floured surface, knead 10-12 strokes (until nearly smooth).
- Pat into 7 inch circle, cut into 8 wedges.
- Arrange wedges on ungreased baking sheet, 1 inch apart.
- Brush tops with egg white, sprinkle with sugar (if desired).
- Bake 12-15 minutes (until light brown).
- Cool on wire rack for 20 minutes, serve warm with nutmeg whipped cream (if desired).
- Optional: Can make these ahead of time, freeze, and reheat on baking sheet at 300 for 20 minutes to serve.

Nutrition Information

- Calories: 241
- Saturated Fat: 4.1
- Sodium: 230.8
- Total Fat: 7
- Fiber: 1
- Sugar: 12.9
- Total Carbohydrate: 40.4
- Cholesterol: 42.8
- Protein: 4.4

69. Gluten Free Yorkshire Pudding

Serving: 8 serving(s) | Prep: 20mins | Ready in:

Ingredients

- 115 g gluten-free self-raising flour
- 142 ml milk
- 142 ml water (half milk and half water)

- 1 pinch salt (optional)
- 1 medium egg
- 30 g vegetable oil

Direction

- Heat the oven to 220°C or 425°F or Gas mark 7.
- Place the flour and salt in a mixing bowl: make a well in the center with a wooden spoon.
- Drop the egg and half the milk and water mixture into it.
- Gradually work the flour into the egg and milk and water mixture to form a smooth creamy texture.
- Slowly add the rest of the milk and water mixture and then beat well.
- Heat the oil in 8-10 patty tins or in a 23x18cm tray (9x7-inch tin) in the oven.
- When the oil begins to smoke, pour in the batter.
- Bake in the top of the oven until well risen and brown; about 20 minutes for the small pudding or 45 minutes for the large pudding.
- Serve immediately with your roast meal or serve it with golden syrup and cream.

Nutrition Information

- Calories: 52.1
- Saturated Fat: 1.1
- Sugar: 0
- Total Carbohydrate: 0.8
- Cholesterol: 22.9
- Protein: 1.3
- Total Fat: 4.9
- Sodium: 16.8
- Fiber: 0

70. Gorgeous Chocolate Muffins

Serving: 18 muffins | Prep: 20mins | Ready in:

Ingredients

- 75 g butter
- 200 g sugar
- 1 teaspoon vanilla sugar
- 1 egg
- 250 ml milk
- 1 teaspoon vinegar
- 300 g flour
- 2 teaspoons baking powder
- 80 g unsweetened cocoa powder
- 75 g chocolate (grated)
- 1 pinch salt

Direction

- In a bowl cream butter, sugar, vanilla sugar and the egg. Mix milk and vinegar and add it to the butter mixture.
- In a second bowl combine flour, baking powder, salt, cacao powder and chocolate.
- Blend the butter mixture into the flour mixture.
- Fill the dough into a lined muffin pan and bake at 170°C in the pre-heated oven for about 30 minutes.
- If you like, melt a bar of chocolate and spread the muffins with it.

Nutrition Information

- Calories: 177.3
- Total Fat: 7.1
- Sugar: 11.3
- Total Carbohydrate: 28.4
- Cholesterol: 21.1
- Protein: 4
- Saturated Fat: 4.3
- Sodium: 91.5
- Fiber: 2.6

71. Healthy Apple Carrot Zucchini Muffins

Serving: 8-10 muffins | Prep: 10mins | Ready in:

Ingredients

- 120 g carrots (1 small)
- 110 g zucchini (1 small)
- 220 g apples (1 big)
- 50 g flour
- 50 g whole wheat flour
- 2 teaspoons baking powder
- 20 g ground hazelnuts
- 30 g oats
- 60 g sugar beet molasses (or honey alternatively)
- 1 egg

Direction

- In a bowl grate zucchini/courgette and carrot. Cut the apple into small chunks.
- Preheat the oven to 170°C/340°F.
- In another bowl cream the egg and molasses with a pinch of salt. Add the grated veggies, oats and grated hazelnuts.
- Mix baking powder and flours and add to the egg mixture. Stir until just combined.
- Now fold in the apples and pour batter into prepared muffin pan.
- Bake for about 30 minutes.

Nutrition Information

- Calories: 130.6
- Sugar: 8.4
- Cholesterol: 26.4
- Total Fat: 2.7
- Saturated Fat: 0.4
- Fiber: 2.9
- Total Carbohydrate: 24.4
- Protein: 3.7
- Sodium: 117.8

72. Honey Biscuits (Cookies)

Serving: 80-100 biscuits | Prep: 1hours | Ready in:

Ingredients

- 2 lbs honey, warmed (just under 1kg)
- 1 lb sugar (500gm)
- 4 eggs, well beaten
- 1 teaspoon ground allspice
- 1 teaspoon cinnamon
- 1/2 teaspoon ground cloves
- 4 teaspoons bicarbonate of soda
- 3 7/8 lbs plain flour (approx 2kg)

Direction

- In a very large bowl thoroughly combine all ingredients except flour.
- Gradually stir in flour until you get a stiff mix that is neither dry nor sticky. Quantity of flour will vary every batch.
- Cover bowl with lid or plastic wrap and set aside overnight.
- Next day. Preheat oven to moderate (180 degrees Celsius). Now, either roll out and cut out shapes or roll into balls. Press halved, skinned almonds onto balls. Either way, allow enough room between biscuits for slight spreading.
- Baking time will vary depending on thickness of biscuit. The biscuit will have a nice golden colour when done and still be soft. Allow to set for a couple of minutes on tray before putting onto a wire rack to cool. A thin biscuit will be crisp whilst a 'ball' will be softer.

Nutrition Information

- Calories: 140.3
- Sodium: 67.4
- Fiber: 0.6
- Cholesterol: 10.6
- Protein: 2.6
- Total Fat: 0.5
- Saturated Fat: 0.1
- Sugar: 15.1
- Total Carbohydrate: 31.9

73. Hugh Yorkshire Puddings

Serving: 8-10 1, 1 serving(s) | Prep: 5mins | Ready in:

Ingredients

- 1 cup milk
- 1/2 cup all-purpose flour
- 1 pinch salt
- 3 eggs
- 1/4 cup vegetable oil

Direction

- Preheat oven to 450F.
- Mix the batter ingredients together let rest 10 minute.
- Preheat a Yorkshire pudding tray or muffin tin with 1/2 inch oil in each section. After about 10 min divide batter into tray. Cook for about 15-20 minutes until crisp and puffy.

Nutrition Information

- Calories: 1079.9
- Sodium: 488.8
- Total Carbohydrate: 60.1
- Cholesterol: 592.2
- Saturated Fat: 17.4
- Fiber: 1.7
- Sugar: 0.7
- Protein: 33.3
- Total Fat: 78.3

74. Italian Wine Biscuits

Serving: 48 biscuit type cookies | Prep: 10mins | Ready in:

Ingredients

- 2 cups flour
- 3 -4 cups flour
- 3 teaspoons baking powder
- 1 cup sugar
- 1 cup oil
- 1 cup dry red wine (like a good table burgundy)
- 1 egg, slightly beaten with 1 tsp water

Direction

- In medium size bowl place sugar, oil and wine; mix together till completely combined.
- Stir 2 cups flour and baking powder together; add to wet mixture and blend well.
- Add 3-4 cups more flour, slowly mixing as you go until mixture pulls away from bowl and holds its shape.
- Pinch off small pieces and roll into logs as thick as your finger and 3-4 inches long. Shape into rings and place on cookie sheet. When sheet is full, brush tops with beaten egg mixture and bake at 350° for 20 minutes.
- Cool on wire rack.
- Don't be alarmed at the colour of the dough- it's kind of grey with a pink blush.

Nutrition Information

- Calories: 109.5
- Saturated Fat: 0.6
- Total Carbohydrate: 14.3
- Cholesterol: 4.4
- Protein: 1.5
- Total Fat: 4.8
- Sugar: 4.2
- Sodium: 24.6
- Fiber: 0.3

75. Kristie's Shortbread Biscuits

Serving: 6-8 serving(s) | Prep: 1hours | Ready in:

Ingredients

- 250 g plain flour
- 1/4 teaspoon salt
- 125 g unsalted butter

- 100 g caster sugar, plus extra for sprinkling
- 1 large egg

Direction

- Sift the flour with the salt, then cream the butter and sugar together until pale and creamy. With the mixer's motor running, gradually add the egg; if the mixture looks like it's curdling, add a tbsp. of sifted flour.
- Put the mixer on its lowest setting and add the flour gradually. Stop mixing as the mixture comes together/leaves the side of the bowl; make sure it isn't sticky.
- Roll out on a floured surface (around 5mm thick) and cut out shapes with your cutter.
- Bake for around 20-30mins until lightly golden in color.
- Let the biscuits cool on a wire rack after sprinkling sugar over the biscuits as soon as they come out of the oven.
- Enjoy!

Nutrition Information

- Calories: 415.7
- Total Fat: 18.2
- Saturated Fat: 11
- Sodium: 111.9
- Fiber: 1.4
- Sugar: 16.9
- Total Carbohydrate: 56.5
- Cholesterol: 80
- Protein: 6.6

76. Lemon Currant Biscuits

Serving: 30 biscuits, 15 serving(s) | Prep: 10mins | Ready in:

Ingredients

- 4 ounces butter
- 6 ounces sugar
- 8 ounces flour
- 1 egg
- 2 ounces currants
- 1 teaspoon baking powder
- 1 large lemon, rind of, grated
- 1/2 teaspoon cinnamon

Direction

- Cream butter and sugar.
- Add egg and mix well.
- Add grated lemon rind and dry ingredients.
- Add currants.
- Roll teaspoonfuls of mixture into balls and place on lightly greased baking tray.
- Press balls lightly with fork.
- (Dip fork in flour and shake off excess).
- Bake 180'-190'C (Gas mark 4) for about 15-20 minutes or until they are just slightly golden in color- not browned.

Nutrition Information

- Calories: 169
- Cholesterol: 28.7
- Fiber: 0.7
- Sugar: 13.9
- Total Carbohydrate: 25.9
- Sodium: 83.7
- Protein: 2.2
- Total Fat: 6.6
- Saturated Fat: 4

77. Lemon Yoghurt Muffins!

Serving: 6-8 muffins | Prep: 15mins | Ready in:

Ingredients

- Wet ingredients
- 1 egg
- 50 g caster sugar
- 50 g unsalted butter
- 100 g yoghurt

- 2 tablespoons lemon juice
- Dry ingredients
- 100 g baking flour
- 1/2 teaspoon baking soda

Direction

- Preheat the oven to 180 degrees Celsius.
- Melt the butter in the microwave.
- Cream the butter and sugar together with a whisk. (Make sure that all the sugar has been dissolved.).
- Add the egg, making sure that the mixture is not too hot to prevent it from cooking the egg entirely. (Alternatively, whisk really quickly!).
- Add the yoghurt followed by the lemon juice. (Depending on individual taste preference, you could add more lemon juice for a richer flavor.
- Mix in the dry ingredients, ensuring that the flour is sifted and the baking soda is evenly mixed so that you have a fluffy muffins.
- Blend the ingredients with a spatula. Do not worry about lumps of batter as they are not clumps of dry flour, and they would disappear with baking.
- Fill the batter into muffin cups or moulds.
- (You could line moulds such as aluminum muffin cups with wax paper or pre-made muffin cups. Just make sure that they can hold their shape to give pretty muffins. (:).
- Pop the filled muffin trays or moulds into the preheated oven for 25 minutes, at 180 degrees Celsius.
- Take note that the yield of this recipe depends on the size of muffin cups used.
- If need be, you could make more of this to suit the number of servings you need.
- Also, if you are using metal muffin cups to hold the muffins while baking, ensure that you remove the muffins from them quickly to prevent moisture from forming at the base of the muffin.
- Enjoy!

Nutrition Information

- Calories: 176.4
- Protein: 3.4
- Total Fat: 8.3
- Saturated Fat: 4.9
- Sugar: 9.3
- Cholesterol: 55.3
- Sodium: 125.5
- Fiber: 0.5
- Total Carbohydrate: 22.3

78. Lemonberry Muffins

Serving: 12 muffins | Prep: 5mins | Ready in:

Ingredients

- 1 cup whole-grain spelt flour
- 1/2 teaspoon baking soda
- 1/4 teaspoon baking powder
- 1/8 teaspoon sea salt
- 1/2 cup unsweetened soymilk
- 1/2 cup brown rice syrup
- 1/4 cup canola oil
- 1/2 teaspoon lemon flavoring
- 3/4 cup raspberries

Direction

- Preheat oven to 375°F.
- In large bowl, whisk together flour, baking soda, baking powder, and sea salt. In small bowl, whisk together soymilk, brown rice syrup, oil, and lemon flavoring.
- Add wet ingredients to dry ingredients, mix well by hand.
- Gently fold in raspberries. Fill the cups of 12-cup muffin tin two-thirds full.
- Bake 20 to 25 minutes, or until toothpick inserted in center comes out clean. Let muffins cool on cooling rack so bottoms do not become soggy.

Nutrition Information

- Calories: 49.5
- Protein: 0.6
- Saturated Fat: 0.3
- Sodium: 89.9
- Sugar: 0.4
- Total Carbohydrate: 1.4
- Total Fat: 4.8
- Fiber: 0.6
- Cholesterol: 0

79. Light Chocolate Chip Scones

Serving: 16 serving(s) | Prep: 20mins | Ready in:

Ingredients

- 2 cups all-purpose flour
- 1 tablespoon baking powder
- 1/2 teaspoon salt
- 2 tablespoons sugar
- 5 tablespoons light butter, cold, cut in chunks
- 3/4 cup chocolate chips
- 1 cup fat-free half-and-half, plus more for brushing the scones
- 1/2 cup confectioners' sugar, sifted
- 1 tablespoon turbinado sugar

Direction

- Preheat oven to 400 degrees F.
- Whisk the flour, baking powder, salt, and sugar together in a bowl. Using a fork, cut in the butter to coat the pieces with the flour. The mixture should look like coarse crumbs.
- Fold the chocolate chips into the batter. Make a well in the center and pour in the half-and-half. Fold everything together just to incorporate; do not overwork the dough.
- Turn the dough out on a lightly floured surface into a rectangle about 12 inches by 3 inches by 1 1/4 inches. Cut the rectangle in half length-wise, then cut in quarters length-wise, giving you 8 squares. Cut the squares in 1/2 on a diagonal to give you the classic triangle shape.
- Place the scones on an ungreased cookie sheet and brush the tops with half-and-half. Bake for 15 to 20 minutes until beautiful and brown. Remove immediately from baking sheet and place on cooling racks.
- While the scones are baking, make the glaze by combining confectioner's sugar with a small amount of water. Let the scones cool a bit before applying the glaze. Whisk the glaze to smooth out any lumps, and brush onto the surface of the scones. Sprinkle with turbinado sugar.

Nutrition Information

- Calories: 147.8
- Saturated Fat: 3.1
- Total Carbohydrate: 23.9
- Total Fat: 5.2
- Sodium: 184.3
- Fiber: 0.9
- Sugar: 10.3
- Cholesterol: 5.6
- Protein: 2.5

80. Low Fat Pumpkin Pie Muffins

Serving: 12 muffins, 12 serving(s) | Prep: 10mins | Ready in:

Ingredients

- 2 eggs
- 1 cup sugar
- 1 cup pumpkin puree
- 1/2 teaspoon vanilla
- 1/2 cup unsweetened applesauce
- 1 1/3 cups whole wheat flour
- 1 teaspoon baking soda
- 1 teaspoon baking powder
- 1 teaspoon cinnamon
- 1/2 teaspoon nutmeg

Direction

- Preheat oven to 400 degrees.
- Line a 12-cup muffin tin with muffin liners.
- In a large mixing bowl, beat eggs, sugar, pumpkin, vanilla, and applesauce until smooth.
- In a small mixing bowl, stir together flour, baking soda, baking powder, cinnamon and nutmeg.
- Pour dry mixture into pumpkin mixture and whisk until a smooth dough forms.
- Fill lined muffin cups 3/4 full with batter.
- Place in the oven for 15-20 minutes or until lightly browned.

Nutrition Information

- Calories: 130.3
- Saturated Fat: 0.3
- Sodium: 147.8
- Total Carbohydrate: 28.4
- Total Fat: 1.2
- Fiber: 1.7
- Sugar: 17.9
- Cholesterol: 31
- Protein: 2.9

81. Low Fat Apple Oatmeal Muffins With Walnuts

Serving: 1 muffin, 6 serving(s) | Prep: 1hours30mins | Ready in:

Ingredients

- 1 cup rolled oats (old fashioned oatmeal)
- 1 cup powdered milk (dry)
- 1 cup warm water
- 1/3 cup agave syrup
- 1/2 cup unsweetened applesauce
- 2 egg whites
- 1 cup whole wheat flour
- 1/2 cup Splenda granular
- 1 teaspoon baking powder
- 1/2 teaspoon baking soda
- 1 teaspoon ground cinnamon
- 1 teaspoon vanilla
- 1 chopped granny smith apple
- 1 cup chopped walnuts
- 1/2 cup raisins

Direction

- Preheat oven to 400 degrees.
- Combine oats, powdered milk, and warm water and set aside to soak for 1 hour.
- In a large bowl, combine remaining ingredients with the oatmeal mixture.
- Spoon into 6 large muffin tins that have been sprayed with non-stick cooking spray.
- Bake for 20-25 minutes until they are done.
- Remove from pan and allow to cool or eat while warm or both!

Nutrition Information

- Calories: 418.9
- Sugar: 18.7
- Total Carbohydrate: 50.1
- Cholesterol: 20.7
- Protein: 15.2
- Saturated Fat: 5
- Sodium: 267.6
- Fiber: 6.5
- Total Fat: 19.8

82. Macadamia Burnt Butter Biscuits

Serving: 25 Biscuits, 25-30 serving(s) | Prep: 15mins | Ready in:

Ingredients

- 100 g unsalted butter (must be at room temperature)
- 50 g unsalted butter
- 75 g caster sugar
- 175 g plain flour

- 30 g rice flour
- 70 g chopped macadamia nuts
- 3 tablespoons marmalade

Direction

- Melt 50g butter in a small saucepan and continue to cook until nut brown, set aside to cool slightly.
- Beat the remaining 100g room temperature butter and castor sugar together in an electric mixer until creamy. Sieve the flour and rice flour together and add to the butter mixture, and mix well by hand.
- Stir in the chopped macadamia nuts and marmalade, and add the cooled nut-brown butter. Stir well to combine, then divide the mixture in two and roll each half into a cylindrical shape on a lightly floured clean work surface. Make sure that there are no cracks in the cylinder shapes, then roll them up tightly in cling film wrap and place on a flat surface and refrigerate for about 2-3 hours or overnight until ready to use.
- Pre-heat the oven to 180°C line a two baking tray's with baking paper. Slice the biscuit dough into even rounds about 1 - 1.5cm thick and bake for 10–12 minutes. Allow to cool before serving.

Nutrition Information

- Calories: 116.9
- Fiber: 0.5
- Sugar: 4.6
- Total Carbohydrate: 12.6
- Cholesterol: 12.9
- Sodium: 2.4
- Protein: 1.2
- Total Fat: 7.1
- Saturated Fat: 3.4

83. Maida Heatter's Blueberry Muffins

Serving: 12 muffins | Prep: 15mins | Ready in:

Ingredients

- 1 cup fresh blueberries, washed and dried
- 1 1/2 cups flour
- 2 teaspoons baking powder
- 1/2 teaspoon salt
- 1/2 cup sugar
- 1 egg
- 2 tablespoons unsalted butter, melted
- 1/2 cup milk
- 1 medium lemon, zest of, finely grated

Direction

- Place rack in center of oven and preheat oven to 400°F. Use a muffin pan with liners or a buttered, nonstick pan (for a better crust).
- Sift together flour, baking powder, salt and sugar in a very large bowl.
- Add blueberries; stir gently to mix.
- In another bowl, beat egg lightly just to mix.
- Add butter, milk and rind. DO NOT OVERMIX.
- Add liquid ingredients all at once to dry ingredients.
- Fold with rubber spatula only a few seconds until dry ingredients are barely moistened. Batter should be lumpy.
- Fill muffin forms 2/3 full.
- Bake 20-25 minutes until golden. Cool in pan 2-3 minutes.
- Then cover with a rack, turn over pan and rack, and remove pan. Turn muffins right side up.

Nutrition Information

- Calories: 126
- Total Fat: 2.9
- Protein: 2.6
- Saturated Fat: 1.6
- Sodium: 168.9

- Fiber: 0.7
- Sugar: 9.6
- Total Carbohydrate: 22.7
- Cholesterol: 24.1

84. Maple/Bran Dog Biscuits

Serving: 150 SMALL approx. | Prep: 25mins | Ready in:

Ingredients

- 1 egg
- 1 teaspoon artificial maple extract
- 1/2 cup oil
- 1/4 cup melted margarine or 1/4 cup butter
- 2 cups fiber 1 cereal (or All Bran cereal)
- 1/2 cup natural bran
- 1/2 cup wheat germ
- 1/2 cup 7 grain cereal
- 1 1/2 cups milk
- 3 cups whole wheat flour, approx

Direction

- In large mixing bowl, with a dough hook, mix all ingredients, EXCEPT the flour Mix well add flour gradually until dough is stiff enough to handle.
- Roll into small balls (for large balls cooking times will be listed differently).
- Place on cookie sheets preheat oven to 300 f flatten balls slightly with bottom of glass or a finger.
- Place lowest oven rack ABOVE middle oven rack For small biscuits bake for 90 minutes, turning over half way through and placing cookie sheets on alternate racks.
- For LARGER biscuits, cook as above, then lower oven temperature to 225 f for another hour.
- To test for doneness, take one out, let cool, break in half and it should be hard and crisp like a milk bone.
- When done, remove from oven and let cool on cookie sheets, store in air tight containers.

Nutrition Information

- Calories: 21.3
- Protein: 0.6
- Saturated Fat: 0.2
- Fiber: 0.4
- Cholesterol: 1.8
- Sugar: 0.1
- Total Carbohydrate: 2.2
- Total Fat: 1.2
- Sodium: 5.9

85. Meemaw's Sweet Cornbread

Serving: 4-6 serving(s) | Prep: 5mins | Ready in:

Ingredients

- 1 cup self-rising cornmeal
- 8 ounces sour cream
- 1 (15 ounce) can cream-style corn
- 3 large eggs, lightly beaten
- 1/4 cup oil

Direction

- Put oil in large cast iron skillet. Place in oven, and turn oven on to 400 degrees. Allow skillet and oil to preheat to 400 degrees along with the oven.
- While skillet heats in oven, mix together corn meal, sour cream, cream-style corn, and eggs.
- When oven is preheated, remove hot skillet and carefully pour mix into sizzling oil. Shake handle to level out the batter.
- Bake for 25-30 minutes, or until golden brown.
- Cut and serve.

Nutrition Information

- Calories: 482
- Sugar: 3.8
- Cholesterol: 184.9

- Saturated Fat: 10.9
- Sodium: 767.8
- Fiber: 3.3
- Total Carbohydrate: 43.6
- Protein: 11
- Total Fat: 31.4

86. Mickey's Quick Sticky Buns

Serving: 8 rolls | Prep: 15mins | Ready in:

Ingredients

- 2 1/2 tablespoons unsalted butter
- 1/2 cup light brown sugar, packed and divided
- 2 tablespoons light corn syrup
- 2 teaspoons fresh lemon juice
- 1/3 cup coarsely chopped walnuts
- 1 (8 ounce) package crescent roll dough
- 3/4 teaspoon ground cinnamon

Direction

- Preheat oven to 375°F. Butter 9-inch cake pan; set aside.
- Melt 2 1/2 tablespoons butter in small saucepan over low heat. Whisk in 1/4 cup brown sugar, corn syrup, and lemon juice.
- Increase heat to medium and whisk until sugar melts and syrup boils. Pour syrup evenly over bottom of prepared pan. Sprinkle with walnuts.
- Unroll dough on floured surface; press perforations together. Roll out dough to 8x-12 inch rectangle. Sprinkle with remaining brown sugar and cinnamon.
- Starting at a short side, roll up dough as for a jelly roll. Cut crosswise into 8 1-inch thick rounds. Arrange rounds in syrup in pan.
- Bake buns until golden brown, about 20 minutes. Cool in pan 1 minute. Place pan over plate. Invert buns onto plate. Remove pan. Spoon any remaining syrup in pan onto buns and serve.

Nutrition Information

- Calories: 219.1
- Cholesterol: 23.7
- Total Fat: 8.6
- Saturated Fat: 3
- Fiber: 1.5
- Protein: 3.5
- Sodium: 164.1
- Sugar: 16.1
- Total Carbohydrate: 33.3

87. Nutella And Banana Bread

Serving: 1 loaf | Prep: 10mins | Ready in:

Ingredients

- 2 cups plain flour
- 2 teaspoons baking powder
- 1 teaspoon ground cinnamon
- 1/2 cup caster sugar
- 1/2 cup brown sugar
- 2 eggs, lightly beaten
- 1/3 cup vegetable oil
- 1 teaspoon vanilla extract
- 4 ripe bananas, mashed
- 1/2 cup nutella

Direction

- Preheat oven to 180°C Grease and line an 11cm x 21cm loaf pan.
- Sift the flour, baking powder and cinnamon into a large bowl. Stir in the sugars.
- In a separate bowl, combine the eggs, oil and vanilla.
- Add to the dry ingredients with mashed banana and fold until just combined.
- Pour the mixture into the loaf pan. Using a teaspoon, drop the Nutella across the top of the mixture, then mix it into the cake mix by inserting a cake skewer or a knife into the cake batter and swirling it around a couple of time.

- Cook for 50 minutes or until a skewer comes out clean. Turn out onto a rack and allow to cool for 10 minutes before slicing and serving.

Nutrition Information

- Calories: 3743.7
- Sodium: 971
- Sugar: 345.9
- Total Carbohydrate: 604
- Protein: 51.8
- Total Fat: 130.2
- Saturated Fat: 55.5
- Fiber: 28.4
- Cholesterol: 372

88. Peanut Butter And Chocolate Chip Muffins

Serving: 15 muffins | Prep: 10mins | Ready in:

Ingredients

- 3⁄4 cup peanut butter
- 1⁄4 cup butter
- 1 cup sugar
- 1⁄2 cup sweetened condensed milk
- 1⁄2 cup evaporated milk
- 2 eggs
- 2 1⁄2 cups flour
- 1 tablespoon baking powder
- 1 pinch salt
- 3 teaspoons vanilla
- milk
- chocolate chips

Direction

- Preheat over at 200 degrees Celsius.
- Cream peanut butter, butter and sugar till light and fluffy.
- Beat in the eggs.
- Mix in flour, baking powder, salt, both milks and vanilla.
- If batter is too thick/stiff keep adding milk until it seems like the right consistency (slightly stiffer than cake batter).
- Mix well.
- Fill muffin cups with batter till quarter full, then drop in chocolate chips to make centre choc filling. Cover/fill with batter till 3/4 full.
- Sprinkle some choc chips on top.
- Bake for about 25 mins or till muffin tops crack.

Nutrition Information

- Calories: 286.8
- Saturated Fat: 4.5
- Fiber: 1.3
- Total Carbohydrate: 38.5
- Cholesterol: 38.8
- Protein: 7.6
- Total Fat: 11.9
- Sodium: 201.1
- Sugar: 20.2

89. Pistachio Banana Bread

Serving: 1 loaf | Prep: 15mins | Ready in:

Ingredients

- 2 cups flour
- 3⁄4 teaspoon baking powder
- 1⁄2 teaspoon salt
- 1⁄2 cup sugar
- 1⁄2 cup packed brown sugar
- 1⁄4 cup butter, softened
- 2 large eggs
- 1 1⁄2 cups mashed bananas (about 3)
- 1⁄3 cup sour cream
- 1⁄2 teaspoon cardamom
- 1⁄2 cup chopped pistachios
- cooking spray

Direction

- Preheat oven to 350°F; spray a 9x5 loaf pan with cooking spray.
- Combine flour, baking powder and salt in a bowl; whisk well.
- Place sugars and butter in a large bowl; mix well.
- Add eggs one at a time, beat well after each addition.
- Add bananas, sour cream, cardamom; beat well.
- Add flour mixture; beat well until a moist batter is formed.
- Stir in pistachios and pour batter into loaf pan. Bake 1 hour until a toothpick inserted into the center comes out clean. Cool on a rack for 10 minutes, remove from pan, and cool on wire rack completely.

Nutrition Information

- Calories: 3077.3
- Total Carbohydrate: 497.7
- Cholesterol: 578.7
- Protein: 57.8
- Sugar: 253.3
- Sodium: 1994.6
- Fiber: 22.1
- Total Fat: 103
- Saturated Fat: 46.4

90. Pistachio Muffins

Serving: 12 muffins, 12 serving(s) | Prep: 5mins | Ready in:

Ingredients

- 1 egg
- 1/2 cup water
- 50 g butter (melted)
- 1 cup unsweetened low-fat yogurt
- 2 cups flour
- 1/4 teaspoon salt
- 2 teaspoons baking powder
- 1/4 cup sugar
- 1 cup pistachio nut, chopped

Direction

- Mix all ingredients together until just combined
- Spoon into well-greased muffin pans and bake at 190°C for 15-20 minutes.

Nutrition Information

- Calories: 198.5
- Protein: 5.9
- Saturated Fat: 3.1
- Sodium: 159.6
- Total Carbohydrate: 24.5
- Total Fat: 8.9
- Fiber: 1.6
- Sugar: 6.5
- Cholesterol: 25.6

91. Pumpkin Raspberry Muffins

Serving: 12 serving(s) | Prep: 15mins | Ready in:

Ingredients

- 1 cup quinoa flour
- 3/4 cup whole wheat flour
- 1 tablespoon baking powder
- 1/2 teaspoon baking soda

Direction

- Preheat oven to 350 degrees. Mix wet ingredients together in a mixing bowl. In a separate bowl add the dry ingredients, stir, then add into the mixing bowl. Beat until mixture looks creamy. Put 2-3 tablespoons into each muffin liner/container. Cook for 20 minutes.

Nutrition Information

- Calories: 26.1
- Protein: 1
- Total Fat: 0.2
- Sugar: 0
- Total Carbohydrate: 5.7
- Fiber: 0.8
- Cholesterol: 0
- Saturated Fat: 0
- Sodium: 143.4

92. Sweet Coffee House Scones II

Serving: 16 scones, 16 serving(s) | Prep: 15mins | Ready in:

Ingredients

- 3 -3 1/4 cups flour (depends on if your mixins are wet)
- 1 tablespoon baking powder
- 1/4 teaspoon salt
- 1/2 cup sugar
- 1/3 cup brown sugar (packed)
- 12 tablespoons butter
- 1/3 cup milk
- 1/2 cup sour cream
- 2 tablespoons vanilla extract
- milk, and
- sugar, for topping

Direction

- Preheat oven to 425°F.
- Mix flour (start with 3 cups), baking powder, salt, sugar and brown sugar, until well incorporated.
- Cut the butter into tiny pieces and mix into the flour mixture (you can also use a food processor for this step). Keep cutting in the butter until you incorporate the butter into the flour and it looks like it's the consistency of cornmeal.
- Add the milk, sour cream and vanilla extract, and mix to form a dough. If dough is too wet to work with, add a little more flour till you have a moist dough, but it's workable. Add your mix in and mix till well distributed. If you have a wet mix in like blueberries, you may need to add a little more flour.
- Cut dough in two (or cut in two before adding the mixins if you want two flavors) and shape into 2 rounds, 1/2 inch thick. Baste the top with a little milk and then sprinkle with sugar. Cut each circle into 8 wedges. Separate slightly to help them cook. Cook for approximately 17 minutes or until golden brown and cooked through in the middle.

Nutrition Information

- Calories: 225.5
- Total Fat: 10.5
- Saturated Fat: 6.5
- Sodium: 190.7
- Sugar: 11.2
- Total Carbohydrate: 29.5
- Fiber: 0.6
- Cholesterol: 27.4
- Protein: 2.8

93. Sweet Molasses Bran Muffins

Serving: 48 serving(s) | Prep: 20mins | Ready in:

Ingredients

- 2 1/2 cups bran flakes
- 1 cup raisins
- 1 cup boiling water
- 1/2 cup oil
- 1 cup molasses
- 2 eggs
- 2 cups buttermilk
- 2 3/4 cups flour
- 2 1/2 teaspoons baking soda
- 1/2 teaspoon salt

Direction

- Mix bran flakes, raisins and water, and set aside.
- Mix all dry ingredients.
- Mix in bran mixture until moist.
- Put in muffin tins, and bake for 20 minutes.
- Enjoy.

Nutrition Information

- Calories: 89.1
- Sodium: 121
- Fiber: 0.7
- Sugar: 6.5
- Total Carbohydrate: 15.2
- Protein: 1.6
- Total Fat: 2.7
- Saturated Fat: 0.5
- Cholesterol: 9.2

94. Sweet Potato Nut Bread

Serving: 8 serving(s) | Prep: 20mins | Ready in:

Ingredients

- 1 cup sugar
- 1/2 cup milk
- 2 eggs (beaten)
- 1/4 cup butter (softened)
- 2 cups flour (sifted)
- 2 teaspoons baking powder
- 1/2 teaspoon baking soda
- 1 teaspoon salt
- 1 teaspoon ground cinnamon
- 1/2 teaspoon ground nutmeg
- 1 cup canned pumpkin
- 1 cup pecans (chopped)

Direction

- In large bowl add flour, baking powder, salt, nutmeg and cinnamon.
- In another large bowl, combine the pumpkin, sugar, milk and eggs.
- Add it to the dry ingredients, and add the butter and mix until well blended.
- Stir in pecans.
- Spread mixture in a loaf pan evenly.
- Bake in a preheated oven at 350 degrees for 45 to 55 min's or until inserted toothpick in the center comes out clean.
- (9x5x3-in loaf pan is what I would use).

Nutrition Information

- Calories: 396.1
- Total Fat: 17.8
- Fiber: 3.2
- Total Carbohydrate: 54.6
- Sugar: 26.8
- Cholesterol: 70.3
- Protein: 7
- Saturated Fat: 5.3
- Sodium: 600.5

95. Sweet And Moist Banana Muffins

Serving: 12 Muffins | Prep: 15mins | Ready in:

Ingredients

- 4 ripe bananas
- 1 cup whole wheat flour
- 1/2 cup unbleached flour
- 2 tablespoons wheat germ
- 1/4 cup oat bran
- 1/2 cup sugar
- 1 egg
- 1 egg white
- 1/3 cup melted butter or 1/3 cup margarine
- 1 teaspoon baking powder
- 1 teaspoon baking soda
- 1/2 teaspoon salt
- 1 teaspoon cinnamon
- 1/2-1 teaspoon orange peel
- 1/4 teaspoon nutmeg

- 1 tablespoon vanilla extract

Direction

- Heat Oven to 350 degrees.
- 1. In a bowl, mash together banana, melted butter, sugar and eggs.
- 2. Add in the vanilla extract, cinnamon, nutmeg, orange peel.
- 3. In a separate bowl, mix together flour, baking soda, baking powder, salt, oat bran and wheat germ.
- 4. Add wet ingredients to the dry ingredients and mix well.
- 5. Make sure to spray your muffin pan with nonstick spray.
- 6. Fill the muffin tray and bake for 20 minutes or golden.

Nutrition Information

- Calories: 186.1
- Saturated Fat: 3.5
- Cholesterol: 31.2
- Protein: 3.8
- Sodium: 280.1
- Fiber: 3
- Sugar: 13.4
- Total Carbohydrate: 30.9
- Total Fat: 6.2

96. Traditional Scottish Pure Butter Shortbread Cookies Biscuits

Serving: 16-24 Shortbread Cookies | Prep: 10mins | Ready in:

Ingredients

- 1 cup confectioners' sugar
- 1 lb salted butter, softened
- 4 1/2 cups all-purpose flour
- caster sugar, for sprinkling (optional)
- 1/4 teaspoon crushed edible lavender flowers (fresh or dried) (optional)

Direction

- Preheat the oven to 325F degrees.
- Blend the confectioner's sugar into the butter, and then gradually add the flour, 1 cup at a time. Dough will be very thick. At this point, you may add crushed lavender flowers or rosemary, if you wish.
- Place dough on floured surface, pat down, and roll out into a square or circle 1/4 to 1/2 inch thick. Cut into 2 1/2 inch squares or Petticoat Tail wedges, and carefully place on an ungreased baking sheet.
- Prick the top of each square or wedge with a fork.
- Bake at 325F degrees for 25 to 30 minutes; cookies should be pale on top, but golden brown on the bottom.
- Remove from oven, sprinkle with sugar if you wish, and cool on wire racks.
- Store in an airtight container.

Nutrition Information

- Calories: 360.6
- Sugar: 7.5
- Protein: 3.9
- Total Fat: 23.4
- Saturated Fat: 14.6
- Fiber: 0.9
- Total Carbohydrate: 34.3
- Cholesterol: 61
- Sodium: 164.2

97. Triple Chocolate Zucchini Loaf, Or Muffins

Serving: 2 loaves, 20 serving(s) | Prep: 30mins | Ready in:

Ingredients

- 2 (1 ounce) unsweetened chocolate squares
- 3 eggs
- 2 cups white sugar
- 1 cup vegetable oil
- 2 1/2 cups zucchini (grated)
- 1 teaspoon vanilla extract
- 2 cups all-purpose flour
- 1 teaspoon baking soda
- 1 teaspoon salt
- 1 teaspoon ground cinnamon
- 3/4 cup semi-sweet chocolate chips
- 1 tablespoon cocoa
- 1 cup sour cream

Direction

- Preheat oven to 350 degrees F (175 degrees C). Lightly grease two 9X5 inch loaf pans, or 24 muffin tins. In a microwave-safe bowl, microwave chocolate until melted. Stir occasionally until chocolate is smooth.
- In a large bowl, combine eggs, sugar, oil, grated zucchini, vanilla, sour cream, and chocolate; beat well.
- In another bowl combine flour, baking soda, salt, cinnamon, cocoa, and chocolate chips. Add to the egg mixture.
- Pour batter into prepared loaf pans.
- Bake in preheated oven for 60 to 70 minutes, (25 minutes for muffins), or until a toothpick inserted into the center of a loaf comes out clean.
- Cool, slice, and enjoy!

Nutrition Information

- Calories: 301.2
- Total Fat: 17.4
- Sodium: 202.2
- Fiber: 1.4
- Total Carbohydrate: 35.6
- Cholesterol: 33.9
- Saturated Fat: 5
- Sugar: 24.3
- Protein: 3.3

98. Valentine Biscuits

Serving: 30-40 biscuits, 30-40 serving(s) | Prep: 20mins | Ready in:

Ingredients

- 2 cups plain flour
- 1 teaspoon mixed spice
- 1/2 teaspoon ground cinnamon
- 1 1/2 teaspoons bicarbonate of soda
- 50 g butter or 50 g soy margarine
- 2/3 cup brown sugar
- 3 tablespoons golden syrup
- 2 tablespoons milk or 2 tablespoons soymilk

Direction

- Line baking tray with baking paper.
- Preheat oven to 160°C.
- Sift flour, spices and bicarb soda into a bowl.
- Place butter, sugar and golden syrup in a saucepan and heat until the butter has melted.
- Remove from heat and stir into the flour mixture with milk (more milk may be needed).
- Mix top form a firm dough.
- Knead the dough lightly on a floured pastry board.
- Roll out to 1cm thickness.
- Cut out with appropriate cookie cutters.
- Re-roll trimming and cut more shapes.
- Place on baking tray.
- Bake for 10 minutes until golden.
- Leave on oven trays to cool and harden.
- Ice with appropriate colored icing sugar and nuts, 100's and 1000's, chocolate, m'n'm's or other favorite decorations.
- For Vegan use only the soy milk and nondairy Vegan margarine. Also make sure any candies are also Vegan containing no dairy or egg products.

Nutrition Information

- Calories: 67.6

- Total Fat: 1.5
- Fiber: 0.2
- Sugar: 5.3
- Cholesterol: 3.7
- Protein: 0.9
- Saturated Fat: 0.9
- Sodium: 76.4
- Total Carbohydrate: 12.9

99. Viennese Biscuits

Serving: 16 biscuits | Prep: 10mins | Ready in:

Ingredients

- 4 ounces soft butter
- 1 ounce sifted icing sugar
- 5 ounces plain flour

Direction

- Beat butter and sugar till pale.
- To quicken it up slightly, beat over a bowl of hot water but not too much it shouldn't be runny Sift in flour.
- Put mixture in a large star piping bag and pipe as you want.
- Traditionally this should be tubes or whirls.
- Chill for 15 minutes.
- Bake 10 minutes at 190°C.
- They should not be brown, they stay pale.
- When cool, melt some chocolate, I use a mixture of 70% cocoa butter and ord. milk. Use a small deep container (egg cup is good).
- Dip each tube or whirl in chocolate.
- Lay on baking parchment and set in fridge.
- Great to serve with ice cream or my.
- SUMMER AVALANCHE (posted too).
- I'm drooling already!

Nutrition Information

- Calories: 91.8
- Total Fat: 5.8
- Fiber: 0.2
- Sugar: 1.8
- Cholesterol: 15.2
- Saturated Fat: 3.7
- Sodium: 41
- Total Carbohydrate: 8.9
- Protein: 1

100. Viennese Shortbread Biscuits

Serving: 35 cookies | Prep: 25mins | Ready in:

Ingredients

- 250 g butter
- 1/4 cup caster sugar
- 1/2 teaspoon vanilla essence
- 1 3/4 cups plain flour
- 1/4 cup rice flour
- 1 pinch salt

Direction

- Cream together butter and sugar until light and fluffy.
- Add essence.
- Beat well.
- Fold in sifted flours and salt.
- Fill into piping bag fitted with fluted tube.
- Pipe into straight lengths or different shapes on greased oven tray.
- Bake in a moderate oven for 12- 15 minutes or until golden.
- Cool on tray.
- Leave plain or dip one end in about 125 gm (4oz) of melted dark chocolate for a pretty effect.
- Serve and enjoy!

Nutrition Information

- Calories: 83.5
- Total Carbohydrate: 7.1

- Protein: 0.8
- Total Fat: 5.8
- Saturated Fat: 3.7
- Sodium: 45.5
- Cholesterol: 15.3
- Fiber: 0.2
- Sugar: 1.5

101. Wheat Banana Walnut Chocolate Chip Bread

Serving: 1 loaf, 10 serving(s) | Prep: 10mins | Ready in:

Ingredients

- 2 cups whole wheat flour
- 1 teaspoon baking soda
- 1 teaspoon baking powder
- 1 teaspoon salt
- 1/2 cup honey
- 4 ripe bananas, mashed
- 1 cup brown sugar
- 1 tablespoon vanilla extract
- 1 cup applesauce or 1/2 cup vegetable oil
- 2 large eggs
- 3/4 cup walnuts
- 3/4 cup chocolate chips

Direction

- Preheat oven to 350.
- Spray a loaf pan with Pam and set aside.
- In a bowl, stir together flour, baking soda, baking powder, and salt and set aside.
- In a separate large mixing bowl, whisk together mashed banana, sugar, honey, vanilla applesauce (or veg oil) and eggs.
- Slowly add dry ingredients to wet and fold together until just combined.
- Fold in walnuts and chocolate chips.
- Pour batter into loaf pan and bake in center of oven for 1hr to 1hr 10min, until center of bread is set.
- Allow to cool in pan ten minutes, then cool completely on a wire rack.
- Slice and serve.

Nutrition Information

- Calories: 414.3
- Cholesterol: 37.2
- Protein: 6.9
- Fiber: 5.5
- Total Carbohydrate: 78.3
- Saturated Fat: 3.2
- Sodium: 425.5
- Sugar: 48.4
- Total Fat: 11.3

102. Yorkshire Pudding With Blue Cheese

Serving: 8 serving(s) | Prep: 10mins | Ready in:

Ingredients

- 1 cup all-purpose flour
- 3/4 cup milk
- 1 1/3 ounces crumbled blue cheese
- 1 1/2 teaspoons sugar
- 1/8 teaspoon salt
- 1 large egg
- 1 large egg white
- 1 tablespoon vegetable oil

Direction

- Preheat oven to 450 degrees.
- Combine first 7 ingredients in a bowl. Beat at medium speed with electric mixer until smooth. Beat at high speed 15 seconds; set aside.
- Divide oil evenly among 8 muffin or popover cups. Coat sides of cups with cooking spray. Place muffin cups in oven for 3 minutes. Divide batter evenly among hot prepared cups. Bake for 10 minutes.

- Reduce oven temperature to 350 degrees. Bake additional 15 minutes or until golden. Serve immediately.

Nutrition Information

- Calories: 117.4
- Protein: 4.6
- Total Fat: 4.7
- Sugar: 0.9
- Total Carbohydrate: 14
- Cholesterol: 30
- Saturated Fat: 1.8
- Sodium: 129.6
- Fiber: 0.4

103. Yorkshire Puddings I

Serving: 12-16 puddings, 12 serving(s) | Prep: 5mins | Ready in:

Ingredients

- 3 ounces plain flour
- 1 egg
- 3 fluid ounces milk
- 2 fluid ounces water
- salt and pepper
- 4 tablespoons oil

Direction

- Sift flour into a bowl.
- Make a "well" in the middle.
- Break an egg into it and gradually incorporate the flour, milk, water and seasoning.
- Put your muffin tins in the oven at a very high heat for about 10 or 15 minutes with the oil in them.
- The oil should be smoking when you take the tin out of the oven.
- Pour the batter into the tins and put them in the oven for between 10 and 20 minutes.
- This depends on your oven, how well insulated it is, how hot it gets and many other things.
- If you take them out and they droop, put them back in for another few minutes to crisp them up, and remember to leave them longer next time.

Nutrition Information

- Calories: 78.4
- Total Fat: 5.3
- Saturated Fat: 0.9
- Sodium: 9.8
- Total Carbohydrate: 6.1
- Fiber: 0.2
- Sugar: 0.1
- Cholesterol: 18.7
- Protein: 1.6

104. Yummy And Easy Raisin Muffins

Serving: 12 muffins, 12 serving(s) | Prep: 10mins | Ready in:

Ingredients

- 2 cups all-purpose flour
- 3 teaspoons baking powder
- 1/2 teaspoon salt
- 3/4 cup sugar
- 1 large overripe banana, mashed
- 3/4 cup finely chopped raisins
- 1 cup milk
- 1 egg, beat well
- 1/4 cup canola oil (or any vegetable oil)
- 12 pieces raisins, for topping (optional)

Direction

- Heat oven at 400 Fahrenheit.
- Mix the dry ingredients together: flour, baking powder, salt, and sugar.

- In a separate bowl, mix milk, oil, egg, banana, and raisins together. Mix very well.
- Pour mixture on dry ingredients. Mix only until the dry ingredients are moistened.
- Put the batter on muffin pan (with muffin liners!) carefully. Top with one raisin per muffin, if desired.
- Bake for 20 minutes or until light to medium brown.

Nutrition Information

- Calories: 221.3
- Total Carbohydrate: 39.4
- Protein: 3.8
- Total Fat: 6
- Saturated Fat: 1
- Sugar: 19.3
- Cholesterol: 20.5
- Sodium: 205
- Fiber: 1.2

105. Zesty Blueberry Muffins

Serving: 12 muffins, 12 serving(s) | Prep: 20mins | Ready in:

Ingredients

- 1 1/2 cups flour
- 1/4 teaspoon salt
- 3/4 cup milk
- 1/2 cup sugar
- 2 1/2 teaspoons baking powder
- 1 egg
- 1/3 cup butter, melted
- 1 tablespoon lemon rind, grated
- 1 cup blueberries (fresh or frozen)
- 2 tablespoons sugar

Direction

- Grease and line 12 muffin tins.
- Mix Flour, ½ cup sugar, baking powder, salt in bowl.
- Beat egg.
- Add milk and melted butter.
- Add liquid to dry ingredients.
- Stir till just moist.
- Add blueberries.
- Fill muffin tins ¾ full.
- Combine lemon rind and remaining sugar and sprinkle over batter.
- Bake at 400 for 20 minutes.

Nutrition Information

- Calories: 165.9
- Cholesterol: 33.3
- Fiber: 0.8
- Saturated Fat: 3.7
- Sodium: 174.1
- Sugar: 11.7
- Total Carbohydrate: 25.2
- Protein: 2.8
- Total Fat: 6.3

Chapter 3: Quick Bread Picnic Recipes

***

106. All Bran Pineapple And Fruit Muffins

Serving: 12 muffins, 12 serving(s) | Prep: 10mins | Ready in:

Ingredients

- 1 cup all-purpose flour
- 3⁄4 cup whole wheat flour
- 1 tablespoon baking powder
- 1⁄2 teaspoon salt
- 1 teaspoon cinnamon
- 1⁄4 teaspoon nutmeg
- 1 cup Kellogg's all-bran cereal (Extra Fiber kind)
- 1 (8 ounce) can crushed unsweetened pineapple, undrained
- 1⁄2 cup unsweetened orange juice
- 1 teaspoon orange peel
- 2 egg whites
- 1⁄4 cup vegetable oil
- 1 cup mixed dried fruit, chopped
- For the Filling
- 1⁄3 cup lowfat margarine, softened
- 5 teaspoons artificial sweetener (or 5 packets)
- 1⁄2 teaspoon vanilla

Direction

- Stir together flours, baking powder, salt and spices; set aside.
- In large mixing bowl, combine cereal, pineapple including juice and orange juice. Let stand 3 minutes or until cereal is softened. Add orange peel, egg whites and oil; beat well. Stir in dried fruit.
- Add flour mixture, stirring only until combined. Portion batter evenly into 12 lightly greased 2 1/2-inch muffin-pan cups. Using measuring-teaspoon, make a 1/2-inch indentation in top of each muffin.
- Bake in 400° F oven about 23 minutes or until golden brown. Cool about 15 minutes before adding filling.
- Filling: Beat together margarine, sweetener and vanilla. Fill each muffin top with measuring-teaspoon of filling. Serve warm.

Nutrition Information

- Calories: 162.9
- Cholesterol: 0
- Saturated Fat: 0.7
- Sodium: 212.1
- Total Carbohydrate: 28.4
- Protein: 3.8
- Total Fat: 5.2
- Fiber: 4
- Sugar: 3.2

107. Almond, Orange, And Blueberry Muffins

Serving: 36 mini muffins, 1 serving(s) | Prep: 20mins | Ready in:

Ingredients

- 2 large eggs
- 1⁄2 cup olive oil
- 3⁄4 cup palm sugar
- 1⁄2 teaspoon vanilla extract
- 1 1⁄2 cups blueberries
- 1 orange, juice and zest of 1 large orange
- 1 teaspoon cinnamon
- 1 cup flour
- 1 cup almond meal
- 1 teaspoon baking powder
- 1⁄2 teaspoon salt

Direction

- Preheat oven to 350.
- In large bowl, mix together eggs, oil, sugar, vanilla, blueberries, orange zest, orange juice, and cinnamon.
- In a separate bowl, sift together flour, almond meal, baking powder, and salt.
- Stir the dry ingredients into the wet ingredients until just combined, being careful not to over mix the batter.
- Spoon the batter into oiled muffin tins and bake until golden brown. 20 to 25 minutes for standard tins, 12-15 minutes for mini tins.
- Makes 24-36 mini muffins or 12-18 standard.
- Enjoy!

Nutrition Information

- Calories: 2882.4
- Protein: 48.6
- Sodium: 1677.6
- Fiber: 24.8
- Sugar: 188.8
- Total Carbohydrate: 317.7
- Cholesterol: 372
- Total Fat: 166.6
- Saturated Fat: 21.9

108. Applesauce Banana Bread

Serving: 12 serving(s) | Prep: 20mins | Ready in:

Ingredients

- 4 bananas
- 1 cup sugar
- 1/2 cup applesauce
- 1 teaspoon vanilla
- 2 eggs
- 1 teaspoon baking soda
- 1 tablespoon baking powder
- 1 teaspoon salt
- 2 cups flour

Direction

- Preheat oven to 350 degrees F. Place bananas in a large bowl and mash with electric mixer. Stir in sugar and let stand 15 minutes.
- Add applesauce and eggs and beat well. Add remaining ingredients and mix thoroughly. Pour into a 9"x5" loaf pan coated with non-stick vegetable spray. Bake for 45 minutes, or until toothpick inserted in the center of the loaf comes out clean. Remove from oven and let stand 10 minutes before removing from pan.

Nutrition Information

- Calories: 197.3
- Total Fat: 1.2
- Saturated Fat: 0.3
- Sodium: 404.9
- Sugar: 21.6
- Protein: 3.6
- Fiber: 1.7
- Total Carbohydrate: 44
- Cholesterol: 35.2

109. Banana Muffins With Chocolate Hazelnut Crunchies

Serving: 12 muffins, 12 serving(s) | Prep: 20mins | Ready in:

Ingredients

- 3/4 cup unsweetened vanilla almond milk
- 1/3 cup agave nectar
- 1/4 cup canola oil
- 1/4 cup unsweetened apple juice
- 2 large overripe bananas, mashed roughly
- 1 cup flour
- 1 cup spelt flour
- 1 1/2 tablespoons baking powder
- 1/2 teaspoon nutmeg
- 3/4 teaspoon salt
- 1/4 cup chocolate, hazelnut crunchies (Recipe #533215) or 1/4 cup miniature chocolate chip

Direction

- Heat the oven to 375F and line a muffin tin.
- In a bowl, beat together milk, agave, canola, apple juice and bananas.
- Stir in the flours, baking powder, nutmeg and salt until just combined.
- Fold in the Chocolate Hazelnut Crunchies.
- Bake for 25 - 30 minutes, until they test done.

Nutrition Information

- Calories: 115.8

- Fiber: 1.4
- Sugar: 3.4
- Total Carbohydrate: 15
- Saturated Fat: 1.3
- Sodium: 282.8
- Total Fat: 6.2
- Cholesterol: 0
- Protein: 1.7

110. Chocolate Chip It Snackin Muffins

Serving: 8 serving(s) | Prep: 5mins | Ready in:

Ingredients

- 1 1/2 cups flour
- 1 cup sugar
- 2 tablespoons cocoa
- 1 teaspoon baking powder
- 1/2 teaspoon salt
- 1/4 teaspoon oil
- 1 teaspoon vanilla
- 1 tablespoon vinegar
- 1 cup warm water
- 1/2 cup chocolate chips

Direction

- Mix flour, sugar, cocoa, baking powder salt.
- Make a well in the center and add wet ingredients.
- Stir until moist.
- Stir in chocolate chips.
- Fill paper baking cups to top.
- Bake 20 minutes @ 400*.

Nutrition Information

- Calories: 240.7
- Protein: 3.1
- Saturated Fat: 1.9
- Fiber: 1.5
- Sugar: 30.8
- Cholesterol: 0
- Total Fat: 3.6
- Sodium: 193
- Total Carbohydrate: 50.5

111. Cosmic Chocolate Chip Banana Muffins

Serving: 12 muffins | Prep: 15mins | Ready in:

Ingredients

- 1 egg
- 2 cups Bisquick
- 1 1/4 cups mashed very ripe bananas (2 to 3 medium)
- 1/3 cup sugar
- 3 tablespoons vegetable oil
- 1/3 cup miniature semisweet chocolate chips

Direction

- Preheat oven to 400°F.
- Beat egg slightly in mixing bowl.
- Mash bananas and deposit in mixing bowl.
- Combine rest of ingredients with egg and banana until just moist.
- Spoon mixture into 12 paper muffin cups or pour directly into greased muffin pan Bake for 15 minutes or until golden brown.

Nutrition Information

- Calories: 180.2
- Fiber: 1.1
- Total Fat: 8.4
- Saturated Fat: 2.2
- Cholesterol: 18
- Protein: 2.5
- Sodium: 261.7
- Sugar: 12.4
- Total Carbohydrate: 24.8

112. Cream Cheese Muffins

Serving: 8 serving(s) | Prep: 10mins | Ready in:

Ingredients

- Filling
- 4 ounces cream cheese, softened
- 1/4 cup sugar
- 1/2 teaspoon grated lemon, rind of
- 1/8 teaspoon vanilla
- 1 egg
- Batter Ingredients
- 1 egg
- 3/4 cup milk
- 1/2 cup vegetable oil
- 2 cups flour
- 1/3 cup sugar
- 3 teaspoons baking powder
- 1/2 teaspoon salt
- powdered sugar

Direction

- Mix filling ingredients with mixer.
- Set aside.
- Preheat oven to 350 degrees.
- Oil bottoms only of medium muffin tins.
- Beat eggs; stir in milk and oil; set aside.
- Mix together flour, sugar, baking powder, and salt until well blended.
- Pour liquids, all at once, into flour mixture; stir until moistened.
- Fill muffin cups about 1/2 full.
- Spoon 1 teaspoon filling onto batter.
- Top with batter to 3/4 full.
- Bake 30-35 minutes.
- Don't brown; should be light in color.
- Roll hot muffins in powdered sugar.

Nutrition Information

- Calories: 374.2
- Total Fat: 20.9
- Sodium: 352.8
- Sugar: 14.8
- Total Carbohydrate: 40.4
- Cholesterol: 71.7
- Saturated Fat: 5.8
- Fiber: 0.9
- Protein: 6.6

113. Flax Morning Glory Muffins

Serving: 12 muffins | Prep: 10mins | Ready in:

Ingredients

- 1 cup Fiber One cereal
- 2/3 cup milk
- 1 cup all-purpose flour
- 3/4 cup ground flax seed
- 3/4 cup apple, finely chopped
- 1/2 cup brown sugar, packed
- 1/2 cup carrot, finely shredded
- 1/4 cup sugar
- 1/4 cup unsweetened coconut
- 1 tablespoon canola oil
- 3 teaspoons baking powder
- 2 teaspoons cinnamon
- 1 teaspoon vanilla extract
- 1/2 teaspoon salt
- 2 eggs

Direction

- Crush cereal with a rolling pin. Mix with milk and let stand 5 minutes.
- Combine flour, flax meal, brown sugar, carrot, sugar, coconut, baking powder, cinnamon and salt. Stir in apple.
- Beat eggs. Stir in vanilla.
- Stir oil into cereal mixture. Stir egg mixture into cereal mixture.
- Stir in dry mixture, just until combined.
- Spoon into a greased or paper cup lined 12-cup muffin pan.

- Bake in a preheated 375F oven for 22 minutes or until done. Immediately remove from pan.

Nutrition Information

- Calories: 225.5
- Fiber: 6.8
- Sugar: 14.7
- Total Carbohydrate: 32.1
- Total Fat: 10.2
- Saturated Fat: 3.8
- Sodium: 239.5
- Cholesterol: 37.1
- Protein: 5.3

114. Flying Biscuit Cafe Low Fat Banana Muffins

Serving: 12 muffins | Prep: 20mins | Ready in:

Ingredients

- 1 1/4 cups mashed ripe bananas
- 3/4 cup sugar
- 2/3 cup low-fat vanilla yogurt
- 4 1/2 tablespoons unsalted butter, melted and cooled
- 1/2 teaspoon vanilla extract
- 2 large eggs
- 2 2/3 cups all-purpose flour
- 3/4 teaspoon baking powder
- 1 teaspoon baking soda
- 1/4 teaspoon salt

Direction

- Preheat oven to 350° F.
- Lightly grease a dozen muffin tins or line with paper cups.
- Place bananas, sugar, yogurt, melted butter, vanilla, and eggs together in a large mixing bowl and beat with a wooden spoon until smooth.
- In a second bowl sift together flour, baking powder, baking soda, and salt.
- Add dry ingredients to wet and mix until just combines.
- Do not overmix, or the muffins will be tough.
- Fill muffin cups three-quarters of the way full.
- Bake for 25 to 35 minutes.
- A toothpick inserted in the center of the muffins will come out clean when they are cooked.
- Remove from the oven and cool slightly before eating.

Nutrition Information

- Calories: 226.2
- Saturated Fat: 3.2
- Fiber: 1.2
- Sugar: 16.4
- Cholesterol: 47.4
- Protein: 4.8
- Total Fat: 5.6
- Sodium: 198
- Total Carbohydrate: 39.3

115. Good For You Banana Bread

Serving: 1 loaf | Prep: 10mins | Ready in:

Ingredients

- 2 cups flour (I use 1 cup white and 1 cup whole wheat)
- 1/4 teaspoon salt
- 1/2 teaspoon baking powder
- 1/2 teaspoon baking soda
- 1/4 cup butter or 1/4 cup margarine
- 3/4 cup brown sugar (I use molasses)
- 1 cup mashed banana (I use three medium bananas)
- 3 tablespoons milk or 3 tablespoons soymilk
- 1 teaspoon vanilla

Direction

- Preheat oven to 350°F; grease loaf pan.
- Sift together first four ingredients.
- In separate bowl, cream butter and sugar (or molasses) until light.
- Beat bananas into butter mixture.
- In small bowl, mix milk and vanilla together.
- Alternate adding banana mixture to flour mixture in 3 equal parts with milk mixture; stir only until blended.
- Pour batter into greased loaf pan.
- Bake 1 hour.
- For Vegan use only the soy milk and a Vegan margarine.

Nutrition Information

- Calories: 2181.8
- Fiber: 12.6
- Sugar: 187.5
- Protein: 30.3
- Total Fat: 50.9
- Saturated Fat: 30.8
- Sodium: 1813.5
- Total Carbohydrate: 406
- Cholesterol: 128.4

116. Grannies Cheese Scone Recipe

Serving: 16 triangular scones, 8 serving(s) | Prep: 10mins | Ready in:

Ingredients

- 175 g self raising flour
- 1 pinch salt and pepper
- 2 1/2 ml mustard powder (1/2 tsp)
- 25 g margarine
- 75 g cheese, grated
- 1 medium egg
- 30 ml milk (2 tbsp)
- 1 tablespoon grated parmesan cheese (to sprinkle on top) or 1 tablespoon dry hard Italian cheese (to sprinkle on top)

Direction

- Heat oven to 220ºC, 425ºF, Gas Mark 7. Grease a baking tray.
- Mix flour and seasonings, rub in margarine and stir in cheese.
- Mix to a soft dough with the egg and milk, reserving a little for glazing.
- Roll out to a round 1.5 cm (½ inch) in thickness and cut into 8 triangles.
- Place on the baking tray and brush with egg and milk and sprinkle with parmesan cheese. Bake for about 10-15 minutes until golden brown.

Nutrition Information

- Calories: 176.1
- Saturated Fat: 2.3
- Sodium: 139.7
- Fiber: 1.1
- Cholesterol: 30.3
- Protein: 6.3
- Total Fat: 6.5
- Sugar: 0.3
- Total Carbohydrate: 22.6

117. High Fiber Bran Muffins

Serving: 12 serving(s) | Prep: 20mins | Ready in:

Ingredients

- 1 cup wheat bran
- 1 1/2 cups whole wheat flour
- 1/2 cup raisins
- 1 teaspoon baking powder
- 1 teaspoon baking soda
- 3/4 cup milk
- 1/2 cup molasses or 1/2 cup honey

- 2 tablespoons oil
- 1 egg, beaten

Direction

- Preheat oven to 400°F.
- Stir together: bran, flour, soda and baking powder.
- Then stir in raisins and set aside.
- Blend milk, molasses, oil and egg.
- Add to dry ingredients and stir JUST UNTIL MOISTENED.
- Spoon into greased muffin tins and bake for 15 minutes or until muffins pull away from sides of cups.

Nutrition Information

- Calories: 156.2
- Sodium: 155.2
- Fiber: 4.1
- Sugar: 11.5
- Total Carbohydrate: 30.1
- Saturated Fat: 0.9
- Cholesterol: 19.8
- Protein: 4
- Total Fat: 3.8

118. Honey Graham Muffins

Serving: 10 muffins | Prep: 5mins | Ready in:

Ingredients

- 3 cups crushed honey graham crackers
- 1/4 cup sugar
- 2 teaspoons baking powder
- 1 cup skim milk
- 2 egg whites
- 2 tablespoons honey
- 1 dash cinnamon (optional)

Direction

- Preheat oven to 400°F.
- Place cupcake liners in muffin pan and set aside.
- In a medium mixing bowl combine crackers, sugar and baking powder.
- In a separate bowl lightly beat milk, egg whites, honey, and cinnamon.
- Add the milk mixture to the cracker mixture and stir just until moistened.
- Spoon batter into muffin pan and bake for about 15 minutes.
- Let stand 5 minutes; remove from pan.

Nutrition Information

- Calories: 152.7
- Total Fat: 2.6
- Saturated Fat: 0.4
- Protein: 3.5
- Sodium: 250.7
- Fiber: 0.7
- Sugar: 16.3
- Total Carbohydrate: 29.4
- Cholesterol: 0.5

119. Honey Mustard And Cheddar Muffins

Serving: 12 muffins | Prep: 20mins | Ready in:

Ingredients

- 2 cups all-purpose flour
- 1 tablespoon baking powder
- 1/4 teaspoon salt
- pepper
- 1 cup grated sharp cheddar cheese
- 1 egg
- 3 tablespoons honey mustard
- 2 tablespoons honey
- 1 1/4 cups milk
- 1/4 cup butter, melted

Direction

- Combine flour, baking powder, salt and pepper in a large mixing bowl.
- Whisk together cheese, egg, mustard, honey, milk and butter.
- Gently but thoroughly fold into the dry ingredients.
- Fill greased muffin tin and bake at 400 degrees for 20 minutes or until done.

Nutrition Information

- Calories: 188.9
- Total Carbohydrate: 21.5
- Cholesterol: 39.1
- Total Fat: 8.9
- Saturated Fat: 5.2
- Sodium: 284.1
- Fiber: 0.6
- Sugar: 3.7
- Protein: 5.9

120. Hungarian Biscuits

Serving: 16-20 biscuits, 16-20 serving(s) | Prep: 15mins | Ready in:

Ingredients

- 200 g flour
- 25 g cocoa
- 200 g margarine
- 100 g sugar
- 1 tablespoon vanilla essence

Direction

- Pre-heat oven to 180° c. Put 100g margarine and 50g sugar into a bowl and cream it. Add 100g of flour and ½ a teaspoon of Vanilla essence into the mixture and mix to form a stiff dough.
- Do the same with the other ingredients (in a separate bowl), only add the cocoa.
- Now, with the two separate mixtures, take the first one, and roll it out onto a floured surface. Roll it to a 5mm thickness.
- Put the second mixture (the cocoa one) on top, and roll it out to relatively the same shape. You now have two different colored layers.
- Take the longest side of the dough and roll it so that the dough now forms a cylinder shape with a spiral visible on either end.
- Cut the dough vertically into 16 pieces and lay them on a baking tray that is lined with greased greaseproof paper.
- Put in the oven for 15 minutes and take out when they are golden and still slightly soft, as they will set hard.

Nutrition Information

- Calories: 165.6
- Total Fat: 10.4
- Saturated Fat: 1.9
- Fiber: 0.9
- Sugar: 6.4
- Total Carbohydrate: 16.9
- Cholesterol: 0
- Protein: 1.7
- Sodium: 118.5

121. Jalapeño Cornbread

Serving: 8 serving(s) | Prep: 5mins | Ready in:

Ingredients

- 1 cup cornmeal
- 2 egg whites (equivalent to 2 eggs) or 2 Egg Beaters egg substitute, egg substitute (equivalent to 2 eggs)
- 1 (12 ounce) can creamed corn
- 1 cup grated fat-free cheddar cheese
- 1/2 teaspoon salt
- 1/4 cup flour
- 1/2 cup fat-free buttermilk

- 1/2 cup Butter Buds or 1/2 cup i can't believe it not butter-flavored cooking spray
- 1 (14 ounce) can Rotel Tomatoes, drained
- 1 1/2 teaspoons baking powder

Direction

- Beat "Egg Beaters" or egg whites, and add remaining ingredients, mixing well.
- Pour into large cast iron skillet (or large baking dish) that has been sprayed with a nonfat cooking spray.
- Bake at 350°F for 50-60 minutes.

Nutrition Information

- Calories: 115.2
- Protein: 3.7
- Saturated Fat: 0.1
- Sodium: 575.3
- Total Carbohydrate: 25.2
- Total Fat: 0.8
- Fiber: 1.8
- Sugar: 1.7
- Cholesterol: 0

122. Jana's Grandmother's Cornbread

Serving: 2 eight inch or nine inch pans (round), 8-10 serving(s) | Prep: 10mins | Ready in:

Ingredients

- 1 1/2 cups self-rising cornmeal mix (White Lily brand preferred)
- 1 1/2 cups self-rising flour (White Lily brand preferred)
- 2 cups milk
- 1/2-1 cup melted butter
- 2 eggs, beaten
- 1/3 cup sugar (pinch of extra sugar makes it taste sweeter)

Direction

- Preheat oven to 425°F.
- Combine ingredients.
- Spray pan: Bake for 20 minutes.

Nutrition Information

- Calories: 350.7
- Sodium: 712
- Cholesterol: 91.9
- Total Carbohydrate: 44.7
- Protein: 7.9
- Total Fat: 16
- Saturated Fat: 9.2
- Fiber: 2.2
- Sugar: 8.5

123. Lemon Verbena Blueberry Scones

Serving: 10 scones | Prep: 20mins | Ready in:

Ingredients

- 1 large free-range egg
- 3/4 cup heavy whipping cream
- 2 cups all-purpose flour
- 2 tablespoons granulated sugar
- 1 tablespoon baking powder
- 1/4 teaspoon salt
- 5 tablespoons unsalted butter, cut into small pieces and chilled
- 6 -8 medium fresh lemon verbena leaves, finely chopped
- 1 lemon, zest of, finely grated
- 1 cup fresh blueberries, coated with a little flour
- 2 -3 tablespoons extra cream, for brushing tops
- turbinado sugar (raw sugar)
- lemon glaze (see my Fresh Lemon Glaze for Scones, Cookies - Biscuits and Cakes #411928) (optional)

Direction

- Centre a rack in the oven and preheat the oven to 400°F.
- Line a baking sheet with parchment or a silicone mat.
- Stir the egg and cream together in a small bowl.
- Whisk the flour, baking powder, and salt together in a large bowl.
- In a separate bowl add the sugar, lemon zest, and lemon verbena leaves. Rub everything together with your fingers to bring out the lemon flavour.
- Stir lemon mixture into the flour mixture. Add the butter to the flour/lemon sugar mixture. Using your fingers, toss to coat the pieces of butter with flour. Quickly, working with your fingertips or a pastry blender, cut and rub the butter into the dry ingredients until the mixture is pebbly. You will have some little butter clumps and some larger clumps-the size of peas.
- Pour the egg and cream over the dry ingredients and stir with a fork just until the dough comes together. It will be sticky. Don't over mix. Still in the bowl, gently knead the dough by hand, 8 to 10 times.
- Gently fold in the blueberries.
- Lightly dust a work surface with flour and turn out the dough. Divide it in half. Working with one piece at a time, pat the dough into a rough circle that's about 5 inches in diameter, cut it into wedges or use a round cookie cutter and cut out the scones.
- Brush the scones with cream and sprinkle Turbinado sugar on top.
- Bake the scones for 20 to 22 minutes, or until their tops are golden brown. Transfer them to a rack and cool.
- Glaze with my lemon glaze recipe #411928, if desired.
- These are best eaten warm and on the day they are made.

Nutrition Information

- Calories: 238.3
- Saturated Fat: 8.5
- Sodium: 183.4
- Fiber: 1
- Sugar: 4.1
- Total Carbohydrate: 24.7
- Total Fat: 14.1
- Cholesterol: 61.6
- Protein: 3.8

124. Lemonade Muffins

Serving: 8-9 large muffins | Prep: 20mins | Ready in:

Ingredients

- 1 1/2 cups flour
- 1/4 cup sugar
- 2 1/2 teaspoons baking powder
- 1/2 teaspoon salt
- 1 beaten egg
- 1 (6 ounce) can frozen lemonade, thawed
- 1/4 cup milk
- 1/3 cup cooking oil
- 1/2 cup chopped walnuts

Direction

- Mix dry ingredients in a bowl.
- In another bowl, mix only 1/2 cup lemonade, egg, milk, and oil.
- Add to dry mix, stirring until just moistened.
- Gently stir in nuts.
- Spoon into prepared pans and bake and bake at 375°F for 15-20 mins or tests clean.
- While hot, brush with remaining lemonade and sprinkle with white sugar.
- Makes 8-9 large muffins.

Nutrition Information

- Calories: 293
- Sugar: 16.6
- Total Carbohydrate: 36.5

- Cholesterol: 27.5
- Protein: 4.6
- Saturated Fat: 2
- Sodium: 272.8
- Fiber: 1.2
- Total Fat: 15

125. Lincolnshire Poacher Cheese Scones Strictly For Grown Ups!

Serving: 8-12 Scones, 4 serving(s) | Prep: 15mins | Ready in:

Ingredients

- 700 g plain flour
- 2 teaspoons baking powder
- 1 teaspoon salt
- 5 ounces butter (softened)
- 2 eggs
- 1/3 pint milk
- 7 ounces grated lincolnshire poacher cheese
- 1 egg yolk (egg-wash)

Direction

- Pre-heat oven to 180°C.
- Sieve flour baking powder and salt, then add butter and rub together.
- Then add 5oz of the grated cheese followed by the eggs.
- Continue to work the mixture together by hand.
- With the ingredients worked in, pour the mixture out of the bowl onto the worktop.
- Gradually add the milk into the mixture as it is worked together.
- Use a little flour to stop the dough sticking to the worktop.
- Gently roll out the dough to about 1" - 1 1/2" inch thick, then using a pastry cutter (2" diameter).
- Cut out, arrange on a greased baking tray.
- Brush with egg-wash, as an option the remainder of the cheese could be sprinkled on top, bake for 10-12 minutes.
- Serve hot, split and spread with butter!

Nutrition Information

- Calories: 1126.6
- Cholesterol: 234.8
- Total Carbohydrate: 169.7
- Sodium: 1028.2
- Fiber: 5.9
- Sugar: 0.8
- Protein: 28
- Total Fat: 35.9
- Saturated Fat: 20.6

126. Low Fat (But You Wouldn't Know It) Banana Bread

Serving: 22 slices | Prep: 15mins | Ready in:

Ingredients

- 3/4 cup white sugar
- 1/2 cup unsweetened applesauce
- 2 eggs, beaten
- 3 bananas, mashed
- 1 cup all-purpose flour
- 1 cup whole wheat flour
- 1 teaspoon baking soda
- 1/2 teaspoon salt
- 1/2 teaspoon baking powder

Direction

- Beat the sugar and applesauce together.
- Add eggs and mashed banana and beat well.
- In another bowl combine both flours, baking soda, baking powder and salt. Add this to the banana mixture and mix well.
- Pour the batter into a greased and floured 9x5x21/2" loaf pan.

- Bake at 350oF for about 1 hour. If a wooden tester inserted into the center of the bread comes out clean the bread is done. Turn the bread out of the loaf pan and allow cake to cool on a wire rack. Wrap the bread in tin foil and store overnight before slicing.
- Enjoy!

Nutrition Information

- Calories: 89
- Fiber: 1.3
- Saturated Fat: 0.2
- Sodium: 125.3
- Cholesterol: 19.2
- Protein: 2.1
- Total Fat: 0.7
- Sugar: 8.8
- Total Carbohydrate: 19.5

127. Low Fat Peachy Oatmeal Muffins

Serving: 12 Muffins | Prep: 15mins | Ready in:

Ingredients

- 1 cup quick-cooking oats
- 1 cup buttermilk
- 1⁄3 cup brown sugar
- 1⁄3 cup applesauce
- 1⁄4 cup molasses
- 2 eggs
- 1 1⁄3 cups all-purpose flour
- 1 teaspoon baking soda
- 1 teaspoon baking powder
- 1 1⁄2 cups pitted and diced fresh peaches
- 2 tablespoons white sugar
- 1⁄2 teaspoon ground cinnamon

Direction

- Preheat oven to 400 degrees.
- Grease muffin cups or line with paper muffin liners.
- In a large bowl, mix together oats, buttermilk, brown sugar, applesauce, molasses and eggs.
- In a separate bowl, stir together flour, baking soda and baking powder.
- Stir flour mixture into eggs mixture, just until moistened.
- Fold in peaches and spoon batter into prepared muffin cups.
- Place in preheated oven.
- While muffins are baking, combine 2 tablespoons sugar and 1/2 teaspoon cinnamon.
- After 15 minutes of baking, remove muffins from oven and sprinkle with cinnamon sugar.
- Return to oven and continue baking for 3 minutes, until a toothpick inserted into center of a muffin comes out clean.

Nutrition Information

- Calories: 162.5
- Total Fat: 1.6
- Fiber: 1.5
- Cholesterol: 36.1
- Protein: 4.5
- Saturated Fat: 0.5
- Sodium: 175.8
- Sugar: 14.8
- Total Carbohydrate: 33

128. Moist Apple Muffins With Pecan Topping

Serving: 17 muffins | Prep: 15mins | Ready in:

Ingredients

- cooking spray
- 3⁄4 cup plus 2 tablespoons packed brown sugar
- 1⁄4 cup chopped pecans
- 1 teaspoon ground cinnamon, divided

- 1 cup all-purpose flour
- 1 cup whole wheat pastry flour or 1 cup whole wheat flour
- 1 teaspoon baking soda
- 1/2 teaspoon salt
- 1/4 cup canola oil
- 2 large eggs
- 1 cup plain applesauce
- 1 teaspoon vanilla extract
- 3/4 cup low-fat buttermilk
- 1 golden delicious apple, peeled, cored and cut into 1/4-inch pieces

Direction

- Preheat oven to 400°F and prepare muffin tins with liners and cooking spray (use both or muffins will stick).
- In a small bowl, mix together 2 tablespoons of the brown sugar, the pecans and 1/2 teaspoon cinnamon.
- In a medium bowl, whisk together the all-purpose and whole-wheat flour, 1/2 teaspoon cinnamon, baking soda and salt.
- In a large bowl, whisk the remaining 3/4 cup sugar and oil until combined. Add the eggs, 1 at a time, whisking well after each addition. Whisk in the applesauce and vanilla.
- Whisk in the flour mixture in 2 batches, alternating with the buttermilk. Whisk just until combined. Gently stir in the apple chunks.
- Pour the batter into a prepared muffin pan and sprinkle with the pecan mixture. Tap the pan on the counter a few times to remove any air bubbles. Bake for about 20 to 25 minutes or until a wooden pick inserted in center of 1 of the muffins comes out clean. (Cooking time may be shorter or longer, depending on muffin size.).
- Let cool on a wire rack for 15 minutes. Run a knife around the muffins to loosen them and unmold. Cool completely on the rack.

Nutrition Information

- Calories: 156.3
- Sodium: 170.6
- Fiber: 1.7
- Saturated Fat: 0.6
- Sugar: 10.9
- Total Carbohydrate: 25.2
- Cholesterol: 25.3
- Protein: 3
- Total Fat: 5.3

129. Moist Jumbo Banana Wheat/Oat Bran Muffins

Serving: 6 muffins, 6 serving(s) | Prep: 25mins | Ready in:

Ingredients

- 1 eggs or 1 egg substitute
- 3/4 cup light brown sugar
- 1 1/3 cups mashed bananas
- 1/2 cup nuts (optional) or 1/2 cup dried fruit (optional)
- 1/3 cup vegetable oil
- 1 teaspoon vanilla extract
- 3/4 cup all-purpose flour
- 3/4 cup whole wheat flour
- 1/2 cup oat bran or 1/2 cup wheat bran
- 2 teaspoons baking powder
- 1/2 teaspoon baking soda
- 1/4 teaspoon salt
- 1 teaspoon cinnamon
- nonstick cooking spray

Direction

- Preheat oven to 375 degrees.
- Grease jumbo pan of 6 muffin cups with non-stick spray or line with paper cups.
- Mash ripe bananas with fork or puree in food processor.
- Chop nuts or dried fruit, if using.
- In a medium size bowl, beat egg and sugars. When smooth add banana, oil and vanilla. Rest.

- In a large bowl mix the flours, bran, baking powder, baking soda, salt and cinnamon. Stir in nuts or dried fruit till coated with the flour.
- Pour the banana mixture onto the flour mixture, folding until flour is just moistened.
- Place into muffin cups immediately and put into oven.
- Bake for 21 - 23 minutes or until springy to the touch. A toothpick should come out of the center with a few crumbs sticking to it.

Nutrition Information

- Calories: 398.9
- Saturated Fat: 2.1
- Cholesterol: 31
- Sugar: 33.1
- Total Carbohydrate: 67.2
- Protein: 6.6
- Total Fat: 14.1
- Sodium: 343.9
- Fiber: 4.8

130. Muffins A Vegetable Medley

Serving: 12 each | Prep: 15mins | Ready in:

Ingredients

- 2 cups self-rising flour
- 1/2 cup finely chopped zucchini
- 1/2 cup finely chopped tomatoes, peeled,seeded,and drained
- 1 tablespoon dried onion
- 1/2 teaspoon celery salt
- 1/2 teaspoon dill weed
- 1 egg, beaten
- 3/4 cup water
- 3 tablespoons vegetable oil
- 4 Tabasco sauce or 4 hot sauce, of your choice

Direction

- Preheat your oven to 425* Grease the muffin cups.
- In a large bowl, stir in the flour, zucchini, tomato, onion, salt, and dill weed together.
- Blend egg, water, Tabasco sauce and oil.
- Add this to your flour mixture.
- Stir all until well blended.
- Fill the prepared muffin cups 2/3 full.
- Bake for 15 to 20 min. or until golden brown.

Nutrition Information

- Calories: 113.6
- Saturated Fat: 0.6
- Sodium: 271.7
- Fiber: 0.8
- Cholesterol: 17.6
- Protein: 2.8
- Total Fat: 4
- Sugar: 0.5
- Total Carbohydrate: 16.3

131. Oaty Banana Mini Muffins (Oamc)

Serving: 24 mini muffins | Prep: 10mins | Ready in:

Ingredients

- 8 ounces all-purpose flour
- 3 ounces porridge oats, plus a spoonful for decoration
- 2 teaspoons baking powder
- 3 eggs, beaten
- 6 ounces superfine sugar
- 1 cup corn oil
- 2 bananas, finely chopped

Direction

- Preheat the oven to 350°F Line a mini muffin tray with 24 cases.
- Place the flour, oats and baking powder into a bowl. In a separate bowl, beat the eggs, sugar

and oil together until pale and fluffy. Fold into the dry ingredients with the bananas.
- Spoon into the muffin cases and sprinkle with the remaining oats. Bake for 15 minutes until risen and golden. Cool and serve.

Nutrition Information

- Calories: 174.2
- Protein: 2.5
- Saturated Fat: 1.4
- Sodium: 39.4
- Sugar: 8.4
- Total Carbohydrate: 19.1
- Total Fat: 10.1
- Fiber: 0.9
- Cholesterol: 26.4

132. Onion And Red Pepper Corn Muffins

Serving: 18 muffins | Prep: 10mins | Ready in:

Ingredients

- 1 red pepper, seeded and chopped
- 1 medium onion, chopped
- 2 tablespoons butter
- 1 1/2 cups milk
- 4 tablespoons butter, melted
- 2 eggs
- 1 1/2 cups yellow cornmeal
- 1 cup unbleached flour
- 1/3 cup sugar
- 3 teaspoons baking powder
- 1 teaspoon salt

Direction

- Heat oven to 400°F.
- Grease bottoms only of 18 muffin cups (2 1/2inches x 1 1/2 inches in size).
- Cook onions and peppers in butter for 2 minutes, stirring occasionally, until softened.
- In a large bowl, using a fork, beat milk, 4 Tablespoons melted butter and eggs until well combined.
- Stir in cornmeal, flour, sugar, baking powder and salt until flour is moistened.
- (Batter will be slightly lumpy).
- Fold in the peppers and onions.
- Divide batter evenly among the muffin cups (batter will be almost level with rims of muffin cups).
- Bake muffins for about 20 minutes or until light golden brown.

Nutrition Information

- Calories: 136.2
- Saturated Fat: 3.1
- Fiber: 1.1
- Total Carbohydrate: 19
- Cholesterol: 36.5
- Protein: 3.1
- Total Fat: 5.6
- Sodium: 238.7
- Sugar: 4.4

133. Popcorn Muffins

Serving: 12 serving(s) | Prep: 15mins | Ready in:

Ingredients

- 1 1/2 cups flour
- 3/4 cup ground popcorn
- 4 teaspoons baking powder
- 1 teaspoon salt
- 1 tablespoon sugar
- 2 tablespoons butter, melted
- 1 cup milk
- 1 egg

Direction

- Sift flour, powder, salt and sugar together.

- Add milk, popcorn and egg, well beaten, and melted butter.
- Bake at 25 minutes at 350* in greased or lined muffin tins.

Nutrition Information

- Calories: 97.8
- Fiber: 0.4
- Total Carbohydrate: 14.3
- Cholesterol: 25.6
- Sodium: 344.6
- Saturated Fat: 1.8
- Sugar: 1.1
- Protein: 2.8
- Total Fat: 3.2

134. Raisin Pumpkin Muffins

Serving: 12 muffins | Prep: 15mins | Ready in:

Ingredients

- 2 cups flour
- 1/2 cup raw sugar
- 2 teaspoons baking powder
- 1 teaspoon baking soda
- 1 1/2 teaspoons ground mixed spice
- 400 g pumpkin, pieces
- 1 cup large sticky raisins
- 2 eggs
- 1 cup milk
- 50 g butter
- 1/2 cup pumpkin seeds
- 2 teaspoons raw sugar

Direction

- Sift flour into a bowl.
- Stir through brown sugar, baking powder, baking soda and mixed spice.
- Remove seeds from pumpkin pieces and microwave on high for 5 minutes until just cooked but still firm.
- Remove skin and cut into 1cm slices.
- Toss through dry ingredients with raisins. Beat eggs together in a bowl.
- Add milk.
- Melt butter.
- Make a well in the centre of the dry ingredients.
- Add egg mixture, then butter.
- Mix through gently.
- Three-quarter fill greased muffin tins or line with muffin cases.
- Sprinkle over pumpkin seeds and raw sugar. Bake at 200 degrees C for 20-25 minutes or until muffins spring back when lightly touched.

Nutrition Information

- Calories: 274.9
- Total Carbohydrate: 47.9
- Cholesterol: 47
- Protein: 6.8
- Total Fat: 8.9
- Saturated Fat: 3.7
- Sodium: 223.6
- Fiber: 4.1
- Sugar: 16.8

135. Raisinet Banana Muffins

Serving: 12 serving(s) | Prep: 5mins | Ready in:

Ingredients

- 1 (14 ounce) package banana muffin
- 1 cup milk chocolate-covered raisins

Direction

- PREHEAT oven to 400° F.
- Grease or paper-line 12 muffin cups.
- PREPARE muffin mix according to package directions; stir Raisinets into batter.

- Spoon into prepared muffin cups, filling 3/4 full.
- BAKE for 15 to 18 minutes or until golden.
- Cool in pan on wire rack for 5 minutes.
- Gently loosen and remove from pan.
- Cool on wire rack.

Nutrition Information

- Calories: 0
- Sodium: 0
- Fiber: 0
- Total Carbohydrate: 0
- Cholesterol: 0
- Protein: 0
- Saturated Fat: 0
- Sugar: 0
- Total Fat: 0

136. Raspberry Vanilla Nut Muffins

Serving: 12 muffins | Prep: 10mins | Ready in:

Ingredients

- 2 1/2 cups flour
- 1 1/2 teaspoons baking powder
- 1 teaspoon baking soda
- 1/4 teaspoon salt
- 1/2 cup granulated sugar
- 1 (8 ounce) container vanilla yogurt
- 2 large eggs
- 1 1/2 tablespoons pure vanilla extract
- 1/2 tablespoon pure hazelnut extract or 1/2 tablespoon almond extract
- 1/4 cup vegetable oil
- 1/2 cup milk
- 1/2 cup toasted finely chopped hazelnuts
- 1 1/2 cups fresh red raspberries

Direction

- Preheat oven to 350 degrees.
- Grease a 12 count muffin tin.
- In a medium bowl mix flour, baking powder, baking soda, salt and sugar together and set aside.
- In a large bowl mix together the yogurt, eggs, extracts, oil and milk.
- Whisk well.
- Add the liquid ingredients to the dry ingredients, stirring constantly until well incorporated.
- Fold in Raspberries.
- Fill each muffin tin 3/4 full and bake for 25 minutes, or until set and golden brown.

Nutrition Information

- Calories: 247.4
- Saturated Fat: 1.8
- Sodium: 225
- Fiber: 2.2
- Cholesterol: 39.1
- Protein: 5.8
- Total Fat: 10.1
- Sugar: 10.6
- Total Carbohydrate: 32.8

137. Red Pepper Corn Muffins

Serving: 12 muffins, 12 serving(s) | Prep: 10mins | Ready in:

Ingredients

- 1/3 cup finely chopped sweet red pepper
- 1 cup yellow cornmeal
- 1 cup flour
- 2 1/2 teaspoons baking powder
- 1/2 teaspoon baking soda
- 1/2 teaspoon salt
- 2 large eggs
- 1 1/4 cups buttermilk
- 1/4 cup butter, melted

Direction

- Preheat oven to 400 degrees.
- Generously butter muffin tin -- 12 muffin regular size.
- Whisk together cornmeal, flour, baking powder, baking soda and salt in a large mixing bowl.
- Whisk together eggs, buttermilk and melted butter in a medium bowl.
- Add buttermilk mixture and red peppers to the flour mixture and stir until just combined; do not overmix.
- Place about 1/3 cup mixture into each of 12 muffin cups.
- Bake for 12 minutes or until a toothpick inserted in the middle of a muffin comes out clean.
- Carefully remove muffins from tin to a wire rack to cool.

Nutrition Information

- Calories: 132.7
- Total Carbohydrate: 17.5
- Cholesterol: 46.4
- Protein: 3.9
- Total Fat: 5.4
- Saturated Fat: 2.9
- Sodium: 294.5
- Fiber: 1.1
- Sugar: 1.6

138. Rosemary Scones

Serving: 10-12 scones approx. | Prep: 10mins | Ready in:

Ingredients

- 2 cups plain flour (can use wholemeal but they will be denser)
- 4 teaspoons baking powder
- 1/4 teaspoon salt
- 1 teaspoon sugar
- 1 tablespoon butter
- 1 tablespoon freshly chopped rosemary (1tsp dried)
- 1 cup milk (have use soya milk too, also good)

Direction

- Sift dry ingredients in a bowl and rub in butter, add rosemary and milk and combine to form a soft dough.
- Roll out on to a floured board to 1 1/2-inch thickness and cut into 2-inch rounds.
- Place on a greased baking tray, brush with a little milk and bake in a pre-heated oven 220c (425f) for12 minutes.

Nutrition Information

- Calories: 119.6
- Saturated Fat: 1.3
- Sodium: 224.1
- Sugar: 0.5
- Cholesterol: 6.5
- Total Fat: 2.3
- Fiber: 0.7
- Total Carbohydrate: 21.1
- Protein: 3.4

139. Round Up Valley Muffins #RSC

Serving: 16 Muffins, 16 serving(s) | Prep: 10mins | Ready in:

Ingredients

- 2 1/2 cups all-purpose flour
- 1 (1 ounce) Hidden Valley Original Ranch Seasoning Mix
- 2 tablespoons granulated sugar
- 4 teaspoons baking powder
- 1 teaspoon baking soda
- 2 large eggs
- 1 cup buttermilk
- 3 tablespoons melted butter

- 1 cup thawed frozen corn or 1 cup drained canned corn
- 1 cup cooked finely diced baby carrots
- 1 1/2 cups cooked cleaned bay shrimp (canned ok)
- 2 tablespoons chopped fresh chives
- 2/3 cup favorite barbecue sauce
- 3/4 cup grated parmesan cheese
- butter-flavored nonstick cooking spray

Direction

- Mix together the flour, seasoning mix, sugar, baking powder and baking soda in a large bowl. In another bowl, combine the eggs, buttermilk and melted butter. Stir in the corn, carrots, shrimp and chives.
- Make a well in the dry ingredients and quickly add the moist ingredients, stirring briefly. Batter will be lumpy.
- Spoon into greased muffin tins, filling them 2/3 full. Top each with 2 teaspoons BBQ sauce and 2 teaspoons parmesan cheese.
- Heat oven to 400° F, and place shelf in center of the oven.
- Bake until golden, cooked through (a toothpick inserted in the center should come out clean), 15-20 minutes. Cool in the pans 5 minutes, then on a wire rack.
- Note: if any muffin tins are unfilled, fill them with water before baking the others.

Nutrition Information

- Calories: 168.8
- Fiber: 1.3
- Total Carbohydrate: 26.5
- Cholesterol: 33.7
- Total Fat: 4.6
- Saturated Fat: 2.5
- Sodium: 380.6
- Sugar: 5.5
- Protein: 5.8

140. Soaked Grain Muffins Or Quick Bread

Serving: 24-36 muffins | Prep: 7hours | Ready in:

Ingredients

- 2 cups buttermilk or 2 cups homemade kefir
- 1 cup honey
- 1 cup coconut oil
- 3 cups wheat berries (soft white, spelt, kamut, hard red, etc.)
- 2 teaspoons salt
- 2 teaspoons baking soda
- 2 teaspoons baking powder
- 2 eggs

Direction

- Put first 4 ingredients into blender in order and blend for 3 minutes on high (1 1/2 minutes in a Vitamix).
- Cover and let stand on counter for at least 7 hours, overnight, or 12 hours.
- After soaking, add salt, soda, powder and eggs. Blend until mixed. Stir in any additions.
- Put into prepared muffin pans and bake at 400 degrees for 20-25 minutes.
- Mini muffins: Bake at 400 degrees for 10-15 minutes. Loaves: bake at 350 degrees for 55 minutes or until tests done. (Makes 2 loaves).
- Additions:
- ~For Blueberry/Millet: 2 C blueberries, 2 t cinnamon, 1/2 C millet.
- ~For Banana: 4-6 mashed bananas, 2 t cinnamon, 1/2 C - 1 C walnuts.
- ~For Carrot or Zucchini: 2 C grated carrot or zucchini, 2 t cinnamon, 1/2 c - 1 C oats.
- ~ For Chocolate: 6-7 T cocoa powder, 1-2 C chocolate chips.
- ~ For Apple: 2 diced apples, 2 t cinnamon, 1 t nutmeg, optional.
- ~ For Poppy seed: 4 T poppy seeds, 2 t vanilla.
- ~For Pumpkin: 2 C pureed pumpkin, 2 t cinnamon, 1/2 t nutmeg, 1/4 t ground cloves.

Nutrition Information

- Calories: 135.7
- Fiber: 0
- Sugar: 12.6
- Total Carbohydrate: 12.7
- Saturated Fat: 8.1
- Sodium: 356.8
- Total Fat: 9.7
- Cholesterol: 18.4
- Protein: 1.2

141. Southern Cheesy Date Biscuits

Serving: 30-35 biscuits | Prep: 25mins | Ready in:

Ingredients

- 1 (8 ounce) packagewhole pitted dates
- 1 1/2 cups all-purpose flour
- 1/2 teaspoon cayenne
- 1/2 teaspoon salt
- 1/2 cup extra-sharp cheddar cheese, grated
- 1/2 cup unsalted butter, room temperature
- 1/2 cup milk

Direction

- Preheat oven to 375^F.
- Sift together the flour, cayenne and salt.
- Set aside.
- In the medium bowl of a mixer, beat butter and cheese until well blended.
- Mix in the flour mixture.
- Add milk making a stiff dough.
- Completely enclose each of 35 dates with 1 tablespoon dough.
- Place each dough covered date on an ungreased baking sheet.
- Bake 15 minutes, or until golden brown.
- These can be formed in advance and baked as needed.
- Serve warm.

Nutrition Information

- Calories: 82.8
- Fiber: 0.8
- Sodium: 55.1
- Sugar: 4.8
- Total Carbohydrate: 10.7
- Cholesterol: 11
- Protein: 1.6
- Total Fat: 4
- Saturated Fat: 2.5

142. Spice Oat Muffins Weight Watchers Point Value 3

Serving: 12 muffins, 12 serving(s) | Prep: 10mins | Ready in:

Ingredients

- 1 cup whole wheat flour
- 1/2 cup cornmeal
- 1/2 cup rolled oats, quick cooking
- 1/4 cup brown sugar, packed
- 3 teaspoons cinnamon sugar
- 1 teaspoon baking powder
- 1/2 teaspoon baking soda
- 1/2 teaspoon salt
- 1 1/4 cups fat-free buttermilk
- 1/2 cup dried cherries (or cranberries, whatever you prefer)
- 1/4 cup fat free egg substitute
- 2 tablespoons canola oil (or vegetable oil)
- 2 tablespoons wheat germ

Direction

- Preheat the oven to 400 degrees.
- Line a 12-cup muffin pan with paper liners.
- Combine the flour, cornmeal, oats, brown sugar, 1 teaspoon of the cinnamon sugar, baking powder, baking soda and salt in a large bowl. Make a well in the center.
- Combine the buttermilk, cherries (or cranberries), egg substitute and oil in a small

bowl, beating with a whisk until blended. Add the buttermilk mixture to the flour mixture, folding with a rubber spatula just until the flour mixture is moistened.
- Fill the muffin cups evenly with the batter; sprinkle with the remaining 2 teaspoons of cinnamon sugar and the wheat germ (I just love wheat germ, don't you?). Bake until a toothpick inserted into the center comes out clean, about 15 minutes.
- Cool in the pan 5 minutes. Unmold the muffins and cool completely.

Nutrition Information

- Calories: 116.1
- Total Fat: 3.2
- Saturated Fat: 0.3
- Sodium: 193.2
- Sugar: 5.6
- Total Carbohydrate: 19.7
- Protein: 3.2
- Fiber: 2.1
- Cholesterol: 0.1

143. Sugar And Spice! Glazed Lemon Tea Scones

Serving: 8 Glazed Lemon Scones, 8 serving(s) | Prep: 10mins | Ready in:

Ingredients

- Scones
- 2 cups self raising flour
- 1/3 cup white caster sugar
- 1 teaspoon baking powder
- 1 teaspoon cream of tartar
- 1/4 teaspoon mixed spice (or a mixture of cinnamon, nutmeg and cloves)
- 1/8 teaspoon salt
- 1 lemon, zest of, finely grated
- 3 tablespoons cold unsalted butter, cut into small pieces
- 1 cup double cream or 1 cup whipping cream, plus a little for brushing
- 1 egg, beaten
- Glaze
- 1 cup icing sugar (confectioners' sugar)
- 1 -2 tablespoon fresh lemon juice
- 1 tablespoon melted unsalted butter
- 2 tablespoons double cream or 2 tablespoons whipping cream

Direction

- Heat the oven to 200C/400°F Grease a large, heavy baking sheet.
- Sift the flour, sugar, baking powder, cream of tartar, mixed spice and salt into a large mixing bowl. Add the lemon zest and lightly mix with your hands.
- Using your fingertips, rub the butter into the dry ingredients until the mixture resembles fine crumbs.
- Make a well in the center of the dry ingredients and add the cream and the beaten egg; mix with a knife; then using a wooden spoon, combine all the ingredients together, just until the dough holds together.
- Scrape the dough onto a floured surface and using floured hands, knead it gently three or four times to form a ball. Flatten the ball into a disk about 1 inch thick, then using a pastry (biscuit or cookie) cutter, cut out 8 rounds, for 8 scones. Transfer the scones to the baking sheet, leaving plenty of space between them. Brush the tops lightly with extra cream.
- Bake the scones in the center of the oven until golden brown, about 15 to 20 minutes. Allow them to cool on the sheet for a few minutes and then transfer them to a wire rack.
- While the scones continue to cool, make the glaze. Combine all the ingredients in a small mixing bowl and whisk them until the mixture is smooth. If necessary, you can thin the glaze with more lemon juice, stirring in a 1/2 teaspoon at a time. When the scones have cooled for another 5 to 10 minutes, drizzle each one generously with the lemon glaze.

- Serve them with butter, cream or lemon curd for a tea-time treat!

Nutrition Information

- Calories: 381.7
- Saturated Fat: 11.6
- Sodium: 105
- Protein: 4.8
- Fiber: 0.8
- Sugar: 23.2
- Total Carbohydrate: 48.6
- Cholesterol: 87.6
- Total Fat: 19.1

144. Tahini Sunflower Seed Scones

Serving: 9 scones | Prep: 10mins | Ready in:

Ingredients

- 1 1/2 cups flour
- 1/4 cup whole wheat flour (I use spelt)
- 1/4 teaspoon salt
- 2 tablespoons sugar
- 2 1/2 teaspoons baking powder
- 9 tablespoons tahini or 9 tablespoons nut butter
- 1/2 cup roasted sunflower seeds or 1/2 cup chopped nuts
- 1 egg
- 1/2 cup milk

Direction

- Heat oven to 375°F.
- Combine flours, sugar, salt and baking powder until well blended.
- Add tahini or nut butter by tbsp., covering each spoonful with flour mixture. Using a pastry blender or wire whisk, cut tahini or nut butter into flour mixture until it resembles coarse crumbs. Fold in roasted sunflower seeds or chopped nuts of your choice.
- In a separate bowl combine egg and milk and whisk until blended. Pour into tahini flour mixture reserving 1 tbsp. full for glaze and combine until just blended.
- On a floured surface flatten dough using your hands or a rolling pin. Using a glass cut out scones of desired size.
- Place on a paper-lined baking sheet and glaze with reserved egg mixture. If you like sprinkle some seeds or chopped nuts on top.
- Bake for about 15 minutes until slightly golden on top. Enjoy!

Nutrition Information

- Calories: 242.3
- Total Fat: 12.1
- Saturated Fat: 1.9
- Sodium: 191.8
- Cholesterol: 25.4
- Fiber: 3.2
- Sugar: 3.1
- Total Carbohydrate: 27.7
- Protein: 7.8

145. Toblerone Cream Cheese Muffins

Serving: 4-8 muffins | Prep: 10mins | Ready in:

Ingredients

- Filling
- 3 ounces cream cheese, softened
- 50 g swiss Toblerone chocolate bars or 50 g dark Toblerone chocolate bar, chopped into very small pieces
- 3 tablespoons sugar
- 1 teaspoon flour
- 1/8 teaspoon vanilla
- 1 egg
- Batter

- 1 egg
- 3/4 cup milk
- 1/2 cup vegetable oil
- 2 cups flour
- 1/3 cup sugar
- 3 teaspoons baking powder
- 1/2 teaspoon salt
- powdered sugar

Direction

- Preheat oven to 350 degrees.
- Combine the filling ingredients with electric mixer; set aside.
- Oil the bottoms only of medium-sized muffin tins.
- Next, begin the batter mixture; beat eggs; stir in milk and oil, and set aside.
- Mix together the flour, sugar, baking powder, and salt until well blended.
- Pour batter liquids, all at one time, into the flour mixture and stir until moistened.
- Fill the muffin cups about 1/2 full with batter mixture, then spoon 2 teaspoons of filling onto the batter, then top with batter until the cup is 3/4 full.
- Bake muffins for 30 to 35 minutes; completed muffins should be light in color, not too dark.
- Roll the tops of the hot muffins in powdered sugar.
- Makes about 8 medium muffins, or 4 in large muffin tins.
- Other candies can be substituted for the Toblerone. Experiment and enjoy!

Nutrition Information

- Calories: 714.1
- Total Fat: 39.4
- Sodium: 684.6
- Fiber: 1.7
- Protein: 12.8
- Saturated Fat: 10.1
- Sugar: 26.5
- Total Carbohydrate: 78
- Cholesterol: 135.5

146. Tortilla Chip Cornbread

Serving: 16 pieces, 16 serving(s) | Prep: 10mins | Ready in:

Ingredients

- 1 1/4 cups corn tortilla chips, finely crushed (see note)
- 1 cup flour
- 1/2 cup sugar
- 1 tablespoon baking powder
- 1/4 cup butter or 1/4 cup margarine, melted
- 1 cup milk
- 1 egg, slightly beaten

Direction

- Note: pulse tortilla chips in a blender or food processor to get them finely crushed. It's okay if they aren't as finely crushed as cornmeal; just get them as small as you can.
- Mix dry ingredients in a medium bowl.
- In a separate bowl, mix butter/margarine, milk and egg.
- Pour wet ingredients into dry, and stir just until combined. Mixture may be slightly lumpy. Pour batter into a greased 8x8-inch square baking dish.
- Bake at 400 degrees for 20-25 minutes or until a toothpick inserted in the center comes out clean.

Nutrition Information

- Calories: 92.8
- Protein: 1.7
- Total Fat: 3.8
- Sodium: 100.5
- Fiber: 0.2
- Total Carbohydrate: 13.2
- Cholesterol: 23
- Saturated Fat: 2.3

- Sugar: 6.3

147. Very Tasty Cheesy Cheddar And Oat Scones

Serving: 12 Scones, 12 serving(s) | Prep: 10mins | Ready in:

Ingredients

- 200 g self raising flour
- 50 g butter, softened
- 25 g porridge oats
- 75 g grated mature cheddar cheese
- 150 ml milk
- 1 pinch salt

Direction

- Preheat oven to 220C - gas 7.
- In a large roomy bowl rub softened butter into flour until they resemble breadcrumbs.
- Stir in oats cheese, then add the milk - if it feels too dry, add a touch more milk.
- Bring it all together and make a soft dough.
- Lightly dust a surface with flour and roll out the dough until NO thinner than 2cm.
- Using a 4cm scone/cookie cutter firmly stamp out the rounds. Do NOT twist as you stamp as it stops the scones from rising evenly!
- Re-roll all the trimmings and stamp out some more rounds until the dough is finished.
- Place on a non-stick baking tray/sheet or one which has been lined with non-stick baking paper. Dust with a little more flour OR glaze with a little milk add some extra grated cheese for the topping if desired.
- Bake for 12-15 minutes until well risen and golden.
- Cool on a wire rack - if you can manage it!
- Serve on their own or with Boursin soft cheese, Philadelphia cream cheese, sliced ham, cucumber, cress or just with BUTTER!
- Cheese variation for the topping is grated parmesan mixed with a little paprika or cayenne pepper.

Nutrition Information

- Calories: 146.5
- Fiber: 0.8
- Total Carbohydrate: 17.9
- Cholesterol: 17.2
- Protein: 4.5
- Total Fat: 6.2
- Saturated Fat: 3.8
- Sodium: 82.1
- Sugar: 0.1

148. Whole Grain Spelt Biscuits

Serving: 6 serving(s) | Prep: 10mins | Ready in:

Ingredients

- 2 cups whole grain spelt flour
- 1 tablespoon baking powder
- 1/2 teaspoon salt
- 2 tablespoons sunflower seeds
- 2 tablespoons flax seeds
- 1 tablespoon black sesame seed
- 2 tablespoons coconut oil (solid)
- 2 tablespoons butter
- 2/3 cup buttermilk

Direction

- Preheat the oven to 220C (450F).
- In a large bowl, mix together the flour, baking powder, salt, and seeds.
- Cut in the coconut oil and butter to resemble coarse crumbs (a pastry blender can come in handy here, so can your hands).
- Add the buttermilk and mix until blended.
- Cut dough into 6 equal portions and arrange on a baking sheet.

- Bake at 220C for 12-15 minutes, until golden brown.

Nutrition Information

- Calories: 129
- Fiber: 1.4
- Protein: 2.4
- Saturated Fat: 6.9
- Sodium: 439.2
- Sugar: 1.4
- Total Carbohydrate: 3.8
- Cholesterol: 11.3
- Total Fat: 12.3

149. Yeo Valley Lemon Drizzle Cake/Muffins

Serving: 1/8-1/8 cake/muffins | Prep: 15mins | Ready in:

Ingredients

- 125 g butter
- 150 g caster sugar
- 200 g plain flour
- 1 teaspoon bicarbonate of soda
- 3 eggs
- 150 g whole milk natural yogurt
- 1 large lemon, zest and juice
- lemon zest from icing
- To make the Icing
- 150 g icing sugar
- 1 large lemon, juice only
- water, to adjust consistency

Direction

- Preheat the oven to 190*C/375*F/Gas mark 5.
- Beat together the butter and sugar until light and creamy.
- Add the eggs one at a time beating well between additions.
- Sieve the flour and bicarbonate together. Add alternate spoons of yogurt and flour mix and blend gently between additions.
- Finally stir in the lemon zest and juice (add poppy seeds now too if using) Pour into a greased and floured 18cm cake tin. Bake for 40-45 minutes until well risen and golden brown.
- Or a 12 pan muffin tray and bake for about 25 minutes.
- While the cake is baking prepare the icing, stir the lemon juice into the icing sugar to make an icing that coats the back of the spoon.
- Just before the cake is baked warm the icing gently to approx. 40°C Remove the cake from the oven, and remove from the tin. Prick the surface of the cake with a fork and pour over the warmed drizzle icing. Allow to cool.

Nutrition Information

- Calories: 39835
- Total Fat: 1474.5
- Saturated Fat: 865.3
- Fiber: 137.4
- Sugar: 3706.9
- Protein: 633.3
- Sodium: 29286.7
- Total Carbohydrate: 6170.4
- Cholesterol: 10135.6

150. Yogurt Bran Muffins

Serving: 12 muffins, 12 serving(s) | Prep: 10mins | Ready in:

Ingredients

- 1 cup Fiber One cereal, original all bran
- 2 egg whites, slightly beaten or 1 egg
- 1/4 cup vegetable oil
- 2 (6 ounce) containers fat free french vanilla yogurt, Yoplait
- 1 1/2 cups Gold Medal all-purpose flour

- 1/3 cup brown sugar, packed
- 1 1/4 teaspoons baking soda
- 1/2 teaspoon salt
- 1/2 cup fresh raspberries or 1/2 cup blueberries

Direction

- Heat oven to 400°F Place paper baking cup in each of 12 regular-size muffin cups, or grease bottom of each muffin cup with shortening. Place cereal in resealable food-storage plastic bag; seal bag and crush with rolling pin or meat mallet (or crush in food processor).
- In medium bowl, stir together egg whites, oil and yogurt. Add cereal, flour, brown sugar, baking soda and salt; stir just until dry ingredients are moistened. Gently stir in berries. Divide batter evenly among muffin cups, filling each 3/4 full.
- Bake 18 to 20 minutes or until golden brown. Immediately remove from pan.

Nutrition Information

- Calories: 135.4
- Cholesterol: 0
- Total Carbohydrate: 22.6
- Protein: 2.7
- Total Fat: 4.9
- Saturated Fat: 0.6
- Sodium: 261.3
- Fiber: 3.2
- Sugar: 6.2

Chapter 4: Quick Bread Chocolate Recipes

***

151. Awesome Chocolate Chocolate Chip Muffins

Serving: 17 muffins, 17 serving(s) | Prep: 10mins | Ready in:

Ingredients

- 1 3/4 cups flour
- 3/4 cup sugar
- 2 tablespoons cocoa powder
- 2 teaspoons baking powder
- 1/2 teaspoon baking soda
- 1 egg
- 1/2 cup sour cream
- 1/2 cup milk
- 1/3 cup vegetable oil
- 2 tablespoons butter
- 1 teaspoon vanilla
- 3/4 cup semi-sweet chocolate chips

Direction

- Preheat oven to 400 degrees.
- Combine the flour, sugar, baking powder, baking soda and cocoa powder in a large mixing bowl.
- In a separate mixing bowl, whisk together the egg, oil, milk, sour cream and vanilla.
- Pour the wet ingredients into the dry ingredients and stir by hand until well blended. Batter should be a bit lumpy.
- Add the chocolate chips and stir till well distributed.
- Spoon into prepared muffin cups and top with 5-8 chocolate chips.
- Bake for 20 minutes and enjoy.

Nutrition Information

- Calories: 190.6
- Protein: 2.5
- Total Fat: 9.9
- Saturated Fat: 3.8
- Sodium: 106.1

- Fiber: 1
- Sugar: 13.2
- Total Carbohydrate: 24.5
- Cholesterol: 19.1

152. Banana Bran Muffins With Lindt Chocolate Inside

Serving: 12 cupcake sized muffins, 12 serving(s) | Prep: 20mins | Ready in:

Ingredients

- 1 1/2 cups bran flakes
- 1 cup mashed banana
- 1/2 cup milk
- 1 lightly beaten egg
- 3 tablespoons corn oil
- 1 cup all-purpose flour
- 1/4 cup sugar
- 2 teaspoons baking powder
- 1/4 teaspoon baking soda
- 1/8 teaspoon ground nutmeg
- 1 piece lindt chili chocolate

Direction

- Preheat oven to 400 degrees F. Paper line 12 (2-1/2 inch) muffin cups. Combine egg, oil, milk, mashed banana, and crushed bran cereal. Mix well and let stand for five minutes. Combine flour, sugar, baking powder, baking soda and nutmeg in a separate bowl. Add cereal banana mixture all at once to flour mixture, stirring just until moistened. Divide evenly among the muffin cups, making sure that the chocolate is covered by batter. Bake 20 to 25 minutes at 400 degrees F or until tester inserted in center comes out clean.
- Any dark chocolate will do, but my favorite is Lindt. I break the slices in half.

Nutrition Information

- Calories: 121.1
- Total Fat: 3.4
- Sodium: 133.4
- Total Carbohydrate: 21.6
- Protein: 2.9
- Saturated Fat: 1.4
- Fiber: 2
- Sugar: 7.3
- Cholesterol: 16.9

153. Banana Bran Muffins With A Hint Of Chocolate

Serving: 12 muffins, 12 serving(s) | Prep: 10mins | Ready in:

Ingredients

- 1 cup whole wheat flour
- 1 cup all-bran cereal
- 1 teaspoon baking powder
- 1 teaspoon baking soda
- 1/2 teaspoon salt
- 2 tablespoons cocoa powder
- 1/4 cup applesauce
- 1/2 cup sugar
- 2 eggs
- 1/4 cup sour milk
- 1 cup mashed banana

Direction

- Mix first six ingredients into mixing bowl.
- In a separate bowl, mix apple sauce, sugar and eggs. Mix in milk and bananas. Pour into dry ingredients until moistened. Ignore lumps. Fill muffin pans 3/4 full. Bake 400F for 20-25 minutes.

Nutrition Information

- Calories: 117.4
- Protein: 3.6
- Saturated Fat: 0.5

- Sodium: 260.2
- Fiber: 3.5
- Total Fat: 1.6
- Sugar: 11.8
- Total Carbohydrate: 25.5
- Cholesterol: 35.8

154. Banana Carob Chocolate Muffins

Serving: 12 muffins, 12 serving(s) | Prep: 10mins | Ready in:

Ingredients

- 1 1/2 cups all-purpose flour
- 1/4 cup toasted carob powder
- 1/4-1/2 cup sugar (adjust according to your sweetness preference)
- 1 teaspoon baking soda
- 1/2 teaspoon salt
- 1/2 teaspoon cinnamon (prefer canela cinammon)
- 1 cup mashed overripe banana
- 4 ounces unsweetened berry applesauce (1 of those prepackaged snack cups)
- 1/3 cup coconut oil
- 1 egg
- 1/2 cup semi-sweet chocolate chips
- 1/2 cup carob chips

Direction

- Mix dry ingredients in a large bowl.
- Mix wet ingredients in a separate bowl. Make a well in dry ingredients and add wet ingredients. Stir until just mixed. Add chocolate and carob chips and stir until incorporated. Bake in regular sized muffin tin at 350 degrees for 20 to 25 minutes, until a toothpick tests clean. Makes 1 dozen muffins.

Nutrition Information

- Calories: 183.3
- Saturated Fat: 6.7
- Protein: 2.6
- Fiber: 1.3
- Sugar: 9.6
- Total Carbohydrate: 25.4
- Cholesterol: 15.5
- Total Fat: 8.8
- Sodium: 211.6

155. Banana Chocolate Muffins

Serving: 4 muffins, 4 serving(s) | Prep: 10mins | Ready in:

Ingredients

- 1 1/2 cups flour
- 1 cup sugar
- 1/4 cup cocoa
- 1 teaspoon baking soda
- 1/2 teaspoon salt
- 1/4 teaspoon baking powder
- 1 1/3 cups bananas, mashed
- 1/3 cup vegetable oil
- 1 egg
- 1 cup semi-sweet chocolate chips

Direction

- In a large bowl, combine the flour, sugar, cocoa, baking soda, salt and baking powder.
- In a small bowl, combine the mashed bananas, oil and egg; stir into dry ingredients just until moistened.
- Fold in chocolate chips.
- Fill greased or paper-lined muffin cups.
- Bake at 350 F for 20-25 minutes or until done.

Nutrition Information

- Calories: 808.8
- Total Carbohydrate: 126.8

- Cholesterol: 52.9
- Total Fat: 33.1
- Saturated Fat: 10.3
- Protein: 9.7
- Sodium: 651.6
- Fiber: 6
- Sugar: 79.2

156. Banana Muffins With Chocolate Peanut Frosting

Serving: 12 serving(s) | Prep: 30mins | Ready in:

Ingredients

- Muffins
- 2 cups unbleached all-purpose flour
- 3⁄4 cup brown sugar (I used 1/2 cup and it was perfect)
- 1 teaspoon baking powder
- 1⁄2 teaspoon baking soda
- 3 ripe bananas
- 1 tablespoon lemon juice
- 1⁄2 cup milk
- 1⁄2 cup canola oil
- 2 eggs
- Chocolate peanut frosting
- 1⁄2 cup peanut butter
- 2 ounces dark chocolate, melted
- 2 tablespoons 35% cream
- unsalted peanuts, toasted and crushed or banana, slices for garnish

Direction

- Muffins: With the rack in the middle position, preheat the oven to 180 °C (350 °F). Line 12 muffin cups with paper liners.
- In a bowl, combine the dry ingredients. Set aside.
- In another bowl, using a fork, mash the bananas with the lemon juice. Add the milk, oil and eggs and stir to combine. Add to the dry ingredients and stir gently with a spatula until the dry ingredients are just moistened.
- Spoon the batter into the cups and bake for about 25 minutes or until a toothpick inserted in the center of a muffin comes out clean. Let cool. Remove from the pan and cool completely on a wire rack.
- Chocolate peanut frosting: In a bowl, combine the peanut butter and chocolate with a spatula. Stir in the cream. Frost the cooled muffins and sprinkle with peanuts or garnish with a banana slice.
- Tips: You can replace the chocolate peanut frosting with whipped peanut butter.

Nutrition Information

- Calories: 347.7
- Total Fat: 19.2
- Sodium: 155.4
- Protein: 7.2
- Sugar: 18.1
- Total Carbohydrate: 40.4
- Cholesterol: 35.2
- Saturated Fat: 4.4
- Fiber: 2.8

157. CHOCOLATE RASPBERRY MUFFINS

Serving: 9 serving(s) | Prep: 10mins | Ready in:

Ingredients

- 2 cups self raising flour
- 1⁄3 cup cocoa, sifted
- 1⁄4 teaspoon salt
- 1 cup caster sugar
- 150 ml oil
- 1 cup buttermilk
- 2 eggs
- 200 g fresh raspberries

Direction

- Preheat oven to 180 Celsius. Line 2 x 6 hole XL muffin tins with 9 XL muffin wrappers.
- Place the flour, cocoa, salt and sugar into a large bowl.
- In a smaller bowl, whisk the eggs ten add the oil and buttermilk. Whisk all together.
- Tip the egg mixture into the flour mixture and stir till well combined. Stir in raspberries 3/4 fill muffin wrappers.
- Cook for approximately 25 - 30 minutes or until they spring back when lightly tapped and a skewer comes out clean.
- NOTE. For smaller muffins follow above directions but just use smaller muffin papers and tins.

Nutrition Information

- Calories: 373.5
- Cholesterol: 42.4
- Fiber: 2.8
- Sugar: 24.6
- Total Carbohydrate: 49.2
- Protein: 6
- Total Fat: 17.4
- Saturated Fat: 2.5
- Sodium: 110

158. COLOSSAL Chocolate Chunk Muffins

Serving: 12 muffins | Prep: 10mins | Ready in:

Ingredients

- 2 eggs
- 3 cups biscuit mix (Bisquick)
- 1/2 cup sugar
- 3/4 cup milk
- 3 tablespoons vegetable oil
- 1 cup semi-sweet chocolate chips or 1 cup semisweet chocolate, coarsely chopped

Direction

- Preheat oven to 400*.
- Line 12 muffin cups (2 1/2 x 1 1/4 inches) with paper baking liners.
- Beat eggs slightly in a large bowl and stir in remaining ingredients except for chocolate, until moistened.
- Fold in chocolate.
- Divide dough evenly among muffin cups.
- Bake for 17 to 19 minutes or until golden.

Nutrition Information

- Calories: 279.8
- Fiber: 1.5
- Cholesterol: 38
- Protein: 4.5
- Saturated Fat: 4.7
- Sodium: 403.5
- Total Fat: 13.6
- Sugar: 19.5
- Total Carbohydrate: 36.9

159. Cappuccino Chocolate Chunk Muffins.

Serving: 12 muffins, 12 serving(s) | Prep: 15mins | Ready in:

Ingredients

- 2 cups flour
- 1/2 cup caster sugar
- 1/2 cup demerara sugar
- 2 1/2 teaspoons baking powder
- 2 tablespoons instant espresso powder (I use Percol)
- 1 teaspoon cocoa powder
- 1/2 teaspoon ground cinnamon
- 1/2 teaspoon salt
- 1 egg (lightly beaten)
- 3/4 cup milk
- 1/4 cup sour cream
- 1/2 cup butter (melted)

- 1 teaspoon vanilla extract
- 100 g semisweet chocolate (min 60% cocoa solids, chopped)
- 1 tablespoon demerara sugar
- 1⁄8 teaspoon ground cinnamon

Direction

- Preheat oven to 190C/375F/Gas 5.
- In a small dish mix 1 tablespoon brown sugar with 1/4 teaspoon cinnamon. (This is to sprinkle over muffin tops prior to baking).
- Chop chocolate into small chunks and set aside.
- Bring milk, egg and sour cream to room temperature.
- Melt butter in a medium sized bowl (I give it a blast in the microwave) and set aside to cool a little.
- Into a large mixing bowl sift flour, baking powder, salt, cocoa powder and cinnamon. Whisk together, add sugars and whisk together again. Make a well in the center and set aside.
- In a measuring jug combine milk and sour cream, mix in espresso powder then vanilla extract. Whisk in egg and finally melted butter.
- Pour into flour and mix with a gentle hand until batter is lumpy.
- Finally fold in chocolate chunks.
- Spoon into muffin cups and sprinkle with cinnamon sugar.
- Bake for 22 - 25 minutes or until toothpick comes out clean.

Nutrition Information

- Calories: 282.3
- Total Fat: 14.2
- Sodium: 260.1
- Total Carbohydrate: 37.7
- Cholesterol: 40.5
- Protein: 4.5
- Saturated Fat: 8.6
- Fiber: 2.1
- Sugar: 18.1

160. Chocolate Almond Scones

Serving: 12 serving(s) | Prep: 40mins | Ready in:

Ingredients

- 3 1⁄2 cups all-purpose flour
- 5 teaspoons baking powder
- 2 tablespoons sugar
- 1 teaspoon salt
- 4 ounces butter, cold
- 3 eggs, divided
- 2 teaspoons almond extract
- 3⁄4 cup cream
- 1 cup chocolate chips
- 1⁄2 cup almonds, sliced, toasted

Direction

- Preheat oven to 425 degrees Fahrenheit.
- Combine flour, baking powder, sugar and salt.
- Cut in butter until it resembles course meal.
- Add 2 eggs (1 egg is reserved for later use), almond extract and cream.
- Stir until soft dough forms; mix in chocolate chips and toasted almonds.
- Pat out dough until 3/4 inch thick.
- Cut into diamond shape; brush with reserved egg.
- Place on baking pan coated with cooking spray.
- Bake for 10 minutes until lightly browned.
- Serve warm.

Nutrition Information

- Calories: 375
- Saturated Fat: 10.9
- Sugar: 10.3
- Cholesterol: 89.8
- Total Fat: 21.1

- Sodium: 443.9
- Fiber: 2.5
- Total Carbohydrate: 41
- Protein: 7.6

161. Chocolate Anzac Biscuits

Serving: 24 BISCUITS, 24 serving(s) | Prep: 10mins | Ready in:

Ingredients

- 1 cup rolled oats
- 1 cup plain flour
- 3/4 cup caster sugar
- 1 cup shredded coconut
- 125 g butter
- 2 tablespoons golden syrup
- 1 tablespoon boiling water
- 1/2 teaspoon bicarbonate of soda
- 400 g dark cooking chocolate, melted

Direction

- Preheat the oven to 160°C Place the oats, flour sugar and coconut in a bowl and stir to combine; set aside.
- Place the butter and golden syrup in a small saucepan over a low heat and stir until melted and combined. Place the water and bicarbonate of soda in a bowl, stir to combine and add the butter mixture. Pour the butter mixture in with the oats mixture and stir until well combined.
- Place tablespoons of the mixture onto baking trays lined with baking paper, allowing room for spreading. Flatten slightly and bake for 10-12 minutes or until golden in color. Allow to cool on the tray. Spread 1 tablespoon of melted chocolate on the base of each biscuit and place the biscuit chocolate side up, on a wire rack until set. Make about 24.

Nutrition Information

- Calories: 141.9
- Total Fat: 8.4
- Sugar: 8.5
- Saturated Fat: 5.5
- Sodium: 76
- Fiber: 1.5
- Total Carbohydrate: 17.2
- Cholesterol: 11.1
- Protein: 1.8

162. Chocolate Banana Muffin

Serving: 18 muffins | Prep: 1hours | Ready in:

Ingredients

- 3/4 cup unsalted butter
- 2/3 cup whole milk
- 2 large eggs
- 2 large egg yolks
- 1 1/2 teaspoons vanilla extract
- 3 cups all-purpose flour
- 1 cup brown sugar
- 2 tablespoons cocoa powder
- 1 tablespoon baking powder
- 1 teaspoon salt
- 3 large bananas

Direction

- Preheat oven to 375 degrees. (190C).
- Place rack in top third of oven.
- Place muffin cups on the trail.
- Melt butter in a small saucepan over moderately low heat, then remove from heat.
- Whisk in milk, then whisk in whole egg, yolk, and vanilla until combined well.
- Whisk together flour, sugar, baking powder, cocoa powder, and salt in a bowl, then add milk mixture and stir until just combined. Notice: NEVER over mix the ingredients, for muffins, the best way is to mix by hand with a fork :).
- Cut bananas into small cubes, and then fold them in and mix slightly.

- Divide batter among the muffin cups, spreading evenly. I tend to fill the cups a bit full so that the muffins will get over the cup top after baking - just like what we get from the shops!
- Bake about 18 to 20 minutes, or until a toothpick inserted in the center of a muffin comes out clean.
- Open the oven a bit to let the muffins settle before move out. Then cool in pans on a rack 15 minutes.
- Serve warm or at room temperature.

Nutrition Information

- Calories: 232.3
- Total Fat: 9.4
- Sodium: 208.6
- Cholesterol: 68
- Protein: 3.9
- Saturated Fat: 5.5
- Fiber: 1.4
- Sugar: 15.2
- Total Carbohydrate: 34

163. Chocolate Banana Nut Muffins

Serving: 12 serving(s) | Prep: 15mins | Ready in:

Ingredients

- 2 cups all-purpose flour
- 2/3 cup sugar
- 1/3 cup unsweetened baking cocoa
- 3 teaspoons baking powder
- 1 teaspoon salt
- 1 egg, slightly beaten
- 1 cup milk
- 1/3 cup vegetable oil
- 1 cup mashed ripe banana (about 2 very large)
- 1 teaspoon vanilla
- 1 cup chopped nuts

Direction

- Set oven to 400 degrees.
- Line 12 muffin tins with paper liners.
- In a large bowl, sift together flour, sugar, cocoa, baking powder and salt.
- In a medium bowl, whisk together egg, milk, oil, bananas and vanilla; mix well to combine.
- Add the dry ingredients to the wet ingredients, stir JUST until moistened (don't worry about any small lumps remaining).
- Gently stir in the nuts.
- Divide batter evenly between the lined muffin tins (filling to the top!).
- Bake for 20-25 minutes, or until muffins test done).

Nutrition Information

- Calories: 277.3
- Sugar: 13.3
- Total Fat: 13.6
- Saturated Fat: 2.4
- Fiber: 2.7
- Protein: 5.9
- Sodium: 378
- Total Carbohydrate: 35.4
- Cholesterol: 18.4

164. Chocolate Breakfast Muffins

Serving: 17 muffins | Prep: 25mins | Ready in:

Ingredients

- 2/3 cup Dutch-processed cocoa powder (2 ounces)
- 1 3/4 cups unbleached all-purpose flour (7 1/4 ounces)
- 1 1/4 cups light brown sugar (9 3/8 ounces)
- 1 teaspoon baking powder
- 3/4 teaspoon espresso powder (optional)
- 1 teaspoon baking soda

- 3⁄4 teaspoon salt
- 1 cup chocolate chips (6 ounces)
- 2 eggs
- 1 cup milk (8 ounces)
- 2 teaspoons vanilla
- 2 teaspoons vinegar
- 1⁄2 cup butter, melted (4 ounces, 1 stick)

Direction

- Preheat the oven to 400°F Line a standard muffin pan with paper or silicone muffin cups, and grease the cups.
- In a large mixing bowl, whisk together the cocoa, flour, sugar, baking powder, espresso powder, baking soda, salt and chocolate chips. Set aside.
- In a large measuring cup or medium-sized mixing bowl, whisk together the eggs, milk, vanilla and vinegar. Add the wet ingredients, along with the melted butter, to the dry ingredients, stirring to blend; there's no need to beat these muffins, just make sure everything is well-combined.
- Scoop the batter into the prepared muffin tin; fill 3/4 way with batter. (Sprinkle with pearl sugar, if desired.).
- Bake the muffins for about 12 minutes, or until a cake tester inserted in the center of a muffin comes out clean. Remove the muffins from the oven, and after 5 minutes remove them from the pan, allowing them to cool for about 15 minutes on a rack before peeling off the muffin papers or silicone cups.

Nutrition Information

- Calories: 230.3
- Total Fat: 10.1
- Sodium: 260.1
- Total Carbohydrate: 34.5
- Cholesterol: 41.2
- Protein: 3.7
- Saturated Fat: 6
- Fiber: 2
- Sugar: 21.2

165. Chocolate Brownie Muffins

Serving: 12 serving(s) | Prep: 5mins | Ready in:

Ingredients

- 1 (18 ounce) box chocolate cake mix
- 1 (16 ounce) can pumpkin

Direction

- Mix together, add some chopped walnuts if you like. I use an ice cream scoop to put the batter into the muffin cups.
- Bake 20 minute.

Nutrition Information

- Calories: 191.8
- Total Carbohydrate: 33.5
- Protein: 2.9
- Total Fat: 6.7
- Sodium: 351.2
- Fiber: 1.2
- Cholesterol: 0
- Saturated Fat: 1.4
- Sugar: 16.8

166. Chocolate Carrot Squash Muffins

Serving: 16 muffins, 16 serving(s) | Prep: 20mins | Ready in:

Ingredients

- 4 eggs, beaten
- 1⁄4 cup canola oil
- 1⁄2 cup non-fat Greek yogurt (or homemade yoghurt)

- 1 tablespoon vanilla extract
- 1 cup sugar
- 3/4 cup brown sugar
- 1/2 cup cocoa powder, sifted
- 2 cups white whole wheat flour
- 2 teaspoons baking powder
- 1/2 teaspoon baking soda
- 1 cup finely shredded yellow squash, peel left on (or zucchini)
- 1 1/2 cups finely shredded carrots
- 1 small sweet apple, finely shredded, peel left on (I used Red Prince)
- 8 teaspoons coarse raw sugar (for topping)

Direction

- Preheat the oven to 350°F. Line two muffin tins with cupcake liners, and set aside.
- In a bowl, combine the eggs, oil, yogurt and vanilla.
- Beat in the sugars and cocoa until smooth.
- Stir in the flour, baking powder and baking soda until just combined, then add the squash, carrots and apple and fold in until evenly distributed.
- Scoop the prepared batter into the muffin tins ¾ of the way up.
- Sprinkle with sanding sugar.
- Bake for approximately 20 minutes, until a toothpick inserted in the center comes out clean.

Nutrition Information

- Calories: 214.5
- Cholesterol: 46.5
- Total Carbohydrate: 40.1
- Sodium: 115.4
- Fiber: 3.1
- Sugar: 26.6
- Protein: 4.3
- Total Fat: 5.4
- Saturated Fat: 0.9

167. Chocolate Cherry Nut Muffins

Serving: 15 muffins, 15 serving(s) | Prep: 20mins | Ready in:

Ingredients

- 2 cups flour
- 1/2 cup sugar
- 1 tablespoon baking powder
- 1/2 teaspoon salt
- 1 tablespoon lemon zest, grated
- 3/4 cup semi-sweet chocolate chips, miniature
- 1 cup cherries, pitted and chopped (about 22)
- 1/2 cup almonds, slivered and blanched
- 1 cup milk
- 1/3 cup oil
- 1/3 cup butter, melted and cooled
- 1 egg, beaten lightly

Direction

- In a bowl, sift together the flour, sugar, BP and salt.
- Stir in the zest, chips and almonds.
- Combine the mixture well and stir in the chopped cherries.
- In a small bowl, whisk together the milk, oil, butter and egg.
- Add this to the flour mixture.
- Stir until batter is just combined.
- Fill sprayed muffin cups.
- Bake at 400 deg. for 20-25 minutes.
- Makes 15 muffins.

Nutrition Information

- Calories: 255.4
- Total Carbohydrate: 28.4
- Total Fat: 14.9
- Saturated Fat: 5.4
- Sugar: 12.8
- Cholesterol: 25.5
- Protein: 4.2
- Sodium: 215.8

- Fiber: 1.7

168. Chocolate Chocolate Banana Bread

Serving: 1 loaf | Prep: 10mins | Ready in:

Ingredients

- 2 cups flour
- 1 cup sugar
- 1/4 cup unsweetened cocoa
- 1/2 tablespoon cinnamon
- 1 teaspoon baking soda
- 1/2 teaspoon salt
- 1/2 cup butter or 1/2 cup margarine, softened
- 2 eggs
- 1/3 cup milk
- 1 cup mashed well-ripened banana (2medium)
- 1 teaspoon vanilla extract
- 1/2 cup semi-sweet chocolate chips

Direction

- Preheat oven to 350 degrees and grease bottom only of 8x4 or 9x5 loaf pan. Blend margarine/butter with sugar until light fluffy. Beat in eggs. Mix in bananas, vanilla, and milk.
- Combine flour, cocoa, baking soda, salt, and chocolate chips. Add flour mixture to banana mixture and combine until ingredients evenly distributed and all dry ingredients just moistened (do not over mix).
- Pour batter into pan and bake for 50-65mins or just until you can insert a toothpick into the center and it comes out clean without wet batter (toothpick might get some melted chocolate on it-which shouldn't be mistaken for batter).
- Cool on a rack for 5mins, then remove the bread from the pan, wrap it in plastic wrap tightly and store in the fridge. Leaving it in there for about a day will allow the flavors to blend and mellow.

Nutrition Information

- Calories: 3300.2
- Sodium: 3436.5
- Sugar: 265.8
- Total Carbohydrate: 499.4
- Cholesterol: 627.4
- Total Fat: 135.7
- Saturated Fat: 80.5
- Protein: 51.5
- Fiber: 24.8

169. Chocolate Cinnamon Scones

Serving: 12 serving(s) | Prep: 15mins | Ready in:

Ingredients

- 2 1/2 cups flour
- 2/3 cup sugar
- 2 1/2 teaspoons baking powder
- 2 teaspoons ground cinnamon
- 1/2 teaspoon baking soda
- 1/4 teaspoon salt
- 1/2 cup cold butter, cut into chunks
- 2 eggs
- 3/4 cup sour cream
- 2 teaspoons pure vanilla extract
- 6 ounces semisweet baking chocolate, chopped

Direction

- Preheat oven to 375°F Mix flour, sugar, cinnamon, baking soda and salt in large bowl. Cut in butter with pastry blender or 2 knives until mixture resembles coarse crumbs.
- Beat eggs, sour cream and vanilla in medium bowl with wire whisk until well blended.
- Add to flour mixture; stir until a soft dough forms. Stir in chopped chocolate.
- Place dough on lightly floured surface. Knead about 1 minute or until smooth.

- Place dough on greased baking sheet and pat into a 10-inch circle. Score top of dough with sharp knife into 12 wedges. Bake 30 minutes or until golden brown.
- Cool slightly on wire rack.
- Melt and drizzle additional semi-sweet chocolate over scones, if desired. Cut into 12 wedges to serve.

Nutrition Information

- Calories: 320
- Sugar: 19.1
- Cholesterol: 61.9
- Protein: 4.9
- Total Fat: 16
- Sodium: 252.5
- Saturated Fat: 9.6
- Fiber: 1.8
- Total Carbohydrate: 41.2

170. Chocolate Cornbread

Serving: 12 serving(s) | Prep: 15mins | Ready in:

Ingredients

- 2/3 cup cocoa powder, unsweetened
- 2/3 cup flour
- 2/3 cup fine cornmeal
- 2/3 cup sugar
- 1 teaspoon salt
- 1 tablespoon baking powder
- 1 large egg
- 1/3 cup corn oil
- 1 cup milk

Direction

- Mix all dry ingredients together.
- Mix all wet ingredients together.
- Combine both til mixed well.
- Pour into a greased 8x8 inch baking dish.
- Bake at 400 degrees for about 25-35 minutes or til center of bread springs back when light pressed.

Nutrition Information

- Calories: 177
- Sodium: 303.9
- Fiber: 2.3
- Total Carbohydrate: 25.5
- Protein: 3.4
- Saturated Fat: 1.8
- Sugar: 11.3
- Cholesterol: 20.5
- Total Fat: 8.2

171. Chocolate Fruit Muffins

Serving: 12 muffins | Prep: 10mins | Ready in:

Ingredients

- 358 g chocolate cake mix
- 3 eggs
- 1/2 cup plain yogurt
- 1 cup pomegranate juice
- 1 1/2 teaspoons allspice
- 1 teaspoon cinnamon
- 1/2 teaspoon nutmeg
- 1/2 cup dried mango, chopped
- 1/2 cup raisins
- 1/2 cup maraschino cherry

Direction

- Preheat oven 350 degrees F. Grease a 12 cup muffin pan with butter or margarine.
- In a large bowl, mix the dry and wet ingredients together. Make sure the cake mix is properly incorporated into the batter, by scraping the bottom of the bowl.
- Add the fruit, and mix well. Fill the muffins cups 3/4 of the way through (filling the cups

to the top will make for a messy spillover). Bake for 15-20 minutes.

Nutrition Information

- Calories: 183
- Total Fat: 6.3
- Fiber: 1.1
- Cholesterol: 47.8
- Sugar: 18.2
- Total Carbohydrate: 30.3
- Protein: 3.9
- Saturated Fat: 1.6
- Sodium: 271.8

172. Chocolate Hazelnut Crinkle Biscuits

Serving: 20-30 biscuits | Prep: 15mins | Ready in:

Ingredients

- 2/3 cup hazelnuts
- 2 tablespoons sugar
- 180 g bittersweet chocolate, finely chopped
- 2 3/4 cups flour
- 2 tablespoons unsweetened cocoa powder
- 2 teaspoons baking powder
- 3/4 teaspoon salt
- 1 teaspoon cinnamon, ground
- 1/2 cup butter, softened
- 1 1/2 cups brown sugar
- 2 large eggs
- 1/4 cup milk
- 1 teaspoon vanilla bean paste
- 3/4 cup icing sugar

Direction

- Put oven rack in middle position and preheat oven to 350°F
- Toast hazelnuts in a shallow baking pan in oven until skins split and nuts are pale golden, about 10 minutes. Remove from oven (turn oven off), then wrap hazelnuts in a kitchen towel and rub to remove any loose skins. Cool nuts completely.
- Pulse nuts with granulated sugar in a food processor until finely chopped.
- Melt chocolate in top of a double boiler, stirring until smooth. Remove bowl from heat and set aside.
- Sieve flour, cocoa powder, baking powder, and salt in a bowl.
- Beat butter and brown sugar in another bowl with an electric mixer at medium-high speed until creamy, about 3 minutes.
- Add eggs 1 at a time, beating well after each addition, then beat in melted chocolate until combined.
- Add milk and vanilla, beating to incorporate. Reduce speed to low and add flour mixture, mixing until just combined.
- Stir in nut mixture. Cover bowl with plastic wrap and chill dough until firm, 2 to 3 hours.
- Put oven racks in upper and lower thirds of oven and preheat oven to 350°F Line 2 large baking sheets with parchment paper.
- Sift confectioners' sugar into a bowl. Halve dough and chill 1 half, wrapped in plastic wrap.
- Roll remaining half into 1-inch balls, placing them on a sheet of wax paper as rolled. Roll balls, 3 or 4 at a time, in confectioners' sugar to coat generously and arrange 2 inches apart on lined baking sheets.
- Bake, switching position of sheets halfway through baking, until cookies are puffed and cracked and edges feel dry (but centers are still slightly soft), 12 to 18 minutes total.
- Transfer cookies (still on parchment) to racks to cool completely.

Nutrition Information

- Calories: 227.2
- Sodium: 171.7
- Sugar: 21.8
- Total Carbohydrate: 36.4
- Cholesterol: 33.8

- Protein: 3.3
- Total Fat: 8.2
- Saturated Fat: 3.4
- Fiber: 1.1

173. Chocolate Lava Muffins

Serving: 6 muffins, 6 serving(s) | Prep: 15mins | Ready in:

Ingredients

- 8 ounces bittersweet chocolate
- 1/2 cup butter
- 1/2 teaspoon vanilla
- 1/2 cup sugar
- 3 tablespoons all-purpose flour
- 1/4 teaspoon salt
- 4 eggs

Direction

- Melt chocolate and butter together in a large bowl over a saucepan of simmering water.
- Stir in the vanilla.
- In a separate bowl, combine the sugar, flour, and salt.
- Sift dry ingredients into the chocolate mixture and blend with an electric mixer.
- Add eggs, one at a time, fully incorporating each egg before adding the next.
- Beat on high until batter is creamy and begins to lighten in color (approximately 4 minutes.).
- Chill batter.
- Preheat oven to 375.
- Coat 6 muffin tins with butter or nonstick cooking spray.
- Spoon batter into the muffin tins, using 1/3 to 1/2 cup batter for each muffin.
- Bake for 12-13 minutes. Outside should be cake-like and centers should be gooey.

Nutrition Information

- Calories: 263.8
- Sugar: 17
- Protein: 4.7
- Total Fat: 18.7
- Sodium: 252.6
- Fiber: 0.1
- Total Carbohydrate: 19.8
- Cholesterol: 181.7
- Saturated Fat: 10.8

174. Chocolate Lovers Wheat Bran Muffins

Serving: 12 muffins, 12 serving(s) | Prep: 20mins | Ready in:

Ingredients

- 1 cup wheat bran
- 1 3/4 cups white flour
- 1 tablespoon baking powder
- 1/2 cup sugar
- 1/2 cup butter
- 1 teaspoon vanilla
- 1 egg
- 3/4 cup milk
- 1 cup semi-sweet chocolate chips

Direction

- Preheat oven to 375 degrees F.
- In a bowl, mix wheat bran, flour, baking powder.
- Cream together the sugar, butter, vanilla, and egg until smooth then blend in milk.
- Add dry ingredients and chocolate chips to the creamed mixture and stir until just moistened.
- Bake at 375 degrees for 20 - 22 minutes or until done.

Nutrition Information

- Calories: 261.4
- Total Fat: 13.2

- Protein: 4.3
- Cholesterol: 40.1
- Saturated Fat: 7.9
- Sodium: 160.6
- Fiber: 3.4
- Sugar: 16.1
- Total Carbohydrate: 35.3

175. Chocolate Nut Wafers

Serving: 5-6 dozen cookies, 20 serving(s) | Prep: 30mins | Ready in:

Ingredients

- 1 cup sugar
- 3⁄4 cup butter
- 2 ounces unsweetened chocolate, melted
- 1 teaspoon vanilla
- 1 egg
- 2 1⁄4 cups flour
- 1⁄4 teaspoon salt
- 1⁄4 teaspoon baking soda
- 1⁄4 teaspoon cinnamon
- 1⁄2 cup nuts

Direction

- Combine sugar, butter, chocolate, vanilla, and egg. Blend well.
- Stir in remaining ingredients until blended.
- Divide dough in half on 2 sheets of waxed paper, shape each half into roll 2 inches in diameter. Wrap. Refrigerate until firm (about 3 hours).
- Heat oven to 400°F
- Cut dough into 1/4 inch slices. Place 2 inches apart on ungreased cookie sheets.
- Bake at 400F for 6 to 8 minutes until set. (Do not overbake.) Immediately remove from cookie sheets.

Nutrition Information

- Calories: 189.8
- Saturated Fat: 5.6
- Sugar: 10.3
- Total Fat: 10.5
- Sodium: 121.2
- Fiber: 1.2
- Total Carbohydrate: 22.5
- Cholesterol: 28.9
- Protein: 2.8

176. Chocolate Oatmeal Biscuits

Serving: 12 biscuits, 12 serving(s) | Prep: 15mins | Ready in:

Ingredients

- 1 1⁄2 cups whole wheat flour
- 1⁄2 cup all-purpose flour
- 3⁄4 cup oats
- 1 tablespoon baking powder
- 1⁄2 teaspoon salt
- 3 tablespoons cocoa
- 2 teaspoons cinnamon
- 2 tablespoons reduced-calorie margarine
- 1 1⁄2 cups chocolate yogurt
- 1 cup chocolate chips (optional)

Direction

- Combine dry ingredients.
- Melt margarine and pour into a bowl with yogurt.
- Add wet ingredients to dry ingredients, mix quickly.
- Pour out onto a floured surface and knead 6-8 times.
- Roll out dough 1/4 inch thick.
- Cut into biscuits, place on a lightly greased cookie sheet.
- Bake at 425 F for 12-15 minutes.

Nutrition Information

- Calories: 120.7
- Cholesterol: 0
- Total Fat: 2.1
- Saturated Fat: 0.4
- Sodium: 212.1
- Fiber: 3.7
- Sugar: 0.1
- Total Carbohydrate: 22.6
- Protein: 4.5

177. Chocolate Pudding Zucchini Muffins

Serving: 30 muffins | Prep: 5mins | Ready in:

Ingredients

- 3 eggs, beaten
- 1 cup cooking oil
- 1 1/4 cups sugar
- 1 (6 ounce) package chocolate instant pudding
- 2 cups grated zucchini
- 2 teaspoons vanilla
- 1 cup unbleached flour
- 2 cups whole wheat flour
- 1 teaspoon baking soda
- 1/2 teaspoon baking powder
- 1 teaspoon salt
- 1 teaspoon cinnamon
- 1 cup chopped nuts (optional)

Direction

- Beat eggs, oil, sugar, pudding mix, vanilla and zucchini together.
- Blend dry ingredients and add to zucchini mixture; mix well.
- Scoop into greased muffin tins.
- Bake 17-20 minutes at 350Â°.
- ** Makes 2 1/2 dozen muffins. I made 2 dozen regular plus 1 dozen mini muffins.
- ** You could also grease two loaf pans and bake 1 hour at 350Â° for Chocolate Pudding Zucchini Bread.

Nutrition Information

- Calories: 169.5
- Saturated Fat: 1.2
- Sodium: 213.1
- Sugar: 12.4
- Total Carbohydrate: 22.6
- Total Fat: 8.1
- Cholesterol: 18.6
- Protein: 2.4
- Fiber: 1.3

178. Chocolate Pumpkin Muffins

Serving: 12 Muffins, 12 serving(s) | Prep: 5mins | Ready in:

Ingredients

- 1 (18 ounce) box chocolate cake mix
- 1 (15 ounce) can pumpkin

Direction

- Mix together ingredients, do not add anything from the cake mix directions.
- Bake at 400 degrees for 20 minutes.
- Makes 12 muffins. They are 3 Weight Watchers Points each.

Nutrition Information

- Calories: 191.5
- Sodium: 351.8
- Protein: 2.9
- Saturated Fat: 1.4
- Fiber: 1.2
- Sugar: 16.8
- Total Carbohydrate: 33.4
- Cholesterol: 0
- Total Fat: 6.7

179. Chocolate Streusel Pecan Muffins

Serving: 12 Muffins | Prep: 15mins | Ready in:

Ingredients

- 1/4 cup all-purpose flour
- 1/4 cup packed brown sugar
- 1/4 teaspoon ground cinnamon
- 2 tablespoons butter, melted
- 1/4 cup chopped pecans
- 1 3/4 cups milk chocolate chips, divided
- 1/3 cup milk
- 3 tablespoons butter
- 1 cup all-purpose flour
- 2 tablespoons granulated sugar
- 2 teaspoons baking powder
- 1/4 teaspoon ground cinnamon
- 3/4 cup chopped pecans
- 1 large egg
- 1/2 teaspoon vanilla extract

Direction

- FOR TOPPING:
- COMBINE flour, brown sugar, cinnamon and 2 tablespoons melted butter in small bowl with fork until mixture resembles coarse crumbs; stir in pecans.
- FOR MUFFINS:
- PREHEAT oven to 375° F; grease or paper-line 12 muffin cups.
- COMBINE 1 cup morsels, milk and 3 tablespoons butter in a microwave safe bowl; microwave on full power for about 60 seconds and then stir until morsels are melted and mixture is smooth; if not fully melted, put back in for 10 second intervals.
- COMBINE flour, sugar, baking powder, cinnamon, pecans and remaining morsels in large bowl.
- COMBINE egg, vanilla extract and melted morsel mixture in small bowl; stir into flour mixture just until moistened.
- Spoon into prepared muffin cups, filling 2/3 full then sprinkle with Topping.
- BAKE for 20 to 25 minutes then cool in pan for 5 minutes; remove to wire rack to cool completely.

Nutrition Information

- Calories: 211.7
- Cholesterol: 32.2
- Protein: 3.3
- Total Fat: 13.4
- Sodium: 109.1
- Fiber: 1.4
- Sugar: 9.1
- Saturated Fat: 4.5
- Total Carbohydrate: 20.8

180. Chocolate Viennese Biscuits

Serving: 1 batch of cookies | Prep: 0S | Ready in:

Ingredients

- 225 g self-raising flour
- 90 g cocoa
- 30 g cornflour
- 225 g unsalted butter, softened
- 90 g icing sugar, sifted
- 1 teaspoon vanilla essence
- icing sugar, for, dusting
- 115 g chocolate, melted

Direction

- Preheat oven to 180 degrees C.
- Grease 2 large baking sheets.
- Into a bowl sift together the flour, cocoa and corn flour.
- In another large bowl beat the butter and icing sugar until fluffy.

- With the beater on low speed gradually add in the flour mixture and vanilla essence until it becomes a soft dough.
- Shape into 'bar' shapes about 10cm long by 5cm wide.
- Bake about 15-20 minutes, rotating baking sheets at half-time.
- Keep an eye on them as they should only be slightly firm and all ovens are different.
- Cool on wire cooling rack until cool and firm.
- Dust with icing sugar.
- Dip one end of each cookie into melted chocolate and place back onto greaseproof paper and allow chocolate to set.
- Store in container with waxed paper between layers.

Nutrition Information

- Calories: 3816.5
- Fiber: 45.4
- Sugar: 90.4
- Cholesterol: 483.8
- Protein: 59.1
- Total Fat: 255
- Saturated Fat: 153.3
- Sodium: 2913.8
- Total Carbohydrate: 368.8

181. Dee's Chocolate Banana Bread

Serving: 1 loaf bread | Prep: 30mins | Ready in:

Ingredients

- 1 1/3 cups sugar
- 7 tablespoons baking cocoa
- 1/2 teaspoon baking soda
- 1/2 teaspoon salt
- 1 teaspoon baking powder
- 1 teaspoon cinnamon
- 2 large eggs
- 1/2 cup lard
- 2 bananas
- 1/2 cup pecans
- 1 1/2 cups flour

Direction

- In food processor mix everything except the flour.
- When mixed together, fold in the flour.
- Bake in a bread pan at 375 degrees Fahrenheit for 30 minutes or until toothpick comes out clean.

Nutrition Information

- Calories: 3463
- Sodium: 2314
- Fiber: 30.3
- Sugar: 298.7
- Saturated Fat: 50.3
- Total Carbohydrate: 496.8
- Cholesterol: 469.4
- Protein: 47
- Total Fat: 159

182. Dee's Chocolate Muffins

Serving: 12 serving(s) | Prep: 30mins | Ready in:

Ingredients

- 2/3 cup shortening
- 1 cup sugar
- 1/4 cup cocoa
- 1/4 cup molasses
- 2 eggs
- 2/3 cup sour cream
- 2 teaspoons vanilla
- 2 cups flour
- 1 teaspoon baking soda
- 1/2 cup coffee
- 1/4 cup chocolate chips

Direction

- Cream the shortening, sugar and cocoa together.
- Add molasses, eggs, sour cream and vanilla. Add flour and baking soda.
- Add coffee and chocolate chips.
- Bake at 400 degrees Fahrenheit for 10 to 15 minutes until done.

Nutrition Information

- Calories: 324
- Sodium: 127.3
- Fiber: 1.4
- Total Carbohydrate: 41.7
- Protein: 4.1
- Total Fat: 16.4
- Saturated Fat: 5.6
- Sugar: 22.7
- Cholesterol: 40.9

183. Double Chocolate Banana Oatmeal Muffins (Fiber)

Serving: 25-30 muffins | Prep: 10mins | Ready in:

Ingredients

- 2 cups flour
- 1 cup oatmeal
- 1/4 cup wheat bran
- 1/2 cup cocoa
- 1 1/2 cups sugar
- 1 teaspoon salt
- 2 teaspoons baking soda
- 1/2 teaspoon baking powder
- 2 teaspoons vanilla
- 2 eggs
- 100 ml vegetable oil
- 3 cups mashed bananas (nice and ripe)
- 1 1/2 cups chocolate chips (I usually use around 2 cups of the dark chocolate type)
- Optional
- 1/2 cup slivered almonds

Direction

- Preheat oven to 350 degrees Fahrenheit.
- Mix together the first six ingredients.
- Mix together all of the wet ingredients in a separate bowl, make sure to mix well.
- Stir the two separate mixtures together using the "dump" method until just moistened (It will be lumpy).
- Fold in the chocolate chips and the nuts if using.
- Fill greased on paper lined muffin tins 3/4 full.
- Bake for 20 to 25 min, test before taking out.

Nutrition Information

- Calories: 225.2
- Sugar: 21
- Total Carbohydrate: 36.3
- Protein: 3.5
- Saturated Fat: 2.5
- Sodium: 208.6
- Fiber: 2.7
- Total Fat: 8.5
- Cholesterol: 14.9

184. Double Chocolate Muffins

Serving: 12 serving(s) | Prep: 15mins | Ready in:

Ingredients

- TRUFFLE FILLING
- 3 ounces dark chocolate, chopped
- 1/3 cup heavy cream, plus
- 1 tablespoon heavy cream
- 1/2 teaspoon vanilla

- MUFFINS
- 1 cup flour
- 1/2 cup cocoa powder
- 2 teaspoons baking powder
- 1/2 teaspoon baking soda
- 1/4 teaspoon salt
- 1 cup sour cream, plus
- 1 tablespoon sour cream
- 1 egg, lightly beaten,room temperature
- 6 tablespoons butter, melted and cooled
- 2/3 cup sugar

Direction

- FILLING: Place chocolate in bowl.
- In small saucepan, heat cream to boil.
- Pour over chocolate and let stand for 30 seconds to melt chocolate.
- Stir until chocolate is completely melted.
- Stir in vanilla extract.
- Scrape filling into small container and cover with plastic wrap.
- Freeze filling for at least 1 hour (or up to 3 days) or until firm.
- Remove filling from freezer.
- Divide filling into 12 portions.
- Shape each portion into a ball and place on plate.
- Loosely cover with plastic wrap and freeze truffles until ready to use.
- MUFFINS: Preheat oven to 350°F.
- Lightly butter 12 (3-inch) muffin cups.
- Sift together flour, cocoa, baking powder, baking soda and salt into medium bowl.
- Whisk together sour cream, egg, butter and sugar in medium bowl until combined.
- Make well in center of flour mixture; add sour cream mixture and stir with wooden spoon just until combined.
- Fill each muffin cup 1/3 full.
- Place frozen truffle in center of each cup on top of batter.
- Spoon remaining batter into cups, making sure each truffle is covered.
- Bake 15 minutes or until toothpick inserted into batter part of muffins comes out clean.
- Cool muffins in pan set on wire rack for 5 minutes.
- Remove muffins from cups.
- Serve warm or cool completely.
- Store in airtight container.

Nutrition Information

- Calories: 252.8
- Cholesterol: 52.5
- Protein: 4.1
- Total Fat: 17.6
- Sodium: 224.5
- Fiber: 2.6
- Sugar: 11.4
- Saturated Fat: 10.8
- Total Carbohydrate: 24.4

185. Eggless, Milkless Chocolate Muffins

Serving: 24 muffins, 24 serving(s) | Prep: 15mins | Ready in:

Ingredients

- 4 1/2 cups all-purpose flour
- 3 cups white sugar
- 1 cup unsweetened cocoa powder
- 1 cup vegetable oil or 1 cup canola oil
- 3 cups water
- 3 teaspoons baking soda
- 1/2 teaspoon salt
- 3 tablespoons vanilla extract

Direction

- Preheat oven to 350°F (175 01456C), grease 12 muffin cup tins or line with muffin liners.
- In a large bowl, sift together flour, cocoa powder, soda and salt. Add sugar and mix together.
- Add oil, water and vanilla and mix thoroughly.

- Spoon batter into prepared muffin cups until full. Bake at 350°F (175°C) for 20-30 minutes or until toothpick inserted in center comes out clean.

Nutrition Information

- Calories: 275.2
- Total Fat: 9.8
- Sodium: 207.7
- Fiber: 1.8
- Total Carbohydrate: 45
- Cholesterol: 0
- Saturated Fat: 1.5
- Sugar: 25.3
- Protein: 3.1

186. English Scones With Chocolate Chunks

Serving: 12 serving(s) | Prep: 5mins | Ready in:

Ingredients

- 2 cups flour
- 1 tablespoon baking powder
- 1/3 cup sugar
- 5 tablespoons slightly chilled butter (use bluebonnet margarine)
- 3/4 cup semisweet chocolate chunk
- 1 cup heavy whipping cream

Direction

- Mix first four ingredients together with a fork like you would pastry dough. Cut the dough till the margarine is pretty much unnoticeable.
- Mix in Chocolate chunks.
- Stir in the cream, if it seems a little dry add a little more cream, but NO more than 1/4 cup.
- Use your hands to roll the dough till all flour is mixed in (adding cream if needed).
- Form into a flat, even circle. Cut into 12 "pie" pieces.
- Place each piece separately on a sprayed cookie sheet allowing enough space for each to raise a bit. Brush tops with more cream. Sprinkle with sugar crystals and bake in a 350 oven no more than 19 minutes. The bottom edges will just be turning brown. DO NOT over bake or they will harden.

Nutrition Information

- Calories: 282.3
- Fiber: 1.5
- Sugar: 13.2
- Total Carbohydrate: 31.6
- Protein: 3.2
- Total Fat: 16.1
- Saturated Fat: 9.9
- Sodium: 133.2
- Cholesterol: 40.3

187. Fat Free Chocolate Banana Muffins

Serving: 12 serving(s) | Prep: 10mins | Ready in:

Ingredients

- 2 cups whole wheat flour
- 1/2 cup sugar
- 1/4 cup unsweetened cocoa
- 1 tablespoon baking powder
- 1 teaspoon baking soda
- 1/2 teaspoon salt
- 3 bananas, mashed
- 1 cup nonfat milk
- 4 teaspoons vinegar

Direction

- Preheat oven to 350 degrees.
- Spray muffin pan with non-stick spray and set aside.
- Mix dry ingredients together in a bowl.

- In a separate bowl, mash bananas, milk and vinegar and mix well.
- Add liquid ingredients to dry and gently stir until just mixed -- mixture will be quite thick. Divide equally among 12 muffin cups. Bake for 18 - 20 minutes. Let rest in pan for 10 minutes, then cool on a wire rack.

Nutrition Information

- Calories: 138.4
- Protein: 4
- Total Fat: 0.9
- Sodium: 302.3
- Sugar: 13.1
- Cholesterol: 0.4
- Saturated Fat: 0.3
- Fiber: 3.5
- Total Carbohydrate: 31.8

188. Fat Free Chocolate Muffins

Serving: 18 regular sized muffins | Prep: 10mins | Ready in:

Ingredients

- 1 cup unbleached white flour
- 1 cup whole wheat flour
- 2/3 cup unsweetened cocoa powder
- 1 cup sugar
- 2 teaspoons baking soda
- 1/2 teaspoon salt
- 1 teaspoon vanilla
- 2 cups pumpkin (or 1 can)
- 1 (4 ounce) package instant chocolate pudding mix (makes them moister) (optional)

Direction

- Spray muffin pans with non-stick coating.
- Mix all ingredients together. You will need to use an ELECTRIC MIXER, the batter is very dry, like brownie batter, KEEP MIXING it WILL mix together. DO NOT ADD EGGS OR MILK.
- Baking soda is your leavening agent, and pumpkin substitutes your fats (much like applesauce does).
- Bake at 350°F for 15 minutes, for regular muffin pans, 20 minutes for jumbo pans. Test with a toothpick to see if they are done.

Nutrition Information

- Calories: 102.2
- Sugar: 11.4
- Total Carbohydrate: 23.9
- Cholesterol: 0
- Protein: 2.4
- Saturated Fat: 0.3
- Sodium: 205.6
- Total Fat: 0.7
- Fiber: 2

189. Ginger Chocolate Chewy Biscuits

Serving: 20-30 biscuits | Prep: 10mins | Ready in:

Ingredients

- 1 1/2 cups flour
- 1/2 teaspoon ginger
- 1/2 teaspoon cinnamon
- 1/2 teaspoon nutmeg
- 1/2 teaspoon clove
- 125 g butter
- 1 tablespoon ginger, grated
- 1/2 cup brown sugar
- 1/2 cup treacle
- 1 1/2 teaspoons hot water
- 1 teaspoon bicarbonate of soda
- 210 g dark chocolate, chopped
- 50 g glace ginger, fine dice

Direction

- Cream butter and ginger for 4 minutes. Add brown sugar and beat inches
- Sift dry ingredients and add to butter mix.
- Mix hot water and bicarb and add.
- Fold chopped chocolate.
- Chill for 2 hours and the roll into balls.
- Refrigerate again for at least ½ hour. Roll in sand sugar and bake at 160C for 12-15 minutes.

Nutrition Information

- Calories: 186.6
- Cholesterol: 13.4
- Saturated Fat: 7.2
- Fiber: 2.4
- Sugar: 10.1
- Total Carbohydrate: 22.8
- Total Fat: 11.6
- Sodium: 107.3
- Protein: 2.6

190. Gluten Free Chocolate Peanut Butter Banana Bread

Serving: 2 loafs, 24 serving(s) | Prep: 20mins | Ready in:

Ingredients

- 1/2 cup butter, room temp
- 2 eggs, large
- 2 teaspoons vanilla
- 3 tablespoons peanut butter
- 1/2 cup applesauce
- 4 bananas, overripe and smashed
- 1 cup sugar
- 1/4 cup brown sugar, packed
- 1 1/2 cups brown rice flour
- 1 cup sorghum flour, sweet sorghum flour
- 2 teaspoons baking powder
- 1 teaspoon baking soda
- 1 teaspoon xanthan gum
- 3/4 teaspoon salt
- 1/2 cup baking cocoa

Direction

- Preheat oven to 350.
- Grease (2) 9x5 non-stick loaf pans.
- Cream together butter, eggs, vanilla peanut butter, applesauce, bananas and Sugar.
- In a separate bowl combine flour, baking powder, baking soda, xanthan gum, salt and baking cocoa.
- Gradually add the dry ingredients to the wet ingredients, mix/stir until smooth (batter will be a little thick).
- Spoon batter into greased loaf pans; Bake at 350 for 50-60 minutes until a knife inserted into it comes out clean. Let cool 10 minutes and remove from loaf pans and cool.
- ** Can be made egg free buy substituting an egg replacer or using more applesauce.
- *** Try adding your favorite things like chocolate chips, nuts or raisins. And top with brown sugar before baking.

Nutrition Information

- Calories: 155.4
- Total Fat: 5.8
- Saturated Fat: 3
- Sodium: 201.4
- Fiber: 1.7
- Total Carbohydrate: 25.2
- Protein: 2.4
- Sugar: 13.3
- Cholesterol: 27.8

191. Gluten Free, Protein And Fiber Rich Chocolate Strawberry Muffin

Serving: 12 muffins | Prep: 15mins | Ready in:

Ingredients

- 2 1/2 cups oat flour (or powder old fashioned oats with mill blade)
- 1/2 cup agave nectar (you can use less since it is very sweet)
- 1/2 cup canola oil
- 2 large eggs
- 1/2 cup Greek yogurt
- 1/2 cup strawberry (mashed or gently pureed)
- 1 scoop chocolate protein powder
- 1 teaspoon vanilla
- 1/2 teaspoon cinnamon
- 1 teaspoon baking powder
- 1 teaspoon salt
- 1/2 cup sliced almonds (optional)

Direction

- First preheat oven to 350 degrees.
- Next, in s large mixing bowl sift together flour, salt, baking soda, cinnamon, and protein powder.
- In a medium mixing bowl, first mix agave nectar and oil, then add eggs, yogurt, and strawberries.
- Add flour mixture and thoroughly mx together with whisk or electric mixer.
- If using nuts, you can now mix into the batter.
- Pour batter into greased muffin pan (or use cupcake liners for less cleanup).
- Put muffin pan in oven and bake for 18-20 minutes or until toothpick comes out clean when inserted in one of the muffins.

Nutrition Information

- Calories: 179.4
- Total Carbohydrate: 18.4
- Cholesterol: 31
- Protein: 4.2
- Saturated Fat: 1.1
- Fiber: 2.7
- Sodium: 238.7
- Sugar: 1
- Total Fat: 10.7

192. Healthy Low Fat Blueberry (Or Chocolate) Oatmeal Muffins

Serving: 12 muffins, 12 serving(s) | Prep: 25mins | Ready in:

Ingredients

- 1 cup toasted quick-cooking oats
- 1 cup skim milk
- 1 cup blueberries (thawed and VERY well drained if frozen) or 1 cup semi-sweet chocolate chips
- 14 tablespoons unsweetened applesauce
- 2 tablespoons canola oil
- 2 egg whites
- 1 teaspoon vanilla
- 1/2 cup brown sugar
- 1/2 cup white pastry flour
- 1/2 cup whole wheat flour
- 2 teaspoons baking powder
- 1/2 teaspoon salt
- 3/4 teaspoon cinnamon
- 1/4 teaspoon nutmeg

Direction

- Toast oats in a dry saucepan over medium heat until browned.
- Combine oats and milk in a bowl and let stand for 20-35 minutes.
- Preheat oven to 350°F.
- Add brown sugar, applesauce, egg, and vanilla to the oat and milk mixture and mix well.
- Whisk the flours, baking powder, salt, cinnamon, and nutmeg.
- Mix the dry into the wet until JUST combined, and fold in the blueberries (or chocolate chips).
- Scoop batter into greased muffin tin and bake for 27-35 minutes. Cool for 10 minutes before removing muffins from tin and putting on cooling rack.

Nutrition Information

- Calories: 146.6
- Sugar: 10.3
- Protein: 3.8
- Total Fat: 3
- Sodium: 183.4
- Fiber: 2
- Total Carbohydrate: 26.8
- Cholesterol: 0.4
- Saturated Fat: 0.3

193. High Fiber Chocolate Zucchini Muffins

Serving: 12 muffins, 12 serving(s) | Prep: 30mins | Ready in:

Ingredients

- 1 1/2 cups zucchini, shredded
- 1 cup reduced-sugar chocolate cake mix
- 3/4 cup whole wheat flour
- 3/4 cup canned pumpkin
- 2/3 cup Egg Beaters egg substitute
- 2/3 cup unsweetened applesauce
- 2/3 cup Splenda sugar substitute
- 2 tablespoons brown sugar
- 1 1/2 teaspoons cinnamon
- 1 teaspoon baking powder
- 1/2 cup dark chocolate chips

Direction

- Preheat oven to 350 degrees.
- Combine all dry ingredients in medium bowl.
- In large bowl combine, eggbeaters, pumpkin, apple sauce and ¼ cup water until blended.
- Combine contents of both bowls.
- Add zucchini and chips.
- Spray 12 cup muffin pan with nonstick spray.
- Evenly distribute cake mixture among cups.
- Bake 20 to 25 minutes (until toothpick comes out clean when poked in center).

Nutrition Information

- Calories: 82.1
- Sodium: 71.1
- Fiber: 2.3
- Sugar: 6.8
- Cholesterol: 0
- Protein: 1.7
- Saturated Fat: 1.3
- Total Fat: 2.3
- Total Carbohydrate: 15.7

194. Hurricane Chocolate Muffins

Serving: 6 Muffins, 6 serving(s) | Prep: 5mins | Ready in:

Ingredients

- 1 cup flour
- 1/2 cup sugar
- 1/4 cup cocoa
- 1/8 teaspoon baking soda
- 1 teaspoon baking powder
- 1/2 cup milk
- 1 teaspoon vanilla essence
- 1 egg
- 1/4 cup oil
- 1/4 cup chocolate chips

Direction

- Preheat oven to 350 F 180 C.
- Mix all dry ingredients.
- Mix all wet ingredients.
- Combine the two, but do not over mix, just bring together.
- Divide the mixture into 6 lined muffin tins.
- Bake at 350 F 180 C for 15 minutes or until a toothpick comes out clean.

Nutrition Information

- Calories: 294.9

- Sugar: 20.6
- Cholesterol: 33.9
- Total Carbohydrate: 40.3
- Protein: 4.8
- Total Fat: 13.3
- Saturated Fat: 3.2
- Sodium: 110
- Fiber: 1.6

195. I Want To Keep This A Secret ? Chocolate Muffins

Serving: 12 muffins, 4 serving(s) | Prep: 25mins | Ready in:

Ingredients

- 1/2 cup butter
- 1/2 cup sugar
- 2 eggs
- 1/3 cup milk (?)
- 2 teaspoons rum (?)
- 1 1/3 cups flour (?)
- 1/3 cup unsweetened cocoa (?)
- 1 teaspoon baking powder (?)
- 1/2 cup chocolate chips

Direction

- Sift the flour, baking powder and cocoa. Combine the milk and rum.
- Put margarine into a bowl, and mix until soft. Add sugar little by little, and mix well with a whisk until white and fluffy.
- Add a beaten egg little by little, and mix well with the whisk.
- Add 1/3 of the ? ingredients →1/2 of the ? ingredients →1/3 of ?→ the remaining ?→ the remaining ?, and chocolate chips in that order, and fold in until the batter is no longer floury!
- Pour the batter into muffin cups about 70 ~ 80 % full with a spoon. Sprinkle sliced almonds or walnuts as toppings if you like.
- Bake in the preheated oven at 350 for about 25 ~ 30 minutes, then it's done.

Nutrition Information

- Calories: 623.6
- Saturated Fat: 20.2
- Cholesterol: 156.8
- Sugar: 36.7
- Total Carbohydrate: 75.8
- Protein: 10.6
- Total Fat: 33.8
- Sodium: 343.7
- Fiber: 4.7

196. Low Fat Chocolate Banana Muffins

Serving: 16-18 muffins, 16-18 serving(s) | Prep: 10mins | Ready in:

Ingredients

- Mix I
- 3 bananas, very ripe, mashed, approx one cup
- 1/2 cup sugar
- 1/2 cup yoghurt, 1% plain
- 1/4 cup butter (melted)
- 1 teaspoon vanilla extract
- 1 egg
- 1 egg white
- Mix II
- 2 cups all-purpose flour
- 1 teaspoon baking powder
- 1/2 teaspoon baking soda
- 1/4 teaspoon salt
- 1/2 cup semi-sweet chocolate chips

Direction

- Preheat oven to 350 F.
- Mix I - mix all ingredients using a hand blender in a large bowl.
- Mix II - combine all ingredients and combine with Mix I until just moist and blended.
- Fill into muffin pans.

- Bake at 350 F and bake for approx. 20 min, until golden on top.

Nutrition Information

- Calories: 162.5
- Total Carbohydrate: 27.1
- Cholesterol: 20.2
- Protein: 3
- Total Fat: 5.2
- Sodium: 136.3
- Fiber: 1.3
- Sugar: 12.3
- Saturated Fat: 3.1

197. Low Fat Double Chocolate Muffins

Serving: 12 muffins, 12 serving(s) | Prep: 10mins | Ready in:

Ingredients

- 90 g pitted prunes
- 125 ml warm water
- 150 g caster sugar
- 180 ml skim milk
- 1 egg
- 1 egg white
- 225 g self raising flour
- 25 g cocoa
- 60 g chocolate chips (Choc Bits)

Direction

- Preheat oven to 180 degrees C (356 degrees F). Line muffin trays (12 x 1/3cup) with paper cases, or coat with cooking oil spray.
- Place prunes and water into a small blender or food processor and blend until smooth. Add sugar and blend until smooth.
- Add milk, eggs and egg white and whizz until just combined. Be careful not to over process. Pour mixture into a bowl.
- Sift flour cocoa together then fold into mixture, until just combined. Fold in the Choc Bits. Again, be careful to not over mix.
- Spoon mixture into prepared tray(s) and bake for about 20 minutes, or until they are firm the touch. Turn on a wire rack to cool.

Nutrition Information

- Calories: 206.9
- Total Fat: 2.5
- Saturated Fat: 1.3
- Cholesterol: 17.9
- Total Carbohydrate: 43.7
- Protein: 4.7
- Sodium: 21
- Fiber: 2.5
- Sugar: 20.2

198. Magic Microwave Muffin Sinless Chocolate Banana (Gluten Free)

Serving: 3 muffins, 3 serving(s) | Prep: 10mins | Ready in:

Ingredients

- Soften the oats (soak overnight or microwave)
- 1/4 cup oats (gluten free)
- 1/2 cup skim milk
- 1 teaspoon vanilla extract
- Dry Mix (make ahead if desired)
- 3 tablespoons brown rice flour
- 2 tablespoons garbanzo bean flour (with fava if available)
- 2 tablespoons cocoa powder (Hershey's Special Dark is good if available)
- 2 tablespoons flax seed meal
- 1 tablespoon sweet white sorghum flour
- 1 1/2 teaspoons tapioca flour (tapioca starch is the same thing)
- 1 1/2 teaspoons cornstarch

- 1/2 teaspoon baking powder
- 1/4 teaspoon baking soda
- 1/4 teaspoon salt, scant
- Wet ingredients
- 1/2 cup mashed overripe banana (1 large overripe banana)
- 2 egg whites (or 1 egg)
- Optional Mix-Ins or Topping Ideas (directions given below)
- uncooked rolled oats (optional) or shredded coconut (optional) or chocolate chips (optional) or sliced almonds or other chopped nuts (optional)

Direction

- Choose one of the following options to soften the oats. OVERNIGHT OPTION: In a small container, combine the oats, milk and vanilla. Cover and let soak overnight in the refrigerator. QUICK OPTION: In a 1.5 cup or larger microwave safe container, combine oats, milk and vanilla and microwave on high for 1 minute to soften the oats.
- Combine dry ingredients in a small bowl and blend together with a wire whisk.
- Mash the overripe banana (more brown than yellow) in a medium bowl with a fork until it is almost like a liquid with very few small clumps and make sure it measures at least a 1/2 cup (a little more is okay). Add 2 egg whites (or 1 egg) and the softened oats mixture and whisk with the fork until well blended. (If the oats are hot from the microwave, stir quickly so they don't cook the eggs).
- Pour the dry mix on top of the banana mixture and stir with a fork until powder is mixed in completely.
- Divide the batter evenly into three 8 oz. ramekins or large coffee mugs so each has about a 1/2 cup of batter. (Batter should never fill its container more than half full or it will bubble over while cooking). Check below for optional toppings and mix-ins you can add here.
- Put all 3 containers in the microwave together with at 1-2" space in between them and microwave on high for 3 to 4 minutes or just until center is dry to the touch (see microwave tips below to determine cook time).
- Carefully remove containers from microwave using oven mitts. Flip over with the serving plate or your hand underneath (ready to catch) and shake muffins lightly side to side and up and down and the muffin should drop right out! Flip so it is right side up and let cool on a paper towel on top of a cooling rack (to prevent soggy bottoms).
- Serve warm, or store in covered containers in the fridge for up to a week (cool muffin completely before storing to prevent soggy bottoms).
- OPTIONAL TOPPINGS: Sprinkle uncooked muffin top with dry rolled oats, flaked coconut, sliced almonds or your favorite chopped nuts. (Since the batter has already been separated you can experiment with a different mix-in or topping for each one!)
- OPTIONAL MIX-INS (add a little sin back in!): Chocolate Whey Coconut - stir in 1 tsp vanilla whey protein powder and 1 tbsp. of coconut per muffin and then sprinkle a little more coconut on top. Chocolate Chip: Stir in an additional tsp of cocoa powder and 1 packet truvia (omit truvia if you already added sweetener to the main mix) and then sprinkle a rounded tsp of chocolate chips on top of the batter of each muffin (do not stir in chips, they will sink into the muffin while it bakes).
- ALSO TRY: A great treat is to pour about a 1/4 cup (or more) of milk over a leftover muffin from the fridge, heat in the microwave for 45 seconds and eat it with a fork like a bread pudding.
- MICROWAVING TIPS: After 3 minutes of baking in the microwave, the muffins should have doubled in height and should be bubbling at the center and possibly the edges. When bubbling stops and centers look dry, stop the microwave and quickly tap the center with your finger. If the batter sticks to your finger, put them back in microwave for another 15-30 seconds and then check again. Repeat until the batter is dry and doesn't stick.

NOTE: Cook time will be reduced if the oats and milk were already hot from the microwave when you mixed the batter.

- OTHER COOKING OPTIONS: ONE AT A TIME - If you prefer to cook them 1 at a time, try 2 minutes in the microwave watching after 1.5 minutes and checking for a dry center like recommended above. BAKING IN THE OVEN - If you prefer to bake in the oven, pour batter into greased muffin pan (they will stick to paper cups) so each muffin only fills the pan 1/2-2/3 of the way so it has room to rise up while baking. Bake in a preheated oven at 350 degrees for 25-35 minutes until the center is dry to the touch.

Nutrition Information

- Calories: 179.6
- Sugar: 3.6
- Protein: 8.8
- Saturated Fat: 0.8
- Fiber: 5
- Total Carbohydrate: 29.2
- Cholesterol: 0.8
- Total Fat: 3.9
- Sodium: 423.6

199. Mexican Chocolate Oatmeal Pepita Mini Muffins

Serving: 24 serving(s) | Prep: 10mins | Ready in:

Ingredients

- 1/2 cup rolled oats
- 1/2 cup butter (cubed)
- 1 cup boiling water
- 1 cup brown sugar
- 2 eggs, beaten
- 1/8 teaspoon vanilla powder
- 1 cup all-purpose flour
- 1 teaspoon baking soda
- 1 teaspoon baking powder
- 1/2 teaspoon salt
- 60 g dark chocolate
- 30 g pepitas
- cooking spray

Direction

- Pre heat oven to 180°C (350F).
- Grind pepitas; set aside.
- I used oil sprayed mini muffin trays. Depending on the size of your tray, baking times will differ.
- The muffins are done when the tops "spring" back and a toothpick comes out clean.
- In a large bowl, mix (with your fingers), oats and butter "well."
- Add boiling water; combine with mixture; stir in finely ground pepitas. Set aside to cool.
- As I "always" like to speed up the process, I placed the bowl in the freezer for about ten minutes; re-whisked to refresh.
- I "gently" whisked all together.
- In separate large bowl, combine xylitol and cinnamon (or "only" sugar if using), eggs and vanilla powder. I used a wooden spoon.
- Add to cooled oats-butter-pepita mixture; combine well.
- In a separate bowl, sift together flour, baking soda, baking powder, salt and dark chocolate.
- I found it easier to mix when I placed the dark chocolate in a small pan on the stove, continuously stirred until melted.
- Add flour-chocolate mixture to wet mixture; combine well.
- Spoon batter into prepared trays.
- Do NOT overfill and make sure the top of the muffin tray is oil sprayed so as to not stick.
- Bake for 10 minutes or until done.

Nutrition Information

- Calories: 119.7
- Cholesterol: 25.7
- Protein: 2
- Total Fat: 6.3
- Sugar: 9

- Sodium: 159.4
- Fiber: 0.8
- Total Carbohydrate: 15.1
- Saturated Fat: 3.5

200. No Fat Chocolate Zucchini Muffins

Serving: 24 serving(s) | Prep: 10mins | Ready in:

Ingredients

- 1 1/4 cups cinnamon applesauce
- 2 cups sugar
- 1 1/2 teaspoons vanilla
- 3 cups zucchini, peeled and grated
- 4 cups flour
- 1 1/2 teaspoons salt
- 1 1/2 teaspoons baking soda
- 3/4 cup cocoa powder
- 1 teaspoon espresso powder
- 3 teaspoons cinnamon
- 1 teaspoon baking powder

Direction

- Mix together flour, salt, soda, cinnamon, espresso powder, cocoa (use a good cocoa powder; I used King Arthur Dark Cocoa) and baking powder.
- In another bowl mix together zucchini, applesauce, sugar and vanilla. Stir well into the dry mixture.
- Fill muffin lined tins 3/4 full with mixture and bake at 350 for 20-25 minutes.

Nutrition Information

- Calories: 160.6
- Saturated Fat: 0.3
- Sodium: 245.2
- Cholesterol: 0
- Protein: 2.9
- Total Carbohydrate: 37.5
- Total Fat: 0.7
- Fiber: 1.9
- Sugar: 17.2

201. Orange And Chocolate Muffins

Serving: 10 muffins | Prep: 20mins | Ready in:

Ingredients

- 1/2 cup unsalted butter
- 1 cup sugar
- 2 to taste x oranges, zest of
- 2 large eggs
- 1/2 cup sour cream
- 1/2 cup orange juice
- 1 teaspoon baking powder
- 2 cups all-purpose flour
- 3 ounces semisweet chocolate, chopped to small bits

Direction

- Preheat oven to 400 degrees.
- Beat butter and sugar together until fluffy.
- Continue beating while you add the orange peel and one egg at a time, then the sour cream and orange juice.
- Measure baking powder, soda and flour.
- Combine with chocolate.
- Add these and fold lightly into the wet batter.
- Fold only until well blended, then fill greased muffin tins.
- Bake for 20 minutes or until done.

Nutrition Information

- Calories: 337.5
- Total Carbohydrate: 43.6
- Cholesterol: 71.8
- Protein: 5.5
- Total Fat: 17.3
- Fiber: 2.1

- Sodium: 60.3
- Sugar: 21.3
- Saturated Fat: 10.4

202. Peanut Butter Chocolate Drops Muffins

Serving: 12 serving(s) | Prep: 10mins | Ready in:

Ingredients

- 1 1/2 cups all-purpose flour
- 1/2 cup whole wheat flour
- 2 teaspoons baking powder
- 1/2 teaspoon sea salt
- 2 tablespoons butter, at room temperature
- 160 g creamy peanut butter
- 100 g light brown sugar
- 2 eggs
- 1 cup milk
- 130 g dark chocolate, drops (or chips)

Direction

- In a medium bowl, sift together the flours, baking powder, and sea salt. Set aside.
- In a large bowl of an electric or stand mixer, cream butter, peanut butter, and brown sugar until smooth and well combined.
- Add the eggs one at a time, mixing thoroughly after each addition. Add the milk and stir until combined.
- Add the dry ingredients to the wet ingredients and stir until just combined - do not over mix. Mix in the chocolate drops.
- Spoon the batter into the into the greased or lined with muffin paper liners muffin tins, filling them evenly. Sprinkle the tops with some chocolate drops.
- Bake the muffins at 220° C for 5 minutes. Reduce temperature to 190° C and bake for additional 12 - 15 minutes until a toothpick inserted in the center comes out clean. Allow muffins to cool for about 5 minutes. Take out of the tins and allow to cool completely.

Nutrition Information

- Calories: 280.9
- Fiber: 3.6
- Saturated Fat: 6.9
- Sodium: 262.7
- Sugar: 9.6
- Total Carbohydrate: 30.8
- Cholesterol: 38.9
- Total Fat: 16.1
- Protein: 8.8

203. Peanutty Chocolate Banana Bread

Serving: 1 loaf, 12 serving(s) | Prep: 30mins | Ready in:

Ingredients

- 2 cups all-purpose flour
- 1 cup sugar
- 1 tablespoon baking powder
- 1/2 teaspoon salt
- 2 very ripe bananas, mashed
- 1/3 cup milk
- 1/3 cup peanut butter
- 3 tablespoons vegetable oil
- 1 egg
- 1 cup milk chocolate chips, divided
- 1/3 cup peanuts, chopped

Direction

- Preheat oven to 350°F.
- Spray loaf pan with nonstick cooking spray.
- Combine flour, sugar, baking powder and salt in large bowl.
- Combine bananas, milk, peanut butter, oil and egg in small bowl.
- Add to dry ingredients, mixing just until moistened.
- Stir in 3/4 cup chocolate chips.
- Spoon batter into loaf pan.

- Sprinkle peanuts and remaining 1/4 cup chocolate chips evenly over batter.
- Bake 60 minutes or until tested done.
- Cool in pans 10 minutes.
- Loosen sides of loaf from pan; remove, cool on rack.
- Cool completely before slicing.

Nutrition Information

- Calories: 276.6
- Sodium: 232.9
- Fiber: 1.9
- Total Carbohydrate: 41.1
- Protein: 6.1
- Total Fat: 10.6
- Saturated Fat: 2.1
- Sugar: 21.2
- Cholesterol: 19.1

204. Pomegranate And Chocolate Chunk Scones

Serving: 6 serving(s) | Prep: 5mins | Ready in:

Ingredients

- 2 cups flour
- 1/4 cup butter
- 2 tablespoons sugar
- 2 teaspoons baking powder
- 60 ml milk
- 2 eggs
- 1 cup pomegranate seeds
- 1/2 cup semisweet chocolate chunk

Direction

- Cut the butter (which must be cold) into small cubes.
- Place the flour, baking powder, lemon zest, sugar and butter into a bowl. Mix until the mixture resembles fine breadcrumbs.
- Add the milk and the eggs. Mix until they form a dough, but be careful not to overwork, add the chocolate and pomegranates.
- Place the mixture onto a floured work service and roll out to a thickness of 1 inch.
- Dip a 2 ¼ inch round pastry cutter in flour, then cut out the scones and then turn the scones over onto a baking sheet.
- Allow to rest for 5 minutes, then bake in a preheated oven set at 400°F.
- Bake for 5 minutes then turn the temperature down to 350°F and bake for a further 5 to 10 minutes.
- Take out of the oven and rest them on a cooling rack.

Nutrition Information

- Calories: 387.2
- Sodium: 219.1
- Cholesterol: 84.3
- Protein: 8.1
- Total Fat: 15.2
- Saturated Fat: 8.6
- Fiber: 3.5
- Sugar: 18.2
- Total Carbohydrate: 54.7

205. Pumpkin Chocolate Muffins

Serving: 12 serving(s) | Prep: 15mins | Ready in:

Ingredients

- nonstick cooking spray, for the pan
- 2 cups unbleached all-purpose flour
- 1/2 teaspoon salt (rounded measure)
- 1 1/2 teaspoons baking powder
- 1 1/2 teaspoons cinnamon
- 1 teaspoon ground ginger
- 1/4 teaspoon allspice
- 1 tablespoon granulated sugar

- 1 tablespoon orange zest, grated or chopped
- 1/3 cup dark brown sugar (packed measure)
- 1 cup mashed pumpkin (or squash or sweet potato)
- 1 large egg
- 1/2 cup milk (plain soy milk will also work)
- 1 tablespoon vanilla extract
- 4 tablespoons unsalted butter, melted
- 2 cups chocolate chips
- 1 cup pecans

Direction

- Preheat the oven to 400°F.
- Lightly spray 12 standard-sized muffin cups with nonstick spray or use cupcake liners.
- Combine the flour, salt, baking powder, spices, granulated sugar, and orange zest in a medium-sized bowl, and stir until well blended.
- Crumble in the brown sugar, and mix with a fork and/or your fingers until thoroughly combined.
- Measure the pumpkin (or squash or sweet potato) into a second medium-sized bowl.
- Add the egg, milk, and vanilla, and beat with a fork or a whisk until well blended.
- Slowly pour this mixture, along with the melted butter, into the dry ingredients.
- Stir with a spoon or a rubber spatula from the bottom of the bowl until you have a uniform batter.
- Don't overmix.
- Fold in chocolate chips and nuts.
- Spoon the batter into the prepared muffin cups.
- (I find it easiest to use two soup spoons for this: One to scoop up the batter and the other to push it into the cup.) For smaller muffins, fill the cups about 4/5 of the way.
- For larger muffins, fill them even with the top of the pan.
- If you have leftover batter, spray one or two additional muffin cups with nonstick spray, and put in as much batter as you have.
- Bake in the center of the oven for to 20 to 25 minutes, or until lightly browned on top, and a toothpick inserted all the way into the center comes out clean.
- Remove the pan from the oven, then remove each muffin from the pan, and place on a rack to cool.
- Wait at least 30 minutes before serving.

Nutrition Information

- Calories: 354.1
- Protein: 5.2
- Saturated Fat: 8.4
- Sodium: 159.9
- Fiber: 3.4
- Total Fat: 19.8
- Sugar: 22.9
- Total Carbohydrate: 43.7
- Cholesterol: 29.2

206. Quick Chocolate Drop Scones

Serving: 15 scones, 7-8 serving(s) | Prep: 5mins | Ready in:

Ingredients

- 90 g self-raising flour
- 1 teaspoon baking powder
- 3 tablespoons golden caster sugar
- 4 tablespoons cocoa powder
- 1 large egg, beaten
- 150 ml full-fat milk
- 65 g unsalted butter, plus extra
- unsalted butter, for frying, melted
- 200 g cherry compote
- heavy cream, to serve

Direction

- Sieve the flour, baking powder, sugar and cocoa powder into a large bowl.
- Make a well in the center of the dry mix and pour in the beaten egg.

- Using a wooden spoon, beat the egg, gradually drawing in the flour. Add the milk a little at a time, while continuously mixing, until a smooth batter is achieved.
- Add the melted butter.
- Melt half the extra butter in a heavy-based frying pan and drop spoonfuls of the batter in the pan.
- Cook for 1 minute or so, until bubbles begin to rise to the surface.
- Flip over, and cook for 1-2 minutes.
- Repeat for the rest of the scones.
- Warm the cherry compote in a small pan.
- Serve the scones with the warm compote and thick cream.

Nutrition Information

- Calories: 163.4
- Protein: 3.5
- Total Fat: 9.5
- Sugar: 6.6
- Total Carbohydrate: 17.8
- Saturated Fat: 5.7
- Sodium: 235.2
- Fiber: 1.4
- Cholesterol: 52.3

207. Simple Chocolate Biscuits

Serving: 12-16 serving(s) | Prep: 15mins | Ready in:

Ingredients

- 75 g softened unsalted butter
- 75 g caster sugar
- 100 g dark chocolate (I use one containing 70% cocoa solid)
- 75 g plain white flour
- 50 g plain whole wheat flour (or just substitute for white)
- 1 tablespoon cocoa powder
- 1/2 teaspoon baking powder

Direction

- Preheat the oven to 180°C, and line a baking sheet with nonstick paper.
- Put the butter and sugar in a bowl and beat until fluffy.
- Melt 75g of the chocolate. Chop the remaining chocolate into little chunks.
- Add the melted chocolate into the butter mixture and mix until smooth.
- In a separate bowl sift the flours, cocoa and baking powder. Beat it into the chocolate mixture. Stir in the chocolate chunks.
- Drop teaspoon size balls onto baking sheet, press down slightly. Bake for 20-25 minutes until crisp on the outside. They may be a little soft in the middle--this is the melted chocolate. Allow to cool on the tray.

Nutrition Information

- Calories: 148.7
- Saturated Fat: 6
- Sodium: 18.2
- Fiber: 2.1
- Cholesterol: 13.4
- Sugar: 6.4
- Total Carbohydrate: 16.8
- Protein: 2.4
- Total Fat: 9.7

208. Sour Cream Banana Bread With Chocolate Glaze

Serving: 8 serving(s) | Prep: 10mins | Ready in:

Ingredients

- 1/2 cup butter, at room temperature
- 1 1/4 cups sugar
- 2 eggs
- 1/2 cup sour cream

- 1 teaspoon vanilla
- 1 cup mashed ripe banana (about 2 medium sized)
- 1 3⁄4 cups flour
- 1 teaspoon baking soda
- 1 teaspoon baking powder
- 1 pinch salt
- 1⁄2 cup semi-sweet chocolate chips
- 3⁄4 cup chopped walnuts
- CHOCOLATE GLAZE
- 1⁄2 cup semi-sweet chocolate chips, melted
- 3 tablespoons butter, melted

Direction

- FOR THE BREAD: Beat together first 6 ingredients until blended. Stir in the remaining ingredients until dry ingredients are just moistened. Do not over-mix.
- Divide batter between 4 greased and lightly floured mini-loaf foil pans (6x3x2 inches), place pans on a cookie sheet, and bake in a 325°F oven for 45 to 50 minutes, or until a cake tester, inserted in center, comes out clean.
- Allow to cool in pans for 15 minutes and then remove from pans and continue cooling on a rack. When cool, drizzle top with Chocolate Glaze (optional, but very good, indeed). Yields 4 mini-loaves.
- You can make this into 12 muffins (2 1/2 x 1 1/4 inches) Or 2 (8x4-inch loaf pans), Or 1 (9x5-inch loaf pan. Adjust cooking time and check with a cake tester, inserted in center, until it comes out clean.
- For the chocolate Glaze: Stir together chocolate and melted butter until well blended.
- Easiest Best! Coffee Cakes and Quick Breads.

Nutrition Information

- Calories: 600.3
- Total Fat: 33.9
- Saturated Fat: 16.8
- Fiber: 3.2
- Sugar: 45.5
- Sodium: 362.9
- Total Carbohydrate: 72.1
- Cholesterol: 101.2
- Protein: 7.8

209. Sour Cream Chocolate Chocolate Chip Banana Bread

Serving: 8-10 slices | Prep: 15mins | Ready in:

Ingredients

- 1⁄2 cup salted butter, room temperature (1/4 lb.)
- 1⁄2 cup sugar
- 1 egg
- 2 large ripened bananas, mashed
- 1 teaspoon vanilla
- 1 cup flour
- 1 teaspoon baking soda
- 2 tablespoons cocoa powder
- 1⁄2 cup sour cream
- 1 cup mini chocolate chip (regular sized will work, also)
- 1⁄2 cup walnuts, chopped (optional)

Direction

- Preheat oven to 350 degrees F. Lightly grease a 9- x 5-inch loaf pan with non-stick spray.
- In a large bowl, cream butter and sugar together until light and fluffy. Stir in egg, mashed bananas, sour cream, and vanilla until well blended. Add baking soda, cocoa, and flour. Mix everything until well incorporated (about 3 minutes in a Kitchenaid mixer). Add chocolate chips and walnuts, if used.
- Transfer batter into loaf pan and bake for 50-60 minutes. Test by inserting a toothpick into center of loaf and checking to see if it comes out clean when you pull it out.
- Remove from heat and allow bread to rest in loaf pan for 10 minutes. Invert the loaf pan onto a cooling rack. Serve bread warm or cold.

Nutrition Information

- Calories: 382.3
- Fiber: 3
- Sugar: 29.1
- Total Carbohydrate: 47.3
- Cholesterol: 61.2
- Protein: 4.4
- Saturated Fat: 13.2
- Sodium: 282.5
- Total Fat: 21.9

210. Triple Chocolate Quick Bread

Serving: 4 mini loaves | Prep: 20mins | Ready in:

Ingredients

- 1/2 cup butter or 1/2 cup margarine, softened
- 2/3 cup packed brown sugar
- 2 eggs
- 1 cup miniature semisweet chocolate chips, melted
- 1 1/2 cups applesauce
- 2 teaspoons vanilla extract
- 2 1/2 cups all-purpose flour
- 1 teaspoon baking powder
- 1 teaspoon baking soda
- 1 teaspoon salt
- 1/2 cup miniature semisweet chocolate chips
- GLAZE
- 1/2 cup miniature semisweet chocolate chips
- 1 tablespoon butter or 1 tablespoon margarine
- 2 -3 tablespoons half-and-half
- 1/2 cup confectioners' sugar
- 1/4 teaspoon vanilla extract
- 1 pinch salt

Direction

- In a mixing bowl, cream butter and sugar.
- Add eggs and melted chocolate; mix well.
- Add applesauce and vanilla.
- Set aside.
- Combine flour, baking powder, baking soda and salt; add to creamed mixture and mix well.
- Stir in chocolate chips.
- Spoon the batter into four greased 5-1/2-in x 3-in. x 2-in. loaf pans.
- Bake at 350 for 35-40 minutes before removing to wire racks to cool completely.
- For glaze, melt chocolate chips and butter in a saucepan; stir in cream.
- Remove from the heat; stir in sugar, vanilla and salt.
- Drizzle over warm bread.

Nutrition Information

- Calories: 1251.5
- Total Fat: 56.1
- Sugar: 98
- Protein: 15.5
- Saturated Fat: 33.2
- Sodium: 1300.1
- Fiber: 8.4
- Total Carbohydrate: 185.2
- Cholesterol: 177.2

211. Triple Chocolate Zucchini Muffins

Serving: 12 Muffins | Prep: 35mins | Ready in:

Ingredients

- 1 1/4 cups whole wheat flour (white is fine)
- 1 cup rolled oats
- 2 scoops chocolate protein powder
- 1 1/2 teaspoons baking powder
- 1/2 teaspoon baking soda
- 1/4 teaspoon salt
- 1/2 teaspoon cinnamon (optional)
- 2 tablespoons cocoa powder

- 1 cup buttermilk
- 2 eggs
- 1 teaspoon vanilla extract
- 2 tablespoons coconut oil, melted
- 1 1/2 cups finely grated zucchini
- 2 tablespoons honey
- 1/4 cup brown sugar
- 2/3 cup mini chocolate chip

Direction

- Preheat oven to 400 degrees F. Spray a 12 cup muffin tin with non-stick spray or line with paper baking cups.
- Mix dry ingredients in a medium bowl with a wire whisk.
- Mix liquid ingredients and shredded zucchini in a small bowl with whisk.
- Make a well in the dry ingredients, then pour in liquid mixture. Stir a few times with a wooden spoon or scraper to incorporate gently.
- Fold in chocolate chips.
- Scoop 1/3 batter per muffin into muffin tin.
- Bake for 20-22 minutes until a toothpick inserted in the center of a muffin comes out clean. Let cool for at least 10 minutes before taking muffins out or they may fall apart.

Nutrition Information

- Calories: 187.9
- Sugar: 14.1
- Total Carbohydrate: 29.3
- Total Fat: 7
- Saturated Fat: 4.2
- Sodium: 184.1
- Fiber: 3
- Cholesterol: 31.8
- Protein: 5

212. Vegan Chocolate Chunk Muffins

Serving: 6 serving(s) | Prep: 20mins | Ready in:

Ingredients

- 1 cup soymilk
- 1/4 cup unsweetened applesauce
- 1/4 cup canola oil
- 1 teaspoon vanilla extract
- 2 cups whole wheat flour
- 1/2 cup white sugar
- 1/2 tablespoon baking soda
- 1/2 cup of chopped vegan dark chocolate bar (I Used Divine Dark Chocolate)

Direction

- Preheat oven to 350F for 15 minutes. Lightly grease a muffin tin.
- In a large bowl, whisk together the dry ingredients and make a well in the center.
- Add the milk, applesauce, oil and vanilla extract. Mix together until the batter is silky. Fold in the chunks of chocolate.
- Scoop out about 1/3rd cup of batter in each muffin cup.
- Bake for 23 minute.

Nutrition Information

- Calories: 308.9
- Sodium: 335
- Sugar: 19.5
- Total Carbohydrate: 49.2
- Total Fat: 10.8
- Saturated Fat: 0.9
- Fiber: 4.6
- Cholesterol: 0
- Protein: 6.6

213. Vegan Chocolate Nut Butter Muffins

Serving: 6 Muffins, 6 serving(s) | Prep: 10mins | Ready in:

Ingredients

- 3⁄4 cup multigrain flour
- 1⁄4 teaspoon baking powder
- 1⁄4 teaspoon baking soda
- 2 tablespoons cocoa powder
- 2 tablespoons nut butter
- 1 tablespoon flourless oil
- 2 tablespoons liquid sweetener (Maple Syrup, Agave)
- 1⁄2-3⁄4 cup almond milk

Direction

- Preheat oven to 350°F or 180°C.
- In a bowl add oil, sweetener, milk, nut-butter and combine well.
- Take another bowl sieve flour, baking soda, baking powder, cocoa powder and salt. Mix well.
- Add dry ingredients to well and mix well.
- Grease your muffin tin with oil and add muffin batter.
- Bake for 15-18 minutes.

Nutrition Information

- Calories: 93.6
- Total Fat: 2.7
- Cholesterol: 0
- Saturated Fat: 0.5
- Sodium: 68.3
- Fiber: 1
- Sugar: 2.8
- Total Carbohydrate: 16.1
- Protein: 2

214. Whole Wheat Vegan Chocolate Zucchini Mini Muffins

Serving: 36 mini muffins, 36 serving(s) | Prep: 15mins | Ready in:

Ingredients

- 1 tablespoon ground flax seeds
- 3 tablespoons warm water
- 1 1⁄4 cups whole wheat flour
- 1⁄4 cup unsweetened cocoa
- 1 1⁄4 teaspoons baking powder
- 3⁄4 teaspoon baking soda
- 1⁄2 teaspoon salt
- 1 teaspoon cinnamon
- 1 cup sugar
- 1⁄2 cup unsweetened applesauce
- 1⁄4 cup almond milk
- 1 teaspoon vanilla extract
- 1 cup zucchini, shredded

Direction

- Preheat oven to 350°F
- Grease mini muffin pan.
- Mix ground flax seed and water and set to the side.
- Mix flour, cocoa, baking powder, baking soda, salt and cinnamon together.
- In a separate bowl, cream flax seed mixture with applesauce and sugar.
- Add in almond milk, vanilla, zucchini.
- Stir until evenly combined.
- Add wet mixture to dry flour mixture and mix well.
- Spoon into mini muffin pan and bake for 12-15 minutes or until a toothpick inserted into the center comes out clean.

Nutrition Information

- Calories: 40.6
- Sodium: 72
- Sugar: 5.7

- Cholesterol: 0
- Total Carbohydrate: 9.6
- Protein: 0.8
- Total Fat: 0.2
- Saturated Fat: 0.1
- Fiber: 0.9

215. Yummy Chocolate Biscuits

Serving: 6 serving(s) | Prep: 15mins | Ready in:

Ingredients

- 2 cups flour
- 2 teaspoons baking powder
- 1 cup sugar
- 1 tablespoon cocoa powder
- 2 eggs, beaten
- 1/2 cup ghee
- grated coconut, to garnish

Direction

- Mix all the ingredients lightly in a bowl.
- Cover the bowl and refrigerate it for 30 minutes.
- Once the time is up, remove dough from the refrigerator.
- Roll into small balls.
- Lightly press each ball.
- Preheat oven and bake the chocolate round balls (biscuits) for 15 minutes.
- Just before serving, garnish each biscuit with a little grated coconut.

Nutrition Information

- Calories: 460.5
- Total Fat: 19.5
- Fiber: 1.4
- Cholesterol: 115.1
- Saturated Fat: 11.4
- Sodium: 145.7
- Sugar: 33.6
- Total Carbohydrate: 66.1
- Protein: 6.6

Chapter 5: Quick Bread Fruit Recipes

***

216. 5 Ingriedient Banana And Brown Butter Muffins

Serving: 12 muffins, 12 serving(s) | Prep: 15mins | Ready in:

Ingredients

- 4 ripe bananas
- 1/3 cup raw agave syrup
- 1/2 cup unsalted butter
- 1 large egg
- 1 3/4 cups self-rising flour

Direction

- Preheat the oven to 375 degrees F. Line a 12-cup muffin tin with paper muffin liners.
- Peel the bananas and add to a large bowl. Add the agave syrup and mash the bananas with a fork until very liquefied but still a little lumpy.
- Melt the butter in a small saucepan or skillet over medium heat. Cook, stirring occasionally, until the milk solids have turned a nutty golden brown.
- To the brown butter, add about 1 cup of the mashed banana mixture and whisk to combine. Cook for a few more minutes until a darker golden color is achieved. Add to the remaining mashed banana mixture and whisk to combine, then whisk in the egg. Fold in the

flour, in 2 batches, with a rubber spatula, until just combined; do not over mix. With an ice cream scoop, evenly divide the batter among the muffin tin cups.

- Bake in the center of the oven until golden brown and the tops spring back when pressed, about 25 minutes. Cool for 5 minutes in the pan, then transfer the muffins to a rack to cool completely. Serve warm or at room temperature.

Nutrition Information

- Calories: 173.5
- Protein: 2.8
- Total Fat: 8.4
- Saturated Fat: 5.1
- Sodium: 238.8
- Fiber: 1.5
- Total Carbohydrate: 22.6
- Sugar: 4.9
- Cholesterol: 38

217. Any Fruit Muffins

Serving: 12 muffins, 12 serving(s) | Prep: 10mins | Ready in:

Ingredients

- 10 ounces all-purpose flour
- 3 teaspoons baking powder
- 1/2 teaspoon salt
- 1 3/4 ounces light brown sugar
- 3 1/2 ounces white sugar
- 1 cup buttermilk
- 1/4 cup unsalted butter (melted)
- 1/4 cup apricot preserves

Direction

- Preheat oven to 400 degrees F (205 degrees C).
- Stir together the flour, baking powder, salt and sugars in a large bowl. Make a well in the center.
- In a small bowl beat egg. Stir in buttermilk and melted butter.
- Add milk mixture to flour mixture. Mix gently with a rubber spatula until moistened, but do not beat. The batter will be lumpy.
- Spoon one tablespoon of batter into paper lined muffin pan cups. Add one teaspoon of jam to each cup. Fill cups with remaining batter.
- Bake for 20 minutes, or until golden.

Nutrition Information

- Calories: 193.1
- Sugar: 15.7
- Cholesterol: 11
- Protein: 3.2
- Total Fat: 4.3
- Fiber: 0.7
- Total Carbohydrate: 36
- Saturated Fat: 2.6
- Sodium: 214.4

218. Apple Hazelnut Muffins (Gf, Vegan)

Serving: 12 muffins, 12 serving(s) | Prep: 30mins | Ready in:

Ingredients

- 2 tablespoons ground flax seeds
- 1/4 cup hot water
- 1/4 cup millet flour
- 1/4 cup sorghum flour
- 1/2 cup rice flour
- 1/4 cup potato starch (NOT potato flour)
- 1/4 cup cornstarch
- 1 tablespoon baking powder
- 1/2 teaspoon baking soda
- 1 teaspoon guar gum

- 1/2 teaspoon sea salt
- 1/2 tablespoon cinnamon
- 1/2 teaspoon nutmeg
- 1/2 teaspoon ginger
- 3/4 cup dark brown sugar
- 1/3 cup canola oil
- 1 teaspoon pure vanilla extract (make sure it's GF)
- 1 teaspoon rice vinegar
- 1/4 cup soymilk
- 1 apple, with peel, coarsely grated
- 3/4 cup hazelnuts, toasted and chopped finely (not ground, though)

Direction

- Preheat oven to 350F, line 12 muffin cups with paper cups.
- In a small bowl, mix together flaxseed and hot water. Let stand for 10 minutes.
- In a medium bowl, whisk together flours, starches, baking powder, baking soda, guar gum, cinnamon, nutmeg and ginger. Set aside.
- In a large bowl beat together brown sugar, oil, vanilla and rice vinegar.
- Add flaxseed mixture and blend in well.
- Add the dry mixture and stir in gently, then add the soy milk and stir just to combine all the ingredients.
- Fold in shredded apple and hazelnuts.
- Portion into the prepared muffin cups.
- Bake 35 minutes, until they test done.
- Remove from the pans immediately and cool on wire racks.

Nutrition Information

- Calories: 245.4
- Fiber: 2.7
- Sugar: 15.8
- Protein: 3
- Total Fat: 12.3
- Saturated Fat: 1
- Sodium: 249.7
- Total Carbohydrate: 32.7
- Cholesterol: 0

219. Apple And Cheddar Cheese Muffins

Serving: 12 serving(s) | Prep: 15mins | Ready in:

Ingredients

- 2 cups all-purpose flour
- 1/3 cup sugar
- 1 teaspoon baking powder
- 1/2 teaspoon baking soda
- 1/4 teaspoon salt
- 1/4 teaspoon cinnamon
- 1 cup sharp cheddar cheese, grated
- 1/3 cup parmesan cheese, grated
- 1 egg
- 1 cup buttermilk or 1 cup sour milk
- 1/4 cup oil
- 1 medium tart apple, finely chopped
- 1/4 cup grated cheddar cheese (optional)

Direction

- Preheat oven to 400F.
- Grease muffin pans.
- COMBINE flour, sugar, baking powder, baking soda, salt, cinnamon and cheeses in large mixing bowl.
- BEAT egg, buttermilk, oil and apple together thoroughly.
- ADD liquid ingredients all at once to dry ingredients.
- Stir just until moistened.
- FILL greased muffin cups 3/4 full.
- SPRINKLE tops with 1/4 cup cheddar cheese if desired.
- BAKE at 400°F for 18-23 minutes or until top springs back when lightly touched.

Nutrition Information

- Calories: 208
- Sodium: 259.9

- Total Fat: 9.3
- Saturated Fat: 3.3
- Sugar: 7.9
- Total Carbohydrate: 24.4
- Cholesterol: 30.8
- Protein: 6.8
- Fiber: 0.9

220. Apple And Cheddar Scones

Serving: 6-8 serving(s) | Prep: 1hours | Ready in:

Ingredients

- 2 firm tart apples
- 1 1/2 cups all-purpose flour
- 1/4 cup sugar, plus 1 1/2 tablespoons for sprinkling
- 1/2 tablespoon baking powder
- 1/2 teaspoon salt plus additional for egg wash
- 6 tablespoons unsalted butter, chilled and cut into 1/2-inch cubes plus additional for baking sheet if not lining it with parchment
- 1/2 cup sharp cheddar cheese, shredded (white is recommended, I assume for aesthetics)
- 1/4 cup milk
- 2 large eggs

Direction

- Position a rack at the center of oven and preheat oven to 375 °F. Line baking sheet with parchment paper.
- Peel and core apples, then cut them into one-sixteenths. (I assumed this meant chunks, not slivers.) Placed them in a single layer on a baking sheet lined with parchment paper and bake them until they take on a little color and feel dry to the touch, about 20 minutes. They will be about half-baked. Let them cool completely. (You can speed this up in the fridge, as I did.) Leave oven on.
- Sift or whisk flour, sugar, baking powder and salt together. Set aside. Place butter in the bowl of an electric mixer with a paddle attachment, along with cooled apple chunks, cheese, cream and one egg. Sprinkle flour mixture over the top and mix on low speed until the dough just comes together. Do not overmix. [Don't have a stand or hand mixer? I'd rub the cold butter into the flour mixture with my fingertips or with a pastry blender, hand-chop the apples coarsely and mix the rest together with a wooden spoon until combined. It might feel awkward, but it should all come together. Again, don't overmix it though it will be harder to do this by hand.].
- Generously flour your counter top and place the scone dough on top of it. Sprinkle with flour. Use a rolling pin to gently roll (or use your hands to pat) the dough into a 1 1/4-inch thick, 6-inch circle. Cut circle into 6 wedges. Transfer them to a baking sheet that has either been buttered or lined with a fresh sheet of parchment paper. Leave at least 2 inches between each scone.
- Beat remaining egg in a small bowl with a pinch of salt. Brush the scones with egg wash and sprinkle them with remaining tablespoon of sugar. Bake until firm and golden, about 30 minutes. With a spatula, lift them to a wire rack to cool for 10 minutes.

Nutrition Information

- Calories: 348.2
- Sugar: 14.8
- Total Carbohydrate: 41.6
- Protein: 8.3
- Saturated Fat: 10.1
- Sodium: 180.8
- Fiber: 2.3
- Cholesterol: 103.8
- Total Fat: 17

221. Apple And Cinnamon Breakfast Muffins (Nigella)

Serving: 12 muffins, 12 serving(s) | Prep: 30mins | Ready in:

Ingredients

- 2 apples, any kind that you like best
- 250 g spelt flour
- 2 teaspoons baking powder
- 2 teaspoons ground cinnamon
- 125 g brown sugar, use an extra 4 for sprinkling
- 125 ml honey
- 60 ml plain fat-free yogurt
- 60 ml vegetable oil
- 65 ml applesauce
- 2 eggs
- 75 g natural almonds, roughly chopped

Direction

- Preheat oven to 300 degrees Fahrenheit, line 12 tin muffin tin with paper liners.
- Peel and core apples, then chop into small pieces about 1cm each and put them to one side.
- Measure the flour, baking powder and 1 teaspoons of the ground cinnamon into a bowl.
- Whisk together 125g brown sugar, honey, yogurt, veg. oil and eggs in another bowl.
- Use the chopped almonds and add 1/2 of them to the flour mix, put the leftover almonds into a small bowl and add the 1 teaspoons of cinnamon and the 4 teaspoons of brown sugar.
- Fold wet ingredients into the dry, add apples but just stir to combine.
- Spoon into the muffin cups, then add some of that topping you made for each muffin
- Bake about 20min or until finished.
- Let stand in tin for 10 min before placing them onto a cooling rack.

Nutrition Information

- Calories: 181.7
- Sugar: 22.3
- Protein: 2.8
- Sodium: 81.6
- Fiber: 1.8
- Saturated Fat: 1.1
- Total Carbohydrate: 26.3
- Cholesterol: 31.1
- Total Fat: 8.3

222. Apple And Orange Muffins

Serving: 12 muffins | Prep: 10mins | Ready in:

Ingredients

- 250 g flour
- 11 g instant yeast, powder
- 1/2 teaspoon baking soda
- orange zest from 1 orange
- 250 g apples, peeled, cored and cut into small pieces (1 1/2 apple)
- 1 egg
- 125 g demerara sugar
- 1 teaspoon vanilla essence
- 250 g plain yogurt
- 80 ml olive oil
- 1/2 orange, juice of

Direction

- In a bowl, mix the flour with the instant yeast powder, baking soda, orange zest and apple pieces.
- In another bowl whisk the egg, and add sugar, vanilla essence, yogurt and olive oil. Dilute with the juice of half an orange.
- Add egg mixture to dry ingredients and apple pieces and stir just until moistened. Batter should be lumpy.
- Spoon batter into greased or lined muffin cups, filling just below the top. Bake in the

oven at 180°C for about 30 minutes or until lightly golden.

- Cool muffins on wire rack for about 5 minutes, then remove from the pan.

Nutrition Information

- Calories: 206.6
- Saturated Fat: 1.4
- Sodium: 69.4
- Sugar: 14.8
- Cholesterol: 18.2
- Total Fat: 7.2
- Fiber: 1.5
- Total Carbohydrate: 32.1
- Protein: 3.9

223. Apple, Apricot And Raisin Muffins

Serving: 18 muffins, 18 serving(s) | Prep: 15mins | Ready in:

Ingredients

- 2 cups bran flakes
- 1 1/2 cups milk
- 2 eggs, lightly beaten
- 1/2 cup vegetable oil
- 2 cups plain flour
- 1/2 cup sugar
- 2 tablespoons baking powder
- 1/2 teaspoon salt
- 1 tablespoon cinnamon
- 1 apple, peeled, diced
- 1/2 cup dried apricot, diced
- 1/2 cup raisins

Direction

- Soak bran flakes in milk for 5 minutes in large bowl.
- Add eggs and oil, combine well.
- Sift all dry ingredients into the bowl and mix well.
- Stir in apples, apricots and raisins.
- Divide batter in 18 well-greased 1/3 cup muffin tins.
- Bake at 375 F for 18 - 20 minutes or till tester comes out clean.
- Turn out onto wire racks.

Nutrition Information

- Calories: 186.9
- Total Fat: 7.6
- Saturated Fat: 1.5
- Sodium: 235.3
- Fiber: 1.9
- Sugar: 11.5
- Total Carbohydrate: 27.7
- Protein: 3.5
- Cholesterol: 26.4

224. Apricot And Cheese Danish Muffins

Serving: 1 dozen | Prep: 10mins | Ready in:

Ingredients

- 1 1/2 cups all-purpose flour
- 2 1/2 teaspoons baking powder
- 1/4 teaspoon salt
- 1 cup oat bran
- 1/2 cup packed light brown sugar
- 1 cup milk
- 1/3 cup vegetable oil
- 2 eggs, lightly beaten
- 1 teaspoon vanilla extract
- 1 (3 ounce) package cream cheese
- 3/4 cup apricot-pineapple jam (or other flavor)

Direction

- Preheat oven to 425 F degrees.
- Grease 12 muffin cup pan.

- Sift flour, baking powder, and salt.
- Stir in oat bran and brown sugar, set aside.
- In another bowl, combine milk, oil, eggs, and vanilla.
- Stir milk mixture into dry ingredients, just until moistened.
- Cut cream cheese into 12 equal pieces.
- Spoon 1/2 of batter into prepared muffin cups, filling about 1/3 full.
- Spoon about 1 tablespoon of jam on top of batter in each cup.
- Top with 1 piece of cream cheese in each cup.
- Spoon remaining batter into each cup, over the jam and cheese, until each cup is about 2/3 full.
- Bake for 14-16 minutes until browned.

Nutrition Information

- Calories: 2588.1
- Sodium: 2051.2
- Fiber: 19.6
- Cholesterol: 550.7
- Total Fat: 129.6
- Saturated Fat: 38.3
- Sugar: 109.2
- Total Carbohydrate: 330.1
- Protein: 62.6

225. Avocado And Bacon Muffins

Serving: 12-24 serving(s) | Prep: 10mins | Ready in:

Ingredients

- 2 cups flour
- 4 teaspoons baking powder
- 1/2 teaspoon salt
- 1 tablespoon sugar
- 1 pinch cayenne pepper
- 1 cup grated tasty cheese
- 4 spring onions (chopped)
- 3 slices bacon
- 75 g butter
- 1 egg
- 1 cup milk
- 1 avocado
- 1 tablespoon lemon juice

Direction

- Sieve the first four dry ingredients into a large bowl and add the pepper, cheese and spring onions.
- Stir to combine.
- Chop the bacon finely and cook in a pan or under the grill until crisp.
- Keep the bacon drippings.
- Melt the butter and add the egg, milk bacon dripping and beat to combine.
- Halve the avocado, scoop out the flesh and cut into small cubes.
- Sprinkle with lemon juice to prevent browning.
- Then add them to the liquid mixture.
- Add the bacon then mix into dry ingredients.
- Stir only to just combine.
- Put about 1/4 cup of mixture into each sprayed or greased muffin cup.
- Bake at 200 deg C (400F) for approx. 10 mins or until the muffins spring back when pressed lightly in centre.
- I make either 24 mini or 12 medium muffins and serve them warm.

Nutrition Information

- Calories: 226.4
- Saturated Fat: 6.8
- Total Carbohydrate: 20.3
- Cholesterol: 44.6
- Protein: 6.8
- Total Fat: 13.4
- Sodium: 365.5
- Fiber: 1.8
- Sugar: 1.4

226. Banana Applesauce Blueberry And Walnut Fat Free Quick Bread

Serving: 16 slices (from two loaves), 8-10 serving(s) | Prep: 10mins | Ready in:

Ingredients

- 3 over-ripe bananas
- 2 tablespoons lemon juice
- 1/2 cup unsweetened applesauce (I've used up to a total of 1 cup of applesauce if the mixture seems too stiff or dry)
- 1/2 cup packed brown sugar
- 2 cups flour
- 3/4 teaspoon baking powder
- 3/4 teaspoon baking soda
- 1/2 teaspoon salt
- 1/8-1/4 teaspoon cardamom
- 1 cup fresh blueberries
- 1/2 chopped walnuts

Direction

- Pre-heat oven to 350.
- Spray two 8 x 4 loaf pans with non-stick spray.
- In large bowl, blend together bananas, lemon juice, applesauce and brown sugar. I use a hand-held blender, which purees everything quickly and evenly.
- In another large bowl, wisk together dry ingredients.
- Add to dry mixture blueberries and nuts and toss until flour coated. This helps to prevent the berries and nuts from settling to the bottom during baking.
- Add flour-berry/nut mixture to the moist-banana mixture. Mix together by hand folding contents until all is moistened being careful not to overmix.
- Divide final mixture into the two loaf pans, spreading contents evenly. Place in oven center for about 35 to 40 minutes, until tooth pick comes out clean and the tops are lightly golden brown. I've found the tooth pick test happens first but wait about 5 or so more minutes for the tops to brown.
- Remove from oven and cool. Even better when served the next day. I cut the loaves into 1 inch thick slices, serving 2 per person.
- I've also substituted coarsely chopped sweet cherries (1 cup) and cinnamon (1 tsp) for the blueberries and cardamom. Very, Very good too, for all those cherry lovers out there!

Nutrition Information

- Calories: 225.2
- Total Carbohydrate: 52.3
- Cholesterol: 0
- Total Fat: 0.7
- Sodium: 302.8
- Fiber: 2.6
- Sugar: 22.2
- Protein: 4
- Saturated Fat: 0.1

227. Banana Yogurt Protein Muffins

Serving: 12 muffins | Prep: 15mins | Ready in:

Ingredients

- 2 small ripe bananas
- 1 egg
- 7 ounces 2% low-fat Greek yogurt, strained
- 1/4 cup blackstrap molasses
- 1 cup whole wheat flour
- 1 cup whole wheat pastry flour
- 1/2 cup egg white powder
- 2 teaspoons baking powder
- 1 teaspoon baking soda
- 1/2 teaspoon nutmeg
- 1 teaspoon cinnamon
- 1/2 cup chopped raisins
- 1/2 cup chopped walnuts

Direction

- Mix bananas, egg, yogurt, and molasses well in electric mixer.
- Add flours, egg white powder, baking powder, baking soda, nutmeg and cinnamon. Mix well, scraping down the sides of the bowl as necessary.
- Stir in chopped raisins and walnuts.
- Spoon batter into greased muffin cups.
- Bake at 375 degrees for 10-15 minutes.

Nutrition Information

- Calories: 183.5
- Protein: 8.9
- Fiber: 3.5
- Sodium: 243.8
- Sugar: 7.3
- Total Carbohydrate: 29.8
- Cholesterol: 18.6
- Total Fat: 4.3
- Saturated Fat: 0.7

228. Banana And Maple Muffins

Serving: 12 serving(s) | Prep: 5mins | Ready in:

Ingredients

- 1 1/2 cups whole wheat flour
- 1 cup quick oats
- 1 tablespoon baking powder
- 2 pinches salt
- 1/2 teaspoon ground coriander (optional)
- 1/2 cup walnuts, minced
- 2 ripe bananas, mashed
- 1 egg
- 1/3 cup canola oil
- 1/3 cup maple syrup
- 1/4 cup maple-flavored butter, 1 teaspoon per muffin
- 12 walnut halves

Direction

- Mix all dry ingredients in one bowl. In another bowl, mix bananas and other wet ingredients, except for the maple butter and walnut halves.
- Add the wet ingredients to the dry. Stir until just moistened.
- Pour batter into muffin cups. Bake for 15 to 20 minutes at 350°F Cool slightly, remove from cups, and glaze with maple butter. Garnish with walnut halves.

Nutrition Information

- Calories: 222.9
- Total Fat: 11.8
- Saturated Fat: 1.1
- Fiber: 3.5
- Cholesterol: 17.6
- Sodium: 124.6
- Sugar: 8.1
- Total Carbohydrate: 27.1
- Protein: 4.9

229. Blueberries And Cream Mall Muffins

Serving: 12 muffins | Prep: 45mins | Ready in:

Ingredients

- 2 1/4 cups sugar
- 1/2 cup vegetable oil
- 1/2 cup unsalted butter, melted
- 4 large eggs
- 1 tablespoon pure vanilla extract
- 1/2 teaspoon lemon extract
- 1/2 teaspoon pure orange extract
- 5 cups all-purpose flour (approx.)
- 1 tablespoon baking powder
- 1/4 teaspoon baking soda
- 1/2 teaspoon salt
- 1 cup buttermilk
- 1/2 cup sour cream

- 2 cups semi-frozen blueberries
- sugar, for dusting tops

Direction

- Preheat oven to 425°; position oven rack to middle position.
- Generously spray a 12-cup large or standard muffin pan or a 24-cup small muffin pan with nonstick cooking spray and then line with paper muffin liners.
- Place pan on a parchment paper-lined baking sheet.
- In a mixer bowl, blend sugar with oil and butter.
- Briskly add eggs, vanilla, and other extracts.
- Fold in 4 cups flour, baking powder, baking soda, and salt.
- Blend somewhat before next blending in buttermilk and sour cream.
- Batter should be quite thick; if not, add a touch more flour.
- Gently fold in berries with a spatula, trying not to break them apart.
- Using a large ice-cream scoop, scoop a very large amount of batter into prepared muffin cups, loading them as full as you can.
- Your need almost a scoop and a half of batter per cup.
- Dust tops of muffins with a little sugar.
- Bake 15 minutes at 425°, then decrease oven temperature to 350° and bake until muffins are golden brown and spring back when gently pressed with fingertips, about 12-16 minutes.
- Let cool 5 minutes before removing from pan.

Nutrition Information

- Calories: 552
- Cholesterol: 88.1
- Protein: 8.6
- Total Fat: 21
- Saturated Fat: 7.9
- Sodium: 269.5
- Fiber: 2
- Sugar: 41.6
- Total Carbohydrate: 82.6

230. Blueberry (or Raisin) Bran Muffins

Serving: 12 muffins | Prep: 15mins | Ready in:

Ingredients

- 1 tablespoon lemon juice
- 1 cup skim milk
- 1 egg, beaten
- 1/4 cup oil
- 1/4 cup molasses
- 1 cup natural bran
- 3/4 cup whole wheat flour
- 3/4 cup all-purpose white flour
- 1/3 cup brown sugar, packed
- 1 1/2 teaspoons grated lemons, zest of
- 1 1/2 teaspoons baking powder
- 1/2 teaspoon baking soda
- 1/2 teaspoon salt
- 1 cup blueberries or 1 cup raisins

Direction

- In bowl, stir lemon juice into milk to sour it.
- Stir in egg, oil and molasses.
- Set aside.
- In another large bowl, combine bran, both flours, sugar, lemon zest, baking powder, baking soda and salt.
- Add milk mixture and blueberries or raisins.
- Spoon mixture into muffin pan sprayed with non-stick spray.
- Bake at 375 F for 20-25 minutes.

Nutrition Information

- Calories: 172.5
- Protein: 3.9
- Saturated Fat: 0.8
- Fiber: 2.9
- Sugar: 11.9

- Total Carbohydrate: 29.5
- Total Fat: 5.5
- Sodium: 230.4
- Cholesterol: 18

231. Blueberry And Pecan Scones

Serving: 15 scones | Prep: 10mins | Ready in:

Ingredients

- 3 cups flour
- 3⁄4 cup sugar
- 1 tablespoon baking powder
- 1⁄2 teaspoon baking soda
- 1⁄2 teaspoon salt
- 3⁄4 cup butter
- 1 cup dried blueberries
- 1⁄2 cup chopped pecans
- 2 teaspoons orange zest
- 1 cup buttermilk
- 1 tablespoon sugar

Direction

- Sift flour, 3/4 cup sugar, baking powder, baking soda, and salt into a large bowl. Mix well.
- Cut in the butter until the mixture is crumbly.
- Stir in blueberries, pecans, and orange zest.
- Stir in buttermilk just until moistened.
- On a floured surface, roll dough 3/4 inches thick. Cut into 2 1/2 inch circles or triangles.
- Place on a greased baking sheet and sprinkle with 1 tablespoon sugar.
- Bake at 400°F for 15-16 minutes.

Nutrition Information

- Calories: 246.7
- Cholesterol: 25.1
- Protein: 3.6
- Total Fat: 12.2
- Saturated Fat: 6.2
- Sodium: 290.9
- Fiber: 1.1
- Sugar: 11.8
- Total Carbohydrate: 31.5

232. Cranberry And White Chocolate Scones

Serving: 8-16 scones | Prep: 15mins | Ready in:

Ingredients

- 1 3⁄4 cups flour
- 1⁄4 cup sugar
- 2 1⁄2 teaspoons baking powder
- 1⁄2 teaspoon salt
- 5 tablespoons chilled unsalted butter, cut into pieces
- 6 tablespoons half-and-half
- 1 large egg, beaten
- 1⁄2 cup fresh or frozen cranberries or 1⁄2 cup dried cranberries (craisins)
- 1⁄2 cup white chocolate chips (or pieces)

Direction

- Preheat oven to 400 degrees F.
- In a bowl by hand or using an electric mixer, blend together the flour, sugar, baking powder, salt, and butter.
- Add the half and half, beaten egg, cranberries (I like the dried ones), and the white chocolate chips, and stir until the dough holds together.
- Turn out onto a lightly floured board and knead for 2 minutes.
- Form into a 1/2-inch thick round, then cut the round into 8 wedges (you can also make two smaller rounds of smaller wedges, if you like).
- Spray a baking sheet with vegetable oil, then transfer the wedges to the sheet.
- Bake the scones at 400 degrees F for 14 minutes or until golden brown.

Nutrition Information

- Calories: 271.8
- Fiber: 1.1
- Sugar: 12.9
- Total Carbohydrate: 35
- Cholesterol: 48.7
- Total Fat: 12.8
- Saturated Fat: 7.7
- Sodium: 283.6
- Protein: 4.7

233. Date And Raisin Muffins

Serving: 12 muffins | Prep: 40mins | Ready in:

Ingredients

- 3/4 cup raisins
- 3/4 cup dates, chopped
- 1 1/2 cups water
- 1/2 butter
- 2/3 cup brown sugar
- 1 egg
- 1 teaspoon vanilla
- 1 1/2 cups all-purpose flour
- 1 teaspoon baking powder
- 1 teaspoon baking soda
- 1/2 teaspoon salt

Direction

- In saucepan, combine raisins, dates and water. Boil gently, uncovered, for 20 minutes, let cool for a few minutes.
- Cream together butter and sugar, beat in egg and vanilla.
- Add fruit and its liquid.
- Combine flour, baking powder, soda and salt, stir into fruit mixture, mixing well.
- Spoon into greased or paper-lined muffin tins, filling 3/4 full.
- Bake at 350°F for 20 -25 minutes.

Nutrition Information

- Calories: 168.8
- Sugar: 24.3
- Total Carbohydrate: 39.5
- Total Fat: 0.7
- Saturated Fat: 0.2
- Sodium: 244.8
- Fiber: 1.6
- Cholesterol: 17.6
- Protein: 2.7

234. Date And Spice Muffins

Serving: 12 muffins, 12 serving(s) | Prep: 10mins | Ready in:

Ingredients

- 1 1/4 cups all-bran cereal
- 1 1/2 cups skim milk
- 2 eggs
- 3 tablespoons margarine spread, melted
- 3/4 cup chopped dates
- 2 tablespoons honey
- 1 1/2 cups wheat flour (self rising)
- 1 teaspoon cinnamon
- 1/2 teaspoon nutmeg
- 1/4 cup sugar

Direction

- Place All-Bran® and milk in a large bowl and stand for 5 minutes until softened.
- Beat in eggs, margarine, honey and dates.
- Sift flour and spices together.
- Stir in the sugar and add to the All-Bran® mixture, being careful not to over beat.
- Fold in stiffly beaten egg whites.
- Spoon mixture into a lightly greased muffin tray and sprinkle each muffin with some All-Bran® cereal.
- Bake at 375F or 190C for 20 minutes or until cool.

Nutrition Information

- Calories: 171.3
- Sugar: 14
- Protein: 5.3
- Saturated Fat: 0.9
- Sodium: 70.8
- Fiber: 4.4
- Total Carbohydrate: 31.6
- Cholesterol: 31.6
- Total Fat: 4.5

235. English Fruit Muffins (Bread Machine)

Serving: 8-10 muffins | Prep: 0S | Ready in:

Ingredients

- 1 cup milk
- 3 tablespoons butter
- 1 egg
- 1/2 teaspoon salt
- 2 teaspoons sugar
- 3 cups plain flour
- 2 teaspoons dried yeast
- 1 teaspoon mixed spice
- 1 cup sultana
- cornmeal

Direction

- Place milk, butter, egg, salt, sugar, flour, and yeast in bread machine, in that order.
- Set to dough setting. When machine beeps, add mixed spice and sultanas.
- When dough cycle has finished, sprinkle cornmeal on your work surface, turn out dough, and press out to a 1/2 inch thick rectangle. Turn, to coat both sides in cornmeal.
- With a large glass or cookie cutter, cut dough into rounds. Place rounds on a tray, cover, and leave to rise for about 30 minutes.
- /heat an electric fry pan to medium heat, and cook muffins until lightly browned on each side.
- Split with a knife, and toast, to serve.

Nutrition Information

- Calories: 306.8
- Saturated Fat: 3.7
- Sodium: 203.6
- Total Carbohydrate: 55.1
- Cholesterol: 42.2
- Total Fat: 6.7
- Sugar: 13.4
- Protein: 7.8
- Fiber: 2.3

236. Fresh Fruit Muffins

Serving: 12 medium muffins | Prep: 5mins | Ready in:

Ingredients

- 2 1/2 cups all-purpose flour, unbleached
- 1/2 cup sugar
- 2 teaspoons baking powder
- 1 teaspoon baking soda
- 1/2 teaspoon salt
- 1 1/4 cups buttermilk
- 1/3 cup butter, melted
- 2 large eggs
- 1 teaspoon vanilla extract
- 1 1/4 cups strawberries, chopped, hulled

Direction

- Preheat oven to 400.
- Lightly butter 12 muffin cups or coat with nonstick spray or line with paper liners.
- Combine the flour, sugar, baking powder, baking soda and salt in a large bowl; stir until well blended.
- In a separate bowl, whisk together the buttermilk, melted butter, eggs and vanilla

until well blended. Add to the dry ingredients all at once, along with strawberries, and fold just until evenly moistened.
- Do not overmix.
- Divide the batter evenly among the muffin cups.
- Sprinkle each muffin with a little sugar, if desired.
- Bake until a toothpick inserted in the centers comes out clean, 22-25 minutes.
- Cool on a wire rack before removing from the pan.

Nutrition Information

- Calories: 200.9
- Saturated Fat: 3.7
- Fiber: 1
- Protein: 4.7
- Total Fat: 6.5
- Sodium: 337.7
- Sugar: 10.4
- Total Carbohydrate: 30.9
- Cholesterol: 49.8

237. Fresh Lemon And Ginger Muffins

Serving: 12 muffins | Prep: 30mins | Ready in:

Ingredients

- 2 tablespoons coarsely chopped peeled fresh ginger
- 1 -2 lemon, well scrubbed and patted dry
- 1/2 cup butter, at room temperature
- 1 cup sugar
- 2 large eggs
- 1 teaspoon baking soda
- 1 cup plain yogurt or 1 cup buttermilk
- 2 cups all-purpose flour
- 1/4 cup freshly squeezed lemon juice
- 2 tablespoons sugar

Direction

- Preheat oven to 375°; grease muffin cups or use foil or paper baking cups.
- Finely chop the ginger; finely grate the lemon peel so you have 2 tablespoons.
- In a big bowl, beat butter and 1 cup sugar with an electric mixer until pale and fluffy.
- Beat in eggs, one at a time; add ginger and lemon peel.
- Stir baking soda into yogurt or buttermilk; it will start to bubble and rise up.
- Fold flour into ginger mixture one third at a time, alternately with the yogurt.
- When well blended, scoop into muffin cups; bake 18-20 minutes, or until lightly browned and springy to the touch.
- While the muffins bake, mix lemon juice and the 2 tablespoons sugar in a small dish; stir until sugar dissolves.
- When muffins are baked, remove from oven and let cool 3-5 minutes in pan.
- Remove from pan and dip top and bottom in the lemon juice and sugar mixture.

Nutrition Information

- Calories: 244.8
- Total Fat: 9.4
- Saturated Fat: 5.6
- Sodium: 181.3
- Total Carbohydrate: 37.3
- Cholesterol: 58.2
- Fiber: 1
- Sugar: 20
- Protein: 4.1

238. Fruit Nut Brown Bread

Serving: 6 mini loaves, 6 serving(s) | Prep: 20mins | Ready in:

Ingredients

- 6 ounces chopped dried cherries
- 2 teaspoons baking soda
- 2 cups boiling water
- 1 cup Splenda brown sugar blend
- 1/2 teaspoon salt
- 1 tablespoon molasses
- 1/2 cup shortening
- 2 eggs
- 4 cups whole wheat pastry flour
- 1 cup chopped walnuts
- 1 cup golden raisin

Direction

- Preheat oven to 325°F Grease the insides of cans well.
- Combine chopped cherries and baking soda in a bowl. Pour in boiling water and let stand 5 minutes.
- Combine sugar, shortening and eggs in a large bowl. Using a mixer, beat at medium-high speed until creamy. Add salt, molasses, the cherry mixture and flour and stir until well blended. Add nuts and raisins; mix well.
- Fill cans about two-thirds full with batter. Bake about 1 hour, or until a wooden toothpick inserted in the center comes out clean. Cool in cans on a wire rack 15 minutes. Remove bread from can and place on wire rack to cool completely.

Nutrition Information

- Calories: 781.2
- Saturated Fat: 6.4
- Fiber: 10.8
- Cholesterol: 62
- Protein: 16.4
- Total Fat: 33.5
- Sodium: 649
- Sugar: 31.7
- Total Carbohydrate: 113.2

239. Fruit Compote Muffins

Serving: 12 muffins, 24 serving(s) | Prep: 20mins | Ready in:

Ingredients

- 1 1/2 cups flour
- 1 teaspoon baking powder
- 1/2 teaspoon baking soda
- 1 teaspoon cinnamon
- 1/2 teaspoon ginger
- 1/2 teaspoon nutmeg
- 1/4 teaspoon salt
- 1 cup granulated sugar
- 1 cup milk
- 2 eggs
- 1/4 cup canola oil
- 1 cup dried fruit
- 1/2 cup walnuts (chopped)

Direction

- Preheat oven to 375 degrees Fahrenheit.
- In a small saucepan add 1/2 cup of water to dried fruit and cook until nice and tender then set aside.
- In a blender or food processor pulse fruit mixture until nicely blended together to form a compote mixture.
- Combine dry ingredients in a medium size bowl and put aside.
- In a large mixing bowl put milk, eggs and oil together and whisk until nice and smooth.
- Put the softened fruit in the egg mixture and stir until well blended.
- Add the chopped walnuts and mix until they are well coated in batter.
- Fill muffin cups 2/3 full and put in the oven for 20 minutes.
- Let cool for 10 minutes before removing from pan to serving plate.

Nutrition Information

- Calories: 131.6
- Protein: 2.3

- Total Fat: 4.8
- Sodium: 78.4
- Fiber: 1.1
- Total Carbohydrate: 21
- Cholesterol: 16.9
- Saturated Fat: 0.7
- Sugar: 8.4

240. Fruit N Nut Muffins

Serving: 12 muffins | Prep: 10mins | Ready in:

Ingredients

- 1 1/4 cups all-purpose flour
- 3/4 cup quick-cooking oats
- 1/2 cup packed brown sugar
- 1/4 cup wheat bran
- 1 tablespoon baking powder
- 1/2 teaspoon ground cinnamon
- 1/2 teaspoon ground allspice
- 1/4 teaspoon salt
- 1 cup halved seedless grapes
- 1/2 cup grated carrot
- 1/2 cup nonfat milk
- 1/2 cup applesauce
- 3 tablespoons canola oil
- 1 egg, beaten
- 1/2 cup chopped walnuts

Direction

- Preheat the oven to 350°F.
- 2. Line 12 muffin cups with paper liners, and set aside.
- 3. Combine the flour, oats, sugar, bran, baking powder, cinnamon, allspice, and salt in a medium bowl, and mix well. Add the grapes, carrots, milk, applesauce, oil, egg, and 1/4 cup of the walnuts. Stir just until combined. Spoon the batter into the prepared muffin cups (they will be very full), and sprinkle with the remaining 1/4 cup walnuts. Bake for 20 to 25 minutes, or until a toothpick inserted in the center comes out clean.

Nutrition Information

- Calories: 196.3
- Fiber: 2.2
- Protein: 4
- Total Carbohydrate: 29.7
- Cholesterol: 15.7
- Total Fat: 7.7
- Saturated Fat: 0.8
- Sodium: 159.7
- Sugar: 11.8

241. Fruit Nut Harvest Muffins

Serving: 12 muffins, 12 serving(s) | Prep: 0S | Ready in:

Ingredients

- 1 cup rolled oats
- 1 cup whole wheat flour
- 1/2 cup oat bran
- 1/2 cup brown sugar, organic
- 2 teaspoons baking powder
- 1 teaspoon baking soda
- 2 cups yogurt
- 1/2 cup butter, melted
- 2 eggs

Direction

- 1. Preheat oven to 400°F Combine oats, whole wheat flour, oat bran, brown sugar, baking powder, and baking soda in a large bowl. Add optional add-ins.
- 2. Whisk together the yogurt and eggs in a small bowl. Add melted butter, whisking to combine. Gently fold the wet ingredients into the dry ones, being careful not to over mix (some lumps are fine).
- 3. Divide batter evenly among 12 muffin cups (I use non-bleached muffin papers to save clean-up time). Bake 20 to 25 minutes, until

muffins are golden and firm to the touch. Allow them to cool for a few minutes, then lift them out of the tin and enjoy.

- Add-Ins (these are how you will make this recipe totally your own, unique, and completely delicious; just use whatever you prefer or have on hand). Choose at least one from each group.
- Fruits: to total one cup.
- 1/2 to 1 cup chopped fresh apple.
- 1/2 to 1 cup chopped fresh pear.
- 1/2 to 1 cup pumpkin puree.
- 1/2 to 1 cup diced banana.
- 1/2 to 1 cup dried cherries or cranberries.
- 1/2 to 1 cup raisins, dark or golden, or currants.
- 1/2 to 1 cup chopped dates.
- Nuts and Seeds: to total 1/2 cup.
- 1/4 to 1/2 cup chopped walnuts, pecans, almonds, or cashews.
- 1/4 to 1/2 cup sunflower seeds, raw or toasted.
- 1/4 to 1/2 cup pumpkin seeds, raw or toasted.
- 1/4 to 1/2 cup flax seeds.
- 1/4 to 1/2 cup sesame or poppy seeds.
- Spices:
- 2 teaspoons grated fresh ginger, or 1 teaspoon ground.
- 1 teaspoon ground cinnamon.
- 1 teaspoon ground allspice.
- 1/2 teaspoon freshly-grated nutmeg.
- Pinch ground cloves.

Nutrition Information

- Calories: 209.4
- Protein: 5.7
- Total Fat: 10.7
- Saturated Fat: 6.1
- Sodium: 254.8
- Fiber: 2.5
- Cholesterol: 60.9
- Sugar: 11
- Total Carbohydrate: 25.4

242. Fruit Upside Down Muffin

Serving: 6 serving(s) | Prep: 10mins | Ready in:

Ingredients

- 3 cups fruit (frozen or fresh)
- 3 cups prepared buttermilk pancake batter
- 1/3 cup brown sugar
- 2 tablespoons butter

Direction

- Preheat oven to 375°F.
- Drain fruit and blot with paper towel to remove excess moisture if using frozen - if using fresh skip this step.
- Spray jumbo sized muffin pan with nonstick cooking spray. Spoon an even amount of butter and brown sugar into the bottom of each muffin pan. Bake for 5 minutes to melt butter and sugar.
- Top with fruit blend and pancake batter. Bake for 12-15 minutes or until golden brown.

Nutrition Information

- Calories: 80
- Total Fat: 3.8
- Sugar: 11.8
- Total Carbohydrate: 11.9
- Protein: 0
- Saturated Fat: 2.4
- Sodium: 32
- Fiber: 0
- Cholesterol: 10.2

243. Gluten Free Apple And Cinnamon Muffins

Serving: 12 serving(s) | Prep: 10mins | Ready in:

Ingredients

- 2 cups of gluten free self-rising flour
- 1 teaspoon gluten free baking powder
- 2 eggs
- 125 g butter, softened
- 2 teaspoons ground cinnamon
- 1 cup caster sugar
- 2 teaspoons vanilla essence
- 1/2 cup milk
- 3 cups of diced apples or 3 cups tinned apples
- for topping 1/2 cup butter
- 1/4 cup raw sugar
- 1/4 cup ground cinnamon

Direction

- Preheat oven at 170-180 c.
- Beat butter and sugar together until light in color and combined well.
- Add one egg at a time and beat until combined.
- Fold through baking powder.
- Add vanilla essence and cinnamon, mix through.
- Add half a cup of flour and a dash of milk each time and fold through until combined.
- Fold through the apples and place into muffin pans baking for 40 mins depending on oven.
- For topping melt butter and mix in sugar and cinnamon in a bowl.
- Dip cooling muffins into mixture and leave to set.
- Enjoy xoxo.

Nutrition Information

- Calories: 272.9
- Sodium: 356.2
- Fiber: 3
- Total Carbohydrate: 43.7
- Cholesterol: 54.7
- Total Fat: 9.9
- Saturated Fat: 5.9
- Sugar: 24.3
- Protein: 3.7

244. Gourmet Scones Add Any Fruit!

Serving: 8-10 scones, 8-10 serving(s) | Prep: 10mins | Ready in:

Ingredients

- 2 cups flour
- 1 tablespoon baking powder
- 1/2 teaspoon salt
- 1/4 cup sugar, but save a little to sprinkle on top
- 6 tablespoons butter, cut semi-soft
- 3/4 cup strawberry, sliced
- 1/2 cup whipping cream
- 1 large egg
- 1 teaspoon lemon juice
- 3 tablespoons cream cheese (optional)

Direction

- Pre-heat oven to 425°F
- Mix dry ingredients together in a mixing bowl.
- Add strawberries, or other fruit of choice.
- In a small bowl, beat egg and add in whipping cream. Mix well. Add lemon juice.
- Add whipping cream mixture into dry ingredients. Stir well, ensuring all flour is incorporated.
- Knead 6-7 times.
- Options: Either put on a baking sheet in spoonfuls, or you can pat the dough out into a large round. Using a knife, cut into triangles.
- Put scones onto an ungreased baking sheet.
- Brush tops with whipping cream and sprinkle on a little sugar.
- Bake for 12-15 minutes. Allow to cool in the pan for a few minutes.
- Enjoy!

Nutrition Information

- Calories: 280.2
- Sodium: 358
- Sugar: 7
- Cholesterol: 69.7
- Saturated Fat: 9.1
- Total Carbohydrate: 32.1
- Protein: 4.5
- Total Fat: 15.1
- Fiber: 1.1

245. Healthy Fruit Muffins

Serving: 12 muffins | Prep: 15mins | Ready in:

Ingredients

- 1 1⁄4 cups all-purpose flour
- 1 1⁄2 teaspoons baking soda
- 1 teaspoon cinnamon
- 1⁄2 teaspoon salt
- 1 (15 ounce) can peaches in light syrup, undrained
- 1⁄2 cup brown sugar, packed
- 1⁄2 cup fat free egg substitute or 2 eggs
- 3 tablespoons canola oil (or other vege oil)
- 4 cups bran flakes
- 1⁄2 cup blueberries (fresh/frozen)

Direction

- Preheat oven to 375F.
- Spray a 12-muffin tin with non-stick spray and set aside, or use muffin liners.
- Combine flour, baking soda, cinnamon and salt in a medium bowl.
- Set aside.
- Drain peaches and reserve 1/3 cup of syrup.
- Puree peaches and reserved syrup in a blender, until smooth.
- Whisk the peach puree, sugar, egg substitute and oil.
- Add Bran Flakes and mix well.
- Add flour mixture and stir until dry ingredients are just moistened.
- DO NOT OVERMIX!
- Gently fold in blueberries.
- Divide batter among the muffin cups (about 2/3 full).
- Bake for 20 mins, or until toothpick test shows doneness.
- Serve warm.

Nutrition Information

- Calories: 182.1
- Protein: 3.9
- Saturated Fat: 0.3
- Fiber: 3.3
- Sugar: 16.6
- Total Carbohydrate: 35.5
- Total Fat: 3.9
- Sodium: 371.6
- Cholesterol: 0

246. Holiday Fruit And Nut Gems

Serving: 3 dozen cookies | Prep: 0S | Ready in:

Ingredients

- 12 ounces red and green glazed cherries, chopped
- 4 slices candied pineapple, chopped
- 1 cup pecans, chopped
- 1 cup walnuts, chopped
- 1 cup brazil nut, chopped
- 1⁄2 cup flour
- 3 egg whites
- 1⁄2 teaspoon salt
- 1⁄2 cup sugar
- 1 teaspoon vanilla

Direction

- In a bowl, combine cherries, pineapple and nuts. Add flour and mix well.
- In another bowl, beat egg whites and salt together until foamy. Gradually add sugar,

beating until mixture is glossy and form stiff peaks. Fold in fruit mixture. Add vanilla.

- Drop by teaspoon on greased cookie sheet. Bake at 350F for 15 minutes or until golden brown. Cool for a few minutes on cookie sheet, then transfer to wire rack to finish cooling.

Nutrition Information

- Calories: 1402.3
- Saturated Fat: 11.7
- Sugar: 128.8
- Total Carbohydrate: 159.6
- Cholesterol: 0
- Total Fat: 82.9
- Sodium: 556.2
- Fiber: 12
- Protein: 22.1

247. Incredible Oat Bran Muffins, Plain, Blueberry Or Banana

Serving: 12 muffins, 12 serving(s) | Prep: 10mins | Ready in:

Ingredients

- 2 cups oat bran hot cereal, uncooked (I use Quaker)
- 1/4 cup firmly packed brown sugar
- 2 teaspoons baking powder
- 1/2 teaspoon salt
- 1 cup milk
- 1 egg
- 1/4 cup honey (I haven't tried molasses yet) or 1/4 cup molasses (I haven't tried molasses yet)
- 2 tablespoons vegetable oil

Direction

- *Blueberry or banana variations are at bottom.
- Pre-heat oven to 425 degrees F. Line 12 medium muffin cups with paper baking cups.
- Combine dry ingredients. Add milk, egg, honey, and oil; mix just until ingredients are moistened.
- Fill muffin cups 3/4 full. Bake 14-17 minutes or until golden brown.
- *NOTE: You can stir in 1/2 cup frozen blueberries or 1 medium ripe mashed banana for a fruity variation.
- These are also great the next day cold if you seal them in a baggy or stick them in a container to keep them fresh.

Nutrition Information

- Calories: 126.8
- Cholesterol: 18.4
- Saturated Fat: 1.1
- Sodium: 175.5
- Fiber: 1.9
- Sugar: 10.4
- Total Carbohydrate: 19.9
- Protein: 3.5
- Total Fat: 4.5

248. Jimmy Griffin's Perfect Raspberry And Raisin Irish Scone

Serving: 12 serving(s) | Prep: 1hours | Ready in:

Ingredients

- Scones
- 2 3/4 cups all-purpose flour (use a flour that's low in gluten, like White Lily flour (but not cake flour!)
- 2 teaspoons baking powder
- 1/2 teaspoon salt
- 1 cup buttermilk
- 1/2 cup olive oil
- 1/2 cup sugar

- 1 egg
- 1/2 cup raisins
- 1/2 cup frozen raspberries (without syrup)
- Glaze
- 2 eggs

Direction

- Preheat oven to 500. (Yes, 500 F.) Place rack in the middle of the oven.
- Spray a cookie sheet with cooking spray, or cut a piece of parchment paper to fit it.
- Whisk the two eggs (for the glaze) together in a small bowl and set aside.
- Combine flour with baking powder and salt. Sift five times. (Yes, that may sound excessive, but it doesn't take long and it makes for a lighter scone.) Set aside.
- Whisk together the buttermilk, olive oil, sugar, and egg.
- Moving very quickly (have all your ingredients ready to go), mix liquid ingredients into flour. This will immediately start to activate the baking powder, so don't loiter! Make a well in the middle of the sifted flour, pour in the milk/oil mixture, and sprinkle the raisins on top. Blend together with a wooden spoon, as lightly as you can.
- Turn dough out onto a large sheet of waxed paper and cover with another sheet of waxed paper. Pat it into a rough rectangle about one inch high.
- Remove the top sheet of waxed paper, scatter the frozen raspberries over half the rectangle, and fold the other half of the rectangle over the raspberries.
- Cover again with waxed paper and pat the rectangle until it is an even 1.5" high.
- Remove the top sheet of waxed paper and cut the dough into rounds with a 3" round cookie cutter.
- Transfer biscuits on to the cookie sheet with a spatula dipped in flour, spacing them about 2" apart.
- Glaze the tops with the beaten egg mixture. Refrigerate scones for 15 minutes, then glaze the scones again.
- Turn the oven temperature down to 425°F. Bake for 18 minutes. Don't bake any longer, even if you're tempted to!
- Cool on baking sheet for 10 minutes, then remove to a cooling rack to finish cooling.
- Scones will stay moist for about two days. They freeze well. They're best served warm, with good butter and jam.

Nutrition Information

- Calories: 271.8
- Protein: 5.5
- Total Fat: 10.8
- Saturated Fat: 1.8
- Fiber: 1.5
- Cholesterol: 53.7
- Sodium: 197.9
- Sugar: 15.3
- Total Carbohydrate: 39

249. Kaak Lebi Hilw (Orange And Cumin Biscuits)

Serving: 4-6 serving(s) | Prep: 15mins | Ready in:

Ingredients

- 2 eggs
- 200 g sugar
- 240 ml oil
- 240 ml orange juice
- 2 teaspoons baking powder
- 700 g flour
- 2 tablespoons roast and ground sesame seeds (tahini)
- 1/2 teaspoon crushed fennel seed (kammon kaak or sweet cumin)
- caster sugar, to decorate

Direction

- Pre-heat oven to 180°C.
- Cream together the sugar and eggs.

- Whisk in the oil, orange juice and tahini.
- Add the flour and baking powder and bring together. You should have a stiff dough.
- Turn the mixture onto a lightly-floured work surface and roll out to about 6mm thickness.
- Cut into ka'ak shapes (typically crescents), transfer to a lightly-greased baking tray.
- Bake for 12-15 minutes, or until a light golden brown. Remove from the oven, sprinkle a little caster sugar over the top then transfer to a wire rack to cool completely.

Nutrition Information

- Calories: 1414
- Total Fat: 62.1
- Saturated Fat: 8.6
- Sodium: 221.4
- Total Carbohydrate: 192
- Cholesterol: 105.8
- Fiber: 5.5
- Sugar: 56
- Protein: 22.5

250. Kittencal's Muffin Shop Jumbo Blueberry Or Strawberry Muffins

Serving: 12-15 jumbo muffins | Prep: 15mins | Ready in:

Ingredients

- 4 1/4 cups all-purpose flour
- 1 1/2 cups sugar
- 3/4 cup butter, softened
- 1 tablespoon baking powder
- 1 teaspoon salt
- 1/2 teaspoon baking soda
- 1 1/2 teaspoons cinnamon (or to taste)
- 1 tablespoon grated lemon zest
- 1 1/2 cups buttermilk (do not substitute milk in place of the buttermilk)
- 2 large eggs
- 1 tablespoon vanilla or 2 teaspoons almond extract
- 2 cups blueberries (fresh or frozen unthawed OR 1-1/2 to 2 cups chopped fresh firm strawberries and 1-2 teaspoons strawb)

Direction

- Set oven to 375 degrees F.
- Set oven rack to second-bottom position.
- Generously grease 12 jumbo muffin tins, then cut out circles of parchment paper (or waxed paper) to fit into the bottom of each muffin tin.
- In a large mixing bowl using an electric mixer blend the flour with sugar, butter and salt until mixture resembles a fine meal (reserve 1/2 cup of the mixture and transfer to a small bowl; set aside to sprinkle on top of muffins).
- In a small bowl mix together baking powder, baking soda, cinnamon and lemon zest to the remaining flour mixture; mix until combined.
- In a bowl whisk together buttermilk with eggs and vanilla to blend; add to the creamed mixture; gently mix just until combined (do not over mix!).
- Carefully fold in the blueberries or chopped strawberries.
- Divide the mixture between the muffin tins.
- Sprinkle the reserved streusel over tops of muffins.
- Bake for about 25-30 minutes, or until muffins test done (if using frozen berries baking time will increase slightly).
- Cool for about 5 minutes in tins then carefully lift out to a rack.

Nutrition Information

- Calories: 402.6
- Saturated Fat: 7.8
- Sodium: 483.8
- Fiber: 2
- Cholesterol: 62.7
- Protein: 7
- Total Fat: 13.1
- Sugar: 29.2

- Total Carbohydrate: 64.7

251. Lemon And Chia Seed Muffins

Serving: 12 muffins, 12 serving(s) | Prep: 10mins | Ready in:

Ingredients

- 2 cups flour
- 3 tablespoons chia seeds
- 1 teaspoon baking powder
- 1/4 teaspoon baking soda
- 1/2 teaspoon salt
- 8 tablespoons butter, softened
- 1 cup sugar (any kind)
- 2 eggs
- 1 lemon, zest of
- 1 teaspoon vanilla
- 1 cup greek vanilla yogurt (non fat)
- For glaze
- 1/2 cup powdered sugar
- 1 -2 tablespoon fresh lemon juice

Direction

- Preheat oven to 350 degrees. Prepare 12 cup muffin tin with non-stock spray or liners.
- In a small bowl combine flour, chia seeds, baking powder, baking soda and salt. Set aside. In an electric mixer, cream butter and sugar together until light and fluffy, about 2 minutes. Beat in eggs, one at a time, mixing well each addition. Mix in lemon zest and vanilla. Using a spatula mix in the flour and yogurt until just combined. Fill muffin tins about 2/3 of the way full. Bake for 18-20 minutes, until a tester comes out clean. Allow the muffins to cool in the pan for a few minutes, before removing to a wire rack.

Nutrition Information

- Calories: 253.5
- Total Fat: 9.3
- Sodium: 242.9
- Fiber: 0.6
- Sugar: 22.6
- Protein: 4
- Saturated Fat: 5.6
- Total Carbohydrate: 38.8
- Cholesterol: 54

252. Low Fat Fruit Muffins

Serving: 12 serving(s) | Prep: 10mins | Ready in:

Ingredients

- 1 cup whole wheat flour
- 1 cup all-purpose flour
- 2 teaspoons baking powder
- 1/2 teaspoon baking soda
- 1 egg
- 4 tablespoons vegetable oil
- 1 cup mixed fruit
- 2/3 cup buttermilk
- 1/2 cup unsweetened fruit juice

Direction

- Sift together dry ingredients.
- Beat wet ingredients together until blended.
- Add to dry ingredients.
- Stir just enough to moisten flour.
- Fill greased muffin tins about 2/3 full.
- Bake at 400F for 20 minutes, or until done.

Nutrition Information

- Calories: 144.3
- Total Fat: 5.4
- Saturated Fat: 0.8
- Total Carbohydrate: 21.1
- Cholesterol: 18.2
- Sodium: 134.4
- Fiber: 1.9

- Sugar: 0.8
- Protein: 3.7

253. Low Fat Fruit And Nut Banana Bread

Serving: 1 loaf, 8-13 serving(s) | Prep: 45mins | Ready in:

Ingredients

- 1/3 cup warmed unsweetened applesauce
- 2 large cage free egg whites (well beaten)
- 1 cup Splenda granular, Splenda is a calorie free ingredient extracted from sugar that is also aspertayme free, do not use a
- 2 tablespoons Smart Balance light butter spread, softened but not melted
- 5 super ripe bananas, if you wrap them in a brown paper bag and put away in a shelf they will ripen faster
- 1 1/2 teaspoons ground cinnamon
- 3/4 teaspoon allspice
- 1 tablespoon lemon juice, orange juice works well too
- 1 tablespoon fruit (the white part under the peal)
- 1/2 teaspoon maple extract
- 1 1/2 teaspoons baking soda
- 2 teaspoons baking powder
- 1 1/4 cups whole wheat flour
- 1/3 cup all-purpose flour
- 1/3 cup pecans (or nuts of your choice)
- 1/2 cup fruit (I used the already dried ones and they worked well. Blueberries and strawberries usually work well t)

Direction

- Tools;
- You will need 3 bowls. 1 small, 1 medium, 1 large.
- You'll need a wisk, an electric beater, a large wooden mixing spoon, a fork, a cutting knife, aluminum foil and wide surface space.
- 1. Make sure oven rack is centered.
- Preheat the oven to 400 degrees F. Pam spray a 9x5x3 loaf pan and one side of the aluminum foil. Poke holes into the center or the foil.
- 2. Smash the bananas with the fork, in the medium bowl [it is ok for bananas to have small lumps]. Then add the spices, maple, and the fruit pith [finely chopped].
- 3. Sift flower in a small bowl. Then use the wisk to stir in the fruits and nuts.-this prevents them from sinking.
- 4. In the large bowl cream the Smartbutter with the electric beater adding in the Splenda a little at a time until fluffy.
- 5. Add the egg whites into the mixture one at a time, beating well after each addition.
- 6. Add the applesauce and then the lemon juice into the creamed mixture, using the electric beater.
- 7. With the fork add the banana mix into the large mix until combined.
- 8. Mix baking powders into the dry ingredients with the wisk and then add them into the large mix. Mix them slowly with large wooden spoon JUST UNTILL FLOWER DISAPEARS. Over mixing is the worst that can happen. Also don't wait too long to put it in the oven.
- 9. Pour the mix into the pan using the wooden spoon. Cover the loaf pan with the aluminum, but make it like a large arch on the top. Then quickly put it in the oven closing it as soon as possible.
- 10. After about 10 minutes lower temperature to 325 and leave it there for 50 min. I like to use the alarm on my phone or you can use a kitchen timer to make sure the times are exact.
- 11. When time is up, check with a rod and see if it comes out clean. If it does, take in out. If it doesn't then just leave it there for another few minutes and then take it out and let it set for 15 minute in the loaf pan. Then take it out onto the serving dish and let it set till it completely cools off, about 8 minutes.
- 12. I sliced it straight across and got about 8 large servings but you can also cut it in half long ways and then cut across that to get smaller slices. It serves well with anything.

Many like it with honey, but it can go with any meal.

Nutrition Information

- Calories: 210.8
- Saturated Fat: 0.8
- Sugar: 9.5
- Total Fat: 5.1
- Sodium: 364.6
- Fiber: 3.4
- Total Carbohydrate: 38.6
- Cholesterol: 0
- Protein: 4.7

254. Mimi's Raspberry And Lemon Muffins With Streusel Topping

Serving: 12 muffins | Prep: 10mins | Ready in:

Ingredients

- 1/2 cup low-fat vanilla yogurt
- 3 tablespoons oil
- 1 tablespoon fresh lemon juice
- 2 egg whites
- 1 1/2 cups flour
- 3/4 cup sugar
- 2 teaspoons baking powder
- 1 teaspoon grated lemon peel
- 1/4 teaspoon salt
- 1 cup frozen raspberries (not in syrup)
- 1/4 cup sugar
- 2 tablespoons flour
- 1 tablespoon butter

Direction

- In a small bowl combine yogurt, oil, lemon juice, and egg whites; blend well.
- In a medium bowl combine the 1 1/2 cups flour, 3/4 cup of sugar, baking powder, lemon peel, and salt; mix well.
- Stir in frozen raspberries.
- Add yogurt mixture to flour mixture stirring just until dry ingredients are moistened--one direction only for muffins.
- Line muffin tins with cupcake papers (or just spray the tins and use them as is).
- Spoon batter evenly into the papers.
- In a small bowl make the streusel topping using the 1/4 cup sugar, 2 tablespoons flour, and 1 tablespoon butter, using a fork till crumbly.
- Sprinkle evenly over batter in muffins tins before baking.
- Bake at 400 degrees for 16-20 minutes or until muffins are golden brown.
- Immediately remove from pan and serve warm.

Nutrition Information

- Calories: 198.4
- Total Fat: 4.7
- Saturated Fat: 1.2
- Sugar: 22.7
- Cholesterol: 3
- Protein: 3
- Sodium: 134
- Fiber: 1.4
- Total Carbohydrate: 36.8

255. Orange, Banana And Oat Bran Breakfast Muffins

Serving: 12 muffins | Prep: 15mins | Ready in:

Ingredients

- melted butter, to grease
- 150 g self-raising flour (1 cup)
- 80 g wholemeal self-rising flour (1/2 cup)
- 1/2 teaspoon ground allspice
- 40 g oat bran (1/3 cup)
- 115 g brown sugar (1/2 cup, firmly packed)

- 2 teaspoons finely grated orange rind
- 125 ml fresh orange juice (1/2 cup)
- 60 ml light olive oil (1/4 cup)
- 2 eggs, lightly whisked
- 1 cup mashed ripe banana (about 2 bananas)
- icing sugar, to dust
- 140 g low-fat ricotta, to serve

Direction

- Preheat oven to 180°C Brush 12 medium (80ml/1/3-cup) non-stick muffin pans with the melted butter to lightly grease.
- Sift the flours and allspice into a medium bowl. Return the husks to the bowl. Add the oat bran and sugar, and mix well.
- Whisk the orange rind, orange juice, oil and eggs together in a large jug until well combined. Add to the flour mixture with the banana and use a wooden spoon to mix until just combined.
- Spoon mixture evenly into muffin pans. Bake in preheated oven for 24 minutes or until a skewer inserted into center of muffins comes out clean.
- Set aside for 5 minutes before turning onto a wire rack to cool slightly. Serve warm or at room temperature, dusted lightly with icing sugar and accompanied by ricotta.

Nutrition Information

- Calories: 157.7
- Sodium: 174.7
- Fiber: 1.2
- Total Carbohydrate: 25
- Cholesterol: 35.2
- Protein: 3.1
- Saturated Fat: 1
- Total Fat: 5.8
- Sugar: 11.8

256. Overnight Banana Sticky Buns With Pecans

Serving: 12 serving(s) | Prep: 3hours | Ready in:

Ingredients

- For the dough
- 1 lb unbleached all-purpose flour, more as needed
- 1 1⁄4 ounces package fast rising yeast (instant)
- 1⁄2 cup very warm milk (about 125Â F) or 1⁄2 cup water (about 125Â F)
- 3⁄4 cup mashed very ripe banana (about 1 large)
- 1 ounce unsalted butter, melted, more for the bowl
- 2 tablespoons granulated sugar
- 1 large egg, lightly beaten
- 1 1⁄4 teaspoons table salt
- For the filling
- 1 1⁄2 ounces unsalted butter, softened
- 1⁄2 cup finely chopped toasted pecans
- 1⁄3 cup packed light brown sugar
- 1 3⁄4 teaspoons ground cinnamon
- For the caramel-pecan sauce
- 1 ounce cold unsalted butter, more softened for the pan
- 1 1⁄2 cups granulated sugar
- 1 large ripe banana, coarsely chopped into 1/2- to 1-inch pieces
- 1⁄2 cup heavy cream
- 1 teaspoon pure vanilla extract
- generous pinch table salt
- 1 cup pecan halves

Direction

- Make the dough:
- In a medium bowl, combine 4-1/2 oz. (1 cup) of the flour with the yeast. Stir in the warm milk or water until combined. Cover the bowl and let sit in a warm spot in the kitchen for 30 minutes. Stir the banana, melted butter, sugar, egg, and salt into the yeast mixture until well combined. Stir in all but 1 oz. (1/4 cup) of the remaining flour to make a stiff, shaggy dough.

Turn the dough out onto a lightly floured surface.

- Knead, folding the dough over onto itself. If the dough sticks, use a dough scraper to pick up the sticky bits and sprinkle a small amount of the remaining flour onto the surface. Continue to knead until the dough becomes smooth and easy to handle, 5 to 10 minutes. Put the dough in a lightly buttered medium bowl, cover with plastic wrap, and let rise in a warm place until doubled, 40 to 50 minutes.
- Fill the rolls:
- Turn the dough out onto a lightly floured surface and shape into a rectangle. Roll out into a 16 x 11-inch rectangle. With an offset spatula, spread the softened butter evenly over the dough to within 1/8 inch of the edge. Combine the chopped pecans, brown sugar, and cinnamon in a small bowl; sprinkle the mixture evenly over the butter.
- Roll up the dough lengthwise, starting from a long edge, and pinch the seam to seal. Turn the log so that it's seam side down. Trim off and discard 1/2 inch from each end; then cut the log into twelve 1-1/4-inch pieces. Cover with plastic wrap.
- Make the caramel-pecan sauce:
- Generously butter a 12-cup standard muffin pan.
- In a medium saucepan over medium-high heat, combine the sugar and 1/4 cup warm water and stir until the sugar dissolves, 2 to 3 minutes. Bring the syrup to a boil and cook, without stirring, until it begins to caramelize. Gently swirl the pan to help the syrup brown evenly. Once the syrup has turned an amber color, remove the pan from the heat and carefully stir in the banana and cold butter. Stir in the heavy cream, returning the pan to low heat if the mixture doesn't smooth out immediately. Add the vanilla and salt and stir until smooth. Strain the sauce, discarding the banana. Let the caramel cool until just warm, about 15 minutes. Drizzle about 1-1/2 Tbs. of caramel into each muffin cup, reserving the extra sauce at room temperature. Sprinkle the pecans evenly among the cups.
- Place the dough slices over the sauce and nuts, cut sides down. Cover with plastic wrap and refrigerate overnight.
- Bake the sticky buns:
- Remove the pan from the refrigerator and let the dough rise in a warm spot until doubled, 1 to 1-1/2 hours.
- Position racks in the center and lower third of the oven and heat the oven to 350°F Put the muffin pan on the center rack and set a foil-lined baking sheet on the rack below to catch any overflowing syrup. Bake until the tops and edges of the buns are browned, 20 to 22 minutes.
- Immediately invert the pan onto a rimmed baking sheet, replace any pecans that fell off, and let cool for 10 minutes. Reheat the reserved caramel sauce and serve the buns drizzled with the sauce.

Nutrition Information

- Calories: 462.6
- Total Fat: 20.9
- Saturated Fat: 7.8
- Fiber: 3.6
- Sugar: 36.2
- Total Carbohydrate: 65
- Protein: 6.9
- Sodium: 262.2
- Cholesterol: 48.3

257. Papaya Or Mango Oat Muffins

Serving: 18 serving(s) | Prep: 10mins | Ready in:

Ingredients

- 1/4 cup raisins
- 1/4 cup rum (to soak raisins) or 1/4 cup water, hot (to soak raisins)
- 1 cup Bisquick or 1 cup krusteaz baking mix

- 1 cup oatmeal (or combination) or 1 cup flour (or combination) or 1 cup whole wheat flour (or combination)
- 1 teaspoon baking soda
- 1 teaspoon baking powder
- 1 1/2 teaspoons cinnamon
- 1/2 teaspoon clove
- 3/4 teaspoon salt
- 1/4 cup vegetable oil
- 1/2 cup milk
- 1/3 cup honey or 1/3 cup light Karo syrup
- 2 cups papayas or 2 cups mangoes, chopped
- 1/2 cup nuts, chopped

Direction

- Preheat oven to 350°F.
- Lightly grease or spray muffin cups or line with papers.
- Set raisins in a bowl of hot rum to soak.
- In a large bowl, mix dry ingredients.
- Make a well, and add oil, milk, and honey.
- Mix just until combined and moistened (Do Not overmix).
- Stir in fruit, nuts, and raisins (drain raisins before adding).
- Drop the batter into muffin tins.
- Bake for 25-30 minutes, testing with toothpick to see if they're done.

Nutrition Information

- Calories: 138.7
- Total Carbohydrate: 17.1
- Cholesterol: 1.1
- Protein: 2.3
- Saturated Fat: 1.1
- Fiber: 1.4
- Sugar: 8.3
- Total Fat: 6.6
- Sodium: 302.2

258. Passion Fruit Raspberry Muffins

Serving: 10 muffins, 10 serving(s) | Prep: 10mins | Ready in:

Ingredients

- 2 cups self raising flour
- 2 egg whites
- 1/2 cup sugar
- 1/2 cup applesauce (in jar)
- 3/4 teaspoon bicarbonate of soda
- 1/4 cup passion fruit pulp
- 3/4 cup frozen raspberries
- 2 tablespoons skim milk

Direction

- Preheat oven 200c.
- Coat a 12 cup muffin tray with cooking spray.
- Beat egg whites and sugar for 1 min in a medium size mixing bowl.
- Stir bicarb soda into the apple sauce (it will froth) then add to bowl.
- Stir in milk.
- Gently fold flour into the mixture in one go, DO NOT BEAT as this will make the muffins tough.
- Carefully fold in passion fruit pulp and raspberries.
- Spoon mixture into prepared muffin tin, dividing into 10 cups.
- Bake 15-20 mins or until firm to touch in centre.
- Allow muffins to sit in the pan for 5 mins before turning onto a wire rack to cool.

Nutrition Information

- Calories: 169.1
- Total Fat: 0.4
- Sodium: 113
- Sugar: 14.8
- Total Carbohydrate: 38.1
- Saturated Fat: 0.1
- Fiber: 2.3

- Cholesterol: 0.1
- Protein: 3.7

259. Peach And Brown Sugar Muffins

Serving: 20 muffins, 20 serving(s) | Prep: 15mins | Ready in:

Ingredients

- 4 cups flour
- 2/3 cup packed brown sugar
- 2 tablespoons baking powder
- 1 teaspoon salt
- 1/2 teaspoon baking soda
- 1/4 teaspoon allspice
- 2 eggs
- 2 cups sour cream
- 1/2 cup vegetable oil
- 1 cup fresh peach, chopped

Direction

- Stir together flour, sugar, baking powder, salt, baking soda, allspice.
- Make a well in center.
- Combine eggs, sour cream and oil.
- Stir in peaches.
- Add to flour mixture. Stir until moistened. Batter will be lumpy.
- Fill muffin cups 2/3 full.
- Bake at 400 for 20-25 minutes.

Nutrition Information

- Calories: 227.5
- Cholesterol: 31.3
- Saturated Fat: 3.9
- Sodium: 279.2
- Fiber: 0.8
- Total Carbohydrate: 28.4
- Protein: 4
- Total Fat: 11
- Sugar: 7.9

260. Peach And Tomato Muffins

Serving: 6 large muffins | Prep: 30mins | Ready in:

Ingredients

- 3 1/2 cups self-rising flour
- 1 teaspoon baking powder
- 1 pinch salt
- 4 tablespoons superfine sugar
- 1/3 cup sweet butter, melted
- 1 egg, beaten
- 1 1/3 cups buttermilk
- 2 ripe peaches, sliced
- 3 tablespoons chopped sun-dried tomatoes

Direction

- Preheat oven to 400°; grease a large 6-cup muffin pan.
- In a mixing bowl, mix the flour, baking powder, salt, and sugar.
- In a large bowl, beat the butter, egg, and buttermilk with an electric mixer.
- Add the flour to the buttermilk mixture, stirring until nearly combined.
- Stir in the peaches and tomatoes.
- Spoon the batter into the prepared pan; bake 18-20 minutes or until test done.
- Remove pan from oven and cool for 5 minutes; remove muffins from pan and cool on a rack.
- **Peach, Tomato, and Lime Muffins: add 1 tablespoon freshly grated lime zest to buttermilk mixture; proceed as directed.
- **Peach, Tomato, and Basil Muffins: add 2 tablespoons chopped fresh basil to the buttermilk mixture; proceed as directed.
- **Peach, Tomato, and Rosemary Muffins: add 1 teaspoon chopped fresh rosemary to the buttermilk mixture; proceed as directed.

Nutrition Information

- Calories: 432.4
- Total Fat: 12.4
- Saturated Fat: 7.2
- Total Carbohydrate: 69.4
- Sodium: 1117.3
- Fiber: 2.7
- Sugar: 14.6
- Cholesterol: 64.5
- Protein: 10.7

261. Pear And Ginger Muffins

Serving: 15 muffins | Prep: 20mins | Ready in:

Ingredients

- 4 ounces dried pear halves
- 1 pear, ripe (Bosc, Bartlett, Anjou)
- 2 cups all-purpose flour
- 2 teaspoons baking powder
- 1/2 teaspoon baking soda
- 1/2 teaspoon salt
- 1/2 teaspoon ground nutmeg
- 2 eggs
- 2/3 cup sugar
- 1/2 cup milk
- 1 teaspoon vanilla extract
- 1/3 cup unsalted butter
- 1/2 cup ginger in syrup or 1/2 cup candied ginger, very finely chopped

Direction

- Preheat oven to 400 F and grease muffin tin.
- Put the dried pears in a small bowl and pour over some boiling water. Let stand for 15 minutes.
- Drain pears and dry with a paper towel. Cut into small pieces (about 1/2 inch).
- Peel and core the fresh pear, and chop into similar pieces.
- In a new bowl, mix dry ingredients.
- In another bowl, whisk together rest of the ingredients (including the pears).
- Mix dry and wet ingredients, stir until mixed but don't overdo it. The batter will be lumpy.
- Fill the tins about 2/3 full. Bake about 20 minutes.
- Cool 5 minutes in the tin, then on a wire rack.

Nutrition Information

- Calories: 173.9
- Sodium: 182.7
- Total Carbohydrate: 29.2
- Cholesterol: 40.2
- Total Fat: 5.3
- Saturated Fat: 3
- Fiber: 1.4
- Sugar: 14.8
- Protein: 3.1

262. Pear And Pumpkin Muffins

Serving: 18 muffins | Prep: 30mins | Ready in:

Ingredients

- 2 1/2 cups all-purpose flour
- 2 1/2 teaspoons pumpkin pie spice
- 1 teaspoon baking soda
- 1 teaspoon salt
- 1 cup sugar
- 2 eggs
- 1 cup pumpkin puree (NOT pie filling)
- 1/2 cup vegetable oil
- 2 cups chopped pears
- 1/3 cup packed light brown sugar

Direction

- Preheat oven to 350°; grease 18 regular muffin cups (need two pans).
- In a large bowl, whisk together the flour, pumpkin pie spice, baking soda, and salt.

- In a medium bowl, whisk together the sugar, eggs, pumpkin and oil until well blended.
- Stir in pears until combined.
- Add the egg mixture to the flour mixture and stir until just blended.
- Divide batter equally among prepared muffin cups.
- Sprinkle with brown sugar.
- Bake for 30-35 minutes or until tops are golden and a pick comes out clean.
- Let cool in pans on a wire rack for 5 minutes, then transfer to the rack to cool.

Nutrition Information

- Calories: 196
- Total Fat: 6.8
- Sodium: 209
- Fiber: 1.1
- Sugar: 17
- Total Carbohydrate: 31.7
- Cholesterol: 20.7
- Saturated Fat: 1
- Protein: 2.6

263. Pineapple Coconut Muffins

Serving: 24 muffins, 24 serving(s) | Prep: 10mins | Ready in:

Ingredients

- 1/2 cup butter
- 1 1/4 cups sugar
- 2 eggs
- 1/2 teaspoon vanilla
- 1/2 teaspoon salt
- 2 1/2 teaspoons baking powder
- 1/2 cup shredded unsweetened coconut
- 2 cups flour
- 1 (20 ounce) can pineapple

Direction

- Preheat oven to 350F, line 2 muffin pans with paper cups.
- In a large bowl, beat butter and sugar until pale and fluffy; add eggs and vanilla, and beat well.
- Combine salt, baking powder, coconut, and flour.
- Drain and chop pineapple, reserving juice (about 7 ounces).
- Add the flour mixture to the butter mixture alternately with the reserved juice.
- Fold in pineapple, and fill muffin cups 2/3 full.
- Bake for 20-25 minutes.
- Note: Sprinkle sugar on top of muffins for crunchy muffin tops.

Nutrition Information

- Calories: 161.6
- Saturated Fat: 5.3
- Cholesterol: 25.7
- Protein: 2.1
- Total Fat: 7.4
- Sodium: 128.3
- Fiber: 1.4
- Sugar: 13.1
- Total Carbohydrate: 22.7

264. Pineapple And Sour Cream Muffins

Serving: 9 muffins, 8-9 serving(s) | Prep: 10mins | Ready in:

Ingredients

- 1/4 cup sugar
- 1 egg
- 1/4 cup butter
- 1 cup sour cream
- 1 1/2 cups flour
- 1 teaspoon baking powder
- 1/2 teaspoon baking soda

- 1/2 teaspoon salt
- 1 cup well drained crushed pineapple

Direction

- Measure sugar, egg, butter and sour cream into bowl and beat.
- Stir flour, baking powder, baking soda and salt together.
- Add cream mixture to dry ingredients and stir until moist.
- Stir in pineapple to mix.
- Fill greased muffin trays and bake 375F degrees for 15-20 minutes.

Nutrition Information

- Calories: 243.8
- Saturated Fat: 7.2
- Sodium: 352.8
- Total Carbohydrate: 30
- Cholesterol: 53.5
- Total Fat: 12.3
- Fiber: 0.9
- Sugar: 11.8
- Protein: 4

265. Pumpkin Fruit Bread/muffins

Serving: 12 serving(s) | Prep: 10mins | Ready in:

Ingredients

- 1 cup flour
- 1 1/2 cups bran flakes (or decrease amount and add oats)
- 1/2 cup brown sugar
- 1 1/2 cups pumpkin puree
- 1/2 teaspoon salt
- 1 teaspoon baking soda
- 2 eggs
- 2 tablespoons sour cream
- 1 tablespoon molasses
- 1/2 teaspoon ground cinnamon
- 1/4 teaspoon ground nutmeg or 1/4 teaspoon ground mace
- 1/8 teaspoon ground cloves
- 1/8 teaspoon ground ginger
- 1/4 cup nuts
- 1/2 cup dried fruits
- 1/4 cup fresh cranberries
- 1/4 cup semisweet chocolate chunk (optional)

Direction

- Preheat oven to 350 and spray muffin pan.
- Combine flour, baking soda, salt, spices, bran and/or oats, and mix.
- Beat eggs slightly and add sugar until dissolved.
- Stir pumpkin into egg mixture, along with dried fruit, nuts, and chocolate.
- Combine wet and dry ingredients.
- Fold in fresh cranberries (if using).
- Divide batter into muffin pan and bake for 20 to 30 minutes until done.
- Allow to cool.
- Eat.
- Repeat steps 1-9.
- Note: You can also use small loaf pans or even an 8 x 8 pan and cut into squares.

Nutrition Information

- Calories: 131.5
- Sodium: 272.8
- Sugar: 11.1
- Total Carbohydrate: 24.1
- Protein: 3.3
- Total Fat: 3
- Cholesterol: 36.1
- Saturated Fat: 0.8
- Fiber: 1.6

266. Pumpkin Fruit And Nut Muffins

Serving: 9 serving(s) | Prep: 20mins | Ready in:

Ingredients

- 1/3 cup raisins
- 10 dried apricot halves, chopped fine
- 1/3 cup water
- 1 cup whole wheat pastry flour
- 1/2 cup old fashioned oats
- 1/3 cup granulated sugar
- 2 teaspoons baking powder
- 1/2 teaspoon salt
- 1/2 teaspoon nutmeg
- 1/2 teaspoon cinnamon
- 3 tablespoons powdered milk
- 1/2 cup unsweetened applesauce
- 1/2 cup pumpkin puree
- 1 egg, lightly beaten
- 1/3 cup cashews, roasted without salt and coarsely chopped
- 1/4 cup apricot preserves

Direction

- Preheat oven to 400 degrees
- Prepare a non-stick muffin tin by spraying with non-stick cooking spray of if you prefer, use paper muffin liners
- In a small microwavable bowl, place the raisins, chopped apricot halves and 1/3 cup water
- Microwave for 45 seconds or until hot
- Cover the bowl and allow fruit to plump while mixing the remaining ingredients
- In a large bowl, mix together the flour, oats, sugar, nutmeg, cinnamon, powdered milk, baking powder and salt
- Add the applesauce, pumpkin puree and egg, mixing until thoroughly combined
- Drain any water from fruit that has not been absorbed and add fruit to muffin batter along with chopped cashews; stir to blend
- Divide batter into 9 muffin cups and bake in preheated oven for 15 to 20 minutes or until toothpick inserted off center comes out clean
- Immediately remove muffins from tin and spread each with a small amount of apricot preserves

Nutrition Information

- Calories: 197.6
- Total Fat: 4.3
- Saturated Fat: 1.2
- Sodium: 265.9
- Fiber: 3
- Sugar: 17.5
- Total Carbohydrate: 37.6
- Cholesterol: 26.1
- Protein: 5.2

267. Quick And Easy English Date And Nut Bread

Serving: 4 1 lb loaves | Prep: 20mins | Ready in:

Ingredients

- 2 cups hot water
- 1 1/4 cups cold milk
- 1 tablespoon granulated yeast
- 1 tablespoon kosher salt (recommend Morton's)
- 1/4 cup malt drink powder
- 1 cup fresh dates, stoned chopped mixed with 1 tbsp flour
- 1 cup pecans or 1 cup walnuts, chopped
- 1 cup whole wheat flour
- 5 cups unbleached all-purpose flour
- flour or parchment paper, for the pizza peel

Direction

- In a 5 or 6 quart bowl or lidded food storage container, mix the water and the milk together and then add the yeast, salt and malt powder.

Because we are mixing in the flour so quickly it doesn't matter that the salt and yeast are thrown in together. If you are using the fresh cake yeast break it up.

- Dump in the flour along with the dates and pecans all at once and stir with a long handled wooden spoon or a Danish dough whisk, which is one of the tools that makes the job so much easier!
- Stir it until all of the wheat is incorporated into the dough. It will be a wet rough dough.
- Put the lid on the container, but do not snap it shut. You want the gases from the yeast to escape. (You could put a little hole in the top of the lid so that you could close the lids and still allow the gases to get out.). Allow the dough to sit at room temperature for about 2 hours to rise. When you first mix the dough it will not occupy much of the container. But, after the initial 2 hour rise it will pretty much fill it. (If you have decreased the yeast you will have to let it go longer than 2 hours.) DO NOT PUNCH DOWN THE DOUGH! Just let it settle by itself.
- The dough will be flat on the top and some of the bubbles may even appear to be popping. (If you intend to refrigerate the dough after this stage it can be placed in the refrigerator even if the dough is not perfectly flat. The yeast will continue to work even in the refrigerator.) The dough can be used right after the initial 2 hour rise, but it is much easier to handle when it is chilled. It is intended for refrigeration and use over the next week and a half, ready for you anytime. The flavor will deepen over that time, developing sourdough characteristics.
- The next day when you pull the dough out of the refrigerator you will notice that it has collapsed and this is totally normal for this type of dough. It will never rise up again in the container.
- Dust the surface of the dough with a little flour, just enough to prevent it from sticking to your hands when you reach in to pull a piece out.
- You should notice that the dough has a lot of stretch once it has rested. (If your dough breaks off instead of stretching your dough is probably too dry and you can just add a few tablespoons of water and let it sit again until the dough absorbs the additional water.).
- At this point, you can divide the dough into 4 one pound balls and freeze them in airtight containers for up to three weeks. Allow 24 hours in refrigerator to thaw before use. You can also leave the dough in its container in the refrigerator for up to 10 days, cutting off pieces as needed.
- When ready to bake, cut off a 1-pound piece of dough using kitchen shears and hold in your hands. Add a little more flour so it will not stick to your hands. Gently stretch the surface of the dough around to the bottom on all four sides, rotating the ball a quarter turn as you go. Most of the dusting flour will fall off; it's not intended to be incorporated into the dough. The correctly shaped final product will be smooth and cohesive.
- Rest the loaf on a generous layer of flour on top of a pizza peel. Let the dough rest for at least 40 minutes, (although letting it go 60 or even 90 minutes will give you a more open hole structure in the interior of the loaf. This may also improve the look of your loaf and prevent it from splitting on the bottom.) You will notice that the loaf does not rise much during this rest, in fact it may just spread sideways, this is normal for this type of dough.
- Twenty minutes before baking, preheat the oven to 400 degrees F with a baking stone on the center rack, with a metal broiler tray on the bottom (never use a glass vessel for this or it will shatter), which will be used to produce steam. (The tray needs to be at least 4 or 5 inches away from your stone to prevent it from cracking.).
- Dust the top of the loaf with more flour. Slide the loaf into the oven onto the preheated stone and add a cup of hot tap water to the broiler tray. Quickly close the oven door. Bake the bread for 35 minutes or until a deep brown color. To insure that you get the best results it

is crucial to have an Oven Thermometer to make sure your oven is accurate.

- Allow the loaf to cool on a rack until it is room temperature.

Nutrition Information

- Calories: 1128.8
- Sugar: 39.2
- Total Carbohydrate: 198.1
- Cholesterol: 10.9
- Sodium: 1834.8
- Fiber: 16.4
- Total Fat: 26.5
- Saturated Fat: 4.4
- Protein: 30.7

268. Raisin Or Date Bran Muffins

Serving: 12 muffins, 12 serving(s) | Prep: 10mins | Ready in:

Ingredients

- 1 cup all-purpose flour
- 2 teaspoons baking powder
- 1/2 teaspoon baking soda
- 3/4 teaspoon salt
- 1 1/2 cups natural bran
- 1/3 cup brown sugar, lightly packed
- 1/2 cup raisins or 1/2 cup dates, chopped
- 1 egg, beaten
- 1 cup sour milk
- 2 tablespoons vegetable oil

Direction

- Preheat oven to 400 degrees Fahrenheit.
- Blend together flour, baking powder, baking soda and salt.
- Blend in bran, brown sugar and raisins or dates.
- Mix a well in the center of dry ingredients.
- Combine and add egg, milk and vegetable oil.
- Stir only until combined.
- Fill paper lined muffin cups 2/3 full.
- Bake for 20 to 25 minutes.

Nutrition Information

- Calories: 137.2
- Sugar: 11.8
- Saturated Fat: 0.9
- Sodium: 293.7
- Fiber: 2.7
- Total Carbohydrate: 25.4
- Cholesterol: 19.7
- Protein: 3.4
- Total Fat: 3.8

269. Raisins And/or Cranberry Scones

Serving: 12 serving(s) | Prep: 15mins | Ready in:

Ingredients

- 4 cups flour
- 1 1/2 tablespoons baking powder
- 1/2 teaspoon baking soda
- 1/2 cup sugar
- 3/4 teaspoon salt
- 2 teaspoons ground cinnamon
- 1 cup butter, cut into pieces
- 1/2 cup raisins (1 cup if not using cranberries)
- 1/2 cup dried cranberries (1 cup if not using raisins)
- 1 teaspoon vanilla
- 1 egg
- 2/3 cup condensed milk or 2/3 cup buttermilk

Direction

- Preheat the oven to 425°F.
- Grease a large baking sheet or cover it with parchment paper.

- In a large bowl, stir together the flour, baking powder, baking soda, sugar, salt and cinnamon.
- Cut the butter into the dry ingredients and continue cutting until the mixture is coarse and uniform.
- Stir in the raisins or cranberries.
- In another bowl, stir together the vanilla the egg, and the milk.
- Form a well in the dry ingredients and pour in the liquid mixture.
- Stir to combine then remove to a floured counter and knead until uniform.
- (Do not over-knead, too much kneading will make the scones tough).
- Divide the dough into two pieces and press each into 3/4 inch thick circles.
- Cut each circle into six wedges and place them on the prepared baking sheet.
- Bake for 15 to 18 minutes or until the tops are lightly browned.

Nutrition Information

- Calories: 403
- Saturated Fat: 10.8
- Sodium: 472
- Fiber: 1.7
- Total Fat: 17.7
- Sugar: 21.5
- Total Carbohydrate: 55.5
- Cholesterol: 64.1
- Protein: 6.5

270. Rosemary, Pear, And Asiago Scones

Serving: 8 wedges, 8 serving(s) | Prep: 18mins | Ready in:

Ingredients

- 2 cups all-purpose flour
- 1 tablespoon baking powder
- 1/2 teaspoon salt
- 1/2 cup cold butter (cut into 1/2-inch cubes)
- 1 cup heavy cream (divided)
- 3/4 cup fresh pear (finely chopped)
- 1/2 cup asiago cheese (grated)
- 1 teaspoon fresh rosemary (chopped)

Direction

- Preheat oven to 450°.
- Stir together first 3 ingredients in a large bowl.
- Cut butter into flour mixture with a pastry blender until crumbly and mixture resembles small peas. Freeze 5 minutes.
- Add 3/4 cup plus 2 tablespoons cream, pear, cheese, and rosemary, stirring just until dry ingredients are moistened.
- Turn dough out onto wax paper; gently press or pat dough into a 7-inch round (mixture will be crumbly). Cut round into 8 wedges.
- Place wedges 2 inches apart on a lightly greased baking sheet. Brush tops of wedges with remaining 2 tablespoons cream just until moistened.
- Bake at 450° for 13 to 15 minutes or until golden.

Nutrition Information

- Calories: 327.1
- Sodium: 394.9
- Fiber: 1.3
- Sugar: 1.5
- Total Fat: 22.8
- Saturated Fat: 14.2
- Total Carbohydrate: 27.3
- Cholesterol: 71.3
- Protein: 4

271. Scrumptious Bran Muffins With Fruit

Serving: 12 muffins, 12 serving(s) | Prep: 15mins | Ready in:

Ingredients

- 1 cup mixed dried fruit (raisins, cranberries, blueberries, cherries, etc.)
- 1 teaspoon water
- 1 cup kellogg's bran buds cereal, finely ground
- 1 1/4 cups kellogg's bran buds cereal
- 2/3 cup light brown sugar
- 3 tablespoons molasses
- 1 large egg
- 1 large egg yolk
- 1 teaspoon vanilla extract
- 6 tablespoons unsalted butter, melted
- 1/2 cup applesauce
- 1/4 cup water
- 16 ounces low-fat sour cream
- 1 1/4 cups all-purpose flour
- 1/2 cup whole wheat flour
- 2 teaspoons baking soda
- 1/2 teaspoon salt
- 1/2 cup shredded coconut

Direction

- Preheat oven to 400°F Lightly coat a 12-cup muffin tin with cooking spray.
- Microwave the raisins and 1 tsp water in a covered bowl for 1 minute. Set aside, covered until needed.
- In a medium bowl, whisk together the sugar, molasses, whole egg, egg yolk, and vanilla until smooth. Whisk in the melted butter, sour cream, apple sauce, water, processed bran, and unprocessed bran. Let sit about 5 minutes until bran cereal is moistened.
- In a large bowl, whisk together the all-purpose flour, whole-wheat flour, baking soda, and salt.
- Add the cereal mixture and combined until just combined. Folded in raisins and coconut.
- Using a 1/3-cup measure coated in cooking spray, portion the batter into the muffin cups.
- Bake 18-20 minutes or until a toothpick inserted into the center comes out with just a few crumbs attached.
- Let the muffins cool in the pan 5-10 minutes, then turn out onto a wire rack to cool. Serve warm.

Nutrition Information

- Calories: 297.6
- Saturated Fat: 8
- Sodium: 350.9
- Fiber: 2.2
- Sugar: 16.5
- Total Carbohydrate: 43.1
- Protein: 4.4
- Total Fat: 12.8
- Cholesterol: 61

272. Spicy Apple And Sultana Muffins

Serving: 1 batch | Prep: 0S | Ready in:

Ingredients

- 3 cups self raising flour
- 1 egg, lightly beaten
- 1/4 cup oil
- 3/4 cup buttermilk
- 1 cup spicy apple mix

Direction

- Mix all ingredients together until just combined.
- Do not over mix.
- Spoon into greased or non-stick muffin tins and bake at 190 C approximately 20 minutes.
- SPICY APPLE MIX; 1 apple, cut into small pieces, 1/2 cup sultanas, 1/4 tsp cinnamon, 1/4 tsp mixed spice, pinch nutmeg, 2 Tbsp. brown sugar and 1/4 cup water. Place all ingredients in a microwave dish.
- Cover with plastic wrap and cook on HIGH four minutes.

- Stir and cook for another minute or until apple is soft.

Nutrition Information

- Calories: 1993.8
- Sodium: 270.4
- Sugar: 10.2
- Cholesterol: 218.8
- Saturated Fat: 10.2
- Total Carbohydrate: 295.4
- Protein: 51.1
- Total Fat: 64.8
- Fiber: 10.1

273. Strawberry And Cream Scones

Serving: 8-18 scones | Prep: 15mins | Ready in:

Ingredients

- SCONES
- 1/2 cup diced fresh strawberries
- 1/4 cup half-and-half or 1/4 cup light cream
- 2 cups king arthur unbleached all-purpose flour or 2 cups mellow pastry blend
- 1/2 teaspoon salt
- 1/4 cup granulated sugar
- 1 tablespoon baking powder
- 6 tablespoons cold butter, cut into pieces
- 1 large egg
- 2 teaspoons vanilla extract
- 2/3 cup diced fresh strawberries
- TOPPING
- 3 tablespoons granulated sugar
- 1 1/2 teaspoons water
- 1 1/2 teaspoons vanilla extract

Direction

- Preheat your oven to 375°F Lightly grease (or line with parchment) two baking sheets, or a full-size or mini-scone pan.
- To make the scones: In a blender or food processor, process 1/2 cup of the strawberries with the half and half or cream until the mixture is smooth. Set it aside.
- In a large bowl, whisk together the flour, salt, sugar, and baking powder. Cut in the butter, using your fingertips, a fork or a pastry blender.
- In a separate bowl, whisk together the strawberry/half and half mixture, the egg, and the vanilla extract. Stir this mixture into the dry ingredients. Add the 2/3 cup diced strawberries and stir just until everything is well-combined. This is a wet, sticky dough, good for drop scones.
- Drop the dough by heaping tablespoonfuls onto the prepared baking sheets; each scone should be about the size of a golf ball. A tablespoon cookie scoop is exactly the right size for this task. Or divide the dough among the compartments of the scone pan of your choice. Bake the scones until they're golden brown, 15 to 16 minutes (on a baking sheet or in a mini-scone pan), or 18 to 20 minutes (in a standard scone pan). Remove the scones from the oven when they're beginning to brown around the edges. Break one open, just to be sure; they should be moist, but not gummy, at the center.
- To make the topping: As soon as you remove the scones from the oven, make the topping. Combine the sugar and water in a very small (e.g., 1/4- to 1/3-cup size) microwave-safe bowl, stirring until the sugar is moistened. Heat in the microwave for 20 to 30 seconds, until the mixture is bubbly. Carefully remove from the microwave (sugar syrup is very hot), and stir in the vanilla. Stir until the mixture smoothes out. Drizzle or brush the topping over the hot scones.
- Yield: 8 to 18 scones, depending on your choice of pan.

Nutrition Information

- Calories: 264.2

- Saturated Fat: 6.3
- Sodium: 370.6
- Total Carbohydrate: 37.5
- Cholesterol: 49
- Protein: 4.5
- Total Fat: 10.5
- Fiber: 1.3
- Sugar: 12.3

274. Tea And Fruit Muffins

Serving: 12 muffins | Prep: 10mins | Ready in:

Ingredients

- 3 tea bags
- 1 cup boiling water
- 2 cups mixed dried fruit
- 1 cup brown sugar
- 1/4 cup glace ginger
- 2 cups self-raising flour
- 1 egg, beaten

Direction

- Place tea bags in jug with boiling water and stand 5 minutes.
- Place dried fruit, ginger and brown sugar in heat proof bowl. Strain tea over fruit. Stand for 2 hours or overnight.
- Preheat oven to 150 degrees Celsius.
- Line 12 hole muffin pan with patty cases.
- Stir flour and egg in to mixture until just combined.
- Pour into prepared patty cases.
- Bake 20-25 minutes until golden brown.

Nutrition Information

- Calories: 210.7
- Fiber: 2.5
- Sugar: 17.7
- Cholesterol: 17.6
- Protein: 3.2
- Total Fat: 0.7
- Saturated Fat: 0.2
- Sodium: 282.5
- Total Carbohydrate: 49.6

275. The Blueberry And Straw Berry Muffins Ever

Serving: 18 Muffins, 18 serving(s) | Prep: 15mins | Ready in:

Ingredients

- 1/2 cup butter or 1/2 cup margarine
- 1 cup granulated sugar
- 2 large eggs
- 1 teaspoon vanilla
- 2 teaspoons baking powder
- 1/4 teaspoon salt
- 2 cups all-purpose flour
- 1/2 cup milk
- 1 1/4 cups frozen blueberries
- 1 1/4 cups frozen strawberries
- 1 tablespoon granulated sugar, mixed with
- 1/4 teaspoon ground cinnamon

Direction

- 1 Heat oven to 375'F.
- 2 Grease 18 regular-size muffin cups or (12 large size muffin cups.
- 3 In bowl, mix butter until creamy. Add sugar and beat until pale and fluffy.
- 4 Add eggs one at a time, beating after each.
- 5 Beat in vanilla, baking powder and salt.
- 6 With spoon, fold in half of flour then half of milk into batter; repeat.
- 7 Fold in blueberries and strawberries.
- 8 Bake 20-25 minutes, until golden brown and springy to touch.
- 9 Sprinkle topping on each muffin.

Nutrition Information

- Calories: 173.1
- Cholesterol: 35.2
- Protein: 2.5
- Total Fat: 6.1
- Saturated Fat: 3.6
- Sodium: 129.8
- Fiber: 1.1
- Total Carbohydrate: 27.9
- Sugar: 15.7

276. Tomato And Parmesan Breakfast Muffins

Serving: 12 muffins | Prep: 5mins | Ready in:

Ingredients

- 2 cups self-raising flour
- 1/2 teaspoon baking powder
- 1/4 teaspoon salt
- 1/2 cup grated parmesan cheese
- 1/2 cup semi sun-dried tomato, roughly chopped
- 3 spring onions, sliced
- 1 garlic clove, crushed
- 125 g philadelphia extra light cream cheese spread
- 1 egg
- 1 cup milk
- 1/4 cup olive oil
- 1/4 cup grated parmesan cheese, extra

Direction

- COMBINE sifted flour, baking powder and salt into a large bowl. Add Parmesan, tomato, spring onion and garlic and mix to combine.
- WHISK together the Philly* and egg until smooth. Whisk in the milk and oil. Add to flour mixture and mix until just combined.
- DIVIDE mixture evenly between 6 × 1 cup capacity greased Texas muffin pans. Sprinkle with extra Parmesan and bake at 190°C for 25 minutes or until cooked through. Serve warm.

Nutrition Information

- Calories: 197.8
- Total Fat: 10.7
- Saturated Fat: 4.2
- Sodium: 557.5
- Sugar: 1.4
- Cholesterol: 35.4
- Fiber: 0.9
- Total Carbohydrate: 18.7
- Protein: 6.8

277. Tropical Fruit Muffins

Serving: 24 muffins | Prep: 0S | Ready in:

Ingredients

- 3 cups flour
- 6 teaspoons baking powder
- 3/4 teaspoon salt
- 1 1/2 cups sugar
- 3/4 cup honey
- 1/2 cup vegetable oil
- 1 1/2 cups milk
- 2 eggs
- 1 -1 1/2 cup mango pulp (2 very ripe mangoes)
- 1 large banana (very ripe)

Direction

- Cut and peel two very ripe (soft to the touch) mangoes and reduce to soft pulp and juice add one mashed very ripe Banana.
- Combine flour, baking powder, salt and sugar in a large bowl.
- In a separate bowl combine oil, milk, and egg.
- Mix liquid ingredients with dry until just moist and stir in the mango and banana pulp.
- Fill greased muffin tins, or paper muffin cups two-thirds full.
- Bake at 400°F for 18 minutes.

- They are done when they are brown on top and a tooth-pick inserted into the center comes out clean.

Nutrition Information

- Calories: 203.6
- Sugar: 23
- Cholesterol: 19.8
- Fiber: 0.7
- Sodium: 177.7
- Total Carbohydrate: 36.6
- Protein: 2.8
- Total Fat: 5.7
- Saturated Fat: 1.1

278. White Chocolate Fruit Scones

Serving: 8 serving(s) | Prep: 15mins | Ready in:

Ingredients

- 6 tablespoons butter, softened
- 2 cups all-purpose flour
- 1/4 cup sugar
- 2 1/2 teaspoons baking powder
- 1/2 teaspoon salt
- 1/2 cup dried fruit (I used cranberries, can also make them with blueberries, apricots)
- 1/2 cup white chocolate chips
- 1 egg (beaten and add buttermilk to make 1 Cup)
- 7/8 cup buttermilk (added to egg, see above)

Direction

- Lightly grease cookie sheets and preheat oven to 400°F.
- Cut butter into dry mixture of flour, sugar, baking powder and salt with pastry cutter.
- Add buttermilk, cranberries and chips. Mix thoroughly.
- Drop by rounded spoonfuls onto cookie sheets as you would cookies, about 12 at a time. (Or, can make a round scone loaf, score and bake).
- Sprinkle with granulated sugar before baking. Bake for 10-12 minutes or till lightly browned. Remove from baking sheet and cool.

Nutrition Information

- Calories: 324.7
- Saturated Fat: 7.9
- Fiber: 1.9
- Sugar: 13.9
- Total Carbohydrate: 46.6
- Cholesterol: 51.9
- Protein: 6
- Total Fat: 13.3
- Sodium: 369.6

279. White Chocolate, Coconut And Banana Muffins

Serving: 12 muffins, 4 serving(s) | Prep: 10mins | Ready in:

Ingredients

- 3 very ripe bananas
- 1 egg
- 125 ml vegetable oil
- 250 g flour
- 100 g caster sugar
- 1 1/2 teaspoons baking powder
- 150 white chocolate chunks
- 2 tablespoons desiccated coconut

Direction

- 1. Preheat the oven to 180C.
- 2. Line a muffin tray with 12 paper muffin cases.
- 3. Mash the bananas well.
- 4. Beat together the eggs and oil.

- 5. Put the flour, baking powder and sugar together in a large bowl, and stir through. Mix in the mashed bananas and beaten egg and oil mixture.
- 6. Fold in the white chocolate chunks and coconut. Spoon evenly into baking cases in muffin tin.
- 7. Bake in the oven for 20 minutes or until the muffins come away from the side of the pan when touched.
- 8. Rest the muffin tray on a wire rack for five minutes then remove the muffins and leave on the rack for another five minutes before serving.

Nutrition Information

- Calories: 674.5
- Cholesterol: 46.5
- Total Fat: 30.1
- Saturated Fat: 4.8
- Sugar: 37
- Total Carbohydrate: 94.8
- Protein: 9.1
- Sodium: 163.7
- Fiber: 4.2

280. Whole Fruit Orange Bran Muffins

Serving: 12 muffins, 12 serving(s) | Prep: 20mins | Ready in:

Ingredients

- 2 cups whole wheat flour
- 1/2 cup wheat bran (not the bran cereal, the real thing)
- 1/4 cup sugar substitute
- 1 teaspoon baking powder
- 1 teaspoon baking soda
- 1 teaspoon ground cinnamon
- 1 pinch salt
- 1 whole navel orange
- 3/4 cup skim milk
- 1/2 cup fresh orange juice
- 1/4 cup non-hydrogenated soft margarine
- 1 egg
- 1 teaspoon vanilla extract

Direction

- Preheat the oven to 400 degrees Fahrenheit.
- In a large bowl, combine the dry ingredients (flour though salt) and whisk to combine.
- Scrub the orange and cut into 8 wedges, peel and all. Place in the work bowl of a food processor and pulse until finely chopped, nearly a puree. Add the milk through vanilla and pulse until combined.
- Pour the wet mixture into the dry ingredients and stir until just combined. Divide into 12 greased or paper-lined muffin cups and bake until golden and firm to the touch, about 20 minutes.

Nutrition Information

- Calories: 144.4
- Sodium: 197.1
- Fiber: 3.6
- Total Carbohydrate: 22.9
- Saturated Fat: 0.8
- Sugar: 4.8
- Cholesterol: 15.8
- Protein: 4.4
- Total Fat: 4.8

281. Wholemeal Fruit Muffins

Serving: 12 muffins, 12 serving(s) | Prep: 10mins | Ready in:

Ingredients

- 3/4 cup desiccated coconut
- 1/2 cup raw sugar
- 1 1/2 cups wholemeal self-rising flour, sifted

- 3/4 cup chopped walnuts (optional)
- 1 cup muesli
- 2 apples, peeled and grated
- 1 cup frozen mixed berries
- 1 banana, peeled and mashed
- 1 egg, lightly beaten
- 1 1/2 cups skim milk

Direction

- Preheat oven to 180 degree Celsius. Lightly grease a 12 x 1/2 cup capacity muffin pan, or use muffin cases.
- Mix together the coconut, sugar, flour, nuts, muesli, apple and berries in a large bowl.
- Combine banana, egg and milk in a jug, and mix together. Add to the dry ingredients, and combine using a large spoon.
- Spoon mixture into prepared muffin pan. And bake for 20 to 25 minutes, or until lightly browned.
- Let stand for 5 minutes before removing from pan. Cool on a wire rack. Serve warm or cold.

Nutrition Information

- Calories: 117.7
- Fiber: 1.5
- Sugar: 16.1
- Protein: 2.8
- Total Fat: 2.4
- Saturated Fat: 1.6
- Sodium: 52.5
- Total Carbohydrate: 23.2
- Cholesterol: 18.2

Chapter 6: Quick Bread Nut Recipes

***

282. Aidan's Banana Nut Bread

Serving: 1 loaf, 8 serving(s) | Prep: 20mins | Ready in:

Ingredients

- 1/2 teaspoon salt
- 1 1/2 cups self raising flour
- 1/2 teaspoon nutmeg
- 1/2 teaspoon cinnamon
- 90 g butter
- 1 cup sugar
- 2 eggs
- 4 bananas, very ripe mashed
- 1 1/2 cups nuts (I use walnuts and sunflower seeds)

Direction

- Sift together salt, flour and spices.
- Cream butter and sugar, then add the eggs one at a time, beating well.
- Beat mixture until light and fluffy.
- Add sifted flour and spices and bananas to creamed mixture, combining lightly.
- Fold in nuts.
- Turn the mixture into a well-greased loaf tin Bake in a moderate oven (180c-200c) for 50 to 60 minutes.
- Cool in the tin.
- Can be iced with a cream cheese frosting or lemon icing.

Nutrition Information

- Calories: 486.9
- Saturated Fat: 8.1
- Sodium: 400.2
- Sugar: 33.6
- Cholesterol: 76.9
- Total Fat: 24
- Fiber: 4.6
- Total Carbohydrate: 63.2
- Protein: 9.2

283. Almond Chocolate Biscuits

Serving: 12 biscuits | Prep: 20mins | Ready in:

Ingredients

- 1 cup whole skin-on almonds
- 1/2 cup sugar
- 2 large egg whites
- 2 ounces bittersweet chocolate, chopped

Direction

- Preheat the oven to 375 degrees F. Put the almonds and sugar in a food processor and blend until the consistency of flour, about 45 seconds. Pour in the egg whites and mix until the dough is smooth and loose, about 30 seconds.
- Line an 8-by-11-inch cookie sheet or pan with parchment. Spread the batter with a wet spatula to evenly cover the pan in a thin layer. Bake until the batter sets and is golden brown, rotating the pan once about halfway through baking, about 18 minutes.
- While still warm, cut the dough into 12 to 14 rectangular biscuits or other desired shape. (A pizza wheel makes cutting very easy.) Transfer to a cooling rack.
- Meanwhile, put the chocolate in a clean microwave-safe bowl. Heat the chocolate at half power, stirring at 30-second intervals until melted, about 2 minutes. Drizzle the chocolate over the biscuits. Cool completely. Serve. Store in an airtight container.

Nutrition Information

- Calories: 103.5
- Total Fat: 6
- Saturated Fat: 0.5
- Fiber: 1.2
- Protein: 3
- Sodium: 48.2
- Sugar: 8.9
- Total Carbohydrate: 10.8
- Cholesterol: 0

284. Anne's Banana Nut Bread

Serving: 2 loaves, 24 serving(s) | Prep: 15mins | Ready in:

Ingredients

- 1 cup butter (at room temperature)
- 2 cups light brown sugar (packed)
- 4 eggs (at room temperature)
- 2 cups plain flour
- 1 cup white whole wheat flour
- 2 teaspoons baking soda
- 1/8 teaspoon baking powder
- 1/8 teaspoon salt
- 3 cups mashed bananas (7 medium VERY RIPE bananas)
- 1 1/2 cups chopped walnuts (TOASTED, or substitute pecans)

Direction

- Preheat oven to 350F (metal) or 325F (glass).
- Cream butter and sugar until light and fluffy.
- Add eggs one at a time, mixing briefly after each.
- Combine flours, baking soda, baking powder, and salt.
- To the creamed mixture, add flours and mashed bananas about one-third at a time, mixing briefly after each.
- Add toasted walnuts (or pecans) and stir until combined.
- Divide batter between two loaf pans sprayed with cooking spray.
- Bake at 350F (metal) or 325F (glass) for 50-55 minutes.

- Cool for 5 minutes, then turn onto a wire rack to completely cool before slicing.
- NOTE: Makes two loaves or bake as one loaf and eight mini loaves (3.7 x 2.4), or as sixteen mini loaves! Bake mini loaves for 20-25 minutes. Cut the recipe in half if you only need one loaf, though the loaves do freeze!

Nutrition Information

- Calories: 277.2
- Sugar: 21.5
- Cholesterol: 51.3
- Protein: 4.3
- Total Fat: 13.6
- Saturated Fat: 5.6
- Sodium: 204.1
- Fiber: 2
- Total Carbohydrate: 37

285. Anzac Biscuits (Cookies)

Serving: 24-36 cookies | Prep: 15mins | Ready in:

Ingredients

- 1/2 cup flour
- 1/3 cup sugar
- 2/3 cup coconut
- 2/3 cup rolled oats
- 2 ounces butter
- 1 tablespoon light molasses
- 1/2 teaspoon baking soda
- 2 tablespoons boiling water

Direction

- Mix the flour, sugar, coconut and oats.
- Melt the butter with the molasses.
- Dissolve the baking soda in boiling water; add to the butter mixture.
- Make a well in the center of the flour; add the liquid and stir well to combine.
- Place spoonfuls on greased cookie trays and bake at 350 degrees F for 15-20 minutes.

Nutrition Information

- Calories: 63.8
- Cholesterol: 5.1
- Total Fat: 3.6
- Saturated Fat: 2.6
- Fiber: 0.7
- Total Carbohydrate: 7.5
- Sodium: 41.2
- Sugar: 3.5
- Protein: 0.8

286. Atwood Inn Breakfast Scones

Serving: 8 Large Scones | Prep: 15mins | Ready in:

Ingredients

- 2 cups flour
- 1/2 cup sugar
- 2 teaspoons baking powder
- 1/2 teaspoon baking soda
- 1/4 teaspoon salt
- 1/2 cup buttermilk
- 1/2 cup Crisco shortening
- 1 egg
- 1 teaspoon vanilla flavoring or 1 teaspoon orange flavoring or 1 teaspoon maple flavoring
- 1/2 cup nuts (walnuts, pecans, or hazelnuts)
- 1/2 cup fruit (blueberry, cranberry, dates, or raisins, if using only nuts or fruit alone should total 1 cup.)

Direction

- The night before mix dry ingredients together in a medium size bowl.
- The next morning add buttermilk, Crisco, egg, flavoring, and nuts and/or fruit.

- Stir together gently kneading to complete mixing ingredients.
- Shape into a large ball and flatten, into a circle, on a cookie sheet or baking stone.
- Score into 8 pieces with serrated knife.
- Bake at 400 degrees for 18 to 22 minutes, until lightly browned and toothpick comes out clear.
- Serve warm with butter, honey, jam, or flavored cream cheese.
- Enjoy.

Nutrition Information

- Calories: 343.4
- Sodium: 324.9
- Sugar: 13.8
- Total Carbohydrate: 39.6
- Cholesterol: 27.1
- Protein: 6
- Total Fat: 18.3
- Saturated Fat: 4.1
- Fiber: 1.6

287. Aunt Cora's Nut Bread

Serving: 2 loaves, 8-12 serving(s) | Prep: 20mins | Ready in:

Ingredients

- 1 egg
- 1 cup sugar
- 1 cup nuts, chopped
- 1/2 cup raisins
- 4 cups unbleached flour
- 3 teaspoons baking powder
- 1 teaspoon salt
- 1 1/2 cups whole milk

Direction

- Cream together the egg and sugar.
- Sift together the flour, salt and baking powder, and add alternately to the egg/butter mixture with the milk.
- The batter will be very stiff.
- Lastly, mix in the nuts and raisins.
- Preheat oven to 375°F.
- Place batter in two buttered loaf pans.
- Give pans a good thump to make sure batter has settled.
- Let stand twenty minutes before putting in the oven.
- Bake for about one hour, or until tester comes out clean and top is lightly browned.
- Cool on rack.
- Note: I generally use walnuts, but pecans would work also. My grandmother chopped her walnuts in a little metal hand - cranked chopper that fed the nuts into a glass jar. The nuts were relatively finely chopped, but still a textural presence in the bread.

Nutrition Information

- Calories: 490.6
- Total Fat: 11.6
- Saturated Fat: 2.3
- Fiber: 3.6
- Cholesterol: 31
- Protein: 12
- Sodium: 570.7
- Sugar: 33.8
- Total Carbohydrate: 86.7

288. Banana Bread With Coconut Rum

Serving: 1 loaf | Prep: 5mins | Ready in:

Ingredients

- 1/4 cup margarine, softened
- 1 cup brown sugar
- 1 egg, slighty beaten
- 3 bananas, mashed

- 1 teaspoon coconut rum
- 2 cups flour
- 1/2 teaspoon salt
- 1 teaspoon baking soda

Direction

- Beat the margarine and brown sugar together until fluffy.
- Add the egg, beating until smooth.
- Stir in the mashed bananas and rum.
- In a large mixing bowl, stir the flour, salt and baking soda together.
- Gradually stir the egg mixture into the dry ingredients, stirring until the batter is moistened and blended.
- Spray a loaf pan with cooking spray.
- Spoon the batter into the loaf pan, spreading the top until smooth.
- Bake at 350 for one hour.
- Place loaf pan on cooling rack for 10 min's then remove loaf and continue to cool to room temperature.
- Banana bread is always better the day after it is made.
- Store in a loose plastic bag, loaves do not like to be in sealed bags.

Nutrition Information

- Calories: 2544.2
- Fiber: 15.9
- Sugar: 256
- Total Carbohydrate: 486.6
- Protein: 36.5
- Total Fat: 54
- Sodium: 3117.5
- Cholesterol: 211.5
- Saturated Fat: 10.2

289. Banana Crunch Muffins (w/grape Nuts)

Serving: 12 serving(s) | Prep: 15mins | Ready in:

Ingredients

- 1 1/2 cups flour
- 1/2 cup sugar
- 1/2 teaspoon baking powder
- 1/4 teaspoon salt
- 1 egg
- 2 medium ripe bananas, mashed
- 1/2 cup plain yogurt
- 1/2 teaspoon vanilla
- 1 cup Post Grape-Nuts cereal

Direction

- Preheat oven to 350.
- Mix flour, sugar, baking powder, baking soda and salt in a large bowl.
- Beat the egg in a small bowl; stir in bananas, yogurt and vanilla.
- Add to flour mixture; stirring until just moistened (batter will be lumpy; do not overmix!).
- Stir in cereal.
- Spoon batter into a 12-cup muffin tin that has been sprayed with cooking spray, filling each cup 2/3 full.
- Bake in preheated oven for 25 minutes or until golden brown.
- Serve warm.
- NOTE: Muffins can be frozen for up to 6 months.
- Just thaw at room temperature and reheat until warm.

Nutrition Information

- Calories: 154.3
- Fiber: 1.8
- Total Fat: 1.1
- Saturated Fat: 0.4
- Sodium: 133.6

- Sugar: 12.5
- Total Carbohydrate: 33.2
- Cholesterol: 18.9
- Protein: 3.8

290. Banana Macadamia Nut Bread (Abm)

Serving: 1 700g | Prep: 5mins | Ready in:

Ingredients

- 2 1/2 teaspoons dry yeast
- 3 1/4 cups plain flour
- 3 tablespoons sugar
- 1/2 teaspoon salt
- 1 egg
- 2 tablespoons margarine
- 2 medium bananas, mashed
- 1/2 cup water
- 1/2 cup macadamia nuts, chopped

Direction

- Add all ingredients (except macadamias) to your bread-maker in the order as per your instruction manual.
- Select sweet bread option crust light and large loaf setting, press start.
- When your machine is ready for add-ins (mine beeps) add the macadamias.

Nutrition Information

- Calories: 2621.9
- Saturated Fat: 14.5
- Cholesterol: 211.5
- Total Fat: 83.7
- Sodium: 1519.9
- Fiber: 25
- Sugar: 71.2
- Total Carbohydrate: 415.4
- Protein: 60.2

291. Banana Macadamia Nut Muffins

Serving: 12 muffins | Prep: 20mins | Ready in:

Ingredients

- 1 1/2 cups flour
- 1 1/2 teaspoons baking soda
- 1/4 teaspoon salt
- 1 teaspoon cinnamon
- 1 1/4 cups mashed bananas (about 3 large)
- 1/2 cup sugar
- 1/4 cup dark brown sugar
- 1/2 cup melted butter
- 1/4 cup milk
- 1 large egg
- 1 teaspoon vanilla
- 1 cup unsalted macadamia nuts, toasted and chopped

Direction

- Preheat oven to 350° and grease or place cupcake liner papers in 12 muffin cups.
- Sift first 4 ingredients into a large bowl.
- Combine bananas, both sugars, butter, milk, egg and vanilla in a medium bowl.
- Mix into dry ingredients, then fold in half of nuts.
- Divide batter among prepared muffin cups and sprinkle tops with remaining macadamia nuts.
- Bake until muffins are golden brown and tester inserted into center comes out clean, about 25 minutes.
- Transfer muffins to wire rack and let cool.

Nutrition Information

- Calories: 278
- Total Carbohydrate: 30.3
- Saturated Fat: 6.5
- Sodium: 284
- Fiber: 1.8

- Sugar: 15.2
- Cholesterol: 36.5
- Total Fat: 16.8
- Protein: 3.4

292. Banana Nut Cake/Bread

Serving: 1 loaf, 12 serving(s) | Prep: 20mins | Ready in:

Ingredients

- 1/2 cup butter
- 1 1/2 cups sugar
- 2 eggs, beaten
- 1 cup banana, mashed
- 1 teaspoon vanilla or 1 teaspoon lemon extract
- 2 cups flour
- 1/2 teaspoon baking soda
- 1/2 teaspoon salt
- 1/2 cup milk
- 1/2 cup nuts, chopped

Direction

- Cream butter.
- Add sugar gradually.
- Add eggs and beat thoroughly.
- Add bananas and flavoring.
- Sift dry ingredients together and add alternately with milk.
- Add nuts.
- Bake in greased loaf pan at 350 for 20-30 minutes.

Nutrition Information

- Calories: 305.2
- Total Fat: 12.1
- Fiber: 1.4
- Total Carbohydrate: 45.8
- Cholesterol: 57
- Protein: 4.7
- Saturated Fat: 5.8
- Sodium: 259.2
- Sugar: 26.9

293. Banana Nut Chocolate Chip Bread

Serving: 12 serving(s) | Prep: 20mins | Ready in:

Ingredients

- 1/3 cup butter
- 3/4 cup sugar
- 1 egg
- 1 cup mashed banana
- 2 cups flour
- 2 1/2 teaspoons baking powder
- 1/4 teaspoon baking soda
- 1/2 teaspoon salt
- 1 cup chopped walnuts or 1 cup pecans
- 1/2 cup chocolate chips
- 1/2 cup buttermilk

Direction

- Cream butter and sugar.
- Mix in egg and banana.
- Stir together flour, baking powder, baking soda, salt, nuts and chocolate chips.
- Add this to the creamed mixture alternately with the buttermilk.
- Stir until just blended.
- Bake at 350 degrees in a greased and floured loaf pan for 60 minutes.
- Cool in pan 10 minutes.

Nutrition Information

- Calories: 294
- Saturated Fat: 5.3
- Sodium: 262.1
- Fiber: 2.1
- Total Carbohydrate: 39.2
- Total Fat: 14.3
- Cholesterol: 29.4
- Protein: 5

- Sugar: 19.4

294. Banana Nut Crunch Muffins

Serving: 12 muffins, 12 serving(s) | Prep: 15mins | Ready in:

Ingredients

- Muffins
- 1 1/4 cups flour
- 1 tablespoon baking powder
- 1/8 teaspoon salt
- 1 egg, slightly beaten
- 1/2 cup milk
- 1/3 cup packed brown sugar
- 3 tablespoons vegetable oil
- 1 1/2 cups post Banana Nut Crunch cereal
- 1 cup mashed ripe banana
- Streusal Topping
- 1/2 cup post Banana Nut Crunch cereal, lightly crushed
- 1 tablespoon brown sugar
- 1/2 teaspoon ground cinnamon
- 1 tablespoon melted butter

Direction

- In a small bowl, combine flour, baking powder and salt.
- In another bowl, whisk together egg, milk, brown sugar, and oil; add flour mixture; stir just until moistened (batter will be lumpy) then stir in cereal and banana.
- Spoon batter into muffin tin that has been lightly sprayed with no-stick cooking spray or lined with paper muffin cups, filling each cup 2/3 full.
- Combine remaining cereal, brown sugar, and cinnamon; drizzle melted butter over cereal mixture and stir until crumbly; sprinkle topping evenly over muffins.
- Bake at 400° for 20 minutes or until golden-brown.

Nutrition Information

- Calories: 179.4
- Sugar: 10.6
- Total Fat: 6.3
- Saturated Fat: 1.6
- Cholesterol: 21.6
- Protein: 3.2
- Sodium: 177.9
- Fiber: 1.4
- Total Carbohydrate: 28

295. Banana Nut French Toast

Serving: 3 slices, 1 serving(s) | Prep: 5mins | Ready in:

Ingredients

- 1 banana (medium sized, ripe)
- 1/2 cup rice milk (I use unflavored Rice Dream)
- 1/2 teaspoon cinnamon
- 1/4 teaspoon nutmeg
- 1 teaspoon maple syrup (or your preferred sweetener)
- 3 slices bread (whole grain, multi-grain)

Direction

- In blender mix: banana, rice milk, cinnamon, nutmeg and syrup.
- Pour into small flat container to dredge bread.
- Coat bread on both sides and cook on griddle that has been oiled lightly.
- Served warm with your favorite nut toppings and a little more maple syrup.

Nutrition Information

- Calories: 388
- Cholesterol: 0
- Sodium: 555.8
- Fiber: 5.6

- Total Carbohydrate: 83
- Sugar: 21.8
- Protein: 7.3
- Total Fat: 4.1
- Saturated Fat: 0.9

296. Banana Nut Scones

Serving: 4 Scones, 4 serving(s) | Prep: 10mins | Ready in:

Ingredients

- 1/2 cup oatmeal, preferably large flake but quick oats will work
- 1/2 cup all-purpose flour
- 1/2 cup whole wheat flour
- 1 tablespoon brown sugar, packed (optional)
- 2 teaspoons baking powder
- 1/2 teaspoon cinnamon
- 1 tablespoon oil
- 1 banana, ripe, mashed
- 1/4 cup cinnamon baking chips
- 1/4 cup walnuts, chopped
- 1 teaspoon vanilla extract
- 1/3 cup milk (or more, if necessary)
- turbinado sugar or demerara sugar, for sprinkling on top
- oats, for sprinkling on top

Direction

- Heat oven to 400.
- Mix dry ingredients together (oatmeal, flours, baking powder, cinnamon). Stir oil into dry ingredients well. Add cinnamon chips and walnuts and stir. In a clear measuring cup, add mashed banana, milk to 3/4 cup (banana plus milk should equal 3/4 cup), and vanilla. Combine wet and dry ingredients; stir until the dry ingredients are damp.
- Drop dough onto parchment paper lined or greased baking sheet, and form into a 5" diameter circle. Cut into four triangles - it's ok to leave them in a circle. Sprinkle with oats and sugar.
- Bake at 400 for 20 minutes, until lightly browned.

Nutrition Information

- Calories: 268.4
- Saturated Fat: 1.6
- Sodium: 193.3
- Sugar: 4.1
- Total Carbohydrate: 39.2
- Cholesterol: 2.8
- Total Fat: 10.2
- Protein: 7
- Fiber: 4.5

297. Banana Nut Snack Muffins For Bill

Serving: 12 serving(s) | Prep: 10mins | Ready in:

Ingredients

- 3 bananas, very ripe
- 1 cup wheat flour
- 1 cup all-purpose flour
- 1/2 cup oatmeal
- 1/2 cup sugar
- 1 teaspoon baking soda
- 1/2 teaspoon baking powder
- 1 dash salt
- 3/4 cup egg substitute
- 1/4 cup extra virgin olive oil
- 2 tablespoons water
- 1 tablespoon vanilla
- 1/4 cup black walnut, chopped

Direction

- Mash bananas in med sized bowl. Add flours, oatmeal, soda, powder and salt. Mix well.
- In 2 c measuring cup mix egg sub, olive oil, water and vanilla.
- Add to dry ingredients, mix well, batter will be thick and slightly lumpy.

- Stir in walnuts.
- Spray standard size muffin tin with cooking spray. Divide batter between cups equally (each will be 3/4 full).
- Bake at 400 for 18 to 20 mins till golden or till tooth pick comes out clean.
- Immediately turn out onto cooling rack and enjoy warm or allow to cool.

Nutrition Information

- Calories: 215.6
- Saturated Fat: 0.9
- Sodium: 162.1
- Fiber: 2.8
- Sugar: 12.3
- Protein: 5.8
- Total Fat: 7.2
- Total Carbohydrate: 33.1
- Cholesterol: 0.2

298. Banana Snack Muffins

Serving: 12 muffins, 12 serving(s) | Prep: 15mins | Ready in:

Ingredients

- 1 cup whole wheat flour
- 1/2 cup quick-cooking oats
- 1 teaspoon baking soda
- 1 teaspoon baking powder
- 1 teaspoon cinnamon (can add cloves and nutmeg tooÃ¢ whatever makes you happy!)
- 1/2 cup honey (you can also substitute a sweetener such as Stevia-in-the-Raw or Ideal, but then also add 1/3 cup li)
- 3 tablespoons natural applesauce or 3 tablespoons light vanilla yogurt
- 2 tablespoons brummel brown margarine
- 4 mashed ripened bananas
- 1/2 cup toasted pecans (toasting really helps to bring out the flavor) or 1/2 cup walnuts (toasting really helps to bring out the flavor)
- 1 egg
- 1 teaspoon vanilla extract
- 1/4 cup muesli, opt (to sprinkle on top before cooking)

Direction

- Mix Brummel Brown and honey (or sweetener of choice) together until creamed. Next add in the egg and beat, add in bananas (if really ripe just add in whole and let the mixer do the work if not mash them in a separate bowl), add in vanilla.
- In another bowl, stir together all dry ingredients. Add to liquid and stir till just combined. Fold in toasted nuts.
- Scoop into 12 muffin tins sprayed with nonstick cooking spray (or can make as a bread in bread loaf). Top with muesli (if you have it). Bake at 350 degrees F for 20 minutes, until cooked through.

Nutrition Information

- Calories: 186.9
- Sodium: 168.9
- Fiber: 3.3
- Sugar: 17.3
- Protein: 3.5
- Total Fat: 6.2
- Saturated Fat: 0.9
- Total Carbohydrate: 32.5
- Cholesterol: 17.6

299. Banana, Coconut Lime Bread

Serving: 1 loaf | Prep: 15mins | Ready in:

Ingredients

- 1/2 cup shortening
- 3/4 cup coconut, grated
- 3/4 cup brown sugar

- 1 teaspoon baking powder
- 2 tablespoons white vinegar
- 2 cups white flour
- 3 ripe bananas, mashed
- GLAZE
- 3 tablespoons water
- 1/4 cup brown sugar
- 1 tablespoon lime juice
- 1 tablespoon oil
- 1/2 teaspoon salt
- 1 tablespoon rum
- 1/2 teaspoon ginger powder
- 3 tablespoons lime juice

Direction

- Beat shortening for a few seconds.
- Add brown sugar and beat till well blended creamy.
- Stir in vinegar, bananas, water lime juice.
- Mix all ingredients well.
- Add salt, ginger grated coconut. Mix well.
- Stir in baking powder.
- Sift flour beat with a wooden spoon till well blended smooth.
- Transfer into a greased loaf pan bake at 350°F for 1 hour.
- Let cool for 10 minutes before removing from pan to a wire rack.

Nutrition Information

- Calories: 3559.7
- Sodium: 1647.8
- Sugar: 261.5
- Total Carbohydrate: 508
- Protein: 34.4
- Total Fat: 160.9
- Saturated Fat: 64.7
- Fiber: 26.7
- Cholesterol: 0

300. Banana, Orange Pecan Muffins

Serving: 12 muffins, 12 serving(s) | Prep: 15mins | Ready in:

Ingredients

- 4 mashed bananas (ripe)
- 1/3 cup melted butter
- 1 large egg
- 1 teaspoon vanilla
- 1 teaspoon grated orange rind
- 1 1/2 cups whole wheat flour
- 1/2 cup granulated sugar
- 1 teaspoon baking soda
- 1 teaspoon baking powder
- 1/2 teaspoon salt
- 1 cup chopped pecans

Direction

- In a large bowl, beat together bananas, butter, egg, vanilla and orange rind.
- In a medium bowl, stir together flour, sugar, baking powder, baking soda and salt. Pour the dry ingredients in the banana mixture and mix until combined. Add chopped pecans stir again.
- Spoon batter into 12 greased or paper-lined muffin cups.
- Bake muffins in 350 degrees F oven for 15 to 20 minutes or until risen and firm to the touch. Let cool on wire racks.
- Store in airtight containers for up to 3 days of freeze for up to 3 months.

Nutrition Information

- Calories: 233.5
- Saturated Fat: 4
- Sodium: 275.3
- Total Carbohydrate: 29.7
- Cholesterol: 31.2
- Protein: 3.9
- Total Fat: 12.5
- Fiber: 3.7

- Sugar: 13.6

301. Banana Nut Muffins

Serving: 6 serving(s) | Prep: 15mins | Ready in:

Ingredients

- 2 cups white flour
- 3 teaspoons baking powder
- 1/2 teaspoon salt
- 1 teaspoon ground cinnamon
- 1/4 teaspoon ground nutmeg
- 1/2 cup butter or 1/2 cup margarine
- 2/3-1 cup sugar, depending on how sweet you want your muffins (I use 2/3 cup)
- 2 eggs
- 1 teaspoon vanilla extract
- 1 1/2 cups bananas
- 1 cup nuts (walnuts or pecans are good)

Direction

- Sift together flour, baking powder, salt and spices; set aside.
- Cream together butter and sugar in bowl until light and fluffy, using electric mixer at medium speed.
- Beat in eggs, one at a time, blending well after each addition.
- Stir in mashed bananas. Add vanilla to banana mixture.
- Mix nuts with flour and add all at once to banana mixture, stirring gently to just combine
- Spoon batter into 6 greased 3-inch muffin-pan cups.
- Batter will be thick.
- Bake in 375 degree F. oven 20-30 minutes or until golden brown.
- Serve hot with homemade jam or jelly.

Nutrition Information

- Calories: 570.9
- Protein: 10.9
- Total Fat: 29.2
- Sugar: 28.1
- Total Carbohydrate: 69.5
- Saturated Fat: 11.9
- Sodium: 688.4
- Fiber: 4.4
- Cholesterol: 102.7

302. Blueberry Pecan Muffins

Serving: 4-6 serving(s) | Prep: 15mins | Ready in:

Ingredients

- 2 cups flour
- 1 cup sugar
- 1 tablespoon baking powder
- 1 cup milk
- 1/3 cup vegetable oil
- 2 eggs
- 2 teaspoons vanilla extract
- 2 1/2 cups blueberry pecan muesli
- 2 tablespoons blueberry jam

Direction

- Heat oven to 400.
- Grease muffin cups.
- Mix flour, sugar and baking powder.
- Mix oil, eggs, vanilla, and milk with the dry ingredients.
- Add cereal to the mixture.
- Pour in muffin cups and spoon 1/4 teaspoon spreadable fruit on top of batter.
- Pour more batter over the fruit spread.
- Bake 20-25 minutes.

Nutrition Information

- Calories: 692.8
- Saturated Fat: 4.6
- Fiber: 1.8
- Sugar: 55.4

- Total Carbohydrate: 108.7
- Cholesterol: 114.3
- Total Fat: 23.5
- Sodium: 341.8
- Protein: 11.6

303. Braided Banana Date Nut Bread (ABM)

Serving: 1 loaf | Prep: 15mins | Ready in:

Ingredients

- Bread
- 3 cups bread flour
- 1/2 cup chopped pitted dates
- 1/2 cup chopped pecans
- 1/4 cup sugar
- 2 teaspoons bread machine yeast
- 1/2 teaspoon salt
- 3 tablespoons butter, cut up
- 3 tablespoons milk
- 3 tablespoons water (80°)
- 1/2 cup mashed banana
- 1 egg
- Topping
- 1 tablespoon sugar
- 1/4 teaspoon allspice

Direction

- Place all bread ingredients in bread machine pan in order as suggested by your manufacturer.
- Select dough cycle.
- When cycle is complete, remove dough to floured surface.
- If necessary, add extra flour and knead to make dough easier to handle.
- Divide dough into 3 equal pieces and roll each piece into a 15" rope.
- Braid the 3 ropes together, pinching ends to seal.
- Place on greased baking sheet, cover and let rise in a warm place until doubled, about 1 hour.
- Combine topping ingredients in a small bowl and sprinkle on bread.
- Bake at 375° for 25 to 30 minutes or until done.
- Remove from pan and cool on wire rack.

Nutrition Information

- Calories: 2734.7
- Sodium: 1515.8
- Cholesterol: 309.5
- Protein: 58
- Total Fat: 85.1
- Saturated Fat: 28.6
- Fiber: 26.2
- Sugar: 131.7
- Total Carbohydrate: 446.2

304. Buttery Cinnamon Nut Bread With Almond Glaze

Serving: 1 loaf | Prep: 15mins | Ready in:

Ingredients

- Bread
- 1 lb loaf frozen bread dough, thawed
- 3 tablespoons Land o' Lakes Butter, softened
- 1/2 cup sugar
- 1/2 cup chopped pecans
- 1 teaspoon cinnamon
- Orange Bread (omit cinnamon and milk)
- 1 1/2 teaspoons freshly grated orange rind
- 1/2 cup sugar
- 1/2 cup chopped pecans
- 1 tablespoon orange juice
- Glaze Ingredients (Can be used on either variation)
- 1/2 cup powdered sugar
- 1 -2 tablespoon milk or 1 -2 tablespoon water
- 1 teaspoon almond extract (optional)

Direction

- Preheat oven to 375°F.
- Butter a 15x10x1" jelly roll pan.
- Press thawed dough on the bottom of pan.
- Spread dough with butter; prick with a fork.
- In a large bowl, stir together sugar, pecans and cinnamon.
- Sprinkle evenly over dough.
- Bake for 15-20 minutes or until golden brown.
- Stir together all glaze ingredients in a small bowl.
- Drizzle over warm bread.
- Cut into squares; serve warm.

Nutrition Information

- Calories: 1785.9
- Fiber: 12.1
- Total Carbohydrate: 279.6
- Protein: 10.7
- Saturated Fat: 7.1
- Sodium: 8.9
- Sugar: 264.2
- Cholesterol: 2.1
- Total Fat: 79.2

305. Cheddar Apple Nut Bread

Serving: 1 9x5 inch loaf, 12 serving(s) | Prep: 20mins | Ready in:

Ingredients

- 2 1/2 cups flour
- 3/4 cup sugar
- 2 teaspoons baking powder
- 1/2 teaspoon salt
- 1/2 teaspoon cinnamon
- 2 eggs, beaten
- 3/4 cup milk
- 1/3 cup butter or 1/3 cup margarine, melted
- 2 cups sharp cheddar cheese, shredded
- 1 1/2 cups peeled chopped apples
- 3/4 cup chopped pecans or 3/4 cup walnuts

Direction

- Preheat oven to 350.
- Grease and flour a 9 x 5-inch loaf pan or spray it with cooking spray.
- In large mixing bowl, combine flour, sugar, baking powder, salt and cinnamon.
- Add beaten eggs, milk and margarine; mix well.
- Stir in cheese, apples and pecans.
- Mixture will be fairly thick; spoon into loaf pan.
- Bake at 350 degrees for 60- 70 minutes or until it tests done with wooden pick inserted in center.
- Remove from oven and let stand for about 5 minutes.
- Invert and remove loaf from pan.

Nutrition Information

- Calories: 342.1
- Sodium: 330.5
- Fiber: 1.8
- Cholesterol: 70.7
- Protein: 9.7
- Total Fat: 17.9
- Saturated Fat: 8.3
- Sugar: 14.6
- Total Carbohydrate: 36.8

306. Chocolatey Delight Pumpkin Oat Muffins

Serving: 12 muffins, 12 serving(s) | Prep: 8mins | Ready in:

Ingredients

- 1 cup canned pumpkin
- 1 tablespoon sugar-free maple syrup

- 1/2 cup Sugar Twin
- 1 teaspoon vanilla extract
- 1/2 teaspoon almond extract
- 1/4 cup skim milk
- 1/4 cup water
- 3/4 cup oat flour
- 1/3 cup unsweetened cocoa powder
- 2 teaspoons baking powder
- 1/2 teaspoon baking soda
- 1/2 teaspoon salt
- 1 teaspoon cinnamon (or more..enough to taste)

Direction

- Combine the first 7 ingredients.
- In a separate bowl, mix remaining ingredients.
- Add both together, stirring out any clumps.
- Bake at 350 for about 20 minutes.

Nutrition Information

- Calories: 42
- Sodium: 263.6
- Fiber: 2.2
- Protein: 1.9
- Total Fat: 0.6
- Saturated Fat: 0.3
- Sugar: 1
- Total Carbohydrate: 8.9
- Cholesterol: 0.1

307. Cinnamon Coffee Scones

Serving: 8 serving(s) | Prep: 15mins | Ready in:

Ingredients

- 2 cups self-rising flour
- 2 teaspoons cinnamon
- 6 tablespoons Splenda granular, sugar substitute
- 3/4 cup light margarine
- 2 eggs
- 1/4 cup strong brewed coffee
- 1/4 cup milk
- 1/2 cup golden raisins or 1/2 cup chopped dried apricot
- 1/2 cup chopped pecans or 1/2 cup walnuts
- milk, for toppings (optional)
- sugar, for toppings (optional)

Direction

- Stir together the flour, cinnamon, and Splenda.
- Cut the margarine into tablespoon pieces and blend with the pastry blender or two knives into the dry mixture (margarine pieces should be the size of small peas.).
- Mix together the eggs, coffee, and milk.
- Stir into the dry mixture to form a soft dough.
- Stir in the fruit and nuts.
- Turn dough out onto a floured board and gently pat into a circle of dough about 1/2" thick.
- Cut out rounds with floured biscuit cutter and place them on a greased baking sheet.
- Gently brush tops with milk and sprinkle with sugar.
- Bake in a preheated 400° F oven for 12 to 15 minutes or until golden brown.

Nutrition Information

- Calories: 209.5
- Total Fat: 6.7
- Fiber: 2.2
- Total Carbohydrate: 32.3
- Cholesterol: 47.6
- Saturated Fat: 1.1
- Sodium: 419.7
- Sugar: 5.8
- Protein: 5.9

308. Coconut Choc Chip Muffins

Serving: 12 serving(s) | Prep: 10mins | Ready in:

Ingredients

- 1/4 cup butter
- 1/2 cup sugar, plus
- 1/4 cup sugar, for the topping
- 2 eggs
- 1 cup coconut yogurt
- 1/2 cup milk (if you happen to have a fresh coconut on hand you can substitute the milk with the strained liquid f)
- 1/2 teaspoon vanilla
- 2 1/2 cups self raising flour
- 1/4 teaspoon baking powder
- 1 cup macaroon desiccated coconut (if you like a stronger coconut flavour you can increase to 1 1/4 cup)
- 1/4 cup macaroon desiccated coconut, for the topping
- 1/2 cup chocolate chips

Direction

- Preheat oven 180°C and line muffin pans with paper cases or grease them.
- Beat softened butter and sugar until creamy.
- Beat in eggs, yoghurt and milk, and vanilla.
- Fold in chocolate chips.
- Combine dry ingredients and fold into wet mixture, do not overmix.
- Mix together the sugar and coconut for the topping, place batter in prepared pans and sprinkle with topping mixture.
- Bake for 20-25 minutes or until skewer inserted in center comes out clean.

Nutrition Information

- Calories: 266.4
- Saturated Fat: 6.4
- Fiber: 1.4
- Total Carbohydrate: 41
- Protein: 4.7
- Total Fat: 9.9
- Sodium: 72.5
- Sugar: 19.8
- Cholesterol: 46.8

309. Coconut Banana Muffins

Serving: 24 muffins | Prep: 10mins | Ready in:

Ingredients

- 1/2 cup butter
- 2 eggs
- 3 very ripe bananas, mashed together
- 1 teaspoon vanilla
- 2 cups flour
- 1 teaspoon salt
- 1 1/2 teaspoons baking powder
- 3/4 cup sugar
- 1/2 cup grated coconut

Direction

- Cream together the butter and eggs, then mix in the ripe bananas and vanilla.
- In a small bowl, mix the flour, salt, baking powder, and sugar together, then add to the wet ingredients and mix just until all is moistened.
- Add the coconut.
- Spoon the batter into muffin tins and bake at 350 for 30 minutes or so, until done.

Nutrition Information

- Calories: 127.6
- Saturated Fat: 3.6
- Fiber: 0.9
- Total Carbohydrate: 18.1
- Cholesterol: 27.8
- Total Fat: 5.5
- Sodium: 153.7
- Sugar: 8.3
- Protein: 1.9

310. Cranberry Nut Scones

Serving: 6 scones, 6 serving(s) | Prep: 10mins | Ready in:

Ingredients

- 1/2 cup sour cream
- 1/2 teaspoon baking soda
- 2 cups all-purpose flour
- 1 cup sugar
- 1 teaspoon baking powder
- 1/8 teaspoon cream of tartar
- 1/4 teaspoon salt
- 1/2 cup butter
- 1 egg
- 2 teaspoons vanilla extract
- 3/4 cup dried cranberries
- 1/2 cup chopped walnuts
- sugar, to sprinkle

Direction

- Preheat oven to 350°F.
- Spray a baking sheet with nonstick cooking spray.
- Combine the sour cream and baking soda in a small bowl.
- Combine flour, sugar, baking powder, cream of tartar and salt in a large bowl.
- Cut in butter until mixture resembles fine breadcrumbs.
- Combine egg and vanilla extract with sour cream mixture.
- Gently stir into the flour until moistened. DO NOT OVERMIX!
- Knead dough 10 times only.
- Place dough on baking sheet and pat into 3/4" thickness.
- Cut into 6 wedges and separate, so the scones are not touching. Leave adequate space for expansion.
- Dust with sugar.
- Bake 15-20 min or until golden brown.

Nutrition Information

- Calories: 543.4
- Protein: 7.7
- Total Fat: 27
- Saturated Fat: 13.1
- Fiber: 2.3
- Sugar: 34.4
- Cholesterol: 84.3
- Sodium: 394.5
- Total Carbohydrate: 69.2

311. Cranberry Walnut Scones

Serving: 16 scones | Prep: 15mins | Ready in:

Ingredients

- 2 cups flour
- 1/4 cup maple sugar, plus
- 1 tablespoon maple sugar, for sprinkling on top
- 2 teaspoons baking powder
- 1/2 teaspoon salt
- 2 teaspoons butter
- 1/2 cup fresh cranberries or 1/2 cup dried cranberries
- 1/2 cup walnuts
- 1 cup skim milk buttermilk
- 1 tablespoon skim milk

Direction

- Heat oven to 425F, spray a baking sheet with veggie spray or line it with parchment paper Stir together the flour, sugar, baking powder salt.
- Cut in the butter with a pastry blender, two knives or your fingertips until the mixture looks like coarse crumbs.
- Stir in the cranberries walnuts.
- Make a well and gradually stir in the buttermilk to form a ball (handle as little as possible) the ball will be sticky and a bit difficult to work with.

- Divide the dough in half on a lightly floured board and pat each half into an 8" circle about a 1/2" thick.
- Cut each round into 8 triangles.
- Place scones on the prepared baking sheet.
- Brush tops with milk and sprinkle with the tbsp. of sugar.
- Bake for 15 minutes until golden.
- Serve warm.

Nutrition Information

- Calories: 103.1
- Total Fat: 3.2
- Saturated Fat: 0.6
- Sodium: 138.8
- Fiber: 0.8
- Cholesterol: 1.9
- Sugar: 3.4
- Total Carbohydrate: 16.3
- Protein: 2.7

312. Dorothy's Banana Nut Bread

Serving: 1 loaf, 3-6 serving(s) | Prep: 20mins | Ready in:

Ingredients

- 3⁄4 cup Crisco
- 4 1⁄2 teaspoons water
- 1 1⁄2 cups sugar
- 2 eggs (whipped well)
- 3 bananas (very ripe)
- 2 tablespoons vanilla extract
- 1 teaspoon baking soda
- 1 teaspoon salt
- 2 cups whole wheat flour
- 1⁄2 cup buttermilk
- 1 cup walnuts (crushed)
- 1 tablespoon maple syrup
- 1 teaspoon nutmeg (freshly grated)
- 1 teaspoon cinnamon

Direction

- Preheat oven to 300 degrees.
- In a large bowl, mix the Crisco and sugar until smooth.
- Add vanilla and eggs and continue to blend
- Add salt and baking soda.
- Add in mashed bananas and continue to blend while adding buttermilk.
- Stir in flour and walnuts and mix thoroughly.
- Add maple syrup, nutmeg and cinnamon.
- Pour batter into glass loaf pan, leaving about 1/2 inch of space for bread to rise but adding more batter to the center (to get the dome shape).
- Place in oven and bake for 1.5 hours.

Nutrition Information

- Calories: 1585.1
- Protein: 23.8
- Total Fat: 82.6
- Saturated Fat: 19.8
- Sodium: 1292
- Total Carbohydrate: 199.1
- Fiber: 16
- Sugar: 123.2
- Cholesterol: 142.6

313. Double Chocolate Macadamia Nut Muffins

Serving: 14 muffins | Prep: 15mins | Ready in:

Ingredients

- 300 g flour
- 3 teaspoons baking powder
- 1⁄4 teaspoon salt
- 150 g sugar
- 5 tablespoons oil
- 180 ml milk
- 1 egg, beaten
- 70 g white chocolate, chopped

- 70 g dark chocolate, chopped (I used 70% cocoa chocolate)
- 75 g macadamia nuts, chopped (roasted and salted slightly)

Direction

- Combine flour, baking powder, sugar and salt in a big bowl.
- In a second bowl combine egg, oil and milk. Add this to the dry ingredients.
- Fold in chocolate chunks and chopped nuts.
- Spoon batter into prepared muffin tin and bake in the preheated oven at 180°C/350°F for about 25 minutes or muffins are nicely browned on top and a toothpick inserted in the center comes out clean.

Nutrition Information

- Calories: 270.7
- Sodium: 137.1
- Sugar: 14
- Cholesterol: 17.6
- Saturated Fat: 4.5
- Fiber: 2
- Total Carbohydrate: 33.4
- Protein: 4.5
- Total Fat: 14.6

314. Easy Banana Bread Chocolate Nut

Serving: 3 loaves, 30 serving(s) | Prep: 15mins | Ready in:

Ingredients

- 2 1/2 cups sugar (500 gms)
- 1 cup butter, softened (228 gms)
- 4 large eggs (200 gms)
- 3 cups mashed ripe bananas (660 gms, approximately 6)
- 1 cup whole milk (236 gms)
- 2 teaspoons vanilla
- 5 cups flour (700 gms)
- 2 teaspoons baking soda
- 2 teaspoons salt
- 1 -2 cup chopped walnuts (120-240 gms) (optional)
- 1 (12 ounce) bag semi-sweet chocolate chips (340 gms) (optional)

Direction

- Move your oven rack so that the top of the loaf will be in the centre of the oven. Heat the oven to 350ºF. Grease three loaf pans with shortening. Line with parchment if desired.
- Cream sugar and butter in a large bowl until light and fluffy.
- Stir in eggs until blended.
- Add bananas, milk, and vanilla. Beat until smooth.
- Mix remaining dry ingredients in Ziploc bag and gently combine with banana mix. Stir in nuts and/or chocolate.
- Divide into 3 pans (about 1000 grams per pan). Bake for 1 ¼ hours (until toothpick inserted into the centre comes out clean).
- Cool 5 minutes on wire rack still in pan. Then remove from pan and place top side up. Cool completely before slicing. Wrap tightly and store a room temperature for 4 days or in the refrigerator for up to 10 days.

Nutrition Information

- Calories: 223.4
- Sodium: 295.7
- Sugar: 19.1
- Cholesterol: 45.3
- Total Fat: 7.3
- Saturated Fat: 4.3
- Total Carbohydrate: 36.5
- Protein: 3.5
- Fiber: 0.9

315. Easy Low Carb Lemon Blueberry Nut Butter Muffins

Serving: 6-8 muffins, 3-4 serving(s) | Prep: 20mins | Ready in:

Ingredients

- 8 ounces smooth cashew butter or 8 ounces smooth almond butter or 8 ounces smooth peanut butter
- 3 eggs
- 1/4 teaspoon salt
- 1 teaspoon baking soda
- 1 tablespoon lemon juice
- 12 -24 drops liquid stevia
- 1/2 teaspoon lemon extract (or to taste)
- 1/2 pint blueberries (approximately) (optional)
- 2 tablespoons chia seeds (optional) or 2 tablespoons poppy seeds (optional)

Direction

- Mix eggs, nut butter, salt, baking soda, sweetener, flavoring, and seeds if you're using them. You will probably need some sort of power tool as nut butters are hard to get to start to blend.
- Once you have a batter (it'll be pretty thick) add the lemon juice and mix again.
- If you're going to use blueberries, fill each cup of a greased muffin tin about 1/4 full of batter, add blueberries, then some batter on top.
- Otherwise fill cups 1/2 to 2/3 full.
- Bake 20 minutes at 275.

Nutrition Information

- Calories: 74.3
- Fiber: 0
- Cholesterol: 186
- Protein: 6.3
- Saturated Fat: 1.6
- Sugar: 0.3
- Total Carbohydrate: 0.7
- Total Fat: 4.8
- Sodium: 684.4

316. Every Which Way Quick Bread

Serving: 4 loaves | Prep: 20mins | Ready in:

Ingredients

- QUICK BREAD BASE
- 1 1/2 cups flour
- 1/2 teaspoon salt
- 1 cup sugar
- 1 teaspoon baking soda
- 1/2 cup vegetable oil
- 2 eggs, beaten
- PUMPKIN
- 1 cup canned pumpkin
- 2 teaspoons pumpkin pie spice
- 1/3 cup nuts (optional)
- 1/3 cup raisins (optional)
- APPLESAUCE
- 1 cup applesauce
- 1 tablespoon molasses
- 1 teaspoon cinnamon
- BANANA
- 3 ripe bananas, mashed
- 1/2 teaspoon cinnamon
- 1/2 teaspoon ginger
- PEANUT BUTTER BANANA
- 2 ripe bananas, mashed
- 1/2 cup peanut butter
- CRANBERRY
- 1 cup cranberries, chopped
- 1 tablespoon orange juice concentrate

Direction

- Preheat oven to 325°F.
- Gather the ingredients for the Quick Bread Base and one of the variations.
- Coat 4 small loaf pans with vegetable cooking spray.
- Combine dry ingredients; blend well and set aside.

- Combine wet ingredients; blend well.
- Mix together wet and dry ingredients.
- Do not over mix.
- Distribute batter among the 4 pans, and bake for 30 to 40 minutes.

Nutrition Information

- Calories: 1070.1
- Sugar: 78.7
- Protein: 18.8
- Total Fat: 47.4
- Saturated Fat: 8
- Sodium: 959.4
- Fiber: 11.3
- Total Carbohydrate: 153.3
- Cholesterol: 105.8

317. Fiber One Banana Nut Muffins

Serving: 12 muffins, 12 serving(s) | Prep: 20mins | Ready in:

Ingredients

- 3⁄4 cup self rising flour
- 1⁄2 cup whole wheat pastry flour
- 2 -3 ripe to over ripe bananas
- 1 cup Fiber One cereal, crushed (some large pieces are good)
- 1 teaspoon vanilla
- 2 tablespoons Splenda brown sugar blend
- 1 teaspoon cinnamon
- 1⁄4 cup applesauce
- 1 egg, beaten
- 1⁄2 cup skim milk
- 1⁄2 cup pecan pieces

Direction

- Heat oven to 425F degrees.
- In large mixing bowl place 1 cup Fiber One cereal and 1/2 cup milk. Mix in 2 to 3 pureed bananas and let stand 5 minutes.
- After 5 minutes add all ingredients except for flour. Mix well.
- Add flour and mix to even consistency.
- Bake in greased muffin tins for 20 to 25 minutes until tops are lightly browned.
- When done, loosen from muffin tin and let cool.

Nutrition Information

- Calories: 127.6
- Sugar: 3.7
- Cholesterol: 15.7
- Protein: 3.4
- Fiber: 4.2
- Saturated Fat: 0.5
- Sodium: 130.9
- Total Carbohydrate: 22.6
- Total Fat: 4.1

318. Fig, Date, And Walnut Quick Bread

Serving: 12 serving(s) | Prep: 25mins | Ready in:

Ingredients

- 3⁄4 cup low-fat buttermilk
- 1⁄2 teaspoon finely grated lemon rind
- 1⁄4 teaspoon ground nutmeg
- 1⁄8 teaspoon ground cloves
- 2⁄3 cup chopped dried fig
- 1⁄3 cup chopped pitted dates
- 1⁄2 cup packed brown sugar
- 2 tablespoons canola oil
- 2 large eggs
- 3⁄4 cup whole wheat flour
- 3⁄4 cup all-purpose flour
- 1 1⁄2 teaspoons baking soda
- 1⁄8 teaspoon salt

- cooking spray
- 1/3 cup chopped walnuts

Direction

- Preheat oven to 350°.
- Heat first 4 ingredients in a small, heavy saucepan over medium heat just until bubbles begin to form around edge (do not boil).
- Remove from heat; stir in figs and dates.
- Let stand 20 minutes or until fruit softens.
- Combine sugar, oil, and eggs in a large bowl; stir with a whisk until well blended.
- Stir in cooled milk mixture.
- Combine flours, baking soda, and salt in a large bowl; make a well in center of mixture.
- Add milk mixture to flour mixture, stirring just until moist.
- Spoon batter into an 8 x 4-inch loaf pan coated with cooking spray.
- Sprinkle walnuts evenly over batter.
- Bake for 40 minutes or until a wooden pick inserted in center comes out clean.
- Cool 10 minutes in pan on a wire rack; remove from pan. Cool completely on a wire rack.

Nutrition Information

- Calories: 183.6
- Total Fat: 5.8
- Sodium: 214.5
- Total Carbohydrate: 30.6
- Cholesterol: 35.9
- Protein: 4.3
- Saturated Fat: 0.8
- Fiber: 2.6
- Sugar: 16.9

319. Gluten Free Moist Mango And Nut Bread

Serving: 2 small loaves, 6-8 serving(s) | Prep: 15mins | Ready in:

Ingredients

- 1 cup Bob's Red Mill gluten-free all-purpose baking flour (you can substitute with all purpose baking flour for a regluar recipe, and if you can tolerate glute)
- 3 teaspoons baking powder
- 1/2 cup brown sugar
- 2 teaspoons coconut oil
- 1/4 teaspoon salt
- 2 large eggs
- 1/2 cup macadamia nuts or 1/2 cup walnuts, chopped
- 300 g raw mangoes, pureed or 2 -3 mangoes, depending on the size
- 2 teaspoons vanilla extract
- 1 teaspoon cinnamon (optional)

Direction

- 1) Preheat oven to 350 degrees.
- 2) In a large bowl combine flour, baking powder, salt (and cinnamon if added). Whisk well.
- 3) In another bowl separate the egg whites from the yolks.
- 4) With an electric beater (or by hand if you've got it in you) beat the egg whites until stiff.
- 5) Beat the yolks, adding in the oil, vanilla, and sugar.
- 6) Pour your wet yolk mixture into the flour and mix well.
- 7) Add the egg whites to the batter. Folding them in until smooth.
- 8) Mix in the mangoes and nuts into the batter.
- 9) Pour into 2 small greased loaf or cake pans.
- 10) Bake for about 1 hour or until toothpick comes out clean.

Nutrition Information

- Calories: 240.5
- Sodium: 308.7
- Fiber: 2.3
- Total Carbohydrate: 32.5
- Cholesterol: 62
- Total Fat: 11.9

- Saturated Fat: 3.2
- Sugar: 29.6
- Protein: 3.7

320. Golden Harvest Muffins II

Serving: 36 serving(s) | Prep: 20mins | Ready in:

Ingredients

- 2 cups white flour
- 2 cups wheat flour
- 2 cups sugar
- 4 teaspoons baking soda
- 4 teaspoons cinnamon
- 1 teaspoon salt
- 1/2 teaspoon clove
- 4 cups shredded apples (approx 6 medium)
- 1 cup shredded carrot
- 1 cup coconut
- 1 cup raisins
- 1 1/2 cups applesauce
- 1 1/2 cups chopped prunes (12 oz pkg)
- 1/2 cup milk
- 4 teaspoons vanilla
- 2 egg whites

Direction

- Heat oven to 350°F.
- Line 36 muffin tins with papers.
- Combine flour, sugar, baking soda, cinnamon, salt cloves.
- Add apples, carrots, coconut, raisins, applesauce, and prunes.
- Mix well.
- Add milk, vanilla, and eggs; stir just until moistened.
- Fill muffin tins 3/4 full.
- Bake at 350°F for 18-20 minutes.
- Immediately remove from pans to cooling rack.

Nutrition Information

- Calories: 157.3
- Saturated Fat: 1.5
- Sodium: 216.5
- Fiber: 2.7
- Sugar: 18.1
- Cholesterol: 0.5
- Protein: 2.5
- Total Fat: 1.9
- Total Carbohydrate: 34.3

321. Grain Free Blueberry Muffins

Serving: 12 muffins, 12 serving(s) | Prep: 20mins | Ready in:

Ingredients

- 2 cups blueberries (frozen or fresh)
- 1/2 cup water
- 2 1/2 cups almond flour
- 1/2 teaspoon baking soda
- 1/4 teaspoon salt
- 1 teaspoon ground cinnamon
- 1/2 teaspoon pure vanilla extract
- 1/2 cup honey
- 3 eggs

Direction

- Heat oven to 325°F Line a muffin tin with large baking cups.
- In a small saucepan, simmer the blueberries with the water until the berries release their juice and the mixture has thickened slightly. Let cool.
- Combine the almond flour, baking soda, salt, and cinnamon in a bowl.
- Combine the blueberries, vanilla, honey, and eggs in another bowl.
- Add the dry ingredients to the wet and mix well.
- Evenly fill each baking up with the batter.

- Bake for 25 to 30 minutes.

Nutrition Information

- Calories: 75.9
- Cholesterol: 46.5
- Saturated Fat: 0.4
- Fiber: 0.7
- Sugar: 14.1
- Total Carbohydrate: 15.5
- Protein: 1.8
- Total Fat: 1.3
- Sodium: 119.8

322. Great Aunt Marie's Banana Nut Bread

Serving: 2 loaves, 12-20 serving(s) | Prep: 20mins | Ready in:

Ingredients

- 1/4 cup butter
- 1 (8 ounce) package cream cheese
- 2 cups sugar
- 2 large eggs
- 3 cups flour
- 1/4 teaspoon baking powder
- 1/2 teaspoon baking soda
- 1/2 teaspoon salt
- 3 very ripe bananas, mashed
- 1 cup chopped toasted pecans
- 1/2 teaspoon vanilla extract

Direction

- Beat butter and cream cheese with an electric mixer.
- Gradually add sugar and beat until light and fluffy.
- Add eggs one at a time blending after each addition.
- Combine flour and next 3 ingredients.
- Gradually add to butter mixture, beating on low speed.
- Stir in banana, pecans and vanilla.
- Spoon into greased and floured 8x4 inch bread pans.
- Bake at 350 for 1 hour shielding with aluminum foil for last 15 minutes.
- Remove from pans and cool 30 minutes on wire racks.

Nutrition Information

- Calories: 444.4
- Sodium: 252.7
- Fiber: 2.5
- Total Carbohydrate: 65.8
- Protein: 6.9
- Total Fat: 18.2
- Saturated Fat: 7.5
- Sugar: 37.5
- Cholesterol: 66.2

323. Greek Muffins

Serving: 6 muffins | Prep: 10mins | Ready in:

Ingredients

- 100 g flour
- 25 g rolled oats
- 60 g walnuts, chopped (or try almonds, hazelnuts, pecans)
- 1 teaspoon baking powder
- 60 g dried dates, chopped (or try raisins, currants)
- 1/4 teaspoon cinnamon (optional)
- 125 g Greek yogurt (plain yogurt will work as well, you can try different flavours, like e.g. walnut)
- 2 tablespoons honey, runny type
- 1 egg, beaten
- 2 tablespoons oil

Direction

- In a big bowl combine all of the dry ingredients.
- In a second bowl combine yogurt, honey, egg and oil.
- Add the wet to the dry ingredients and stir only until just combined (do not overmix).
- Fill batter into prepared muffin tins and bake in the pre-heated oven at 180°C/350°F for about 25 minutes or until a toothpick inserted in the center comes out clean and muffins are nicely browned.

Nutrition Information

- Calories: 243.7
- Sodium: 73.6
- Total Carbohydrate: 30.4
- Cholesterol: 31
- Protein: 5.1
- Saturated Fat: 1.5
- Fiber: 2.4
- Sugar: 12.5
- Total Fat: 12.3

324. Hartson's Moist Banana Strawberry Nut Bread

Serving: 2 Loafs | Prep: 15mins | Ready in:

Ingredients

- 1/2 cup butter (or margarine)
- 2 cups powdered sugar
- 4 teaspoons vanilla
- 3 eggs (beaten)
- 4 bananas, peel should fall off (smashed)
- 1/4-1/2 cup milk
- 3 cups flour (white)
- 1/2 teaspoon salt
- 1/2 teaspoon baking soda
- 6 ounces chopped pecans
- 2 cups fresh strawberries, chopped (add more if desired)

Direction

- Grate butter if refrigerated, microwave 20 seconds until soft, or use room temperature butter.
- Chop a basket of strawberries (about 2 cups). Important: Do not over chop strawberries. You will want the chew of the Strawberry to come through and deliver the strawberry flavor.
- Chop, lightly, pecans in food processor or use meat tenderizing mallet to break pecans into smaller pieces. Important: Do not over chop pecans. You will want the chew of the pecan to come through.
- In LARGE bowl, combine powdered sugar, salt, baking soda, chopped pecans and only TWO of the three cups of flour together. Set aside third cup of flour. The bowl used should be large enough to combine all ingredients together later.
- Separately, beat three eggs. Add vanilla, milk, and butter. Mix gently together.
- ADD Step 5 (wet mixture) into large bowl used earlier to combine dry ingredients. Fold and mix lightly until combined and smooth.
- Preheat oven to 350 degrees.
- ADD bananas and mix (if bananas have not been blended yet, use a mashing utensil such as one used for mashing potatoes). Do not over mix bananas. You will want small chunks of banana for texture and flavor.
- ADD strawberries to mix and lightly fold.
- Combined mixture should be slightly fluid. ADD remaining flour in small parts until mixture maintains a light form. It should fall off a spatula, a little more formed than making pancake batter.
- Coat well, two bread loaf pans (metal or glass will do).
- Place mixture in equal parts into two loaf bread pans (see pan size in finished loafs picture).
- Place both filled pans in center oven. Bake 50 minutes. REDUCE oven temperature to 325 and continue to cook 30-40 minutes.

- Remove from oven, Cover with cloth and cool. Serve warm or cold.

Nutrition Information

- Calories: 2552
- Protein: 41.6
- Fiber: 22.3
- Sugar: 158.5
- Total Carbohydrate: 342.6
- Total Fat: 118.7
- Saturated Fat: 38
- Sodium: 1433.4
- Cholesterol: 405.3

325. Hawaiian Nut Bread

Serving: 1 loaf, 6 serving(s) | Prep: 15mins | Ready in:

Ingredients

- 3 tablespoons butter, softened
- 1 3/4 cups all-purpose flour
- 1/4 teaspoon baking soda
- 1 tablespoon sugar
- 2 eggs
- 2 teaspoons baking powder
- 3/4 cup macadamia nuts, chopped
- 1/4 teaspoon ground cinnamon
- 3/4 cup brown sugar, packed
- 1/2 teaspoon salt
- 1 cup crushed pineapple

Direction

- In a mixing bowl, beat butter, eggs and brown sugar.
- Combine the flour, baking powder, salt, baking soda and nuts; stir half into egg mixture.
- Add pineapple, then remaining flour mixture.
- Pour into a greased 3x4x2" loaf pan.
- Combine sugar and cinnamon; sprinkle over loaf.
- Bake at 350 degrees for 50-55 minutes or until toothpick inserted into center comes out clean.

Nutrition Information

- Calories: 466.1
- Total Fat: 20.5
- Saturated Fat: 6.2
- Sodium: 444.2
- Fiber: 2.8
- Total Carbohydrate: 66.1
- Sugar: 35.5
- Cholesterol: 85.8
- Protein: 7.4

326. Healthy Delicious Muffins

Serving: 12-15 muffins, 12-15 serving(s) | Prep: 20mins | Ready in:

Ingredients

- 1/2 cup white flour or 1/2 cup brown flour
- 1/2 cup cornflour
- 1/4-1/2 cup oats
- 2 teaspoons natural bran
- 1 cup yoghurt
- orange zest
- 1/4 cup sunflower oil
- 1/4 cup white sugar
- 2 teaspoons honey
- 1 teaspoon baking powder
- 1 teaspoon baking soda
- 2 eggs or 2 egg whites
- 1/4 cup raisins or 1/4 cup dried fruits
- 1 teaspoon vanilla

Direction

- Mix the yoghurt the oats set aside.
- Mix the dry ingredients.
- Beat the oil, sugar honey for 2 minutes.
- Add eggs one by one while beating.

- Add the yoghurt oats while beating.
- Add the dry ingredients beat until well mixed together.
- Add the raisins the orange zest lastly mix by spoon for one minute in one direction.
- Fill cups 2/3 full.
- Bake for 20 to 25 minutes or until toothpick inserted in center comes out clean. Cool 1 minute before removing from pan. Serve warm or cold with coffee.
- Bon appetite.

Nutrition Information

- Calories: 146.7
- Total Fat: 6.3
- Protein: 3
- Total Carbohydrate: 19.7
- Cholesterol: 37.9
- Saturated Fat: 1.3
- Sodium: 157.2
- Fiber: 0.7
- Sugar: 8

327. Healthy Apple Spice Muffins

Serving: 18 Muffins, 18 serving(s) | Prep: 30mins | Ready in:

Ingredients

- 1 cup brown rice syrup
- 1/2 cup sucanat
- 4 tablespoons canola oil
- 2 tablespoons unsweetened apple juice
- 1/3 cup plain low-fat yogurt
- 1 teaspoon vanilla
- 3 eggs
- 1 1/4 cups unbleached flour
- 1/3 cup whole wheat flour
- 1 teaspoon cinnamon
- 1/2 teaspoon nutmeg
- 2 1/2 teaspoons baking soda
- 1/2 teaspoon salt
- 1 apple, diced
- 1/3 cup chopped walnuts
- 1/3 cup raisins
- Frosting (optional)
- 4 tablespoons unsalted butter, softened
- 4 ounces low-fat cream cheese
- 1 tablespoon apple juice
- 1 teaspoon cinnamon
- 1 cup date sugar or 1 cup sucanat

Direction

- Preheat oven to 350ºF and grease or line muffin tins.
- Blend together brown rice syrup, Sucanat, oil, apple juice, yogurt, and vanilla in a large bowl.
- Mix in eggs, one at a time.
- In a medium bowl, sift together flours, cinnamon, nutmeg, baking soda, and salt.
- Add dry ingredients to wet ingredients, stirring until just combined.
- Do not overmix.
- Fold in diced apple, walnuts, and raisins.
- Spoon batter into prepared muffin tins.
- Bake 25 minutes or until a toothpick inserted in the center of a muffin comes out clean.
- Let cool in the tins for about 5 minutes to set then remove to a rack to cool completely.
- If frosting, let muffins cool completely.
- **FROSTING** Mix butter, cream cheese, and apple juice with an electric mixer on medium speed.
- In a separate bowl, mix cinnamon and date sugar/sucanat.
- Gradually add sugar mixture to cream-cheese mixture, blending on medium speed until stiff.
- Use about 1 tablespoon frosting per muffin.

Nutrition Information

- Calories: 149.8
- Cholesterol: 47.1
- Protein: 3.6
- Saturated Fat: 3.2

- Sodium: 280.6
- Total Carbohydrate: 12.8
- Total Fat: 9.6
- Fiber: 1.1
- Sugar: 3.2

328. Healthy Good Morning Muffins

Serving: 12 serving(s) | Prep: 10mins | Ready in:

Ingredients

- 1 1/2 cups whole wheat flour
- 1/2 cup oatmeal
- 1 teaspoon baking powder
- 2 teaspoons cinnamon
- 2 medium carrots, grated
- 1/2 cup raisins
- 1/2 cup walnuts, chopped
- 1/2 cup desiccated coconut (preferably unsweetened to keep it healthy)
- 1 medium apple, 1/2 grated 1/2 chopped into small chunks
- 1/2 cup yoghurt
- 1 banana, mashed
- 1 teaspoon baking soda
- 3 eggs, beaten
- 1/2 cup butter, melted
- 3 teaspoons vanilla essence

Direction

- Preheat oven to 180°C/350°F/Gas 4.
- In a mixing bowl combine wholemeal flour, oatmeal, baking powder, cinnamon, grated carrots, raisins, chopped walnuts, coconut and the grated apple.
- In a second bowl mix the yoghurt, banana and baking soda, once combined add the eggs, melted butter and vanilla essence.
- Blend well and then stir into the flour mixture until the two are combined.
- Don't overbeat.
- Bake in muffin tins for approx. 20 minutes.

Nutrition Information

- Calories: 243.9
- Sodium: 228.8
- Fiber: 3.9
- Sugar: 8.7
- Saturated Fat: 6.8
- Total Carbohydrate: 26
- Cholesterol: 74.5
- Protein: 5.9
- Total Fat: 14

329. Holiday Banana Bread

Serving: 1 loaf | Prep: 20mins | Ready in:

Ingredients

- 1 3/4 cups flour
- 2 3/4 teaspoons baking powder
- 1 teaspoon salt
- 1/2 cup walnuts, chopped
- 1 cup mixed candied fruit, finely chopped
- 1/4 cup fresh raisins
- 1/3 cup butter, room temperature
- 2/3 cup sugar
- 2 eggs
- 2 cups bananas, mashed (about 3 or 4 very ripe bananas)

Direction

- Preheat oven to 350 degrees F. Thoroughly grease a 5 x 9-inch loaf pan.
- Sift the flour, measure, and sift with the baking powder and salt onto a piece of waxed paper. Add the nuts, raisins and candied fruits, and mix until well coated with the flour.
- Cream together the butter and sugar until fluffy. Beat in eggs one at a time until thick and pale-lemon colored. Alternate additions of flour and fruit mixture and the mashed

bananas, stirring after each addition until well blended. Begin and end with flour mixture.

- Spoon into prepared loaf pan and bake in preheated oven for about 60 minutes or until bread pulls away from the sides of the pan.
- Let cool about 20 minutes before turning out on a rack to cool well.

Nutrition Information

- Calories: 2765.9
- Sugar: 194.4
- Cholesterol: 585.5
- Protein: 49.1
- Total Fat: 112.7
- Saturated Fat: 46.2
- Fiber: 19
- Total Carbohydrate: 409.4
- Sodium: 3911.9

330. Holiday Raisin Nut Pumpkin Bread

Serving: 3 loaves, 45-60 serving(s) | Prep: 10mins | Ready in:

Ingredients

- 3 cups white sugar
- 4 eggs
- 2/3 cup water
- 2 teaspoons baking soda
- 1 teaspoon baking powder
- 1 teaspoon ground allspice
- 3 1/2 cups all purpose flour
- 2 teaspoons salt
- 1 teaspoon ground nutmeg
- 1 teaspoon ground cinnamon
- 1/2 teaspoon ground cloves
- 1 (15 ounce) can pumpkin puree
- 1 cup chopped walnuts (can substitue pecans if desired)
- 1 cup raisins (your preference-white or purple)
- 1 cup vegetable oil

Direction

- Preheat oven to 350 degrees F. Grease loaf pans (can make in Bundt pans but need to adjust timing). Mix oil, sugar, and eggs together in a large bowl. Mix in pumpkin puree. Stir together flour, soda, baking powder, salt, and spices. Add to pumpkin mixture and mix until just combined. Fold in nuts and raisins and spread evenly into desired baking pan. Depending on oven, bake for 45 minutes-1 hour or until done. Set aside to cool on wire racks before slicing.

Nutrition Information

- Calories: 166.1
- Saturated Fat: 1
- Total Carbohydrate: 24.4
- Cholesterol: 18.8
- Protein: 2.2
- Total Fat: 7.1
- Sodium: 174.5
- Fiber: 0.7
- Sugar: 15.5

331. Judy's Date Muffins

Serving: 8 muffins, 8 serving(s) | Prep: 15mins | Ready in:

Ingredients

- 1/2 cup dates, chopped
- 1/2 cup boiling water
- 1/4 cup shortening
- 1/2 cup sugar
- 1 egg
- 1 cup all-purpose flour
- 1/2 teaspoon baking powder
- 1/2 teaspoon baking soda
- 1/2 teaspoon ground cinnamon
- 1/4 cup walnuts, chopped

Direction

- Place dates in a small bowl and add boiling water, let stand 10 minutes (do not drain!).
- Meanwhile in a small mixing bowl, beat shortening and sugar until crumbly, about 2 minutes then beat in egg until well mixed.
- Add dates and beat on low speed until blended.
- Combine the flour, baking powder, baking soda and cinnamon and then stir into date mixture with a wooden spoon just until blended.
- Stir in the walnuts.
- Fill paper-lined muffin cups two-thirds full.
- Bake at 350F for 15-20 minutes or until toothpick comes out clean.
- Cool for 5 minutes before removing to wire rack to cool completely.

Nutrition Information

- Calories: 226.8
- Total Fat: 9.6
- Sodium: 111
- Fiber: 1.6
- Sugar: 19.7
- Saturated Fat: 2
- Total Carbohydrate: 33.5
- Cholesterol: 26.4
- Protein: 3.2

332. Lemon Nut Bread

Serving: 1 loaf | Prep: 20mins | Ready in:

Ingredients

- 1/4 cup butter or 1/4 cup margarine, softened
- 3/4 cup sugar
- 2 eggs
- 2 teaspoons finely shredded lemons, rind of
- 2 cups all-purpose flour
- 2 1/2 teaspoons baking powder
- 1 teaspoon salt
- 3/4 cup milk
- 1/2 cup chopped walnuts

Direction

- Cream together butter or margarine and sugar until mixture is light and fluffy.
- Add eggs and shredded lemon peel.
- Beat thoroughly.
- Stir together flour, baking powder and salt.
- Add to creamed mixture alternately with milk, beating well after each addition.
- Stir in walnuts.
- Pour batter into a greased 8 1/2x4 1/2x2/12 inch loaf pan.
- Bake at 350 for 50-55 minutes.
- Cool in pan for 10 minutes.
- Remove and cool on rack.

Nutrition Information

- Calories: 2551.8
- Saturated Fat: 40.4
- Sugar: 153
- Cholesterol: 570.6
- Total Fat: 103.3
- Sodium: 3796.1
- Fiber: 11.1
- Total Carbohydrate: 361.5
- Protein: 53.9

333. Lower Fat Banana Nut Chip Muffins

Serving: 24 serving(s) | Prep: 10mins | Ready in:

Ingredients

- 1/2 cup unsweetened applesauce
- 1 cup sugar
- 2 eggs
- 2 large bananas, mashed
- 2 cups whole wheat pastry flour

- 1 teaspoon salt
- 1 teaspoon baking powder
- 1/2 teaspoon baking soda
- 1/2 cup skim milk
- 1 teaspoon vanilla
- 1/2 cup pecans, chopped
- 3/4 cup chocolate chips

Direction

- Preheat the oven to 400 degrees and spray the muffin tin with cooking spray.
- Place the applesauce and sugar into a mixing bowl. Using an electric mixer, beat until fluffy.
- Add your eggs, beating after each one. Then add the mashed banana and beat well.
- Add one cup of the flour, the salt, the baking powder and baking soda, and mix. Pour in about half the milk and mix.
- Now add the additional 1 cup of flour and the rest of the milk and mix.
- Using a wooden spoon add the vanilla, pecans, and chocolate chips. Mix just until moist.
- Pour into your muffin tins and bake for 13-18 minutes or until just browned. Let cool on a wire rack.

Nutrition Information

- Calories: 128.1
- Cholesterol: 17.7
- Protein: 2.7
- Total Fat: 3.9
- Saturated Fat: 1.2
- Sodium: 148.4
- Fiber: 2.1
- Sugar: 12.8
- Total Carbohydrate: 22.8

334. Mama's Banana Bread

Serving: 12-15 serving(s) | Prep: 20mins | Ready in:

Ingredients

- 6 medium very ripe bananas
- 2 tablespoons vanilla extract
- 2 cups firmly packed brown sugar
- 1 1/2 cups vegetable oil
- 1 cup sour cream
- 4 large eggs
- 3 1/2 cups all-purpose flour
- 2 teaspoons baking soda
- 2 teaspoons baking powder
- 1 teaspoon salt
- 1 cup ground pecans
- 2 cups miniature semisweet chocolate chips

Direction

- Preheat oven to 350. Grease two (6x9 inch) loaf pans.
- In a small bowl, mash bananas together with vanilla.
- In a large bowl combine brown sugar, oil, sour cream, and eggs, stirring until combined.
- In a medium bowl, combine flour, baking soda, baking powder, and salt. Gradually add to sugar mixture, stirring until just combined. Stir in banana mixture, ground pecans, and mini chocolate morsels.
- Pour into pans and bake for 1 hour and 15 minutes, or until wooden pick inserted in center comes out clean. Let cool in pans for 15 minutes; remove from pans, and cool completely on wire racks.

Nutrition Information

- Calories: 837.4
- Total Fat: 48.7
- Saturated Fat: 12.3
- Sodium: 516.5
- Fiber: 5.1
- Cholesterol: 78.9
- Protein: 9.2
- Sugar: 59.1
- Total Carbohydrate: 97.8

335. Maple Nut Muffins

Serving: 12 serving(s) | Prep: 20mins | Ready in:

Ingredients

- 2 cups flour
- 1 cup whole wheat flour
- 1 tablespoon baking powder
- 1/2 teaspoon salt
- 1 teaspoon cinnamon
- 2 eggs, beaten
- 1/4 cup brown sugar
- 1/3 cup maple syrup
- 1 cup milk
- 6 tablespoons butter, melted
- 1/2 cup chopped nuts (optional)

Direction

- In a mixing bowl, combine flours, baking powder, salt and cinnamon; set aside.
- Mix together remaining ingredients till well blended.
- Pour liquid ingredients over dry mixture and stir a few quick strokes till moistened.
- Spoon into muffin cups.
- Bake at 350 degrees F for 25-30 minutes.

Nutrition Information

- Calories: 227.6
- Fiber: 1.9
- Total Carbohydrate: 35
- Protein: 5.3
- Cholesterol: 53.4
- Total Fat: 7.8
- Saturated Fat: 4.4
- Sodium: 253.8
- Sugar: 9.9

336. Maple Pecan Biscuits

Serving: 12 biscuits | Prep: 10mins | Ready in:

Ingredients

- 2 cups all-purpose flour
- 2 tablespoons sugar
- 2 teaspoons baking powder
- 1 teaspoon salt
- 1/2 cup shortening
- 1/3 cup chopped pecans
- 1 cup milk
- 2 teaspoons maple flavoring
- Glaze
- 1/2 cup powdered sugar
- 1/4 teaspoon vanilla extract
- 2 -3 teaspoons milk

Direction

- Preheat oven to 400°F.
- Grease a cookie sheet with cooking spray.
- Mix flour, sugar, baking powder and salt in a bowl.
- Cut in shortening until the mixture is like fine crumbs.
- Add the pecans.
- Combine the milk and maple flavor in another bowl; mix well.
- Add to the flour mixture; stir just until moistened.
- Drop the dough by spoonfuls on the cookie sheet.
- Bake 10-12 minutes or until the biscuits are light golden brown.
- Remove to a wire rack placed over wax paper.
- Combine all glaze ingredients and drizzle over the biscuits.

Nutrition Information

- Calories: 215.7
- Protein: 3.1
- Total Fat: 11.7
- Saturated Fat: 2.8
- Sodium: 265.3

- Fiber: 0.8
- Sugar: 7.2
- Total Carbohydrate: 24.6
- Cholesterol: 3

337. Merry Cherry Nut Yeast Scones

Serving: 1 serving(s) | Prep: 0S | Ready in:

Ingredients

- 1/4 cup water
- 2 (1/4 ounce) envelopes active dry yeast
- 2 teaspoons sugar
- 5 cups all-purpose flour
- 1 tablespoon baking powder
- 2 teaspoons salt
- 1 teaspoon baking soda
- 1 cup shortening
- 2 cups buttermilk
- 1/2 cup dried cherries
- 1/2 cup walnuts, chopped
- to taste jelly (optional)
- Mock Devonshire Cream
- 1 (8 ounce) package cream cheese (optional)
- 1/2 cup unsalted butter, softened (optional)
- 1 (12 ounce) package Cool Whip, thawed (optional)

Direction

- In a small bowl combine warm water, yeast and sugar and let proof 10 minutes.
- In a large bowl combine flour, baking powder, salt and baking soda.
- Cut in shortening until mixture resembles coarse crumbs.
- Gradually add in yeast mixture and buttermilk, stirring just until dry ingredients are moistened.
- Stir in cherries and walnuts, cover and chill at least 1 hour or up to 48 hours.
- Preheat oven to 450 degrees.
- Turn dough out onto a lightly floured surface and knead 3 - 4 times. Flatten to 1/2 inch thickness and cut with a 2 inch round cutter.
- Place on ungreased baking sheet and bake until golden, about 10 minutes.
- Serve hot with Mock Devonshire Cream and, if desired, jelly.
- MOCK DEVONSHIRE CREAM: In a mixer bowl, beat cream cheese and butter at high speed until fluffy.
- Add Cool Whip and beat at medium speed until blended.

Nutrition Information

- Calories: 4751.4
- Saturated Fat: 58.6
- Sugar: 35.1
- Total Carbohydrate: 526
- Protein: 95.4
- Total Fat: 254.7
- Sodium: 7536
- Fiber: 24.6
- Cholesterol: 19.6

338. Mini Pecan Muffins

Serving: 24-26 mini muffins | Prep: 20mins | Ready in:

Ingredients

- 1 cup light brown sugar
- 2 eggs
- 1/2 cup all-purpose flour
- 2/3 cup melted salted butter
- 1 cup chopped pecans

Direction

- Pre-heat oven to 350 degrees Combine all ingredients except pecans using a mixer Fold in chopped pecans.

- Pour mini muffin pan about 2/3 full Sprinkle with more chopped pecans on top Bake for 12-15 minutes.

Nutrition Information

- Calories: 126.9
- Sodium: 53.6
- Total Carbohydrate: 11.6
- Total Fat: 8.8
- Saturated Fat: 3.7
- Fiber: 0.5
- Sugar: 9.1
- Cholesterol: 29.1
- Protein: 1.3

339. Mr. Food's Date Nut Bread

Serving: 1 loaf, 8-10 serving(s) | Prep: 30mins | Ready in:

Ingredients

- 2 cups dates, pitted and chopped
- 2/3 cup firmly packed brown sugar
- 1/2 cup honey
- 2 tablespoons butter or 2 tablespoons margarine
- 1 cup very hot water
- 1 egg, beaten
- 2 teaspoons vanilla extract
- 2 cups all-purpose flour
- 1 teaspoon baking soda
- 1/2 teaspoon salt
- 1 cup chopped walnuts

Direction

- In a large bowl, combine dates, sugar, honey, and butter; add hot water, stir and let stand for 15 minutes.
- Preheat oven to 325 degrees.
- Stir egg and vanilla into date mixture.
- In a separate bowl, combine remaining ingredients.
- Stir the flour mixture into the date mixture.
- Pour batter into a greased 9x5 inch loaf pan.
- Bake for 1 hour or until a toothpick inserted in the center comes out clean.
- Cool in the pan for 10 minutes, then remove and let cool completely on a wire rack.

Nutrition Information

- Calories: 506.1
- Total Fat: 13.5
- Saturated Fat: 3
- Sodium: 342.4
- Fiber: 5.4
- Total Carbohydrate: 94.7
- Cholesterol: 34.1
- Sugar: 63.9
- Protein: 7.4

340. Noe Valley Bakery Blueberry Pecan Scones

Serving: 16 scones, 16 serving(s) | Prep: 50mins | Ready in:

Ingredients

- 7 ounces cold unsalted butter
- 2 1/2 cups all-purpose flour
- 1/3 cup granulated sugar
- 1 teaspoon baking powder
- 1/2 teaspoon salt
- 1/4 teaspoon baking soda
- 1/3 cup toasted pecans, chopped
- 1 cup buttermilk
- 1/2 cup fresh blueberries or 1/2 cup frozen blueberries

Direction

- Preheat the oven to 375°. Line 2 baking sheets with parchment, or grease them with butter.

- Chop the butter into 1/4-inch pieces. (It is important to make the pieces no larger than 1/4 inch because they are difficult to make any smaller once frozen.) Spread on a plate and place in the freezer until hard, about 30 minutes or overnight.
- Combine the flour, sugar, baking powder, salt and baking soda in a large bowl.
- Add the butter, and chop with two butter knives or a pastry blender until it is well blended and some of the butter is crumbly. Mix in the pecans.
- Gradually add the buttermilk, 1/3 cup at a time, and mix gently until all ingredients are incorporated but not completely blended. You might not use up all of the liquid. The end result should be a shaggy mass.
- Sprinkle the blueberries on top of the dough and only mix enough to evenly distribute the berries.
- Gently form the dough into 1/3-cup balls and place them 1 inch apart on the prepared baking sheets. (You may freeze the balls at this point and bake them later. Once frozen, place scones in freezer storage bags.).

Nutrition Information

- Calories: 200.7
- Total Fat: 12
- Saturated Fat: 6.6
- Sodium: 132.9
- Fiber: 0.8
- Sugar: 5.5
- Cholesterol: 27.3
- Total Carbohydrate: 20.9
- Protein: 2.9

341. North Carolina Applesauce Muffins

Serving: 12 muffins | Prep: 20mins | Ready in:

Ingredients

- 1/2 cup butter, softened
- 1/2-2/3 cup packed brown sugar
- 1 egg
- 1 cup unsweetened applesauce
- 1 1/2 teaspoons cinnamon
- 1/2 teaspoon clove
- 1 teaspoon allspice
- 1/2 teaspoon salt
- 1 teaspoon baking soda
- 1 cup unbleached flour
- 1 cup whole wheat flour
- 1/2 cup sliced almonds (or nuts of choice)

Direction

- Cream butter and sugar together.
- Beat in egg.
- Stir in applesauce and spices.
- Combine salt, baking soda, and flour in separate bowl; add to wet ingredients and beat well.
- Stir in nuts.
- Divide batter between 12 sprayed muffin tins and bake for 15-18 minutes, or until test done.
- Cool slightly on rack before serving.

Nutrition Information

- Calories: 212.7
- Sodium: 267.2
- Cholesterol: 38
- Protein: 3.9
- Saturated Fat: 5.2
- Fiber: 2.4
- Sugar: 9.1
- Total Carbohydrate: 27.6
- Total Fat: 10.4

342. Nut Butter Gems

Serving: 40 cookies, 40 serving(s) | Prep: 30mins | Ready in:

Ingredients

- 1 cup all-purpose flour (measured by dip sweep)
- 1 teaspoon baking soda
- 1/8 teaspoon salt
- 1/2 cup firmly packed light brown sugar
- 1/4 cup granulated sugar, preferably superfine
- 1/2 cup unsalted butter, cold
- 1 cup smooth peanut butter (must be smooth!) or 1 cup smooth cashew butter (must be smooth!) or 1 cup smooth almond butter (must be smooth!)
- 1 large egg
- 1/2 teaspoon vanilla extract
- 6 ounces milk chocolate
- 6 ounces bittersweet chocolate or 6 ounces semisweet chocolate
- 6 tablespoons unsalted butter

Direction

- Preheat oven to 375°F at least 15 minutes before baking time.
- •Food processor method:
- Into a small bowl, sift together the flour, baking soda, and salt- whisk to mix evenly.
- Process the sugars for several minutes until very fine.
- Cut the butter into a few pieces and add it with the motor running.
- Add the peanut butter and process until smooth and creamy.
- Add the egg and vanilla extract and process until incorporated, scraping the sides of the bowl.
- Add the flour mixture and pulse in just until incorporated.
- •Electric mixer method or by hand:
- Soften the butter to a cool room temperature.
- In a small bowl, sift together the flour, baking soda, and salt.
- Whisk to combine.
- In a mixing bowl, beat the sugars until well mixed.
- Add the butter and peanut butter and beat for several minutes, until very smooth and creamy.
- Add the egg and vanilla extract and beat until incorporated, scraping the sides of the bowl.
- Gradually beat in the flour mixture just until incorporated.
- •Both methods:
- Scrape the dough into a bowl and refrigerate for at least 1 hour or as long as overnight.
- Measure the dough into a 1 1/4-inch cookie scoop (2 level teaspoons) and roll it to shape 1-inch balls.
- Place the balls 1 1/2-inches apart on ungreased cookie sheets.
- As soon as you roll each ball, use your index finger or the handle of a wooden spoon to make a depression going down almost to the cookie sheet in the center of each ball.
- Bake for 10 to 12 minutes or until lightly browned and set.
- For even baking, rotate the cookie sheet front to back halfway through baking.
- Cool the cookies on the sheets for a few minutes or until firm enough to lift.
- Use a small angled metal spatula to transfer the cookies to wire racks to cool completely.
- If necessary, while the cookies are still hot, use the greased handle of a wooden spoon to deepen the depressions.
- Fill the centers with milk chocolate toppings.
- While the cookies are baking, prepare the chocolate topping, melt the chocolates.
- Whisk in the softened butter.
- The mixture will thicken immediately.
- Do not over whisk.
- Use a reclosable quart-size freezer bag with one corner cut off to pipe the chocolate into the centers the cookies.
- Allow the chocolate to set until firm before storing the cookies in airtight containers.

Nutrition Information

- Calories: 124.9
- Saturated Fat: 3.9

- Fiber: 0.6
- Sugar: 6.7
- Total Fat: 8.7
- Sodium: 75.1
- Total Carbohydrate: 10.1
- Cholesterol: 16.9
- Protein: 2.5

343. Nut Muffins

Serving: 24 Muffins, 10-12 serving(s) | Prep: 10mins | Ready in:

Ingredients

- Wet Ingredients
- 3 bananas
- 3 eggs
- 1 tablespoon vanilla
- 1 cup applesauce, with
- cinnamon
- 1/4 cup margarine, cut into pieces
- Dry Ingredients
- 1 1/2 cups flour
- 1 dash salt
- 3 dashes cinnamon
- 1 cup sugar
- 1 tablespoon baking powder
- 1 (8 -10 ounce) packagechopped walnuts

Direction

- Set oven to 350.
- In muffin pan place Baking cups; spray in center with Mazola no stick Canola/Sunflower Spray.
- In large mixing bowl, place bananas, eggs, vanilla, margin, (you can use butter if you like.) sugar, and applesauce.
- Mix w/ blender, add baking powder, and flour, salt and cinnamon, walnuts, mix well. Set aside a few nuts to place on top.
- Spoon out batter into muffin cups add a few chopped walnuts on top; and set in center of oven, for about 20 minute or so till brown.
- Remove from muffin tin and cool for about 10 minute
- Slice in middle spread w/ your favorite butter and enjoy!

Nutrition Information

- Calories: 412
- Cholesterol: 63.5
- Protein: 7.8
- Sodium: 207.1
- Fiber: 3.3
- Saturated Fat: 2.7
- Sugar: 25.2
- Total Carbohydrate: 51.3
- Total Fat: 21.2

344. Oatmeal Banana Raisin Nut Muffins

Serving: 10-12 muffins | Prep: 10mins | Ready in:

Ingredients

- 1 1/4 cups rolled oats
- 1/4 cup ground roasted soybeans
- 1/4 cup raisins
- 1/4 cup melted butter
- 1/4 soya oil
- 2 cups mashed bananas
- 1 beaten egg
- 1/4 teaspoon salt
- 1 teaspoon baking soda
- 1 1/2 teaspoons baking powder
- 1/2 cup sugar
- 3/4 cup unbleached flour
- 1/4 cup soy flour

Direction

- Heat oven to 375.
- Grease 10-12 muffin cups.
- In large bowl: combine the flours, oats, sugar, baking soda powder salt.

- Stir in beaten egg, mashed bananas, melted butter, and oil.
- Fold in nuts and raisins.
- Combine well.
- Pour batter into greased muffin cups.
- Bake 20-25 minutes or until toothpick in center comes out clean.
- Let muffins cool for at least 15 minutes before removing from tins.

Nutrition Information

- Calories: 207
- Total Carbohydrate: 34.5
- Cholesterol: 33.4
- Protein: 4.5
- Total Fat: 6.4
- Saturated Fat: 3.3
- Sodium: 279.7
- Fiber: 2.2
- Sugar: 16

345. Orange Cranberry Nut Bread

Serving: 1 loaf | Prep: 20mins | Ready in:

Ingredients

- ONE
- 1/3 cup orange juice
- 2/3 cup buttermilk
- 6 tablespoons butter, melted
- 1 egg, beaten
- TWO
- 1 cup sugar
- zest from 1 orange
- 2 cups all-purpose flour
- 1 teaspoon salt
- 1 teaspoon baking powder
- 1/4 teaspoon baking soda
- THREE
- 1 1/2 cups chopped fresh cranberries
- 1/2 cup chopped toasted pecans

Direction

- Preheat oven to 375F, butter and flour a 9-inch loaf pan.
- Combine ONE and stir together.
- Rub orange zest into sugar until aromatic, then add the rest of TWO.
- Stir ONE into TWO.
- Gently stir in THREE, do not overmix.
- Pour into pan, bake 20 mins, reduce heat to 350F, and bake 30-45 mins, until toothpick comes out clean.

Nutrition Information

- Calories: 2916.8
- Sodium: 3864.9
- Total Carbohydrate: 434.5
- Cholesterol: 375.7
- Total Fat: 117.3
- Saturated Fat: 50
- Fiber: 19.1
- Sugar: 223.5
- Protein: 44.4

346. Orange Date Nut Bran Muffins

Serving: 12 serving(s) | Prep: 15mins | Ready in:

Ingredients

- 2 cups shredded bran cereal
- 3/4 cup boiling water
- 1/4 cup vegetable oil
- 3/4 cup buttermilk
- 1/4 cup orange juice
- 2 tablespoons dark molasses
- 2 tablespoons honey
- 1 tablespoon grated orange zest
- 1 large egg (egg substitute optional)
- 3/4 cup all-purpose flour

- 1/2 cup whole wheat flour
- 1 1/2 teaspoons baking soda
- 1/2 teaspoon salt
- 1 cup chopped dates
- 3/4 cup chopped walnuts

Direction

- Heat oven to 400 degrees.
- Grease one 12-cup muffin tin.
- In a large bowl, combine bran cereal, water and oil, stirring until bran softens.
- In a small bowl, whisk buttermilk, orange juice, molasses, honey, orange zest, and egg until blended.
- In a small bowl, combine flours, baking soda and salt.
- Add buttermilk mixture to bran, stirring to combine.
- Add flour mixture, dates and walnuts to bran mixture, stirring just until flour is moistened.
- Spoon into muffin cups, and bake until top springs back when lightly pressed, about 18 minutes.
- Let cool in pan 5 minutes before removing to wire rack.

Nutrition Information

- Calories: 203.2
- Saturated Fat: 1.3
- Sodium: 278.7
- Fiber: 2.3
- Total Carbohydrate: 26.6
- Protein: 4
- Total Fat: 10.1
- Sugar: 13.9
- Cholesterol: 16.1

347. Orange Date Pumpkin Bread

Serving: 2 loaves, 28 serving(s) | Prep: 15mins | Ready in:

Ingredients

- nonstick cooking spray
- 2 cups all-purpose flour
- 1 1/3 cups whole wheat flour
- 2 teaspoons baking powder
- 1 teaspoon ground nutmeg
- 1/2 teaspoon salt
- 1/2 teaspoon baking soda
- 1 cup egg substitute or 4 eggs
- 1 (15 ounce) can pumpkin
- 1/2 cup sugar
- 1/4 cup Splenda sugar substitute, for baking
- 1/3 cup honey
- 3 tablespoons cooking oil
- 7 teaspoons unsweetened applesauce
- 1 teaspoon finely shredded orange peel
- 1/3 cup orange juice
- 1/2 cup chopped walnuts or 1/2 cup pecans
- 1/2 cup pitted dates, diced

Direction

- Preheat oven to 350 degrees. Prepare two loaf pans with a light coating of cooking spray.
- In a large bowl, stir together all-purpose flour, whole wheat flour, baking powder, nutmeg, salt, and baking soda. Set aside.
- In a medium bowl, stir together pumpkin, sugar, egg, honey, oil, applesauce, orange peel, and orange juice.
- Using a spoon, stir pumpkin mixture into flour mixture just until combined. Take care not to overmix as that will toughen the bread. Stir in nuts and dates (or raisins). Divide mixture between the prepared pans.
- (Tip: Dates can be quite sticky and hard to chop. Give your knife a quick shot of cooking spray. Once chopped, mix about 2 tablespoons of the flour mixture with the dates to help the bits separate and become evenly distributed in the bread.).
- Bake about 50 minutes or until a toothpick inserted near centers comes out clean.
- Cool in pans on wire racks for 10 minutes. Remove from pans. Cool completely on wire racks.

- This bread freezes well.

Nutrition Information

- Calories: 124.2
- Total Fat: 3.1
- Saturated Fat: 0.4
- Sugar: 9.8
- Cholesterol: 0
- Sodium: 107.8
- Fiber: 1.3
- Total Carbohydrate: 22.3
- Protein: 3.1

348. Orange Pecan Bran Muffins

Serving: 18 serving(s) | Prep: 20mins | Ready in:

Ingredients

- 1 1/4 cups flour
- 3/4 cup sugar
- 1 1/2 teaspoons baking soda
- 1 teaspoon salt
- 4 oranges
- 2 eggs, beaten
- 1/2 cup vegetable oil
- 4 1/2 cups Raisin Bran cereal
- 1 cup pecans, chopped

Direction

- Preheat oven to 375°F
- Grease or line muffin cups.
- In a large bowl, combine first four (dry) ingredients; set aside.
- Remove the peel and white membrane from two of the oranges; either discard or save the peel for another use.
- Cut all four of the oranges into eighths and remove the seeds; puree in a food processor.
- Measure out 2 cups of puree. If there is any extra, save it for another use.
- Stir oranges, eggs, oil, cereal and nuts into the dry ingredients; blend just until mixed.
- Fill muffin tins 3/4 full.
- Bake for 20 -25 minutes or until they test done with a toothpick.

Nutrition Information

- Calories: 229.7
- Total Carbohydrate: 30.9
- Protein: 3.7
- Total Fat: 11.5
- Fiber: 3.3
- Sugar: 16.2
- Cholesterol: 23.5
- Saturated Fat: 1.4
- Sodium: 332.5

349. Peach And Coconut Muffins

Serving: 10-12 serving(s) | Prep: 8mins | Ready in:

Ingredients

- 400 g canned peaches (sliced into small pieces)
- 250 ml vegetable oil
- 1 cup white sugar
- 3 eggs
- 1 1/2 cups self raising flour
- 1 cup coconut
- 1 teaspoon vanilla essence

Direction

- Whisk oil, eggs and sugar together in a bowl.
- Add sifted flour, vanilla and coconut, combine with a wooden spoon. Stir in peaches.
- Spoon mixture into greased muffin tray and bake in moderate oven (170 degrees Celsius) for 35 minutes.

Nutrition Information

- Calories: 438.9
- Sugar: 26.1
- Total Carbohydrate: 42.3
- Cholesterol: 55.8
- Protein: 4.6
- Total Fat: 28.9
- Sodium: 27.1
- Saturated Fat: 8.2
- Fiber: 2.4

350. Pecan Cinnamon Muffins

Serving: 6-12 serving(s) | Prep: 15mins | Ready in:

Ingredients

- 1 1/2 cups all-purpose flour, Sifted
- 1/4 cup sugar
- 1/4 cup brown sugar, Packed
- 2 teaspoons baking powder
- 1/2 teaspoon salt
- 1 teaspoon cinnamon, Ground
- 1 large egg, Slightly Beaten
- 1/2 cup vegetable oil
- 1/2 cup milk
- 1 teaspoon vanilla extract
- 1/2-1 cup pecans, Chopped

Direction

- Sift together flour, baking powder, salt and cinnamon into mixing bowl; Add white and brown sugar; stir in Pecans.
- Combine egg, oil and milk and vanilla in small bowl; blend well.
- Add all at once to dry ingredients, stirring just enough to moisten; Batter will be thick.
- Spoon batter into 12 greased 2 1/2-inch muffin-pan cups or 6- 3 1/2 muffin cups.
- Bake in 375°F oven about 20 minutes for 12 muffins or about 30 minutes for 6 -3 1/2 inch muffin cups or until tester comes out clean.

Nutrition Information

- Calories: 433
- Protein: 5.8
- Total Fat: 26.6
- Fiber: 1.9
- Sugar: 17.8
- Total Carbohydrate: 44.2
- Cholesterol: 33.9
- Saturated Fat: 3.7
- Sodium: 340

351. Pecan Pie Surprise Muffins

Serving: 12 serving(s) | Prep: 10mins | Ready in:

Ingredients

- 3 slices pecan pie, frozen
- 1 egg
- 1 cup milk
- 1/2 cup unsalted butter, melted and cooled
- 1/2 teaspoon vanilla extract
- 2 1/4 cups all-purpose flour
- 1/2 cup sugar
- 3 1/2 teaspoons baking powder
- 1 teaspoon salt
- Topping
- 2 tablespoons sugar
- 1/4 teaspoon cinnamon

Direction

- Preheat oven to 400 degrees F. Grease a 12 cup muffin tin.
- Cut each frozen pie single into 4 chunks. Place one frozen pie chunk in each muffin tin.
- In a small bowl, beat together egg, milk, melted butter and vanilla extract.
- In large bowl, combine flour, sugar, baking powder, and salt. Add egg mixture; stir just until blended.
- Spoon batter into muffin tins, covering pecan pie chunks. Stir together topping ingredients

(sugar and cinnamon) and sprinkle evenly over muffin tops.
- Bake for 20 minutes. Let cool for 5 minutes; remove from muffin tins.

Nutrition Information

- Calories: 339.6
- Protein: 5.2
- Sugar: 10.6
- Total Carbohydrate: 45.6
- Fiber: 0.7
- Cholesterol: 67.3
- Total Fat: 15.8
- Saturated Fat: 6.7
- Sodium: 396.9

352. Pennsylvania Grange Banana Nut Bread Grange # 1751

Serving: 2 9x5 loaves, 20 serving(s) | Prep: 25mins | Ready in:

Ingredients

- 2 1/2 cups white sugar
- 1 cup shortening
- 3 eggs
- 1 1/2 cups mashed bananas
- 3 cups unbleached flour
- 1 1/4 cups buttermilk
- 1 1/2 teaspoons baking soda
- 1 1/2 teaspoons baking powder
- 1 teaspoon vanilla
- 1/2 cup pecan pieces or 1/2 cup walnut pieces

Direction

- Cream sugar and shortening.
- Add eggs one at a time and then add the mashed bananas and vanilla.
- Add dry ingredients alternately with the buttermilk and chopped nuts.
- Put batter in 2 greased and floured 9x5 inch loaf pans and bake at 350 degrees for 45 - 50 min., or until a wooden toothpick comes out clean when inserted.
- Cool for 10 min., then remove from pans.
- Slice when cold.
- Keeps moist when tightly wrapped.
- Freezes well.
- Delicious toasted!

Nutrition Information

- Calories: 307.1
- Sodium: 149.2
- Fiber: 1.2
- Protein: 3.8
- Total Carbohydrate: 44.4
- Cholesterol: 28.5
- Total Fat: 13.3
- Saturated Fat: 3.1
- Sugar: 28

353. Perfect Pumpkin Mini Muffins

Serving: 75 mini muffins | Prep: 15mins | Ready in:

Ingredients

- Muffin Batter
- 2 eggs
- 1 2/3 cups sugar
- 1 tablespoon vanilla extract
- 1 (15 ounce) can pumpkin puree
- 3/4 cup vegetable oil
- 3/4 cup apricot nectar
- 1 cup pastry flour (this can be substituted with all-purpose, but be more gentle while stirring so as not to create to m)
- 1 3/4-2 cups all-purpose flour
- 1 teaspoon baking powder
- 1 1/2-2 teaspoons cinnamon
- 1/2 teaspoon nutmeg

- 1 teaspoon salt
- Strudel Topping
- 2/3 cup flour
- 2/3 cup sugar
- 2/3 cup ground pecans
- 1/2 teaspoon salt
- 6 tablespoons butter, cold

Direction

- Preheat oven to 375°F.
- Line mini muffin pan with paper (or foil) liners.
- For Muffin Batter:
- Sift together both flours, baking powder, cinnamon, nutmeg, and salt. Set aside.
- Beat eggs, sugar, and vanilla with whisk attachment on stand-up mixer on medium for 2 minutes or until pale yellow.
- Add pumpkin, veg oil, and nectar and whisk on low until just combined.
- Fold in dry ingredients until just combined. Set aside.
- For Strudel Topping:
- Combined first four ingredients.
- Cut in the butter with pastry cutter or fingers until crumbly.
- For Muffins:
- Fill lined mini muffin tins 3/4 to the top with batter then fill to the top with strudel topping.
- Bake for 10-12 minutes.
- Cool and EAT!

Nutrition Information

- Calories: 85
- Sodium: 61.7
- Sugar: 6.7
- Total Carbohydrate: 11.7
- Cholesterol: 7.4
- Total Fat: 4
- Saturated Fat: 1
- Fiber: 0.3
- Protein: 0.9

354. Pineapple Muffins With Coconut And Brown Sugar Topping

Serving: 18 muffins | Prep: 15mins | Ready in:

Ingredients

- 1 1/3 cups flour
- 1/2 cup sugar
- 1/3 cup brown sugar, lightly packed
- 1 teaspoon baking powder
- 1/2 teaspoon baking soda
- 1/2 cup chopped pecans
- 2/3 cup rolled oats
- 1 cup buttermilk
- 1/2 cup melted butter
- 1 egg
- 1 (15 ounce) can crushed pineapple, drained well
- 1/2 cup sweetened flaked coconut
- Topping
- 1/3 cup brown sugar
- 1/4 cup flour
- 1/4 cup sweetened flaked coconut
- 2 tablespoons rolled oats
- 3 tablespoons cold butter, cut up

Direction

- Grease 18 muffin cups, or line with paper liners.
- In a large bowl, mix together flour, sugar, brown sugar, baking powder, baking soda, pecans and oats. Make a well in the center of the mixture.
- In a separate bowl, whisk together buttermilk, melted butter and egg.
- Pour into well in flour mixture, stir to blend just until dry ingredients are moistened, but do not overmix.
- Gently fold in pineapple and coconut.
- Spoon batter into prepared muffin cups, filling about 2/3 full.
- For topping:

- Mix together brown sugar, flour, coconut and oats. Cut in butter with a pastry cutter till coarse crumbs have formed.
- Sprinkle crumb topping over pineapple muffin batter.
- Bake muffins at 400 for about 20 minutes, or till tops are lightly browned and firm.
- Transfer pans to rack to cool for about 5 minutes.
- Gently turn muffins out onto rack to cool completely.

Nutrition Information

- Calories: 232.2
- Protein: 3
- Sodium: 148.4
- Sugar: 19.4
- Cholesterol: 29.5
- Fiber: 1.3
- Total Carbohydrate: 31.1
- Total Fat: 11.3
- Saturated Fat: 6.1

355. Polenta Quick Bread With Lemon And Thyme

Serving: 1 loaf | Prep: 30mins | Ready in:

Ingredients

- 3⁄4 cup butter, softened, plus more for pan
- 1⁄3 cup flour, plus more for pan
- 3⁄4 cup sugar
- 1 tablespoon finely grated lemon zest
- 2 tablespoons fresh lemon juice
- 3 eggs
- 1 tablespoon coarsely chopped fresh thyme leave, plus
- fresh thyme sprig (to garnish)
- 1 cup fine yellow cornmeal (preferably stone-ground)
- 1 teaspoon baking powder
- 3⁄4 teaspoon coarse salt
- 1⁄4 cup pine nuts, toasted, half coarsely chopped and half whole

Direction

- Preheat oven to 325°.
- Butter a 9-by-5-inch loaf pan. Dust with flour, and tap out excess; set aside.
- Put butter and sugar into the bowl of an electric mixer fitted with the paddle attachment. Mix on medium-high speed until pale and fluffy, about 3 minutes.
- Add lemon zest; mix 1 minute.
- Add eggs, 1 at a time, mixing well after each addition.
- Mix in lemon juice and thyme.
- Add flour, cornmeal, baking powder, and salt, and mix until just combined.
- Stir in chopped pine nuts.
- Pour batter into prepared pan. Sprinkle with pine nuts.
- Bake until a pick inserted into center comes out clean, 50 to 55 minutes.
- Let cool completely on a wire rack.
- Garnish with thyme.

Nutrition Information

- Calories: 2856.9
- Total Carbohydrate: 286.4
- Protein: 39.5
- Total Fat: 180.9
- Fiber: 12.4
- Sugar: 154.2
- Cholesterol: 1000.5
- Saturated Fat: 94.5
- Sodium: 3342.9

356. Pumpkin Banana Nut Muffins

Serving: 24 muffins, 24 serving(s) | Prep: 15mins | Ready in:

Ingredients

- 4 cups whole wheat flour
- 1/4 cup wheat bran
- 2 tablespoons flax seeds
- 1/2 teaspoon cinnamon
- 1/8 teaspoon ginger
- 2 teaspoons baking powder
- 1 teaspoon baking soda
- 1/4 teaspoon salt
- 30 ounces pumpkin pie mix
- 1 large banana (overripe, about 3/4 cup)
- 4 large eggs
- 3/4 cup packed brown sugar
- 3/4 cup oil
- 1 cup crushed walnuts or 1 cup pecans

Direction

- Preheat oven to 350F and line muffin tins with paper cups.
- Combine flour, baking powder, baking soda, spices, and salt in a large bowl. Stir until mixed well.
- In a separate bowl combine all the other ingredients and stir until smooth.
- Little by little, add the flour mix to the pumpkin mix. Mix only until combined.
- Divide into muffin pan and sprinkle with graham cracker crumbs or cinnamon sugar if desired.
- Bake for 25 to 30 minutes or until a toothpick will come out of a muffin without batter on it.
- Transfer muffins to a wire rack and cool.
- Enjoy!

Nutrition Information

- Calories: 246.2
- Saturated Fat: 1.6
- Fiber: 6.4
- Sugar: 7.6
- Total Fat: 11.7
- Sodium: 196.4
- Total Carbohydrate: 33.4
- Cholesterol: 35.2
- Protein: 5.2

357. Sarah's Zucchini Nut Bread

Serving: 2 loafs, 24-36 serving(s) | Prep: 10mins | Ready in:

Ingredients

- 1 cup white sugar
- 1 cup brown sugar
- 1 cup cooking oil
- 3 eggs
- 2 cups grated zucchini
- 3 cups flour
- 1 teaspoon salt
- 1/2 teaspoon baking powder
- 2 teaspoons baking soda
- 4 teaspoons vanilla
- 2 teaspoons cinnamon
- 1/2 cup chopped walnuts

Direction

- Mix sugar, oil, vanilla and eggs together.
- Mix dry ingredients together and add to wet mixture.
- Mix in grated zucchini and nuts.
- Bake @325 degrees for 60 minutes in loaf pans.

Nutrition Information

- Calories: 233.3
- Sodium: 223.2
- Sugar: 17.6
- Cholesterol: 26.4
- Protein: 2.9
- Total Fat: 11.5
- Saturated Fat: 1.6
- Fiber: 0.8
- Total Carbohydrate: 30.2

358. Scd Gluten Free Cinnamon Apple Scones

Serving: 6 scones, 6 serving(s) | Prep: 10mins | Ready in:

Ingredients

- 3 3⁄4 cups almond meal
- 1 1⁄2 teaspoons ground cinnamon
- 3⁄4 teaspoon salt
- 3 eggs
- 6 tablespoons honey
- 1⁄2 cup butter, melted
- 2 apples, chopped

Direction

- Heat oven to 180C (350F).
- Mix all ingredients.
- Drop 1/4 cup amounts onto greased tray, shape into triangles.
- Bake for 15 minutes.

Nutrition Information

- Calories: 609.8
- Fiber: 9.1
- Sugar: 26
- Total Carbohydrate: 39.3
- Cholesterol: 133.7
- Protein: 16.1
- Total Fat: 47.2
- Sodium: 463.4
- Saturated Fat: 12.7

359. Slovak Nut Bread

Serving: 4 loafs | Prep: 1hours30mins | Ready in:

Ingredients

- Dough
- 4 cups flour
- 3⁄4 teaspoon salt
- 1⁄2 teaspoon baking soda
- 5 egg yolks
- 1 cup sour cream
- 1⁄4 cup Crisco
- 1⁄4 cup butter
- 1 fresh yeast cake
- Filling
- 5 egg whites
- 1 teaspoon vanilla
- 1 lb ground nuts
- 3⁄4 cup sugar

Direction

- Mix flour, salt, and soda.
- Add egg yolks and sour cream to the flour mixture.
- Cut the dough like pie dough.
- Form the dough into four balls and refrigerate them over night.
- The next day, roll the dough with a rolling pin.
- Mix the nut filling ingredients.
- Spread, thinly on the dough.
- Roll the dough like a jelly roll.
- Brush the dough with an egg white bath.
- Place the dough on an ungreased cookie sheet.
- Bake at 350 deg. for 25 minutes.

Nutrition Information

- Calories: 1028.7
- Fiber: 3.7
- Cholesterol: 291.8
- Total Carbohydrate: 137.2
- Protein: 22.7
- Total Fat: 42.8
- Saturated Fat: 20.7
- Sodium: 787.1
- Sugar: 38.4

360. Sourdough Nut Batter Bread

Serving: 1 loaf | Prep: 2hours | Ready in:

Ingredients

- 2 cups proofed sourdough starter
- 2 tablespoons butter
- 1/2 cup milk
- 1 teaspoon salt
- 2 tablespoons sugar
- 1 teaspoon ground cinnamon
- 1 teaspoon ground nutmeg
- 1 cup raisins
- 1/2 cup chopped nuts
- 3 cups bread flour

Direction

- Measure the starter into a large mixing bowl.
- Melt butter; add milk and warm to 85 degrees F.
- Add the salt and sugar and stir until dissolved.
- Add this mixture to the starter and mix well.
- Stir in nuts, raisins, and spices.
- Add the flour, 1 cup at a time, mixing vigorously for 1 minute or so between cups.
- Grease a 4 1/2 x 8 1/2-inch loaf pan and spoon batter into pan.
- Proof, covered, at 85 degrees F for 1 to 2 hours, or until dough rises 1/2 inch above the edge of the pan.
- Preheat oven to 350 degrees F.
- Bake for about 45 minutes.
- Remove loaf from pan and cool on wire rack.

Nutrition Information

- Calories: 2602.2
- Total Carbohydrate: 452.1
- Cholesterol: 78.1
- Protein: 59.5
- Fiber: 23.4
- Saturated Fat: 23.3
- Sodium: 3031.5
- Sugar: 115.9
- Total Fat: 68

361. Spiced Peach Nut Bread

Serving: 1 loaf, 6-8 serving(s) | Prep: 5mins | Ready in:

Ingredients

- 2 cups all-purpose flour
- 2/3 cup sugar
- 2 teaspoons baking powder
- 1/2 teaspoon salt
- 1/4 teaspoon ground cloves
- 2 tablespoons margarine
- punce cans sliced peach, drained, liquid reserved
- 1/2 cup reserved peach syrup
- 2 eggs
- 1 cup chopped pecans
- 1 cup raisins

Direction

- Blend everything but nuts and raisins on low speed until moistened. Blend on medium for 2 minutes.
- Stir in nuts and raisins.
- Bake at 350 for 1 hour in a greased baking pan.

Nutrition Information

- Calories: 494.2
- Total Carbohydrate: 76.3
- Cholesterol: 62
- Protein: 8.8
- Total Fat: 19
- Saturated Fat: 2.5
- Sodium: 386.7
- Fiber: 3.8
- Sugar: 37.4

362. Strawberry Pecan Scones

Serving: 12 serving(s) | Prep: 20mins | Ready in:

Ingredients

- 2 cups all-purpose flour
- 1⁄4 cup sugar
- 2 teaspoons baking powder
- 1⁄2 teaspoon baking soda
- 1⁄4 teaspoon salt
- 3 tablespoons margarine, chilled and cut into small pieces
- 8 ounces low-fat vanilla yogurt
- 1⁄4 cup sugar-free strawberry jelly
- 2 tablespoons pecans, finely chopped

Direction

- Preheat oven to 400, use center rack.
- Combine first 5 ingredients in a mixing bowl and cut in margarine with a pastry blender till mixture looks like coarse meal. Add yogurt to dry ingredients, stirring till ingredients are just moistened (dough will be sticky).
- Turn dough out onto a floured surface; with floured hands, knead 4-5 times. Pat dough into an 8 inch circle on a baking sheet covered with cooking spray. Cut dough into 12 wedges, cutting to but not through bottom of dough. Make a small slit in the center of each wedge.
- Place 1 tsp of strawberry spread on top of each slit and sprinkle with pecans. Bake at 400 for 13-20 minutes or until golden. Serve warm.

Nutrition Information

- Calories: 141.1
- Sugar: 5.5
- Protein: 2.8
- Cholesterol: 0.4
- Total Fat: 4.8
- Saturated Fat: 0.8
- Sodium: 200.6
- Fiber: 0.8
- Total Carbohydrate: 21.8

363. Strawberry Macadamia Nut Muffins

Serving: 12 serving(s) | Prep: 12mins | Ready in:

Ingredients

- 3⁄4 cup milk
- 1⁄3 cup butter, melted (5 1/3 Tbsp.)
- 1 large egg
- 2 cups flour
- 2⁄3 cup sugar
- 2 teaspoons baking powder
- 1⁄2 teaspoon salt
- 1 cup chopped fresh strawberries
- 1⁄2 cup chopped macadamia nuts

Direction

- Preheat oven to 400*F.
- Grease the bottoms only of 12 standard-size muffin cups, or line with paper wrappers; set aside.
- In a large bowl, beat together the milk, melted butter, and egg.
- Stir in the flour, sugar, baking powder, and salt just until combined; do not overmix.
- Gently fold in the strawberries and macadamia nuts.
- Spoon batter into the prepared tins; sprinkle with sugar, if desired.
- Bake for 20-22 minutes, or until golden and puffed.
- Immediately invert onto wire racks.
- Serve warm or cool.

Nutrition Information

- Calories: 224.2
- Saturated Fat: 4.4
- Cholesterol: 33.3

- Total Fat: 10.6
- Sodium: 207.8
- Fiber: 1.3
- Sugar: 12
- Total Carbohydrate: 29.6
- Protein: 3.8

364. Sun Nut Bread (Bread Machine)

Serving: 1 Extra Large 2lb Loaf, 20 serving(s) | Prep: 1hours30mins | Ready in:

Ingredients

- 1 1/2 cups water
- 2 tablespoons butter
- 1/4 cup honey
- 3 1/2 cups white bread flour
- 1 cup whole wheat flour
- 2 tablespoons dry milk
- 2 teaspoons salt
- 1/2 cup sunflower seeds
- 1 1/4 teaspoons fast rise yeast or 3 teaspoons active dry yeast

Direction

- Add ingredients according to your Bread Machine's manufacturer's instructions.
- Success Hints: This bread makes great croutons!
- Lightly butter bread slices, cube, and bake at 350 degrees until crisp.
- Sunflower seed salt contents varies by brand.
- If using low or unsalted seeds, adjust salt accordingly.
- This recipe can be made with the white, rapid or delay bake cycles.

Nutrition Information

- Calories: 148.1
- Saturated Fat: 1.1
- Sodium: 245.1
- Sugar: 4
- Protein: 4.2
- Total Fat: 3.5
- Fiber: 1.8
- Total Carbohydrate: 25.6
- Cholesterol: 3.8

365. Sunburst Quick Bread

Serving: 4-6 serving(s) | Prep: 0S | Ready in:

Ingredients

- 1 tablespoon baking powder
- 1/2 cup sunflower seeds, chopped coarsely
- 1/2 cup raisins (can sub golden raisins, currants or cranberries)
- 1/2 cup vanilla rice milk (or soy milk)
- 1/2 teaspoon salt
- 1/3 cup sunflower oil
- 2 cups unbleached white flour
- 2 tablespoons flax seeds
- 2 tablespoons poppy seeds
- 3 tablespoons tahini
- 1/2 cup sugar
- 1 lemon, juice and zest of (1/4 cup lemon juice)

Direction

- Preheat oven to 350 degrees.
- Grease and flour a 9x5 loaf pan.
- In electric blender, grind the flaxseeds to fine powder. Add 1/3 cup water; blending until frothy. Set aside.
- In mixing bowl, combine the safflower oil, sesame paste and sugar. Beat with mixer on medium speed until blended. Beat in the flaxseed mixture.
- In another bowl, stir together the flour, baking powder and salt. Add this to the wet mixture, beating on low speed until smooth.

- Beat in the rice milk, fresh lemon juice and peel. Fold in gently the sunflower seeds and raisins just until blended.
- DO NOT over stir.
- Pour the batter into the prepared loaf pan.
- Sprinkle poppy seeds over the top of the batter. Bake the bread until a toothpick inserted in center comes out clean.
- Bake about 50-60 minutes.
- Cook in pan on wire rack for 10 minutes. Invert pan onto wire rack and cool. Cool completely before slicing.

Nutrition Information

- Calories: 776.3
- Saturated Fat: 4.6
- Fiber: 7.2
- Total Carbohydrate: 100.8
- Protein: 14.9
- Total Fat: 37.5
- Sodium: 588.4
- Sugar: 37.3
- Cholesterol: 0

366. Super Almond Banana Bread (Gluten/Grain Free!)

Serving: 1 loaf | Prep: 10mins | Ready in:

Ingredients

- 2 1/4 cups almond flour
- 1 teaspoon salt
- 1 teaspoon baking soda
- 1 tablespoon honey
- 3 bananas (mashed and VERY ripe)
- 12 1/2 ounces almond filling (SOLO brand is what I used)
- 1/4 cup coconut oil (plus extra to grease the pan)
- 3 eggs
- 1 teaspoon cinnamon (can adjust to your preference)

Direction

- Mix first 3 dry ingredients together in a small bowl.
- In a food processor, place the remaining ingredients and mix well (eggs, banana, honey, almond filling, cinnamon, coconut oil).
- Once mixed well, add in (pulse) the dry mixture.
- Grease a loaf pan with coconut oil and then pour the batter inches
- Bake at 350 degrees for an hour. (Time may need to be adjusted, I started with 50 minutes and checked every 5 mins or so until a toothpick came out clean/dry from the center of the loaf.).

Nutrition Information

- Calories: 1069.6
- Saturated Fat: 52.2
- Sugar: 61.1
- Total Carbohydrate: 101.3
- Protein: 22.9
- Cholesterol: 558
- Total Fat: 70
- Sodium: 3801.7
- Fiber: 10.6

367. Super Quick Banana Nana Nut Muffins

Serving: 24 muffins | Prep: 5mins | Ready in:

Ingredients

- 1 (18 1/4 ounce) box yellow cake mix
- 1 (4 ounce) package instant banana pudding mix
- 1/2 cup water
- 1/2 cup vegetable oil

- 2 ripe mashed bananas
- 4 eggs
- 1 cup chopped walnuts

Direction

- Mix first 6 ingredients together well and add chopped walnuts.
- Place batter in paper lined cupcake tins and fill 3/4 full.
- Bake at 350° for about 20 minutes or until tests done with a toothpick.

Nutrition Information

- Calories: 203.3
- Fiber: 0.8
- Total Carbohydrate: 24.2
- Total Fat: 11.1
- Saturated Fat: 1.5
- Sodium: 224.7
- Sugar: 14.3
- Cholesterol: 31.4
- Protein: 2.9

368. Sweet Potato Pecan Biscuits

Serving: 18 biscuits | Prep: 10mins | Ready in:

Ingredients

- 3⁄4 cup cold mashed cooked sweet potato
- 1⁄2 cup butter, melted and cooled
- 1⁄4-1⁄2 cup light brown sugar
- 1⁄2 cup buttermilk
- 2 cups self-rising flour
- 1⁄2 cup chopped pecans

Direction

- Heat oven to 400* F.
- Combine sweet potatoes, butter and brown sugar.
- Stir in milk until smooth.
- Add flour and stir until moistened, Add pecans to dough.
- Turn dough out on lightly floured surface; knead a few times.
- Roll dough to 1/2 inch thickness.
- Cut with floured 2 inch biscuit cutter.
- Bake on lightly greased baking sheet for 15 to 18 minutes.

Nutrition Information

- Calories: 134.3
- Total Fat: 7.5
- Fiber: 0.8
- Total Carbohydrate: 15.2
- Protein: 2
- Saturated Fat: 3.5
- Sodium: 224.1
- Sugar: 3.6
- Cholesterol: 13.8

369. Sweet Potato Raisin Muffins

Serving: 10 muffins, 10 serving(s) | Prep: 15mins | Ready in:

Ingredients

- 1 3⁄4 cups all-purpose flour
- 2 teaspoons baking powder
- 1⁄2 teaspoon baking soda
- 1⁄2 teaspoon nutmeg
- 1⁄2 teaspoon cinnamon
- 1 egg
- 1⁄2 cup brown sugar
- 1⁄4 cup unsweetened applesauce
- 1⁄4 cup evaporated skim milk
- 1⁄2 cup sweet potato, cooked and mashed
- 1⁄2 cup canola oil (or other cooking oil)
- 1⁄2 cup raisins

Direction

- Preheat oven to 350.
- Line muffin pan with liners or spray with cooking spray.
- In a large bowl, blend dry ingredients until well combined.
- In a separate bowl, mix remaining ingredients until well blended; add to dry ingredients and mix until just combined.
- Spoon batter into each muffin cup until 3/4 full.
- Bake for 25 minutes, until golden brown.
- Cool 5 minutes on wire rack.

Nutrition Information

- Calories: 261.2
- Total Fat: 11.7
- Saturated Fat: 1
- Sugar: 16
- Cholesterol: 21.4
- Protein: 3.7
- Sodium: 159.3
- Fiber: 1.2
- Total Carbohydrate: 36.3

370. Terry's Banana Nut Bread

Serving: 2 loafs | Prep: 15mins | Ready in:

Ingredients

- 1 cup whole milk
- 1 cup mashed banana
- 1/2 cup butter
- 1 1/2 cups sugar
- 3 eggs, beaten
- 2 cups all-purpose flour
- 2 teaspoons baking soda
- 1/4 cup jamaican spiced rum
- 1/2 cup chopped walnuts (optional)

Direction

- 1. Pre-heat oven to 350o.
- 2. Cream butter, sugar, and eggs.
- 3. In a separate bowl, mix bananas and milk till creamy. (Note: 2% milk may be substituted).
- 4. Stir banana mixture and creamed butter, sugar, egg mixture together. Sift remaining dry ingredients and gradually add to wet mixture. Mix in rum. Stir in optional walnuts if desired. Pour the final mixture into greased, floured loaf pans.
- 5. Bake for 1 hour, or until toothpick inserted into middle comes out clean.
- This is a very moist banana bread - not dry at all!

Nutrition Information

- Calories: 1788.4
- Sodium: 1828.1
- Fiber: 6.3
- Sugar: 170.3
- Total Carbohydrate: 277.5
- Cholesterol: 413.2
- Total Fat: 58.7
- Saturated Fat: 34.1
- Protein: 27.9

371. Ultimate Banana Nut Bread (Cake?)

Serving: 2-3 loaves, 16 serving(s) | Prep: 15mins | Ready in:

Ingredients

- 2 cups fresh ground wheat flour (or all purpose flour)
- 1 teaspoon salt
- 2 teaspoons baking soda
- 1 teaspoon baking powder
- 1 cup butter
- 1 cup white sugar
- 1 cup brown sugar

- 4 eggs, beaten
- 1 teaspoon cinnamon
- 1 teaspoon pure vanilla extract
- 3 cups mashed overripe bananas
- 1 -2 cup chopped walnuts (to taste) or 1 -2 cup chopped pecans (to taste)

Direction

- Preheat oven to 350 degrees F. Grease two 9X5 pans or three 8X4 loaf pans.
- Mix together the flour, salt, baking soda and baking powder and set aside. In a large bowl or mixer, blend the butter and sugars until well mixed. Add the eggs and blend until smooth. Mix in the bananas, vanilla, and cinnamon until creamy. Add the dry ingredients to the wet ingredient in two batches, mixing completely and scraping sides between additions. Stir in nuts last, then pour into loaf pans.
- Bake for 45 to 65 minutes, depending on oven and altitude. Check at 45 minutes and then at 10 minute intervals until toothpick comes out slightly damp but not wet.
- Let cool in pans for 15 minutes. Turn out of pans, wrap in foil, and cool on cooling rack for 1 hour. The longer this one cools, the better it gets. Enjoy!

Nutrition Information

- Calories: 345.3
- Saturated Fat: 8.2
- Fiber: 3.1
- Sugar: 29.6
- Total Carbohydrate: 44.5
- Total Fat: 17.9
- Sodium: 431.2
- Cholesterol: 83.4
- Protein: 5.2

372. Vanilla Glazed And Pecan Streuseled Date Bread

Serving: 16 serving(s) | Prep: 40mins | Ready in:

Ingredients

- Streusel
- 1/2 cup pecan halves
- 1/2 cup flour
- 1 1/2 tablespoons packed light brown sugar
- 1 tablespoon granulated sugar
- 1/2 teaspoon baking powder
- 1 pinch salt
- 3 tablespoons butter, melted
- Bread
- 3/4 cup whole milk
- 3/4 cup finely chopped pitted dates (4 oz)
- 2 cups flour
- 2 1/4 teaspoons baking powder
- 1/2 teaspoon salt
- 1 cup sugar
- 2 large eggs, at room temperature
- 1/2 cup vegetable oil
- 1 teaspoon vanilla extract
- Glaze
- 1/2 cup powdered sugar
- 2 tablespoons butter, softened
- 1 tablespoon milk
- 1/2 teaspoon vanilla extract

Direction

- Streusel: Preheat oven to 350*F. Grease and lightly flour a 10x5" loaf pan (or 3 mini loaf pans).
- Spread the pecans on a baking sheet and toast until lightly browned, about 8 minutes. Let cool, then break into large pieces.
- In a medium bowl, combine the flour, sugars, baking powder, and salt; stir in the butter and add the pecans, squeezing mixture into large crumbs. Set aside.
- Bread: In a small saucepan, bring the milk and dates to a simmer; let cool slightly.
- In a medium bowl, whisk together the flour, baking powder, and salt.

- In another bowl, beat the sugar, eggs, and oil with an electric mixer on medium speed until well blended.
- Blend in the milk-date mixture and vanilla.
- Add the flour mixture all at once and blend on low speed until batter is smooth.
- Spread the batter in the prepared pan; sprinkle with streusel. Bake 45-55 minutes, or until golden, risen, and a toothpick tests out with a few moist crumbs attached to it.
- Let cool for 20 minutes, then invert onto a wire rack.
- Glaze: In a small bowl, combine the powdered sugar, butter, butter, and vanilla until smooth. Drizzle over the warm bread and cool completely.
- Store leftovers wrapped in foil and kept at room temperature for up to 3 days.
- *The batter can be spread in 3 6x3" loaf pans and baked for 45 minutes at 375*F. The mini loaves make nice additions to brunch tables.*.

Nutrition Information

- Calories: 297.1
- Saturated Fat: 3.8
- Sugar: 24.4
- Fiber: 1.5
- Total Carbohydrate: 40.7
- Cholesterol: 37.3
- Protein: 3.7
- Total Fat: 13.9
- Sodium: 185.2

373. White Chocolate Banana Muffins

Serving: 16 serving(s) | Prep: 10mins | Ready in:

Ingredients

- 1 egg
- 1/4 cup vegetable oil
- 4 bananas, pureed
- 1/2 cup milk
- 2 cups all-purpose flour
- 1/4 cup sugar
- 2 tablespoons baking powder
- 1/3 cup grated white chocolate
- 1/3 cup ground pecans

Direction

- Preheat oven to 400 degrees, F.
- In a bowl, blend the egg, oil, banana, and milk.
- In a separate bowl, mix together the flour, sugar, baking powder, white chocolate, and pecans.
- Make a well in center of the dry ingredients, and pour in the milk mixture.
- Stir until moistened (do not overmix).
- Fill 16 greased muffin cups 3/4 full.
- Bake 15-20 minutes until tops are golden brown.
- TIP: Put a few tablespoons of water in any unused muffin cups to protect the pan and keep the rest of the muffins moist.
- Yield: 16 muffins.

Nutrition Information

- Calories: 170.4
- Sodium: 148.1
- Fiber: 1.4
- Total Carbohydrate: 25
- Cholesterol: 14.8
- Protein: 3
- Saturated Fat: 1.6
- Sugar: 9
- Total Fat: 7

374. Whole Grain Blueberry Muffins (Health Nut!)

Serving: 12-15 muffins, 12-15 serving(s) | Prep: 10mins | Ready in:

Ingredients

- 3⁄4 cup whole wheat flour (or white whole wheat flour)
- 3⁄4 cup all-purpose flour
- 1⁄2 cup quick oats (or instant)
- 1⁄4 cup flax seed meal
- 1 teaspoon baking soda
- 1 teaspoon baking powder
- 1⁄4 teaspoon salt
- 3⁄4 cup sugar
- 1 cup blueberries
- 1⁄2 cup walnuts, chopped
- 1 banana (really ripe, black even)
- 1 egg
- 1 cup buttermilk
- 2 tablespoons honey
- 1 tablespoon oil
- 1 teaspoon vanilla

Direction

- Combine dry ingredients- everything from flour through sugar.
- Stir together wet ingredients- banana through vanilla.
- Toss blueberries and walnuts into the flour mix and stir, then stir in wet ingredients until just combined.
- Pour into muffin tin and bake 18-20 minutes at 350.
- Cool completely and eat (or eat while still a little warm, but careful, they can stick to the paper liners if you use them and they are still too warm!).

Nutrition Information

- Calories: 211.2
- Total Fat: 6.4
- Sodium: 212.8
- Fiber: 2.9
- Protein: 4.8
- Cholesterol: 16.3
- Saturated Fat: 0.9
- Sugar: 19.1
- Total Carbohydrate: 35.5

375. Whole Wheat Healthy Banana Nut Bread

Serving: 15 slices, 15 serving(s) | Prep: 20mins | Ready in:

Ingredients

- 2 cups whole wheat pancake mix
- 2 eggs
- 2 scoops vanilla whey protein powder
- 4 medium bananas, mashed
- 2 tablespoons olive oil
- 1⁄3 cup flax seed meal
- 2⁄3 cup rolled barley
- 1⁄4 cup agave nectar
- 1⁄2 cup walnuts
- 1 1⁄2 cups water

Direction

- Mix dry ingredients in large mixing bowl. Add eggs, olive oil, agave nectar, and water. Mix well. Stir in mashed bananas and walnuts. Pour into loaf pan and bake at 350 for 30-35 minutes. Allow to cool, cut into slices and serve.

Nutrition Information

- Calories: 185.7
- Fiber: 3.2
- Protein: 5.6
- Sodium: 276.8
- Sugar: 4.1
- Total Carbohydrate: 27.8
- Cholesterol: 28.2
- Total Fat: 6.6
- Saturated Fat: 0.9

376. Yogurt Cranberry Nut Muffins

Serving: 12 muffins, 12 serving(s) | Prep: 10mins | Ready in:

Ingredients

- 2 cups all-purpose flour (may substitute 1/2 cup whole wheat pastry, 1 1/2 AP)
- 2 teaspoons baking powder
- 1 teaspoon baking soda
- 1 teaspoon salt
- 1⁄2 cup sugar
- 1 egg
- 3⁄4 cup yogurt whey or 3⁄4 cup milk
- 1 ripe banana
- 1⁄4 cup plain yogurt
- 1⁄2 cup vegetable oil
- 1 teaspoon orange extract
- 1⁄2 cup dried cranberries
- 1⁄2 cup walnuts, coarsely chopped

Direction

- Mix the flour, baking powder, baking soda, and salt together in large bowl until well combined. In another large bowl, combine the sugar, egg, whey, yogurt, oil, extract, and cranberries. Mix until well combined. Fold the wet ingredients into the dry just until mixed.
- Divide batter evenly among 12 greased (or lined with paper baking cups) muffin cups. Bake at 400°F for 12 to 15 minutes or until golden. Cool 5 minutes; carefully remove from pan to cooling rack. Cool completely before storing. Serve warm if desired.

Nutrition Information

- Calories: 241.4
- Sodium: 368.3
- Sugar: 10.2
- Protein: 3.7
- Total Fat: 13.1
- Saturated Fat: 1.8
- Fiber: 1.3
- Total Carbohydrate: 28.1
- Cholesterol: 16.2

377. Zucchini Nut Bread By Sheila

Serving: 2 loaves, 16 serving(s) | Prep: 10mins | Ready in:

Ingredients

- 3 eggs
- 1 cup oil
- 2 1⁄2 cups sugar
- 2 -3 cups zucchini (peeled grated)
- 3 teaspoons vanilla
- 3 cups flour
- 1 teaspoon salt
- 1 teaspoon baking soda
- 1 teaspoon baking powder
- 3 teaspoons cinnamon
- 1⁄2 cup chopped nuts

Direction

- Beat eggs.
- Add oil, sugar, zucchini, and vanilla.
- Mix lightly but well.
- Add other ingredients.
- Beat well.
- Bake in greased loaf pans at 325 for 1 hour.
- Yields 2 loaves.
- Freezes well.

Nutrition Information

- Calories: 371.9
- Sugar: 31.9
- Cholesterol: 39.7
- Protein: 4.5
- Saturated Fat: 2.4
- Fiber: 1.4
- Sodium: 290.7
- Total Carbohydrate: 51.3

- Total Fat: 17

Chapter 7: Awesome Quick Bread Recipes

***

378. Almond And Blueberry Muffins

Serving: 16 muffins, 8 serving(s) | Prep: 20mins | Ready in:

Ingredients

- 625 ml cake flour
- 10 ml baking powder
- 200 ml caster sugar
- 2 eggs
- 200 g butter
- 350 ml milk
- 1 cup fresh blueberries (or 1 tin blueberries in a light syrup, drained)
- 100 g ground almonds
- 5 ml lemon zest

Direction

- Preheat oven to 220°C.
- Sift flour, baking powder and sugar.
- Beat eggs, butter and milk.
- Make a hole in the middle of the flour, and pour the milk mixture into it.
- Add the lemon zest; stir lightly.
- Fold in the berries and almonds.
- The mixture should be lumpy.
- Pour into muffin pans, and bake until cooked.
- For a variation: Substitute the berries with other fruit or 1cup chocolate chips.

Nutrition Information

- Calories: 546
- Saturated Fat: 14.7
- Sodium: 273.5
- Fiber: 2.7
- Total Carbohydrate: 62.3
- Protein: 9.6
- Total Fat: 29.7
- Sugar: 22.6
- Cholesterol: 112.3

379. Amazing Cinnamon Chip Scones

Serving: 12 scones | Prep: 25mins | Ready in:

Ingredients

- Dough
- 3 1/4 cups all-purpose flour
- 1/3 cup sugar
- 2 1/2 teaspoons baking powder
- 1/2 teaspoon baking soda
- 1/2 teaspoon salt
- 3/4 cup cold butter
- 1 cup buttermilk
- 1 (10 ounce) package cinnamon baking chips
- Topping
- 2 1/2 tablespoons melted butter
- 2 tablespoons sugar
- 1 teaspoon cinnamon

Direction

- Combine the flour, sugar, baking powder, baking soda, and salt in a large bowl.
- Cut in the cold butter, with a pastry blender, until it resembles course crumbs.
- Stir in buttermilk until moistened.
- Fold in cinnamon chips.
- Knead gently (10-12 times) or until dough is no longer sticky on a lightly floured surface.
- Cut the dough in half. Then gently roll each portion into a 7 inch circle.

- Brush each circle with melted butter.
- In a separate bowl, combine the sugar and cinnamon for the topping. Then sprinkle the mixture onto the circles (You can add more sugar and cinnamon if you like).
- Cut each circle into six wedges. Then separate the wedges and place on an ungreased baking sheet.
- Bake at 425 degrees for 11-13 minutes or until lightly brown.

Nutrition Information

- Calories: 285
- Saturated Fat: 9
- Fiber: 1
- Sugar: 8.7
- Cholesterol: 37.7
- Total Fat: 14.4
- Sodium: 369.6
- Total Carbohydrate: 34.9
- Protein: 4.3

380. Apple Cinnamon Streusel Muffins Sugar Free

Serving: 18 muffins, 18 serving(s) | Prep: 15mins | Ready in:

Ingredients

- 2 eggs
- 1/4 cup vegetable oil
- 1 1/4 cups sour milk (include 1 Tbsp vinegar to sour the milk)
- 1 1/2 cups finely diced apples
- 1 3/4 cups all-purpose flour
- 2 teaspoons baking powder
- 1 teaspoon cinnamon
- 1/2 teaspoon salt
- 3/4 cup Splenda granular, sugar substitute
- Streusel Topping
- 1/4 cup all-purpose flour
- 1/2 cup Splenda granular, sugar substitute
- 1/4 cup margarine

Direction

- Beat eggs well. Stir in veg. oil, sour milk, and diced apples.
- Sift dry ingredients together. Set aside.
- Streusel Topping:
- Combine flour and Splenda. Rub in the margarine.
- Pour in the semiliquid ingredients into a well-made in the center of the dry ingredients. Stir quickly just until moistened. Spoon the muffin mixture in 18 greased muffin cups, 3/4 full and sprinkle with the streusel topping.
- Bake at 350 F (180 C) for approximately 15 minutes, or until knife inserted in muffin comes out clean.

Nutrition Information

- Calories: 124.2
- Protein: 2.7
- Fiber: 0.7
- Total Carbohydrate: 13.1
- Saturated Fat: 1.3
- Sodium: 149.5
- Sugar: 2.1
- Cholesterol: 25.2
- Total Fat: 6.8

381. Apple Oatmeal Muffins

Serving: 12 muffins | Prep: 10mins | Ready in:

Ingredients

- 2 eggs
- 3/4 cup milk
- 1/2 cup vegetable oil
- 1 cup all-purpose flour
- 1 cup uncooked quick-cooking oats
- 1/3 cup sugar
- 1 tablespoon baking powder

- 1 teaspoon salt
- 1 teaspoon ground nutmeg
- 1/2 teaspoon ground cinnamon
- 2 tart cooking apples, cored,peeled,and chopped

Direction

- Preheat oven to 400 degrees F.
- Grease a 12 cup muffin tin.
- In a mixing bowl, lightly beat eggs; add milk and oil, stirring until just blended.
- Stir in flour, oats, sugar, baking powder, salt, nutmeg, and cinnamon, mixing until only just moistened (do not overmix).
- Gently fold in the apples.
- Spoon batter into the muffin tin, dividing evenly among the cups.
- Bake in a preheated oven for 15-20 minutes or until a toothpick inserted comes out clean.
- Cool in pan 5 minutes before removing to a wire rack to finish cooling.
- Serve warm or cool; store unused portions in an airtight container.

Nutrition Information

- Calories: 204.5
- Sodium: 304.9
- Fiber: 1.8
- Sugar: 8.9
- Total Carbohydrate: 23.5
- Total Fat: 11.1
- Protein: 3.6
- Saturated Fat: 1.9
- Cholesterol: 33.1

382. Apricot Orange Yogurt Muffins

Serving: 10 serving(s) | Prep: 30mins | Ready in:

Ingredients

- 2 cups flour
- 1/2 cup sugar
- 2 teaspoons baking powder
- 1 teaspoon nutmeg
- 1/2 teaspoon baking soda
- 1/2 teaspoon salt
- 2 eggs
- 1 cup plain yogurt
- 1/3 cup melted butter
- 1 cup slivered dried apricot
- 2 tablespoons coarsley grated orange rind

Direction

- In large mixing bowl whisk together the flour, sugar, baking powder, nutmeg, baking soda and salt.
- In separate bowl whisk together eggs, yogurt and butter and pour over dry ingredients.
- Sprinkle with apricots and orange rind.
- Stir just until dry ingredients are moistened.
- Scoop into greased or paper lined muffin cups, filling to top.
- Bake in center of 375 oven for about 20 minutes or until golden and tops are firm to the touch.
- Let stand for 5 minutes before serving warm.

Nutrition Information

- Calories: 247.7
- Cholesterol: 61.7
- Total Fat: 8.3
- Saturated Fat: 4.8
- Fiber: 1.8
- Total Carbohydrate: 39.1
- Protein: 5.2
- Sodium: 322.5
- Sugar: 18.3

383. Aunt Annie's Bran Muffins

Serving: 12 muffins | Prep: 5mins | Ready in:

Ingredients

- 1 1/2 cups natural bran
- 1 cup brown sugar
- 1/2 teaspoon salt
- 1 egg
- 1 cup all-purpose flour
- 1 teaspoon baking soda
- 2 tablespoons butter (melted)
- 1 cup buttermilk

Direction

- Preheat oven to 350°F.
- Whisk together the bran, sugar, salt flour baking soda.
- Add the wet ingredients and mix lightly.
- Bake for 20 minutes or till done.
- Enjoy!

Nutrition Information

- Calories: 158.8
- Saturated Fat: 1.5
- Sugar: 20
- Cholesterol: 21.4
- Total Fat: 3
- Fiber: 2.5
- Total Carbohydrate: 32.7
- Protein: 3.3
- Sodium: 271.5

384. Bacon Cheese Biscuits

Serving: 12 biscuits | Prep: 10mins | Ready in:

Ingredients

- 2 cups flour
- 1 tablespoon baking powder
- 1/2 teaspoon salt
- 2 tablespoons shortening (Crisco)
- 3/4 cup cheddar cheese, shredded (6 oz.)
- 2/3 cup low-fat milk
- 6 slices bacon, cooked and crumbled

Direction

- Preheat oven to 450 degrees.
- Mix flour, baking powder and salt in a large bowl.
- Cut in shortening using a pastry blender.
- Add cheese, milk and bacon, mixing until a soft and sticky dough forms; beat 20 strokes.
- Drop by spoonfuls onto a greased cookie sheet.
- Bake 8 to 10 minutes until golden brown.

Nutrition Information

- Calories: 181.3
- Protein: 5.7
- Total Fat: 9.9
- Saturated Fat: 3.8
- Sodium: 332.3
- Fiber: 0.6
- Total Carbohydrate: 17
- Sugar: 0.8
- Cholesterol: 15.8

385. Baked Creamy Chicken And Cornbread

Serving: 2 serving(s) | Prep: 15mins | Ready in:

Ingredients

- 2 cups cooked chicken or 2 cups cooked turkey, cut up
- 1 (10 3/4 ounce) can cream of chicken soup, with herbs
- 1 (10 3/4 ounce) can milk
- 1 (10 ounce) package frozen peas and carrots

- Cornbread
- 1 (12 ounce) package corn muffin mix
- 1 egg
- 1/3 cup milk

Direction

- Mix together soup and milk in a saucepan and add in the chicken and vegetables.
- Heat until bubbly.
- Turn into an 8x8" baking pan.
- Prepare cornbread by blending together corn muffin mix, egg and milk.
- Spread batter over chicken mixture carefully to cover all the way to the sides of the pan.
- Bake at 425° for about 20 minutes or until browned on top.

Nutrition Information

- Calories: 1325.1
- Sodium: 2814.8
- Sugar: 35.6
- Total Carbohydrate: 154.8
- Protein: 65.2
- Total Fat: 49.4
- Saturated Fat: 15.9
- Fiber: 15.9
- Cholesterol: 242.2

386. Banana Almond Muffins

Serving: 12 serving(s) | Prep: 15mins | Ready in:

Ingredients

- 8 tablespoons unsalted butter, softened
- 1/2 cup light brown sugar, firmly packed
- 1/3 cup granulated sugar
- 2 large eggs, at room temperature
- 3 medium bananas
- 1/4 cup sour cream
- 1 teaspoon pure vanilla extract
- 1 1/2 cups all-purpose flour
- 1/2 cup whole wheat flour
- 2 teaspoons baking powder
- 1/2 teaspoon baking soda
- 1/2 teaspoon ground cinnamon
- 1/4 teaspoon salt
- 1/4 teaspoon nutmeg, freshly grated
- 1/4 teaspoon cardamom
- 3/4 cup whole almond, coarsely chopped and unblanched

Direction

- Center a rack in the oven and preheat it to 375 degrees F. Line each cavity of the muffin pan with a paper muffin cup.
- Place the butter in the bowl of an electric stand mixer or a large mixing bowl. Use the flat beater attachment or a hand-held mixer to beat the butter until light and fluffy, about 2 minutes.
- Add the brown sugar and granulated sugar to the butter, and cream together well. One at a time, add the eggs to the butter mixture, stopping to scrap down the bottom and the sides of the bowl after each addition. At first the mixture may look curdled as the eggs are added, but as your stop and scrape down the bowl, the mixture will smooth out.
- Use a fork to mash the bananas in a bowl. Add the sour cream and vanilla and mix together well. Add to the butter mixture and blend thoroughly.
- Sift together the flour, whole wheat flour, baking powder and baking soda. Add the cinnamon, salt, nutmeg and cardamom and blend together.
- Add to the banana/butter mixture in 3 stages, stopping after each addition to scrape down the sides of the bowl to promote even blending. Add the almonds to the batter and stir to distribute evenly.
- Use a spoon to divine the batter evenly among the muffin cups, filling them to the top. Bake the muffins for 25 to 30 minutes, until they are light golden brown and a tester inserted in the center comes out clean. Remove the pan from the oven and cool on a rack.

Nutrition Information

- Calories: 300.2
- Protein: 5.8
- Cholesterol: 57.7
- Sodium: 181.2
- Fiber: 2.9
- Sugar: 18.6
- Total Carbohydrate: 39.2
- Total Fat: 14.4
- Saturated Fat: 6.2

387. Banana Bran Oat Muffins

Serving: 6 serving(s) | Prep: 15mins | Ready in:

Ingredients

- 1 cup whole wheat flour
- 3/4 cup white sugar
- 1/4 cup rice milk
- 1 teaspoon vanilla extract
- 2 1/2 very ripe bananas, mashed
- 1 egg
- 1/2 cup quick oats
- 1/2 cup unprocessed wheat bran

Direction

- Preheat oven to 350°F.
- Mix wet and dry ingredients separately, and then combine.
- Pour into greased muffin tins (makes 6).
- Bake for 30 minutes at 350°F.

Nutrition Information

- Calories: 263.9
- Saturated Fat: 0.5
- Total Carbohydrate: 59.6
- Protein: 6.2
- Total Fat: 2.1
- Sodium: 17.2
- Fiber: 6.5
- Sugar: 31.3
- Cholesterol: 35.2

388. Banana Muffins By Jenny

Serving: 20 muffins, 20 serving(s) | Prep: 10mins | Ready in:

Ingredients

- 12 ounces vegetable oil
- 20 ml baking soda (1 T plus 1 tsp)
- 2 1/4 cups flour
- 1 1/2 cups sugar
- 3 eggs
- 5 -6 ripe bananas
- 3/4 cup chopped walnuts (optional) or 3/4 cup pecans (optional)

Direction

- Mix flour and baking soda in bowl, set aside.
- Mix oil, eggs and sugar with mixer on medium. Add flour and baking soda mixture and mix 30 seconds. Add bananas (broken into chunks) and mix 1-2 more minutes (mixture will still be a little lumpy). Stir in chopped nuts, if desired.
- Pour into greased muffin pans and bake at 350 F for 16-18 minutes.
- Or pour into two greased bread pans and bake at 300 F for 40-45 minutes.

Nutrition Information

- Calories: 296.9
- Sodium: 266.6
- Sugar: 18.7
- Total Fat: 18
- Saturated Fat: 2.5
- Fiber: 1.1
- Total Carbohydrate: 32.5
- Cholesterol: 31.7

- Protein: 2.7

389. Banana Nut Muffins, Healthy

Serving: 7 Muffins, 6-7 serving(s) | Prep: 15mins | Ready in:

Ingredients

- 1/4 cup plain yogurt
- 1/4 cup vegetable oil
- 1 egg
- 1/4 cup honey
- 3/4 cup mashed ripe banana
- 1 teaspoon vanilla
- 1 teaspoon baking soda
- 1/4 teaspoon salt
- 1 cup all wheat flour (plus or minus almond meal mixed in)
- optional
- frozen blueberries
- almonds
- 1/4 cup oats
- 3 tablespoons flax seeds
- 1/4 cup almond meal

Direction

- Mash bananas into a bowl with a fork.
- Add the yogurt and vegetable oil, mix well.
- Add the egg, honey, and vanilla continue mixing.
- In a separate container mix the flour, almond meal (if using take about 1/4 cup of flour out and add almond meal), oats, flax seeds, salt, and baking soda.
- Add dry ingredients to wet ingredients and stir in chopped almonds and frozen or fresh blueberries.
- Grease muffin tin and fill with batter.
- Bake at 350 degrees for approximately 20 minutes.

Nutrition Information

- Calories: 303.9
- Total Carbohydrate: 37.6
- Cholesterol: 36.6
- Protein: 7.3
- Total Fat: 15.3
- Sodium: 326.6
- Fiber: 5.5
- Saturated Fat: 2.2
- Sugar: 14.9

390. Bananaumpkin Muffins

Serving: 12-15 muffins | Prep: 10mins | Ready in:

Ingredients

- 1 1/2 cups flour
- 1 cup pumpkin puree (I cheated and used the canned kind)
- 1/2 cup evaporated milk
- 1 banana (you could use more if you like)
- 1 1/4 cups dark brown sugar
- 1 egg
- 1 teaspoon baking soda
- 1 teaspoon salt
- 1/2 teaspoon ginger
- 1/2 teaspoon cinnamon
- 1/8 teaspoon nutmeg
- Topping Idea 1
- 1/2 cup brown sugar
- 2 tablespoons flour
- 2 tablespoons butter
- Topping Idea 2
- 1/2 cup brown sugar
- 1 1/2 cups confectioners' sugar
- 3 tablespoons orange juice

Direction

- Preheat oven to 375.
- Combine flour, baking soda, salt, ginger, cinnamon, and nutmeg in a bowl.
- Whisk.

- Add sugar.
- Add pumpkin, milk, egg, and bananas.
- I mushed my bananas, but you can add them chopped up I would think.
- Stir until blended.
- Grease muffin cups.
- Make streusel topping by combining all ingredients.
- Fill muffin cups, I used the large size, until half full.
- If using streusel topping add it next.
- If topping is to buttery it will "melt" into the batter.
- Mine did at first, so I added more flour to the topping mixture.
- Cook for 12-15 minutes.
- Let cool and remove.
- If using icing mixture, blend all ingredients until it is spreadable.
- Then spread or drizzle over muffins.

Nutrition Information

- Calories: 327.3
- Total Fat: 3.3
- Saturated Fat: 1.9
- Sodium: 345.1
- Total Carbohydrate: 72.8
- Cholesterol: 23.6
- Fiber: 0.8
- Sugar: 56.4
- Protein: 3.3

391. Bisquick Cheese Bread Or Biscuits (Like Red Lobster!)

Serving: 1 loaf | Prep: 15mins | Ready in:

Ingredients

- 2 cups original Bisquick baking mix
- 3⁄4-1 cup shredded cheddar cheese
- 3 tablespoons grated parmesan cheese
- 1⁄2-1 teaspoon garlic powder
- 1⁄2 cup water, plus
- 1 tablespoon water
- TOPPING
- 3 tablespoons melted butter
- 1⁄2 teaspoon garlic powder (or to taste)
- 1 teaspoon italian seasoning (or to taste)
- 1 teaspoon dried parsley (or to taste)

Direction

- Set oven to 400°F (convection bake if possible).
- Grease a foil-lined baking sheet.
- In a large bowl mix/toss together the baking mix with grated cheddar cheese, Parmesan cheese and garlic powder.
- Add in the water, and mix with hands until well combined.
- Shape the dough into one oval-shaped loaf, or even better into smaller oval shaped balls, or drop heaping tablespoonfuls onto the baking sheet for biscuits.
- Transfer to cookie/baking sheet.
- Brush the tops and sides with melted butter; sprinkle with garlic powder, Italian seasoning and dried parsley.
- At this point, let dough rest, covered loosely with plastic or a clean tea towel in the refrigerator for 20-25 minutes before baking.
- Remove from fridge and bake for 25 minutes, or until brown in color (bake less time for smaller size balls or biscuits, the dough will spread when baked).
- Remove from oven, cut in slices, serve warm.

Nutrition Information

- Calories: 1819
- Total Fat: 106.4
- Saturated Fat: 52.5
- Total Carbohydrate: 166.3
- Cholesterol: 198.9
- Protein: 48.4
- Sodium: 3658.6
- Fiber: 5.8
- Sugar: 30.5

392. Boosted Banana Muffins

Serving: 24-30 mini-muffins | Prep: 15mins | Ready in:

Ingredients

- DRY INGREDIENTS
- 1 cup whole wheat flour
- 2/3 cup buckwheat flour
- 1/3 cup ground flax seeds
- 1 1/2 teaspoons stevia powder
- 1 1/2 teaspoons baking powder
- 1 teaspoon baking soda
- WET INGREDIENTS
- 1/3 cup unsweetened applesauce
- 1 tablespoon unsweetened applesauce
- 1 cup kefir or 1 cup plain yogurt
- 2 eggs
- 2 ripe bananas, mashed
- 1 teaspoon vanilla extract

Direction

- In medium bowl, combine dry ingredients; set aside.
- In large bowl, combine wet ingredients; mix until light and homogeneous.
- With a wooden spoon, incorporate dry ingredients into the wet ones.
- Spoon into mini-muffin pans and bake at 325F (see note) for 25 minutes, or until a toothpick comes out clean.
- Cool completely before removing from moulds.
- NOTE: I baked these in a convection toaster oven, baking time and temperature may need to be adjusted for a conventional oven.

Nutrition Information

- Calories: 53.7
- Total Fat: 1.3
- Fiber: 1.7
- Sugar: 1.4
- Cholesterol: 17.6
- Protein: 2
- Saturated Fat: 0.2
- Sodium: 82.2
- Total Carbohydrate: 9.2

393. Bread Pudding Muffins

Serving: 12 serving(s) | Prep: 30mins | Ready in:

Ingredients

- 1 lb crusty artisan white bread
- 1/2 teaspoon ground cinnamon
- 6 eggs
- 3/4 cup sugar (5.25 ounces)
- 1 1/2 cups heavy cream (12 fl.oz.)
- 1 1/2 cups milk (12 fl.oz.)
- 2 teaspoons vanilla extract
- powdered sugar, for dusting

Direction

- Slice the bread and cut it into 1-inch cubes; put it in a large bowl and toss with the cinnamon.
- In a bowl, whisk the eggs, sugar, cream, milk, and vanilla together until combined.
- Pour the custard over the bread; cover and refrigerate for at least 4 hours and up to 24 hours.
- Preheat oven to 325°; line a standard 12-cup muffin tin with paper liners, or generously grease with butter.
- Scoop a heaping 1/2 cup of the pudding mixture into each of the 12 muffin cups; each one should be nicely mounded.
- Top off each pudding with any remaining custard.
- Bake for 45 minutes, rotating the tin halfway through the baking time.
- The puddings should be lightly golden brown on top.
- Dust with powdered sugar while they are still warm.

Nutrition Information

- Calories: 310.4
- Sodium: 319.6
- Sugar: 14.4
- Total Fat: 15.9
- Saturated Fat: 8.6
- Fiber: 1
- Total Carbohydrate: 34.3
- Cholesterol: 150.8
- Protein: 7.7

394. Caramelized Butternut Squash Gems

Serving: 4 serving(s) | Prep: 5mins | Ready in:

Ingredients

- 2 1/2 lbs butternut squash (estimated weight)
- 1 tablespoon olive oil
- 1/2 tablespoon brown sugar, packed (can use Splenda brown sugar if desired) (optional)
- 1 teaspoon kosher salt
- 1/2 teaspoon fresh ground black pepper

Direction

- Preheat the oven to 450°F.
- Peel squash, cut in half lengthwise and remove the seeds. Cut the squash into 1" to 1 1/2" cubes (large and uniform is best), and place in a bowl. Drizzle olive oil over the chunks and toss them around with your hands to evenly distribute the oil.
- Mix brown sugar, (if using) salt and pepper together and sprinkle it over the squash pieces. Toss around again to evenly distribute the seasoning. Spray a baking sheet with cooking spray and spread squash in a single layer.
- Roast for 40-45 minutes, until the squash is tender and the glaze begins to caramelize, turning a few times to ensure even browning. Serve.

Nutrition Information

- Calories: 158.5
- Sodium: 447.5
- Protein: 2.9
- Total Fat: 3.7
- Saturated Fat: 0.5
- Fiber: 5.8
- Sugar: 6.3
- Total Carbohydrate: 33.4
- Cholesterol: 0

395. Carrot Cake Muffins (Good For You!)

Serving: 18 serving(s) | Prep: 15mins | Ready in:

Ingredients

- 3 cups carrots, shredded
- 3/4 cup brown sugar
- 3 tablespoons canola oil
- 2 eggs
- 2 teaspoons vanilla
- 1 (8 ounce) can crushed pineapple (including the juice)
- 1/2 cup milk
- 1/2 raisins
- 2 1/2 cups whole wheat pastry flour (half whole wheat four half white flour)
- 2 teaspoons baking soda
- 1 teaspoon cinnamon
- 1 teaspoon pumpkin pie spice
- 1/8 teaspoon salt

Direction

- In a large bowl mix sugar, oil and eggs.
- Add vanilla, pineapple, milk and raisins.
- In another bowl mix flour, baking soda and spices. Add carrots.

- Add the carrot mixture a little at a time, to the large bowl with the sugar mixture.
- Bake at 350°F in sprayed or lined muffin pans about 15-20 minutes.

Nutrition Information

- Calories: 141.3
- Fiber: 2.7
- Total Carbohydrate: 25.4
- Cholesterol: 24.4
- Sugar: 11.7
- Protein: 3.4
- Total Fat: 3.5
- Saturated Fat: 0.6
- Sodium: 184.4

396. Cheddar Green Onion Biscuits

Serving: 12 biscuits | Prep: 10mins | Ready in:

Ingredients

- 2 cups all-purpose flour
- 2 1/2 teaspoons baking powder
- 1/2 teaspoon baking soda
- 1/2 teaspoon salt
- 1/4 cup cold butter
- 1 1/2 cups grated orange cheddar cheese
- 2 -3 green onions, thinly sliced or 1/4 cup snipped fresh chives
- 2 1/4 cups buttermilk or 2 1/4 cups sour cream

Direction

- Sift dry ingredients together; using a pastry cutter, 2 knives or a food processor, cut in butter until only small bits are visible.
- Add cheddar green onions, tossing until evenly distributed; pour in a cup of buttermilk or sour cream stir until dough forms.
- Increase liquid if necessary - I used 11/2 cups of full fat sour cream.
- Turn out onto a lightly floured surface, pat until ½ inch thick cut with a biscuit or cookie cutter or a glass.
- Place about 1 inch apart on a parchment lined baking sheet (or use cooking spray) and bake above the center of a preheated 450F oven for 10 to 12 minutes or until golden.

Nutrition Information

- Calories: 186.3
- Protein: 7.3
- Saturated Fat: 5.7
- Sodium: 389
- Cholesterol: 26.8
- Total Fat: 9.1
- Fiber: 0.6
- Sugar: 2.4
- Total Carbohydrate: 18.7

397. Cheddar Applesauce Muffins

Serving: 12 serving(s) | Prep: 5mins | Ready in:

Ingredients

- 2 cups baking mix (Bisquik)
- 1/4 cup sugar
- 1 teaspoon cinnamon
- 1 egg, well beaten
- 1/2 cup unsweetened applesauce
- 1/4 cup milk
- 2 tablespoons oil
- 1 cup finely shredded sharp cheddar cheese
- 1/2 cup finely chopped walnuts

Direction

- In a large bowl combine baking mix, sugar, and cinnamon.
- In a separate bowl combine egg, applesauce, milk, oil and cheese.
- Add to dry ingredients.

- Fold in walnuts.
- Grease or spray muffin pan.
- Fill each cup 2/3 full.
- Bake in a 400 degree oven for 15-20 min or until light golden.
- Cool muffins in pan for 10 minutes.
- Run sharp knife around muffin to loosen and remove from pan.

Nutrition Information

- Calories: 205.8
- Total Fat: 12.3
- Sodium: 322.4
- Sugar: 6.7
- Saturated Fat: 3.6
- Fiber: 1
- Total Carbohydrate: 19.2
- Cholesterol: 28.6
- Protein: 5.4

398. Cheddar Scones With Dill

Serving: 16 scones, 8 serving(s) | Prep: 10mins | Ready in:

Ingredients

- 2 1/2 cups all-purpose flour
- 1 cup shredded sharp cheddar cheese
- 1/4 cup chopped fresh parsley
- 3 tablespoons minced fresh dill
- 1 tablespoon baking powder
- 1/2 teaspoon salt
- 3/4 cup butter or 3/4 cup margarine, chilled
- 2 eggs, beaten
- 1/2 cup half-and-half cream or 1/2 cup cream

Direction

- Heat oven to 400°F.
- Combine the flour, cheese, parsley, dill, baking powder and salt in a mixing bowl.
- Use a pastry blender to cut in the cold butter or margarine until crumbly.
- Add eggs and half-n-half and stir lightly until just moistened.
- Turn dough onto a lightly floured surface.
- Knead dough gently until smooth, about 1 minute.
- Divide the dough in half and roll each half into an 8-inch circle.
- Cut each circle into 8 wedges, as if cutting a pie.
- Place the wedges 1 inch apart on a cookie sheet. Bake for 15 to 20 minutes, until lightly browned.
- Cool on a rack for 2 minutes before serving.

Nutrition Information

- Calories: 391.4
- Sodium: 517.5
- Fiber: 1.1
- Sugar: 0.3
- Cholesterol: 119.1
- Protein: 9.8
- Total Fat: 25.3
- Saturated Fat: 15.4
- Total Carbohydrate: 31.3

399. Cheese Scones With Gomashio

Serving: 4 scones | Prep: 10mins | Ready in:

Ingredients

- 1 1/4 cups whole grain flour
- 1 1/2 teaspoons baking powder
- 30 g butter
- 2 -4 tablespoons gomashio (use more if you really want to taste the sesame in the scones)
- 1/4-1/2 cup milk
- grated cheese, for sprinkling

Direction

- Preheat the oven to 220°C/425°F.
- In a bowl combine flour, gomashio and baking powder. Rub in butter until mixture resembles coarse crumbs.
- Add liquid little by little until a soft, but not sticky dough forms.
- Pat out on a lightly floured surface and cut out scones of desired size (I use a regular glass for cutting).
- Place on a paper-lined baking sheet, top with grated cheese and bake for about 15 minutes or until golden brown and baked through.
- Enjoy!

Nutrition Information

- Calories: 206.3
- Fiber: 1.1
- Cholesterol: 18.2
- Protein: 4.6
- Total Fat: 7
- Saturated Fat: 4.2
- Sodium: 187.3
- Sugar: 0.1
- Total Carbohydrate: 30.9

400. Cheesy Buttermilk Drop Biscuits

Serving: 12 serving(s) | Prep: 5mins | Ready in:

Ingredients

- 2 1/2 cups all-purpose flour
- 2 tablespoons granulated sugar
- 1 1/2 tablespoons baking powder
- 1/4 teaspoon salt
- 1/2 cup butter or 1/2 cup margarine, softened
- 1/2 cup shredded cheddar cheese
- 1 cup buttermilk

Direction

- Preheat oven to 350, and mix dry ingredients in a bowl.
- Cut in butter until it resembles coarse crumbs.
- Mix in cheese.
- Add buttermilk, and blend until dry ingredients are moistened; DON'T OVERMIX!
- Divide dough between 12 greased muffin tins, and bake for 25 minutes, or until lightly browned.

Nutrition Information

- Calories: 198.8
- Sodium: 303.4
- Total Carbohydrate: 23.4
- Protein: 4.6
- Saturated Fat: 6
- Fiber: 0.7
- Sugar: 3.2
- Cholesterol: 26.1
- Total Fat: 9.7

401. Chicken Chile Cheese Muffins

Serving: 24 serving(s) | Prep: 10mins | Ready in:

Ingredients

- 1 (7 ounce) box oat bran muffin mix
- 1 (8 1/2 ounce) box corn muffin mix
- 1 cup milk
- 2 eggs
- 1 tablespoon margarine
- 1 (15 ounce) can creamed corn
- 2 cups cooked chicken (bite sized peices)
- 1 (4 1/4 ounce) canchopped green chilies
- 1/2 cup shredded cheddar cheese
- 4 ounces cream cheese, cut into 1/2 inch cubes

Direction

- Preheat oven to 400°.

- Combine muffin mixes, milk, eggs, creamed corn and margarine.
- Add chicken, chiles and cheddar cheese, stirring to combine.
- Gently fold in cubes of cream cheese, trying to keep their shape intact.
- Using an ice cream scoop sprayed with non-stick spray scoop mixture into greased muffin pans (I have not had much success with paper liners for this recipe).
- Bake for 20 minutes.

Nutrition Information

- Calories: 120.1
- Saturated Fat: 2.5
- Cholesterol: 35.7
- Protein: 5.9
- Total Fat: 5.8
- Sodium: 220.3
- Fiber: 1
- Sugar: 3
- Total Carbohydrate: 11.6

402. Chocolate Fudge Muffins

Serving: 24 regular muffins | Prep: 30mins | Ready in:

Ingredients

- 400 g plain flour
- 250 g caster sugar
- 100 g light brown sugar (or muscovado)
- 50 g cocoa
- 2 teaspoons baking powder
- 1 teaspoon bicarbonate of soda
- 1/2 teaspoon salt
- 3 eggs
- 150 ml sour cream
- 1 teaspoon vanilla essence
- 125 ml vegetable oil
- 175 g butter, melted and cooled
- 300 ml water
- 175 g dark chocolate
- 250 g unsalted butter
- 275 g icing sugar, sifted
- 1 tablespoon vanilla essence

Direction

- Preheat oven to 180C and line 12 cup muffin tin with papers.
- In a large bowl sift together the flour, sugars, cocoa, baking powder, bicarbonate and salt.
- In another bowl whisk together the eggs, sour cream and vanilla until blended.
- In a third bowl, using a hand mixer, beat together the melted butter and oil until just blended then beat in the water (yes this really works).
- Add the dry ingredients to the oil mixture all at once and mix on low speed.
- Add the egg mixture and beat until everything is blended well.
- Fill each muffin cup 3/4 full and bake in the oven for 20-25 minutes or until a skewer comes out clean.
- Cool on wire rack while making icing.
- -- To make the icing --
- Melt the chocolate in the microwave (2-3 mins on medium) and let in cool slightly.
- In a large bowl beat the butter until it is soft and creamy and then add the sifted icing sugar and beat again until everything is light and fluffy.
- Gently add the vanilla and chocolate and beat until smooth.
- Ice the cupcakes with a spatula or piping bag.

Nutrition Information

- Calories: 413.4
- Fiber: 2.7
- Sugar: 26
- Total Carbohydrate: 46
- Cholesterol: 66.7
- Protein: 4.8
- Saturated Fat: 13.5
- Total Fat: 25.5
- Sodium: 190.5

403. Chocolate Hazelnut Swirled Banana Bread (Or Muffins)

Serving: 1 loaf, 18 serving(s) | Prep: 10mins | Ready in:

Ingredients

- 2 cups all-purpose flour
- 3 teaspoons baking powder
- 1/2 teaspoon salt
- 1 teaspoon ground cinnamon
- 1 dash ground nutmeg
- 1/2 cup unsalted butter, softened or 1/2 cup oil
- 2 eggs
- 3/4 cup brown sugar
- 1 1/2 cups mashed bananas or 3 medium bananas or 3 medium unsweetened applesauce
- 2 teaspoons vanilla extract, 1 teaspoon banana extract for 1 teaspoon of the vanilla extract (for more banana flavor) or 2 teaspoons substitute 1 teaspoon banana extract for 1 teaspoon of the vanilla extract (for more banana flavor)
- 3/4 cup chocolate hazelnut spread (something comparable to Nutella)

Direction

- Preheat oven to 350.
- Sift together, flour, baking powder, salt, cinnamon nutmeg into a large mixing bowl. Set aside.
- Cream butter (or oil) and sugar together until light and fluffy.
- Add in eggs one at a time, and mix until incorporated.
- Mix in banana mash and vanilla (or banana extract if using). Once the mixture is full mixed, fold in try ingredients.
- Mix batter together until everything is combined.
- Heat hazelnut spread in microwave for about 20 seconds or until it is melted.
- Spread half of your banana bread batter into the bottom of a greased bread pan (or paper lined muffin tins), drizzle with half of your hazelnut spread. Top with remaining batter. Drizzle the rest of the hazelnut spread over the top of bread. Using a fork or knife, gently swirl the batter together with the chocolate hazelnut spread.
- Bake for one hour (for bread; 15-20 minutes for muffins) or until a toothpick is inserted and comes out clean.

Nutrition Information

- Calories: 224.1
- Total Carbohydrate: 31.9
- Protein: 3.1
- Total Fat: 9.5
- Sodium: 141.8
- Fiber: 1.6
- Sugar: 18
- Saturated Fat: 7
- Cholesterol: 34.2

404. Cornmeal Cheddar Scones

Serving: 15 scones | Prep: 45mins | Ready in:

Ingredients

- 2 cups all-purpose flour
- 3/4 cup stone-ground cornmeal
- 1 tablespoon sugar
- 1 tablespoon baking powder
- 1/2 teaspoon baking soda
- 1/2 teaspoon salt
- 1/8 teaspoon cayenne pepper
- 3/4 cup unsalted butter, cut into chunks
- 1 cup shredded extra-sharp cheddar cheese (4 oz.)
- 1 large egg

- 3⁄4 cup buttermilk
- unsalted butter, melted
- sea salt

Direction

- Preheat oven to 425°.
- Place the first 7 ingredients in a food processor.
- Add 3/4 cup butter; pulse 3-4 times or until mixture resembles coarse meal.
- Place flour mixture in a large bowl; stir in cheese.
- Wish together egg and buttermilk until blended.
- Make a well in the center of dry ingredients; add egg mixture, stirring just until dry ingredients are moistened.
- Turn dough out onto a floured surface; knead lightly 3-4 times.
- Put dough into a 10 x 7 inch rectangle.
- Cut into 15 squares.
- Place squares on a parchment paper-lined baking sheet.
- Brush tops with melted unsalted butter, and sprinkle with sea salt.
- Bake for 20 minutes or until golden.

Nutrition Information

- Calories: 213
- Fiber: 0.9
- Sugar: 1.6
- Cholesterol: 46.5
- Total Carbohydrate: 19.2
- Protein: 5.3
- Total Fat: 12.9
- Saturated Fat: 7.9
- Sodium: 268.1

405. Cranberry Harvest Muffins

Serving: 18 muffins | Prep: 20mins | Ready in:

Ingredients

- 3 cups all-purpose flour
- 1 tablespoon baking powder
- 1⁄2 teaspoon baking soda
- 1⁄2 teaspoon salt
- 1 tablespoon ground cinnamon
- 2 teaspoons ground ginger
- 1 1⁄4 cups whole milk
- 2 extra-large eggs
- 1⁄2 lb unsalted butter, melted and cooled
- 1 1⁄2 cups coarsely chopped fresh cranberries
- 1⁄2 cup medium-diced calimyrna fig
- 3⁄4 cup coarsely chopped hazelnuts, toasted and skinned
- 3⁄4 cup brown sugar, packed
- 3⁄4 cup granulated sugar

Direction

- Preheat the oven to 375 degrees F.
- Line 18 muffin cups with paper liners.
- Sift together the flour, baking powder, baking soda, salt, cinnamon, and ginger in a large bowl.
- Make a well in the center of the mixture and add the milk, eggs, and melted butter.
- Stir quickly just to combine.
- Add the cranberries, figs, hazelnuts, and both sugars and stir just to distribute the fruits, nuts, and sugar evenly throughout the batter.
- Spoon the batter into the paper liners, filling each one to the top.
- Bake for 20 to 25 minutes, until browned on the top and a toothpick inserted in the center of the muffins comes out clean.

Nutrition Information

- Calories: 293.7
- Total Fat: 15.1

- Saturated Fat: 7.3
- Sugar: 18.7
- Total Carbohydrate: 36.5
- Cholesterol: 56.1
- Protein: 4.5
- Sodium: 181.6
- Fiber: 1.7

406. Curry Spiced Carrot And Date Muffins

Serving: 4 muffins | Prep: 20mins | Ready in:

Ingredients

- 165 g gluten-free flour
- 1 teaspoon baking powder or 1 teaspoon bicarbonate of soda
- 1 teaspoon curry powder
- 1/4 teaspoon salt
- 125 ml coconut oil
- 100 g coconut sugar crystals
- 1 egg
- 70 g carrots, shredded
- 60 g dates, chopped

Direction

- Preheat oven to 190C/375°F.
- Line a muffin tin with paper muffin cases.
- In a bowl, whisk together the dry ingredients – flour, xanthan gum, baking powder, curry powder, and salt.
- In a separate bowl, mix the wet ingredients – coconut oil, sugar, and egg.
- Mix the wet ingredients into the dry.
- Fold in the carrots and dates.
- Scoop 80ml of batter into each muffin case.
- Bake for 20 minutes.
- Transfer to a cooling rack and leave to cool completely.

Nutrition Information

- Calories: 317.8
- Total Fat: 30.1
- Saturated Fat: 25.3
- Sodium: 266.5
- Fiber: 1.9
- Sugar: 10.4
- Total Carbohydrate: 13.6
- Cholesterol: 46.5
- Protein: 2.2

407. Date And Cheddar Good Day Muffins

Serving: 12 serving(s) | Prep: 10mins | Ready in:

Ingredients

- 1 cup white sugar
- 1 cup all-purpose flour
- 1 cup whole wheat flour
- 1 tablespoon baking powder
- 1/2 teaspoon salt
- 1 teaspoon vanilla extract
- 1 whole egg
- 1/4 cup canola oil or 1/4 cup any vegetable oil
- 1 cup whole milk or 1 cup 2% low-fat milk
- 1 cup grated cheddar cheese
- 1 cup peeled and diced granny smith apple
- 2/3 cup chopped dates
- Topping
- 3 tablespoons brown sugar
- 3 tablespoons grated cheddar cheese

Direction

- Combine dry ingredients in a bowl and set aside.
- Combine fruit and cheese in a bowl and set aside.
- Whisk in a bowl the egg, sugar, oil vanilla, and milk until well combined.
- Add the dry ingredients just until moist.
- Fold in the fruit and cheese.
- Place into prepared muffin tins.

- Bake 350 degrees for 20 minutes.
- Combine the topping ingredients of cheddar and brown sugar well.
- Remove the muffins from oven after 20 minutes baking time, and sprinkle topping evenly on each muffin.
- Return to oven for another 10 minutes-- Total baking time for muffins is 30 minutes-- Remove to a wire rack to cool--.

Nutrition Information

- Calories: 287
- Total Fat: 9.6
- Fiber: 2.5
- Sugar: 28.6
- Protein: 6.6
- Saturated Fat: 3.2
- Sodium: 272.8
- Total Carbohydrate: 45.5
- Cholesterol: 29.3

408. Daughter's Banana Bread

Serving: 1 loaf | Prep: 20mins | Ready in:

Ingredients

- 1 1/3 cups flour
- 3/4 teaspoon salt
- 1/2 teaspoon baking soda
- 1/4 teaspoon baking powder
- 5 1/3 tablespoons butter (soft)
- 2/3 cup sugar
- 2 large eggs (slightly beaten)
- 1 cup mashed very ripe banana
- 1/2 cup coarsely chopped walnuts

Direction

- Preheat oven to 350°F.
- Make sure all the ingredients are at room temperature.
- Whisk together the flour, salt, soda, and powder; set aside.
- In a large bowl beat on high speed for 2-3 minutes the butter, and sugar.
- Beat in the flour mixture till blended and is the consistency of brown sugar.
- Gradually beat in the eggs.
- Fold in the bananas and nuts till combined.
- Put into a greased and floured bread pan and bake for 50-60 minutes or until bread tests done.
- Cool pan on rack for 5-10 minutes.
- Take out and cool on rack.

Nutrition Information

- Calories: 2329.4
- Protein: 41
- Total Fat: 111.6
- Sodium: 3046.4
- Total Carbohydrate: 303.9
- Saturated Fat: 46
- Fiber: 12.3
- Sugar: 154.4
- Cholesterol: 585.8

409. Delicious Pumpkin Muffins

Serving: 24 mini muffins, 24 serving(s) | Prep: 20mins | Ready in:

Ingredients

- 2 cups flour
- 2/3 cup brown sugar
- 1/3 cup granulated sugar
- 1 tablespoon baking powder
- 1 teaspoon salt
- 1 teaspoon ground cinnamon
- 1/4 teaspoon baking soda
- 1/4 teaspoon ground ginger
- 1/2 cup butter

- 1/2-2/3 cup Libby's canned pumpkin
- 2 large eggs
- 1/3 cup buttermilk

Direction

- In a large bowl combine all dry ingredients.
- In medium bowl combine all wet ingredients.
- Mix wet mixture with dry mixture.
- Preheat oven to 400 degrees.
- Grease 24 mini muffin cups.
- Scoop into the prepared muffin cups, fill about 3/4 full.
- Bake for 7-10 minutes, or until cooked in the middle.

Nutrition Information

- Calories: 115.4
- Sugar: 9.1
- Cholesterol: 27.9
- Saturated Fat: 2.6
- Sodium: 207
- Fiber: 0.5
- Total Carbohydrate: 17.5
- Protein: 1.8
- Total Fat: 4.4

410. Delicious Whole Grain Muffins

Serving: 48 muffins, 48 serving(s) | Prep: 15mins | Ready in:

Ingredients

- 4 large eggs
- 1 1/3 cups unsalted butter
- 4 cups unbleached flour
- 4 teaspoons salt
- 4 teaspoons baking powder
- 4 teaspoons baking soda
- 2 cups white sugar or 2 cups turbinado sugar
- 1 quart buttermilk
- 4 cups multi grain hot cereal (Bob's Red Mill 10 Grain hot cereal)

Direction

- 1: preheat oven to 350°F.
- 2: Mix Red Mill hot cereal and buttermilk well, let sit for 10 minutes.
- 3: In the meantime, cream butter and sugar in a separate bowl.
- 4: add all ingredients EXCEPT eggs into the butter and sugar. Mix well.
- 5: Combine both mixtures, ADD IN THE EGGS, and mix well AGAIN.
- 6: grease muffin tins, distribute mixture equally and bake for 20 minutes or until golden brown.
- Enjoy!

Nutrition Information

- Calories: 129.8
- Saturated Fat: 3.5
- Fiber: 0.3
- Cholesterol: 32
- Protein: 2.3
- Total Fat: 5.8
- Sodium: 357.1
- Sugar: 9.4
- Total Carbohydrate: 17.4

411. Diabetic Cinnamon Bun Scones

Serving: 1 batch | Prep: 15mins | Ready in:

Ingredients

- SCONES
- 2 cups self-rising flour
- 1 cup quick oats or 1 cup old fashioned oats
- 1/4 cup Splenda sugar substitute
- 2 tablespoons Splenda sugar substitute

- 8 tablespoons butter, chilled and cut into pieces
- 3⁄4 cup milk
- 1 egg, lightly beaten
- 1 teaspoon vanilla
- 1⁄2 cup pecans, toasted and chopped
- 2 teaspoons ground cinnamon
- GLAZE
- 3 -4 teaspoons orange juice or 3 -4 teaspoons milk
- 3⁄4 cup Splenda sugar substitute

Direction

- Heat oven to 425°F Spray cookie sheet with cooking spray.
- In large bowl, combine flour, oats, 1/4 cup Splenda; mix well.
- Cut in butter with pastry blender or two knives until mixture resembles coarse crumbs.
- In small bowl, combine milk, egg and vanilla; blend well. Add to dry ingredients all at once; stir with fork or rubber spatula until dry ingredients are moistened. In small bowl, combine remaining 2 tablespoons Splenda with the pecans and cinnamon; mix well. Sprinkle evenly over dough in bowl; gently stir batter to swirl in cinnamon mixture (Do not blend completely.)
- Drop dough by 1/4 cupfuls 2 inches apart on cookie sheet.
- Bake 11 to 13 minutes or until golden brown. Remove to wire rack; cool 5 minutes.
- GLAZE: In small bowl, combine Splenda and enough liquid for desired consistency; mix until smooth. Drizzle over top of warm scones. Serve warm.

Nutrition Information

- Calories: 2608.4
- Total Fat: 150.7
- Fiber: 22.4
- Protein: 56.2
- Saturated Fat: 68.8
- Sodium: 3994
- Sugar: 6.2
- Total Carbohydrate: 262.1
- Cholesterol: 481.4

412. Double Chocolate Buckwheat Muffins

Serving: 12 serving(s) | Prep: 40mins | Ready in:

Ingredients

- 1 cup gluten-free flour
- 3⁄4 cup buckwheat flour
- 1 cup grated zucchini
- 1⁄2 cup chocolate chips
- 1⁄4 cup cocoa
- 1⁄2 cup brown sugar, packed
- 1⁄2 teaspoon ground cinnamon
- 1 1⁄2 teaspoons baking powder
- 1⁄4 teaspoon baking soda
- 1⁄8 teaspoon salt
- 3⁄4 cup buttermilk
- 3 tablespoons honey
- 2 tablespoons vegetable oil
- 1 egg, lightly beaten
- 1⁄2 cup chopped nuts

Direction

- Combine the flour, buckwheat flour, zucchini, cherries, brown sugar, cinnamon, baking powder, baking soda and salt in a large bowl.
- Make well in the center of the mixture for the liquid ingredients.
- Combine the buttermilk, oil, honey and egg and add to dry ingredients, stirring together just until moistened.
- Stir in the chopped nuts.
- Divide the batter evenly among muffin cups coated with cooking spray.
- Bake at 375°F for 20 minutes.
- Remove from pan immediately.
- Let cool on wire racks.

Nutrition Information

- Calories: 181.7
- Protein: 3.8
- Total Fat: 8.3
- Sodium: 162.7
- Total Carbohydrate: 26.7
- Saturated Fat: 2.3
- Fiber: 2.5
- Sugar: 18.4
- Cholesterol: 18.2

413. Double Pear Muffins

Serving: 12 muffins | Prep: 30mins | Ready in:

Ingredients

- Topping
- 1/2 cup chopped pecans
- 2 tablespoons packed brown sugar
- 1/2 teaspoon ground nutmeg
- Muffins
- 2 cups all-purpose flour
- 1 teaspoon baking soda
- 1/2 teaspoon salt
- 3/4 cup packed brown sugar
- 2 eggs
- 1/3 cup unsalted butter, melted
- 2 (4 ounce) jars pear baby food
- 1 teaspoon vanilla extract
- 3/4 cup buttermilk
- 1 cup diced pear

Direction

- Preheat oven to 400°; grease 12-cup muffin pan.
- Topping-in a small bowl, combine pecans, brown sugar, and nutmeg; set aside.
- Muffins-in a bowl, whisk together flour, baking soda, and salt.
- In a big bowl, whisk together brown sugar, eggs, and butter until well blended.
- Whisk in pear baby food and vanilla until blended.
- Stir the flour mixture into the egg mixture alternately with the buttermilk, making two additions of flour and one of buttermilk, until just blended.
- Gently fold in diced pears.
- Divide batter evenly among prepared muffin cups.
- Sprinkle with topping.
- Bake for 19-23 minutes or until tops are golden and a pick comes out clean.
- Let cool in pan on a wire rack for 5 minutes, then transfer to the rack to cool.

Nutrition Information

- Calories: 248.6
- Total Carbohydrate: 37.3
- Cholesterol: 45.2
- Sodium: 235.7
- Fiber: 2.1
- Sugar: 19.3
- Protein: 4.3
- Total Fat: 9.6
- Saturated Fat: 3.9

414. Drought Buns (Currant Scones)

Serving: 16 serving(s) | Prep: 10mins | Ready in:

Ingredients

- 3 1/2 cups self-raising flour
- 80 g butter or 80 g vegetable fat, chilled and diced
- 1 cup water
- 2 tablespoons currants

Direction

- Mix the flour with the sugar and rub in butter until the mixture resembles breadcrumbs.

- Gradually add the water, stirring until smooth. Stir in the currants.
- Place balls or tablespoons-full on a greased baking tray and bake at 180 degrees for 20 minutes, or until tinged with brown and cooked through.

Nutrition Information

- Calories: 135.6
- Sodium: 376.3
- Fiber: 0.8
- Total Carbohydrate: 21.1
- Total Fat: 4.3
- Saturated Fat: 2.6
- Cholesterol: 10.7
- Protein: 2.8
- Sugar: 0.8

415. Easiest Banana Muffins Ever

Serving: 12 large muffins | Prep: 5mins | Ready in:

Ingredients

- 2 -3 ripe bananas (to make 1 cup)
- 3⁄4 cup sugar
- 1 cup Miracle Whip
- 1 1⁄2 cups all-purpose flour
- 2⁄3 cup whole wheat flour
- 2 teaspoons baking soda
- 1⁄2 teaspoon salt

Direction

- In medium size bowl beat bananas, sugar, and salad dressing. Stir in the flour, baking soda, and salt until it is just moistened. Fill muffin cups three quarters full. Bake at 350 degrees.

Nutrition Information

- Calories: 145.4
- Total Fat: 0.3
- Saturated Fat: 0.1
- Cholesterol: 0
- Sodium: 307.5
- Fiber: 1.8
- Sugar: 15
- Total Carbohydrate: 33.8
- Protein: 2.7

416. Easy Cheese Scones

Serving: 20 scones | Prep: 5mins | Ready in:

Ingredients

- 250 g plain flour
- 3 teaspoons baking powder
- 1 teaspoon salt
- 1 teaspoon cayenne
- 250 g mature cheddar cheese
- 1 egg
- 3 teaspoons sunflower oil
- 130 ml milk

Direction

- Pre-heat your oven to 180°C.
- Mix together the flour, baking powder, salt, cayenne and cheddar, reserving just a little to sprinkle on the tops of the scones.
- In a separate bowl, beat the egg and add the milk and oil.
- Add the liquid mixture to the flour mixture and combine together with a spoon and then your hands. If the mixture won't hold together, add a splash more milk until it does.
- Use your hands to flatten the dough until it's about half a centimeter thick. Fold in half and flatten again to the same thickness.
- Use a cutter of your choice to press out the scones and arrange them on a baking tray. They don't spread much so you don't have to worry about leaving a large gap between each one. Sprinkle the reserved cheddar over the

tops of the scones and place in the oven for 15-20 minutes, until golden.

- Bake until golden.

Nutrition Information

- Calories: 121.6
- Protein: 5.3
- Saturated Fat: 3
- Fiber: 0.5
- Sugar: 0.1
- Total Carbohydrate: 12.6
- Cholesterol: 23.3
- Total Fat: 5.5
- Sodium: 255.5

417. Easy Dog Biscuits

Serving: 6-8 serving(s) | Prep: 5mins | Ready in:

Ingredients

- 2 (2 1/2 ounce) jars turkey baby food
- 1 (2 1/2 ounce) jar beef baby food
- 9 tablespoons powdered milk
- 13 tablespoons wheat germ

Direction

- Preheat oven to 350.
- Mix all ingredients together and form into small balls; place onto lightly greased cookie sheets.
- Bake at 350 degrees for 12 minutes.
- Store in refrigerator.

Nutrition Information

- Calories: 151.6
- Protein: 10.9
- Fiber: 2.1
- Sugar: 4.6
- Cholesterol: 31.5
- Total Fat: 6.5
- Saturated Fat: 2.8
- Sodium: 62.9
- Total Carbohydrate: 13.3

418. Easy Low Fat Whole Wheat Irish Soda Bread

Serving: 8 Wedges, 8 serving(s) | Prep: 5mins | Ready in:

Ingredients

- 2 cups whole wheat flour
- 1 teaspoon baking soda
- 1 teaspoon sugar
- 1/2 teaspoon salt
- 1 cup plain fat-free yogurt

Direction

- Combine all ingredients.
- Shape into ball.
- Bake for 25 minutes at 400 degrees.

Nutrition Information

- Calories: 120.9
- Fiber: 3.7
- Total Carbohydrate: 24.6
- Cholesterol: 0.6
- Total Fat: 0.6
- Saturated Fat: 0.1
- Sodium: 327.7
- Sugar: 3
- Protein: 5.9

419. Elf Biscuits

Serving: 44 cookies | Prep: 15mins | Ready in:

Ingredients

- 1 (5 1/3 ounce) package graham crackers (1 sleeve)
- 3⁄4 cup butter or 3⁄4 cup margarine
- 1⁄2 cup sugar
- 1 cup chopped pecans or 1 cup almonds

Direction

- Preheat oven to 300°F.
- Arrange 11 whole graham crackers on an un-greased 15 x 10 inch jelly roll pan.
- Bring butter, sugar, and nuts to a boil in a medium saucepan, and boil 2 minutes.
- Pour mixture over the graham crackers, spreading quickly to cover.
- Bake for 12 minutes.
- Remove crackers to wax paper to cool.
- Cut with a knife along perforations and serve.

Nutrition Information

- Calories: 68.2
- Protein: 0.5
- Total Fat: 5.3
- Sugar: 3.4
- Total Carbohydrate: 5.3
- Cholesterol: 8.3
- Saturated Fat: 2.2
- Sodium: 43.1
- Fiber: 0.3

420. English Muffins With Eggs, Cheese And Ham

Serving: 1-2 | Prep: 0S | Ready in:

Ingredients

- 2 English muffins
- 2 eggs
- 2 slices cheese slices
- 2 slices ham

Direction

- Toast the English muffin and butter.
- Meanwhile, heat a frying pan, spray with cooking spray or coat with oil or butter. When hot enough crack the eggs into the frying pan and pop the yolks, (you can even beat them if you want), cook until fully cooked flipping about 1/2 way through. Top with cheese slices.
- Cut ham slices into 4 and heat in the frying pan.
- Top English muffins with ham, and one egg and cheese.
- You can also use crisp cooked bacon or sausage patties or even links that have been butterflied.
- Serves one or two.

Nutrition Information

- Calories: 703.9
- Total Fat: 34.4
- Sugar: 4.8
- Fiber: 4
- Total Carbohydrate: 56.6
- Cholesterol: 488.7
- Protein: 40.7
- Saturated Fat: 15.7
- Sodium: 1695.1

421. English Royalty Scones

Serving: 12 serving(s) | Prep: 15mins | Ready in:

Ingredients

- 1 3⁄4 cups all-purpose flour
- 1⁄3 cup sugar
- 2 teaspoons baking powder
- 1⁄2 teaspoon salt
- 5 tablespoons unsalted butter, chilled and cubed
- 1⁄2 cup miniature semisweet chocolate chips (see note)
- 3 tablespoons orange juice

Direction

- Preheat oven to 400 degrees.
- Spray a baking sheet with nonstick cooking spray.
- In a large bowl, whisk together the flour, sugar, baking powder and salt.
- With a pastry blender or a large fork, cut in the butter until the mixture resembles coarse crumbs.
- Stir in the chocolate chips (or whatever you choose).
- Mix in the orange juice to form a dough. Turn out the dough on a floured surface. Pat or roll into a 9" circle about 1/2" thick.
- With a 2 1/2" fluted biscuit cutter, cut out 12 scones, pushing the scraps together for the last few.
- Transfer the scones to the baking sheet. Bake until golden brown, about 12 minutes. Cool on racks.
- Note: I have used white chocolate chips and dried cranberries and I prefer either or both to milk chocolate in these.

Nutrition Information

- Calories: 166.8
- Saturated Fat: 4.3
- Cholesterol: 12.7
- Protein: 2.3
- Total Carbohydrate: 24.6
- Total Fat: 7.2
- Sodium: 159.2
- Fiber: 0.9
- Sugar: 9.8

422. Fat Free, Sugar Free Whole Wheat Blueberry Muffins

Serving: 9 muffins, 9 serving(s) | Prep: 15mins | Ready in:

Ingredients

- 1 cup unsweetened blueberries (fresh or frozen)
- 2 cups whole wheat flour (less 2 tablespoons, see step 4 below)
- 2 7/8 teaspoons baking powder
- 3/8 cup Splenda granular
- 1/4 cup pasteurized pasteurized liquid egg-whites (equals 1 whole egg)
- 1/3 cup unsweetened applesauce
- 5/8 cup nonfat milk
- 1 1/8 tablespoons Splenda granular (to sprinkle on top of muffins)

Direction

- Preheat oven to 400 degrees.
- Lightly spray muffin pan with non-stick spray or use muffin holders.
- Wash and drain blueberries. Set aside. If using frozen blueberries, thaw before using.
- In large bowl, sift flour. VERY IMPORTANT: REMOVE 2 TABLESPOONS OF THE FLOUR BEFORE DOING ANYTHING ELSE! After removing the 2 tablespoons of flour, add in the baking powder and the 3/8 cup Splenda. Mix together.
- In another bowl, mix the liquid egg white, applesauce and milk.
- Combine the wet mixture into the flour mixture. Stir just enough to blend (electric mixers are not necessary). Gently fold in blueberries.
- Using a spoon, fill muffin cups about 2/3 full. Use the last 1 1/8 tablespoon of Splenda to sprinkle on top of each muffin and bake for 15 minutes, or until tops are light brown.
- After baking, allow muffins to cool before removing them from the pan. Please note: 1 serving = 1 muffin. Enjoy! For those on Weight Watchers, each muffin = 1 point!

Nutrition Information

- Calories: 109.8
- Fiber: 3.8
- Sugar: 2.4
- Sodium: 126.5

- Saturated Fat: 0.1
- Total Carbohydrate: 23.6
- Cholesterol: 0.3
- Protein: 4.3
- Total Fat: 0.6

423. Flavorful Sausage Gravy And Biscuits For A Cold Morning

Serving: 3-4 serving(s) | Prep: 5mins | Ready in:

Ingredients

- 1 lb roll jimmy dean's hot breakfast sausage
- 1/4 cup all-purpose flour
- 2 1/2 cups milk
- 3/4 teaspoon salt (approximately, to taste)
- 1/4 teaspoon black pepper (approximately, to taste)
- 6 -8 buttermilk biscuits, already prepared

Direction

- In a large skillet, over medium-high heat, cook sausage until browned and cooked through, crumbling and breaking it up as it cooks.
- Sprinkle flour over the sausage and drippings and stir until all flour is dissolved and incorporated. Cook for a minute or two longer.
- Slowly stir in milk, stirring constantly. Cook, stirring constantly, over medium-high heat until thick and bubbly. **Note** If the gravy is too thick for you at this point you can add more milk in 1/8 cup increments.
- Remove from heat. Taste gravy and season with salt and pepper as desired.
- Serve over hot biscuits that have been split open on the plate.

Nutrition Information

- Calories: 1070.7
- Saturated Fat: 23.2
- Total Carbohydrate: 67.7
- Cholesterol: 155.6
- Protein: 45.5
- Total Fat: 67.8
- Sodium: 3025
- Fiber: 0.3
- Sugar: 0

424. Gelt Biscuits

Serving: 12 cookies | Prep: 12mins | Ready in:

Ingredients

- 1 cup butter
- 2 cups all-purpose flour
- 1 cup grated cheddar cheese
- 1 teaspoon fresh rosemary
- 1 pinch cayenne pepper

Direction

- Place all ingredients in a food processor and pulse until dough forms into a ball.
- Shape dough into a log and wrap it tightly in plastic wrap.
- Chill the dough for at least 2 hours or overnight.
- Preheat oven to 350 degrees F and line a baking sheet with parchment paper.
- Slice log into 1/4 inch coins (5mm) and place on baking sheet.
- Bake until golden brown, 15-18 minutes.
- Cool and store in an airtight container.

Nutrition Information

- Calories: 249.5
- Saturated Fat: 11.7
- Fiber: 0.6
- Sugar: 0.1
- Protein: 4.7
- Total Fat: 18.7

- Sodium: 194
- Total Carbohydrate: 16.1
- Cholesterol: 50.6

425. Gluten Free Irish Soda Bread

Serving: 1 slice, 20 serving(s) | Prep: 20mins | Ready in:

Ingredients

- 2 tablespoons butter
- 1 cup sugar
- 2 eggs
- 3 cups gluten free all-purpose flour, I like Pillsbury brand
- 1 cup whole milk
- 3 teaspoons baking powder
- 1/4 teaspoon salt
- 1 cup raisins, soaked in hot water mixed with cinnamon for 15-20 minutes
- 1 tablespoon caraway seed (optional)

Direction

- Preheat oven to 350 and grease a round cake pan.
- Cream butter and sugar together using a mixer.
- Add eggs and beat until creamy and smooth.
- Stir in Milk
- Slowly add flour, salt and baking powder into the wet ingredients one cup at a time, mix until a dough form.
- Drain raisins and add to the dough along with the caraway seeds (if desired). Mix dough thoroughly (I find using my hands easier than with a spoon/spatula).
- Place dough in cake pan and gently push down the dough to spread.
- Using a sharp knife, cut an "X" on top.
- Sprinkle sugar and bake for 60 minutes or until brown and a knife comes out clean.
- Best when served warm with butter. Cover leftovers to prevent drying.

Nutrition Information

- Calories: 153.8
- Total Fat: 2.2
- Sodium: 107.3
- Cholesterol: 22.9
- Protein: 3.2
- Saturated Fat: 1.1
- Fiber: 0.8
- Sugar: 15
- Total Carbohydrate: 30.8

426. Gluten Free Cheddar Bay Biscuits

Serving: 10 biscuits | Prep: 10mins | Ready in:

Ingredients

- 2 1/4 cups pamela's baking and pancake mix
- 1 1/2 teaspoons baking powder
- 1/4 teaspoon garlic powder
- 4 tablespoons butter, softened
- 1/2 cup cheddar cheese, shredded
- 1 egg, beaten
- 2/3 cup milk

Direction

- Preheat oven to 375 degrees.
- Mix dry ingredients together.
- Cut in butter.
- Stir in cheddar cheese.
- Add the beaten egg and the milk.
- Drop onto an ungreased baking sheet - about a 1/4 cup for each biscuit (I use an ice cream scoop).
- Bake for 15-17 minutes until golden brown.

Nutrition Information

- Calories: 191.7

- Protein: 5.6
- Sodium: 500.6
- Saturated Fat: 4.9
- Fiber: 0.8
- Sugar: 0.1
- Total Carbohydrate: 21.9
- Cholesterol: 45.2
- Total Fat: 9

427. Golden Muffins

Serving: 12 muffins | Prep: 10mins | Ready in:

Ingredients

- 1 (8 1/4 ounce) can crushed pineapple
- 2 cups sifted all-purpose flour
- 1⁄4 cup sugar
- 1 tablespoon baking powder
- 1⁄4 teaspoon salt
- 1⁄4 teaspoon ground nutmeg
- 1 egg
- 1 cup milk
- 1 teaspoon grated orange rind
- 1⁄4 cup butter, melted

Direction

- Drain pineapple well.
- Sift together flour, sugar, baking powder, salt and nutmeg.
- Beat together egg and milk; stir in pineapple and orange rind.
- Blend into dry ingredients, along with melted butter, mixing as little as possible until all particles are just moistened.
- Spoon into lightly greased muffin pans.
- Bake in a preheated 400-degree oven 20- 25 minutes until golden.
- Cool 5 minutes before removing from pan.
- Serve warm!

Nutrition Information

- Calories: 157.7
- Cholesterol: 30.6
- Protein: 3.5
- Total Fat: 5.2
- Saturated Fat: 3.1
- Sodium: 182.9
- Fiber: 0.8
- Sugar: 7.1
- Total Carbohydrate: 24.4

428. Grandma's Scones

Serving: 12 serving(s) | Prep: 15mins | Ready in:

Ingredients

- 1 cup sour cream
- 1 teaspoon baking soda
- 4 cups flour
- 1 cup sugar
- 2 teaspoons baking powder
- 1⁄4 teaspoon cream of tartar
- 1 teaspoon salt
- 1 cup butter
- 1 egg
- 1 cup dried fruit, chopped finely

Direction

- In a small bowl, blend the sour cream and baking soda, and set aside.
- Preheat oven to 350 degrees F.
- Lightly grease a large baking sheet.
- In a large bowl, mix the flour, sugar, baking powder, cream of tartar, and salt.
- Cut in the butter.
- Stir the sour cream mixture and egg into the flour mixture until just moistened.
- Mix in the dried fruit.
- Turn dough out onto a lightly floured surface, and knead briefly.
- Roll or pat dough into a 3/4 inch thick round.
- Cut into 12 wedges, and place them 2 inches apart on the prepared baking sheet.

- Baking 12 to 15 minutes in the preheated oven, until golden brown on the bottom.

Nutrition Information

- Calories: 438.6
- Protein: 5.8
- Total Fat: 20
- Fiber: 2.5
- Total Carbohydrate: 60.7
- Cholesterol: 66.1
- Saturated Fat: 12.1
- Sodium: 519.7
- Sugar: 17.4

429. Grandma's Blueberry Banana Applesauce Bread For The Bread Machin

Serving: 2 pound loaf, 1 serving(s) | Prep: 20mins | Ready in:

Ingredients

- 2 1/2 tablespoons canola oil
- 6 ounces fat-free blueberry yogurt
- 1/2 cup unsweetened applesauce
- 2 ripe bananas, Mashed
- 2 cups bread flour
- 1/2 teaspoon salt
- 2 tablespoons sugar
- 2 cups wheat flour
- 2/3 cup old fashioned oats, Uncooked
- 1/2 teaspoon nutmeg
- 1/2 teaspoon cinnamon
- 1 cup fresh blueberries or 1 cup frozen blueberries, coated with some of the flour
- 2 1/2 teaspoons yeast

Direction

- Bag the bananas and seal the baggie, getting as much air out as possible. Then, using your hands, just start squishing and squashing, mashing the bananas to a pulp. "Smoosh" the bananas out of the baggie and into the Bread Machine's Pan.
- Put about a 1/4 cup of the Bread Flour in a bowl and stir the Blueberries around in it. This helps keep the Blueberries from clumping together in the dough.
- Insert the Bread Pan into the Machine and close the lid. Set the Machine for a Medium Crust, 2 Pound Loaf of Wheat Bread.

Nutrition Information

- Calories: 2886.8
- Sodium: 1286.4
- Sugar: 115.1
- Cholesterol: 3.4
- Total Fat: 49.9
- Saturated Fat: 5.5
- Fiber: 52.5
- Total Carbohydrate: 552.5
- Protein: 80.2

430. Green Chilies Corn Muffins

Serving: 16 muffins | Prep: 10mins | Ready in:

Ingredients

- 8 1/2 ounces corn muffin mix
- 9 ounces yellow cake mix
- 2 eggs
- 1/2 cup milk
- 1/3 cup water
- 2 tablespoons vegetable oil
- 4 ounces green chilies, chopped, drained
- 1 cup cheddar cheese, shredded, divided (4 oz.)

Direction

- In a bowl, combine dry corn bread and cake mixes.

- In another bowl, combine the eggs, milk, water and oil.
- Stir wet ingredients into the dry ingredients just until moistened.
- Add chilies and 3/4 cup cheese.
- Fill greased or paper lined muffin cups two-thirds full.
- Bake at 350 degrees for 20-22 minutes or until muffins test done.
- Immediately sprinkle with remaining cheese.
- Cool for 5 minutes before removing from pans to wire racks.
- Serve warm.

Nutrition Information

- Calories: 192.3
- Protein: 4.7
- Total Carbohydrate: 24.1
- Cholesterol: 35.5
- Total Fat: 8.6
- Saturated Fat: 2.8
- Sodium: 329
- Fiber: 1.3
- Sugar: 10.4

431. Green Pistachio Muffins

Serving: 10 muffins | Prep: 20mins | Ready in:

Ingredients

- 1 1/3 cups all-purpose flour
- 2 teaspoons baking powder
- 1/2 teaspoon salt
- 1/2 teaspoon ground cinnamon
- 1/4 teaspoon nutmeg
- 1 teaspoon lemon zest
- 1/2 cup pistachios, finely chopped
- 1/2 cup butter
- 2/3 cup granulated sugar
- 2 large eggs
- 1 teaspoon vanilla extract
- 1/2 teaspoon rum extract
- 1/2 cup milk
- 1/2 cup pistachios, coarsely chopped

Direction

- Preheat the oven to 425 degrees.
- Prepare the muffin tins by greasing them well.
- Combine the dry ingredients including the zest and finely chopped pistachios in a large bowl.
- Cream the butter and sugar together in a mixer with the paddle attachment. Beat the eggs, one at a time, into the creamed mixture until light and fluffy. Add the vanilla and rum extracts.
- Starting with about 1/4 of the dry mixture, alternately add part of the dry ingredients and the milk, briefly mixing after each addition. Do not over-mix the batter.
- Scoop the batter into the prepared tins. Sprinkle the tops with the coarsely chopped pistachios.
- Place the muffins in the oven and immediately turn the temperature down to 375 degrees. Bake for 15 minutes or until the muffins test done.
- After the muffins have cooled for five minutes, remove them from the tins to cool on a wire rack.
- Baker's Note: It's the finely chopped pistachios that give the muffin a green hue. We used a nut chopper to chop ours finely. You can also chop them in a food processor.

Nutrition Information

- Calories: 287.9
- Total Fat: 16.4
- Saturated Fat: 7.2
- Fiber: 1.8
- Sugar: 14.4
- Protein: 6
- Sodium: 290.8
- Total Carbohydrate: 30.6
- Cholesterol: 63.3

432. Harvest Morning Muffins

Serving: 1 Dozen, 12 serving(s) | Prep: 15mins | Ready in:

Ingredients

- 1 1/2 cups flour (all purpose white or whole-wheat)
- 2 teaspoons pumpkin pie spice
- 1 teaspoon baking powder
- 1/2 teaspoon baking soda
- 1/2 teaspoon salt
- 1 cup canned pumpkin (pure)
- 3/4 cup packed brown sugar
- 2 large eggs, room temperature
- 6 tablespoons unsalted butter, melted
- 1/2 cup sour cream, room temperature
- 3/4 cup chopped walnuts
- 1/2 cup dried cranberries

Direction

- Preheat the oven to 350°F Line a 12-cup muffin tin or two 6-cup muffin tins with paper liners.
- In a medium bowl, whisk the flour, spice, baking powder, baking soda, and salt. In a large bowl, whisk the pumpkin, brown sugar, eggs, butter, and sour cream. Fold in the flour mixture, walnuts, and cranberries until just combined. Divide among muffin cups.
- Bake until a toothpick inserted in the center of a muffin comes out clean, about 25 minutes. Cool in the pan on a wire rack for 5 minutes, then cool on the rack.

Nutrition Information

- Calories: 248.3
- Fiber: 1.7
- Sugar: 14.8
- Total Carbohydrate: 29.2
- Protein: 4.3
- Total Fat: 13.5
- Saturated Fat: 5.5
- Sodium: 253.6
- Cholesterol: 51.2

433. Healthy Butternut Squash Muffins

Serving: 12 muffins, 12 serving(s) | Prep: 35mins | Ready in:

Ingredients

- 1 cup butternut squash, peeled, seeded and cubed
- 1 cup wheat flour
- 1/2 cup all-purpose flour
- 2 teaspoons baking powder
- 1/3 cup brown sugar
- 1/4 teaspoon salt
- 2 teaspoons pumpkin pie spice
- 3/4 cup milk, soy
- 1 egg, beaten
- 1/4 cup applesauce

Direction

- Preheat oven to 400 degrees. Lightly grease a 12 cup muffin pan.
- In a medium saucepan with enough water to cover, boil squash 20 minutes, or until tender. Remove from heat, drain, and puree in a food processor.
- In a large bowl, whisk together flour, baking powder, sugar, salt and pumpkin pie spice.
- In a medium bowl, thoroughly mix together milk, egg and applesauce. Stir in squash. Fold the squash mixture into the flour mixture just until moistened.
- Spoon batter into the greased muffin pan, filling cups about ½ full. Bake 20 minutes.

Nutrition Information

- Calories: 102.4
- Total Fat: 1.3

- Sugar: 6.2
- Total Carbohydrate: 20.7
- Cholesterol: 19.8
- Saturated Fat: 0.5
- Sodium: 127.3
- Fiber: 1.7
- Protein: 3.1

434. Healthy Muffins

Serving: 12 muffins | Prep: 20mins | Ready in:

Ingredients

- 1/2 cup brown sugar
- 1 cup wheat flour
- 1 cup oat bran
- 2 cups oats
- 1 1/2 teaspoons cinnamon
- 1 1/2 teaspoons baking powder
- 1 teaspoon baking soda
- 2 -3 cups blueberries (Fruit of choice or any fruit is great and frozen blueberries work well)
- 1/4 cup non-fat powdered milk
- 1 cup milk
- 1/4 cup nonfat plain yogurt
- 1 egg white

Direction

- Combine ingredients from brown sugar thru powdered milk.
- Combine: milk, yogurt and egg white.
- Mix together.
- Bake 375 degrees for ~20min.
- (I undercook them and refrigerate uneaten muffins. Then pop one in a toaster even when ready to eat and it cooks through without drying them out).

Nutrition Information

- Calories: 230.8
- Saturated Fat: 0.9
- Fiber: 5.8
- Sugar: 13.2
- Cholesterol: 3.5
- Protein: 9.4
- Total Fat: 3.5
- Sodium: 186
- Total Carbohydrate: 45.2

435. High Fiber Cholesterol Free Oat Bran Muffins

Serving: 12 serving(s) | Prep: 10mins | Ready in:

Ingredients

- 3/4 cup flour
- 1 cup oat bran
- 1/2 cup brown sugar
- 1 teaspoon baking powder
- 2 teaspoons ground cinnamon
- 1/2 teaspoon baking soda
- 1/8 teaspoon allspice
- 2 mashed bananas
- 1/4 cup skim milk
- 1/4 cup egg substitute
- 2 tablespoons cooking oil
- 1 teaspoon vanilla

Direction

- In a large mixing bowl, stir together flour, oat bran, brown sugar, baking powder, cinnamon, baking soda, and allspice.
- In a medium mixing bowl combine mashed bananas, milk, egg substitute, cooking oil and vanilla.
- Add all at once to the flour mixture. Stir until moistened.
- Put into muffin pans you have sprayed with cooking spray.
- Bake at 400 degrees for 18 to 20 minutes.
- Makes 12 muffins. You can add raisins, nuts, shredded carrots, etc.

Nutrition Information

- Calories: 128.6
- Cholesterol: 0.1
- Protein: 3.2
- Total Fat: 3.2
- Saturated Fat: 0.5
- Fiber: 2.1
- Sodium: 99.4
- Sugar: 11.4
- Total Carbohydrate: 25.3

436. Honey Vanilla Bran Muffins

Serving: 6 jumbo muffins, 6 serving(s) | Prep: 10mins | Ready in:

Ingredients

- 1 1/4 cups oat bran
- 1 cup all-purpose flour
- 2 teaspoons baking powder
- 1 teaspoon baking soda
- 1 teaspoon ground cinnamon
- 1/2 teaspoon ground nutmeg
- 1 (8 ounce) container low-fat vanilla yogurt
- 6 tablespoons honey
- 2 eggs, beaten
- 3 tablespoons vegetable oil
- 1 teaspoon vanilla extract
- 1/2 cup seedless raisin

Direction

- Preheat oven to 400. Grease 6 large muffins cups.
- Combine oat bran, flour, baking powder, baking soda, cinnamon and nutmeg in large bowl. Combine yogurt, honey, eggs, oil and vanilla in small bowl until blended; stir into flour mixture just until moistened. Fold in raisins. Let stand 5 minutes. Spoon into prepared muffin cups, filling 2/3 full.
- Bake 20 to 25 minutes or until wooden pick inserted in center comes out clean. Cool in pan on wire rack 5 minutes. Remove from pan. Cool on wire rack.

Nutrition Information

- Calories: 327.5
- Total Fat: 10.4
- Fiber: 4.3
- Cholesterol: 71.3
- Protein: 8.9
- Total Carbohydrate: 59
- Saturated Fat: 1.9
- Sodium: 368.7
- Sugar: 27.3

437. Hot Biscuits

Serving: 15 Biscuits, 8 serving(s) | Prep: 8mins | Ready in:

Ingredients

- 3/4 cup water
- 3 cups Bisquick baking mix

Direction

- Stir water into bisquick mix with about 25 strokes.
- Turn onto lightly floured surface, round up dough knead 10 times.
- Pat to 1/2 inch thickness.
- Cut close together with floured 1 inch cutter.
- Place 1 inch apart on greased baking sheet for crusty sides, close together for soft sides.
- Bake 425 oven to 16 minutes, until browned.

Nutrition Information

- Calories: 192.6
- Sodium: 574.6
- Cholesterol: 0.9

- Protein: 3.6
- Saturated Fat: 1.8
- Sugar: 5.2
- Total Carbohydrate: 28.5
- Total Fat: 6.9
- Fiber: 0.9

438. Jalapeno And Bacon Cornbread Muffins

Serving: 12 muffins | Prep: 20mins | Ready in:

Ingredients

- 8 slices bacon
- 2 tablespoons Crisco or 2 tablespoons other vegetable shortening
- 2 eggs
- 1 small onion, chopped
- 5 pickled jalapeno peppers, stemmed, drained and chopped
- 1 tablespoon jalapeno juice
- 1 tablespoon sugar
- 1 teaspoon baking soda
- 1 teaspoon salt
- 1/4 teaspoon cumin
- 1/4 teaspoon pepper
- 2 cups cornmeal
- 1 1/2 cups buttermilk

Direction

- Preheat oven to 425-degrees F.
- Fry bacon in a skillet over medium heat until crisp (10-15 minutes).
- Transfer bacon to paper towels to drain.
- Crumble bacon and set aside.
- Pour bacon fat into a bowl and set aside.
- Melt Crisco and 2 tablespoons of the bacon fat together in the same skillet over medium heat.
- Grease a muffin tin with remaining bacon grease and transfer to oven so muffin tin will be hot.
- In a large bowl beat eggs.
- Add bacon, onions, jalapenos, pickling juice, sugar, baking soda, salt, cumin and pepper and stir well to combine.
- Add cornmeal and buttermilk and stir to combine.
- Add the hot fat (from the skillet) and stir until combined.
- Remove muffin tin from oven.
- Pour batter into muffin tins.
- Bake or 15-20 minutes or until done and toothpick comes clean.

Nutrition Information

- Calories: 195.4
- Total Carbohydrate: 19.4
- Protein: 5.6
- Saturated Fat: 3.5
- Sodium: 628.9
- Fiber: 1.8
- Sugar: 3.2
- Cholesterol: 46.8
- Total Fat: 10.9

439. Kahlua Muffins

Serving: 18 muffins | Prep: 10mins | Ready in:

Ingredients

- 1 box yellow cake mix
- 1 (3 ounce) box vanilla instant pudding mix
- 4 eggs
- 1 cup sour cream
- 1 cup vegetable oil
- 1 cup chopped pecans
- 1 cup brown sugar
- 3/4 cup Kahlua

Direction

- In a small bowl combine pecans, brown sugar and Kahlua.
- Let sit until needed.

- In a large bowl, and I do mean large, combine the cake mix, pudding mix, vegetable oil and sour cream, and mix on low speed until moistened.
- Add the eggs, one at a time and mix well after each.
- Beat for 2 minutes on medium speed, the mixture will be very thick, don't panic.
- Slowly mix in the pecan mixture, until well mixed.
- Pour into very well-greased muffin cups, see note below.
- Bake at 350 for 15 to 20 minutes, or until toothpick comes out clean.
- Pop out of pan and cool on rack, if you can wait that long to eat one.
- NOTE: Make sure you use well-greased muffin tins, if you're using non-stick pans.
- I spray mine with Baker's Ease and am sure to run my finger all around the inside and rim.
- I find the darker the pan, the better the muffin.
- If they stick, you did not grease enough.
- Just run a spatula around the edge to release.
- I noted these make 18 regular size muffins.
- These do not rise a lot so you can fill 2/3 way full without spill over.
- When I make, I make 12 regular muffins and 6 mini-Bundt size, or I might make 48 mini muffins and 6 regular muffins.

Nutrition Information

- Calories: 417.9
- Total Carbohydrate: 44.2
- Cholesterol: 53.2
- Protein: 3.6
- Total Fat: 23.7
- Fiber: 0.9
- Sugar: 32.8
- Saturated Fat: 4.5
- Sodium: 287.3

440. Khanom Puto (A Steamed Sweet Savory Coconut Muffin)

Serving: 30 mini muffins appx | Prep: 10mins | Ready in:

Ingredients

- 1 1/3 cups plain flour
- 1/3 cup desiccated coconut
- 1 tablespoon baking powder
- 1 egg
- 200 ml sugar
- 250 ml coconut milk
- 1/2 cup coconut cream
- 1/8 teaspoon sugar
- 1 teaspoon glutinous-rice flour
- 1 teaspoon cornflour
- 1/8 teaspoon salt
- 1 cup sweet corn
- 6 dried anchovies or 12 dried shrimp, cut and pounded to a dust
- 1 sprig garlic chives, finely chopped

Direction

- MUFFINS: Mix together the 1 1/3 cup of flour, desiccated coconut, baking powder, egg, sugar and coconut milk to make a smooth batter.
- Pour the batter to half fill the mini silicone muffin cups.
- Steam the muffins for 5 minutes.
- TOPPING: Mix together the 1/2 cup coconut CREAM, glutinous rice flour, corn flour, sugar, salt to make the coconut cream topping.
- Take the Muffins at 5 minutes and smear evenly with a small teaspoonful of coconut cream topping mixture, and then sprinkle with dried anchovies dust, corn kernels and garlic chives, then return to steamer for additional 3 minutes.
- Lift from steamer, release gently from silicone molds and serve.

Nutrition Information

- Calories: 66.9
- Total Fat: 3.1

- Saturated Fat: 2.7
- Sodium: 54.8
- Fiber: 0.4
- Sugar: 3.2
- Cholesterol: 6.2
- Total Carbohydrate: 8.9
- Protein: 1.2

441. Kingsbys' No Yeast Biscuits

Serving: 1 biscuit, 12 serving(s) | Prep: 5mins | Ready in:

Ingredients

- 2 cups self-rising flour
- 1 cup milk
- 6 tablespoons mayonnaise
- 6 tablespoons sugar
- 1 teaspoon baking powder
- 1 egg

Direction

- Grease a muffin pan and pre-heat the oven at 350.
- Combine all of the dry ingredients in a medium-large bowl. Add the milk, mayo, and egg. Mix well.
- Fill the greased muffin tins 1/4-1/2 full and bake for 12-25 minutes at 350 until they are golden-brown on the outside and a toothpick comes out clean.
- Serve with butter or jam.

Nutrition Information

- Calories: 146
- Protein: 3.3
- Saturated Fat: 1
- Fiber: 0.6
- Sodium: 363
- Sugar: 6.8
- Total Carbohydrate: 24.6
- Cholesterol: 20.3
- Total Fat: 3.8

442. Lemon Chocolate Chip Muffins

Serving: 12 serving(s) | Prep: 10mins | Ready in:

Ingredients

- 1 medium lemon
- 1 cup sugar
- 1 teaspoon baking soda
- 1 cup plain buttermilk or 1 cup yogurt
- 1⁄4 cup fresh lemon juice
- 1⁄2 cup butter
- 2 large eggs
- 2 cups flour
- 3⁄4 cup chocolate chips

Direction

- Finely grate lemon peel, avoiding pith.
- Beat butter and sugar until pale and creamy. Add eggs, one at a time, beating well after each. Stir in baking soda and grated peel. Fold in half the flour, then half the buttermilk. Repeat. Fold in chocolate chips.
- Scoop 1/4 cup batter into prepared muffin tins.
- Bake at 375 degrees for 20-25 minutes. Remove from oven.
- Brush lemon juice over hot muffins until used up. Sprinkle with sugar. Let stand 5 minutes before removing from pans.

Nutrition Information

- Calories: 281.9
- Total Fat: 12.1
- Sodium: 194.4
- Fiber: 1.6
- Sugar: 23.6
- Cholesterol: 56.4

- Saturated Fat: 7.1
- Total Carbohydrate: 41.6
- Protein: 4.5

443. Lemon Poppy Seed Surprise Snack Muffins

Serving: 6 muffins, 6 serving(s) | Prep: 5mins | Ready in:

Ingredients

- 1 (7 ounce) package fat free muffin mix, lemon poppy seed
- 1/2 cup milk
- 2 ounces cream cheese, softened
- 2 tablespoons sugar
- 2 tablespoons lemon juice

Direction

- Preheat oven to 375°.
- Prepare the muffin mix (I used Lemon Poppy Seed Flavour for this recipe) with 1/2 cup of milk and 2 tablespoons of lemon juice. Blend just until moist with a fork, leave lots of small lumps throughout the dough for best results.
- In a separate bowl blend the cream cheese and sugar.
- Spray a 6 cup muffin tin with non-stick cooking spray.
- Evenly distribute the dough into the six cups filling about 2/3's of the way full.
- Gently press about a teaspoon of the cream cheese mixture onto each muffin. The cream cheese will fall into the centre of each muffin as it bakes.
- Bake for 15 minutes.
- Can serve warm or freeze and serve later, but these are definitely better the next day.

Nutrition Information

- Calories: 63.5
- Sodium: 38
- Fiber: 0
- Total Carbohydrate: 5.8
- Protein: 1.4
- Saturated Fat: 2.5
- Sugar: 4.3
- Cholesterol: 13.2
- Total Fat: 4

444. Lemon Thyme Biscuits

Serving: 6 biscuits | Prep: 25mins | Ready in:

Ingredients

- 1/4 cup cold butter, cut into small pieces
- 1 tablespoon lemon zest, freshly grated
- 2 cups white flour
- 1 tablespoon sugar
- 2 teaspoons baking powder
- 1/2 teaspoon baking soda
- 1/2 teaspoon salt
- 2 -3 tablespoons chopped fresh thyme
- 3/4 cup buttermilk, plus
- 2 tablespoons buttermilk
- buttermilk, for brushing

Direction

- Preheat the oven to 425*F.
- Lightly oil a baking sheet.
- Place the butter pieces and lemon peel in a medium bowl or in food processor.
- Sift the flour, sugar, baking powder, baking soda, and salt over the butter.
- By hand or with the food processor, mix the butter into the flour until evenly distributed.
- Add the thyme and mix well.
- Add the buttermilk and stir or pulse briefly.
- The dough will be soft and a little sticky.
- On a lightly floured surface, pat the dough into a 9-inch circle that is about 1/2 inch thick.
- Slice it into six pie-shaped wedges.
- Place the wedges on the prepared baking sheet and brush the tops with a little buttermilk.

- Bake for 20 minutes, until the biscuits are firm and nice and golden brown.
- Serve immediately.
- Enjoy!

Nutrition Information

- Calories: 243.9
- Sodium: 512.5
- Fiber: 1.4
- Protein: 5.6
- Total Fat: 8.4
- Saturated Fat: 5.1
- Sugar: 4
- Total Carbohydrate: 36.3
- Cholesterol: 21.8

445. Low Fat Sugar Free Zucchini Bread/Muffins

Serving: 24 cupcakes | Prep: 10mins | Ready in:

Ingredients

- 2 cups Equal sugar substitute or 2 cups Splenda granular
- 3 cups flour
- 1 teaspoon baking soda
- 1/4 teaspoon salt
- 1/4 teaspoon baking powder
- 1 tablespoon cinnamon
- 1/2 cup chopped walnuts
- 3 eggs
- 2 cups finely grated zucchini
- 1/4 cup oil
- 3/4 cup applesauce
- 1 tablespoon pure vanilla extract

Direction

- Mix dry ingredients in large bowl.
- Then mix other ingredients in smaller bowl.
- Gently mix other ingredients into dry ingredients, just until moist. (Mix gently, and only until mixed; otherwise the muffins will be tough and dry).
- Spoon into cupcake liners in pan.
- Bake about 15-18 minutes at 400°F degrees.
- (Or pour into 3 loaf pans or 2 if you want larger loaves and bake at 350°F for about 60 minutes).

Nutrition Information

- Calories: 163.1
- Total Fat: 4.7
- Sodium: 92.8
- Saturated Fat: 0.7
- Fiber: 1
- Sugar: 11.8
- Total Carbohydrate: 27
- Cholesterol: 23.2
- Protein: 3.2

446. Maple Oat Nut Scones Starbucks

Serving: 8 serving(s) | Prep: 25mins | Ready in:

Ingredients

- For The Scones
- 1 cup oats (quick or old-fashioned)
- 1 1/2 cups flour
- 2 tablespoons sugar
- 1/2 teaspoon salt
- 1 tablespoon baking powder
- 2 tablespoons maple syrup
- 2 1/2 tablespoons cold butter (small pieces)
- 1 large egg
- 1/2 cup half-and-half or 1/2 cup heavy cream
- 1/2-3/4 teaspoon maple extract
- 2/3 cup coarsely chopped pecans
- Maple Glaze
- 1 1/2 cups powdered sugar
- 1/2 teaspoon maple extract
- 5 teaspoons water

Direction

- Preheat oven to 425°F.
- Using a food processor or blender, finely grind oats.
- In a mixer, mix flour, oats, sugar, salt and baking powder.
- Add maple syrup and butter and mix well.
- In a small bowl, beat the egg with the cream and maple extract.
- Pour the egg mixture into the flour mixture and mix well.
- Add pecans and mix just to incorporate.
- Place dough on a floured surface. Knead and pat dough into an 8 to 10 inch circle and cut into 8 wedges.
- Spray a baking sheet with cooking spray. Place wedges on top and bake for 13 to 15 minutes, or until light brown.
- Remove scones from oven to wire rack. Let cool about 3 to 5 minutes.
- Mix glaze ingredients until smooth. Adjust the amount of water to get to the desired consistency. I like the glaze to be rather thick. Spread lots of glaze over each scone and dry about 15 minutes before serving.

Nutrition Information

- Calories: 399.3
- Sugar: 29
- Total Fat: 14.1
- Saturated Fat: 4.4
- Fiber: 3.6
- Protein: 7.8
- Sodium: 330.3
- Total Carbohydrate: 62.5
- Cholesterol: 38.4

447. Mayonnaise Biscuits (Cookies)

Serving: 20-30 biscuits | Prep: 15mins | Ready in:

Ingredients

- 500 g flour
- 250 g sugar
- 250 ml mayonnaise
- 1 teaspoon vanilla bean paste
- 1 teaspoon baking powder
- 1/8 teaspoon salt
- 1/2 cup sugar, extra

Direction

- Sieve flour and baking powder, set aside.
- Mix the mayonnaise, sugar, salt and vanilla paste.
- Add the flour to the mayonnaise and mix well.
- Depending on the brand of mayonnaise you may need to add an extra tablespoon of flour if it is still sticky.
- Form into small balls and roll in extra sugar.
- Place onto baking tray and bake for 10-12 minutes.

Nutrition Information

- Calories: 204.7
- Saturated Fat: 0.6
- Sodium: 116.9
- Fiber: 0.7
- Sugar: 18.3
- Cholesterol: 3.1
- Protein: 2.7
- Total Fat: 4.2
- Total Carbohydrate: 39.4

448. Melissa's Drop Biscuits With Green Onions

Serving: 12 biscuits | Prep: 0S | Ready in:

Ingredients

- 1/2 cup all-purpose flour
- 1/2 cup whole wheat flour

- 1 teaspoon baking powder
- 1/4 teaspoon salt
- 3 tablespoons unsalted butter, cubed and chilled
- 3 green onions, chopped
- 1 tablespoon finely grated parmesan cheese
- 1/2 cup milk

Direction

- Preheat the oven to 450 degrees F.
- Put the flour, baking powder, and salt in a food processor and pulse briefly to mix. Add the butter and pulse until the mixture is crumbly. Add green onion and Parmesan and pulse just enough to blend. Add the milk and pulse until combined. Drop the dough in rounded tablespoons onto a greased baking sheet, and bake until golden, about 13 to 15 minutes.

Nutrition Information

- Calories: 71.1
- Total Fat: 3.5
- Sodium: 91.2
- Fiber: 0.8
- Sugar: 0.1
- Total Carbohydrate: 8.4
- Cholesterol: 9.4
- Saturated Fat: 2.2
- Protein: 1.8

449. Mile High Biscuits

Serving: 15 Large Biscuits | Prep: 10mins | Ready in:

Ingredients

- 3 cups all-purpose flour
- 1/4 cup sugar
- 4 teaspoons baking powder
- 1/2 teaspoon cream of tartar
- 3/4 teaspoon salt
- 1/2 cup shortening
- 1 egg, beaten
- 3/4 cup milk

Direction

- Combine dry ingredients in a mixing bowl.
- Cut in shortening until mixture resembles coarse crumbs.
- Add egg and milk; mix until dough forms a ball.
- Turn dough out on a lightly floured surface and knead 10- 12 times, only.
- Roll out to 3/4 inch, cut with floured cutter.
- Place on lightly greased baking sheet.
- Bake at 475 degrees for 12- 15 minutes or until light brown.

Nutrition Information

- Calories: 177.8
- Total Fat: 7.8
- Protein: 3.4
- Saturated Fat: 2.1
- Sodium: 224.4
- Fiber: 0.7
- Sugar: 3.4
- Total Carbohydrate: 23.4
- Cholesterol: 14.1

450. Mini Italian Biscuits

Serving: 3 dozen, 12 serving(s) | Prep: 10mins | Ready in:

Ingredients

- 2 cups biscuit mix or 2 cups baking mix
- 1/2 cup cheddar cheese (finely shredded)
- 1/2 teaspoon garlic powder
- 1/2 teaspoon dried oregano
- 1/2 teaspoon dried basil
- 2/3 cup milk

Direction

- Combine the biscuit mix, cheese, garlic powder, oregano, basil. With a fork stir in milk just until moistened.
- Drop by the rounded teaspoonfuls onto a lightly greased baking sheet. Bake at 450degres for 7-8 minutes or until golden brown.
- Serve warm.

Nutrition Information

- Calories: 113.8
- Total Fat: 5.1
- Saturated Fat: 2.1
- Fiber: 0.5
- Sugar: 2.4
- Sodium: 291.1
- Total Carbohydrate: 13.5
- Cholesterol: 7.2
- Protein: 3.2

451. Mom's Bran Muffins

Serving: 12 muffins | Prep: 15mins | Ready in:

Ingredients

- 1⁄4 cup butter
- 1⁄2 cup brown sugar
- 1⁄4 cup molasses
- 2 eggs (unbeaten)
- 3⁄4 cup milk
- 1 1⁄2 cups natural bran
- 1 1⁄4 cups flour
- 1 1⁄2 teaspoons baking powder
- 1⁄2 teaspoon baking soda
- 3⁄4 teaspoon salt
- 1⁄2 cup raisins (optional) or 1⁄2 cup chopped dates (optional)

Direction

- Cream butter and sugar.
- Add eggs and beat well.
- Add molasses and bran and milk.
- Mix well.
- Add dry ingredients and stir just until blended inches.
- Fill Lined muffin tins 2/3 full.
- Bake 375 for 15-20 min.

Nutrition Information

- Calories: 178
- Fiber: 2.5
- Cholesterol: 47.5
- Total Fat: 5.7
- Saturated Fat: 3.1
- Sodium: 314.1
- Sugar: 14
- Total Carbohydrate: 30.6
- Protein: 3.9

452. Mom's Refrigerator Bran Muffins

Serving: 48 muffins, 24 serving(s) | Prep: 10mins | Ready in:

Ingredients

- 1 (18 -20 ounce) box Raisin Bran cereal
- 3 cups sugar
- 5 cups flour (I use part whole wheat)
- 5 teaspoons baking soda
- 4 eggs
- 1 cup oil
- 1 quart buttermilk
- 1 (20 ounce) can crushed pineapple, drained
- 1 1⁄2 cups raisins

Direction

- Mix the dry ingredients together in a large bowl.
- Add the eggs, oil, buttermilk, and pineapple and stir until mixed.
- Mix in the additional raisins.

- Pour into greased muffin tins (don't use liners.).
- Bake at 400 for 18-20 minutes or until golden brown.
- The batter may be stored in a sealed container in the refrigerator for up to three months. I think this recipe improves with age as the raisin bran flakes have time to soak up the liquids more.

Nutrition Information

- Calories: 409.5
- Sodium: 444.6
- Fiber: 3.8
- Total Carbohydrate: 74
- Total Fat: 11.1
- Saturated Fat: 2
- Sugar: 42.6
- Cholesterol: 36.9
- Protein: 7.3

453. Muesli Muffins (21 Day Wonder Diet: Day 20)

Serving: 6 muffins, 2 serving(s) | Prep: 5mins | Ready in:

Ingredients

- cooking spray
- 1/2 cup bran and cranberry muesli, Bran Cranberry Muesli (21 Day Wonder Diet: Day 4)
- 1 teaspoon vegetable oil
- 1/2 cup skim-milk natural yogurt
- 1 egg
- 2/3 cup self-rising flour
- 2 teaspoons orange rind, finely grated
- 1/4 teaspoon mixed spice
- 1 tablespoon demerara sugar
- 1 tablespoon low-fat ricotta

Direction

- Preheat oven to 180°C. Spray 6 muffin pan holes with cooking oil, or line with paper cases.
- Combine muesli, oil, yogurt, egg, flour, rind and spice in medium bowl. Mix with fork.
- Divide mixture among pan holes; sprinkle with sugar. Bake about 25 minutes.
- Serve 2 muffins each with cheese.

Nutrition Information

- Calories: 267.9
- Sodium: 592.7
- Fiber: 1.3
- Protein: 9.4
- Sugar: 9.4
- Total Carbohydrate: 40.8
- Cholesterol: 113.7
- Total Fat: 7.1
- Saturated Fat: 2.4

454. Oatmeal Walnut Muffins

Serving: 12-13 muffins, 12 serving(s) | Prep: 10mins | Ready in:

Ingredients

- 2 eggs, at room temperature
- 1/2 cup canola oil
- 1 cup cooked oatmeal, at room temperature
- 1 teaspoon vanilla extract
- 1 cup flour
- 1 cup brown sugar
- 1 teaspoon baking powder
- 1 teaspoon baking soda
- 1 cup walnuts, chopped

Direction

- Preheat oven to 350°F.
- Place paper liners in each of 12 muffin cups.
- Whisk eggs well, then whisk in oil, oatmeal and vanilla.

- In another bowl, combine flour, brown sugar, baking powder and baking soda until there are no more lumps of brown sugar. Add walnuts and toss to coat.
- Add liquid mixture and fold in, just until the dry ingredients are moistened.
- Spoon into muffin cups, filling 3/4 full. An ice cream scoop works well for this. You may have enough batter for a 13th muffin.
- Bake 18 - 20 minutes or until they test done. Allow to cool 10 minutes in the muffin pan, then turn out onto a wire rack to cool completely.
- These freeze well.

Nutrition Information

- Calories: 276.6
- Total Carbohydrate: 29.4
- Protein: 4.1
- Fiber: 1.3
- Sugar: 18
- Cholesterol: 35.2
- Total Fat: 16.6
- Saturated Fat: 1.6
- Sodium: 185.6

455. Oatmeal Muffins

Serving: 12 small muffins | Prep: 15mins | Ready in:

Ingredients

- 1 cup rolled oats
- 1 cup flour
- 1/2 teaspoon baking soda
- 1 teaspoon baking powder
- 1/3 cup butter, softened
- 1 egg
- 1 cup buttermilk or 1 cup sour milk (1 cup slightly warm milk with 1 tablespoon vinegar)
- 3/4-1 teaspoon salt
- 1/2 cup white sugar or 1/2 cup brown sugar (little bit less if the muffins are going to be topped with cinnamon sugar)
- cinnamon sugar, as topping (optional)

Direction

- Combine oats and buttermilk or sour milk in a bowl, mix and let stand 1 hour.
- Sift together flour, baking soda, baking powder and salt.
- Cream together butter and sugar with an electric mixer.
- Add the egg and beat until light and fluffy.
- Add to the flour mix and stir.
- Add the oat and sour milk mix and stir until just combined.
- Fill a greased muffin tin (mine is for 12 small muffins, 2 and 3/4 inches in diameter in the widest part).
- Top with a little cinnamon sugar if desired.
- Bake at 400o Fahrenheit for 20 minutes.
- The muffins are ready when a stick inside them comes out clean.

Nutrition Information

- Calories: 155.2
- Sugar: 9.4
- Cholesterol: 29.9
- Sodium: 301.1
- Fiber: 1
- Total Carbohydrate: 21.9
- Protein: 3.2
- Total Fat: 6.2
- Saturated Fat: 3.6

456. Orange Blueberry Scones

Serving: 8 serving(s) | Prep: 10mins | Ready in:

Ingredients

- 1 3/4 cups all-purpose flour

- 1/2 cup sugar
- 1/4 cup cornmeal
- 1 1/2 teaspoons baking powder
- 1/2 teaspoon salt
- 2 tablespoons cold butter, cut into pieces
- 2 1/2 teaspoons grated orange zest
- 2/3 cup buttermilk
- 1 egg white, slightly beaten
- 1 cup blueberries
- 1/2 cup confectioners' sugar

Direction

- Preheat oven to 425 Line a jellyroll pan with foil; coat with cooking spray.
- Combine flour, sugar, cornmeal, baking powder and salt.
- With a pastry blender or 2 knives cut in butter and 1 tsp of the zest until well combined.
- Stir in buttermilk and egg white until a soft dough forms.
- Gently stir in blueberries.
- With Moist hands transfer dough to a floured surface and shape into an 8 in round.
- Cut into wedges and place 2 inches apart on pan.
- Bake 8-12 minutes or until golden brown
- Cool Completely.
- In a small bowl combine the confectioners' sugar with 1/2 tsp zest and 1- 2 tbsp. water stir until smooth.
- Drizzle over scones.

Nutrition Information

- Calories: 238.2
- Sodium: 269.4
- Fiber: 1.5
- Sugar: 22.8
- Protein: 4.4
- Total Fat: 3.5
- Saturated Fat: 2
- Total Carbohydrate: 47.8
- Cholesterol: 8.4

457. Orange Cranberry Cream Scones

Serving: 16-20 scones | Prep: 10mins | Ready in:

Ingredients

- 3 cups all-purpose flour
- 1 1/2 teaspoons baking powder
- 1 teaspoon salt
- 3 tablespoons sugar
- 1 cup dried cranberries
- 2 oranges, zest of, only
- 15 ounces heavy cream

Direction

- Preheat the oven to 350°F.
- Combine the flour, baking powder, salt, 2 Tbsp. of sugar, cranberries, and orange zest together in a mixer fitted with a dough hook.
- Mix well until combined.
- While mixing on a low speed, slowly drizzle the cream in just until the mixture comes together into dough. **You may not use all of the cream.
- Roll dough out on a lightly floured surface to about 1/2" thickness and cut into rounds with a cookie cutter.
- Place the rounds on a sheet pan lined with parchment paper.
- Brush lightly with any remaining cream and sprinkle with remaining Tbsp. of sugar.
- Bake until lightly golden about 12-20 min depending on the size of the rounds.

Nutrition Information

- Calories: 193.8
- Saturated Fat: 6.5
- Fiber: 0.9
- Total Carbohydrate: 21.9
- Cholesterol: 38.3
- Total Fat: 10.6
- Sodium: 190.6

- Sugar: 2.7
- Protein: 3

458. Orange Marmalade Muffins

Serving: 6 muffins, 6 serving(s) | Prep: 0S | Ready in:

Ingredients

- 1 1/8 cups whole wheat flour
- 1 1/2 teaspoons baking powder
- 1/4 cup Splenda granular
- 1/2 tablespoon orange peel, finely grated
- 1/4 cup sugar-free orange marmalade, warmed
- 1/4 cup orange juice
- 1 medium egg, beaten
- 3 1/2 tablespoons unsweetened applesauce
- 2 tablespoons sugar-free orange marmalade, for topping

Direction

- Preheat oven to 350 degrees F (180 degrees C) and grease a 6 hole muffin tin.
- Sift flour and baking powder into a mixing bowl and stir in Splenda and orange peel.
- In another bowl combine warmed marmalade, juice, egg and applesauce, mix well.
- Add wet ingredients to the dry, being careful not to overmix, (some lumps are OK).
- Divide the batter between the muffin holes and place a dollop of the reserved marmalade on top of each muffin.
- Bake for 15 to 20 minutes or until a skewer inserted comes out clean.
- Carefully remove from tin. Eat as soon as possible.
- NOTE: If you wish to use sugar instead of Splenda add another 16 calories to each muffin.
- Serve with either no fat cream cheese or extra applesauce.

Nutrition Information

- Calories: 96.6
- Fiber: 2.9
- Sugar: 1
- Total Carbohydrate: 18.9
- Cholesterol: 31
- Protein: 4.1
- Total Fat: 1.2
- Saturated Fat: 0.3
- Sodium: 102.5

459. Paleo Apple Cinnamon Muffins

Serving: 12 muffins, 12 serving(s) | Prep: 10mins | Ready in:

Ingredients

- 2 1/4 cups almond meal
- 4 eggs
- 1 apple, peeled and chopped
- 1 banana, very ripe
- 1/4 cup coconut oil
- 1/3 cup water
- 1/2 teaspoon baking soda
- 1 tablespoon cinnamon

Direction

- Preheat oven to 350. Grease muffin cups or use paper liners.
- Mash banana.
- Add all ingredients and mix well.
- Fill muffin cups 3/4 full.
- Bake 15-17 minutes.

Nutrition Information

- Calories: 183.7
- Cholesterol: 62
- Fiber: 3.1
- Sugar: 3.5

463. Peanut Butter Oatcakes

Serving: 4 oatcakes, 4 serving(s) | Prep: 5mins | Ready in:

Ingredients

- 2 cups quick-cooking oats
- 1 1/2 cups all-purpose flour
- 1 teaspoon baking powder
- 1/4 teaspoon salt (or 2 pinches)
- 3/4 cup brown sugar, packed
- 3/4 cup peanut butter
- 3/4 cup cold water
- 1 1/2 teaspoons vanilla extract
- 1/4 cup chocolate chips (optional)

Direction

- Preheat oven to 350°F.
- Using a food processor or blender, grind 1 cups of oats until fine.
- In a large bowl, mix ground oats, the remaining 1/2 cup of oats, all-purpose flour, baking powder, salt, and brown sugar.
- Add peanut butter to dry ingredients and mix with spoon or hands. Texture will be crumbly.
- Add cold water and vanilla extract and mix well to combine.
- Grease an 8x8" baking dish. Press oatcake batter into dish.
- Bake 15 to 20 minutes, or until top is lightly browned.
- If desired, melt 1/4 cup of chocolate chips and drizzle over oatcakes.
- Enjoy!

Nutrition Information

- Calories: 771.2
- Total Carbohydrate: 113
- Cholesterol: 0
- Protein: 23.5
- Total Fat: 27.4
- Fiber: 8.1
- Saturated Fat: 5.5
- Sodium: 477.8
- Sugar: 45.1

464. Pecan Cheese Biscuits

Serving: 48 biscuits | Prep: 1hours | Ready in:

Ingredients

- 3/4 cup butter, at room temperature
- 1 1/2 cups grated extra-sharp cheddar cheese
- 1/4 cup grated parmesan cheese
- 1 1/2 cups all-purpose flour
- 1 teaspoon salt
- cayenne pepper
- 1 cup finely chopped pecans

Direction

- Combine the butter and cheeses in a food processor and process until smooth.
- Sift the flour, salt, and cayenne directly into the food processor and process until the mixture begins to form a ball.
- Add the pecans and pulse just until the pecans are mixed.
- The mixture will be very soft.
- Divide the dough into three equal parts and place each on a piece of wax paper.
- Fold the paper over the mixture and roll into logs about 1 inch (3 cm) in diameter.
- Refrigerate until thoroughly chilled, about 1 hour.
- Roll the chilled dough into a more regular round shape if desired.
- Unwrap the logs immediately prior to baking and slice into rounds 1/4 inch (5 mm) thick.
- Place 1/2 inch (1 cm) apart on an ungreased baking sheet and bake in a preheated 350F oven until light golden brown, about 15 minutes.
- Cool on a wire rack and store in an airtight container.

Nutrition Information

- Calories: 74.2
- Total Fat: 6.1
- Sugar: 0.1
- Cholesterol: 12.4
- Protein: 1.9
- Saturated Fat: 2.9
- Sodium: 102.5
- Fiber: 0.3
- Total Carbohydrate: 3.4

465. Pineapple Carrot Muffins

Serving: 12 serving(s) | Prep: 10mins | Ready in:

Ingredients

- 1 cup sugar
- 2/3 cup oil
- 2 eggs
- 1 1/2 cups flour
- 1 teaspoon baking powder
- 1 teaspoon baking soda
- 1 teaspoon cinnamon
- 1/2 teaspoon salt
- 1 teaspoon vanilla
- 1 cup carrot, grated
- 1 cup crushed pineapple

Direction

- Mix in order given and bake at 350 degrees for 20-25 minutes.
- You can use paper lined muffin cups, if you wish.

Nutrition Information

- Calories: 258.6
- Fiber: 0.9
- Sugar: 20.2
- Total Carbohydrate: 33.1
- Total Fat: 13.1
- Saturated Fat: 1.9
- Sodium: 250.6
- Cholesterol: 35.2
- Protein: 2.8

466. Pumpkin Bread / Muffins

Serving: 2 loaves, 24 serving(s) | Prep: 30mins | Ready in:

Ingredients

- 1 (16 ounce) can pumpkin
- 1 2/3 cups sugar
- 2/3 cup vegetable oil
- 2 teaspoons vanilla
- 4 large eggs
- 3 cups flour
- 2 teaspoons baking soda
- 1 teaspoon salt
- 1 teaspoon ground cinnamon
- 1/2 teaspoon ground cloves
- 1/2 teaspoon baking powder

Direction

- Preheat oven to 350°F
- Mix all ingredients together.
- Pour into 2 bread pans sprayed with non-stick spray or lined muffin tins.
- Bake loaves about 1 hour, muffins about 45 minutes. Check frequently after half hour and add or lessen time as needed.

Nutrition Information

- Calories: 182.5
- Total Fat: 7
- Saturated Fat: 1.1
- Cholesterol: 31
- Sodium: 222
- Fiber: 0.6
- Sugar: 14.2
- Total Carbohydrate: 27.3
- Protein: 2.9

467. Pumpkin Muffins [vegan]

Serving: 6 large muffins | Prep: 7mins | Ready in:

Ingredients

- 1 3⁄4 cups flour
- 1 1⁄4 cups sugar
- 1 tablespoon baking powder
- 1⁄4 teaspoon salt
- 1 teaspoon cinnamon
- 1⁄2 teaspoon nutmeg
- 1⁄2 teaspoon ginger
- 1⁄4 teaspoon allspice
- 1⁄8 teaspoon ground cloves
- 1 cup pumpkin puree (fresh or from a can)
- 1 tablespoon soy yogurt
- 1⁄2 cup soymilk
- 1⁄2 cup vegetable oil
- 2 tablespoons molasses

Direction

- Preheat oven to 400°F; grease muffin tins with vegetable shortening or spray on oil.
- Sift together dry ingredients (flour through cloves). In a separate bowl, whisk together wet ingredients (pumpkin through molasses). Pour wet into dry and combine. Fill muffin tins 2/3 of the way. Bake for 27-30 minutes, till a toothpick inserted in the center comes out clean.

Nutrition Information

- Calories: 493.6
- Saturated Fat: 2.5
- Sugar: 45.9
- Cholesterol: 0
- Protein: 4.9
- Total Fat: 19.1
- Sodium: 293.4
- Fiber: 1.6
- Total Carbohydrate: 77.9

468. Quick Gluten Free Scones

Serving: 12 serving(s) | Prep: 10mins | Ready in:

Ingredients

- 3 cups gluten-free bread mix (I use Orgran brand)
- 1 cup cream (single or pouring cream)

Direction

- Preheat oven to 200°C.
- Mix ingredients and very lightly knead to form a soft dough. It is important to only knead until the mixture is combined.
- Roll dough out gently, between two sheets of cling-wrap or baking paper. Roll to 2.5cm (1 inch) thickness. Cut with a scone or biscuit cutter into rounds.
- Bake on lightly floured trays. Place scones fairly close together to assist rising. Brush tops of scones with milk. Bake 10 minutes or until cooked.
- Enjoy!

Nutrition Information

- Calories: 58.2
- Fiber: 0
- Sugar: 0
- Total Carbohydrate: 0.6
- Cholesterol: 22.1
- Protein: 0.4
- Total Fat: 6.2
- Saturated Fat: 3.9
- Sodium: 6.8

469. Quick Mix Muffins

Serving: 18 serving(s) | Prep: 15mins | Ready in:

Ingredients

- 3 1/2 cups Raisin Bran cereal
- 2 1/2 cups all-purpose flour
- 1 cup sugar
- 1 teaspoon baking soda
- 1 teaspoon salt
- 2 eggs, beaten
- 2 cups buttermilk
- 1/2 cup vegetable oil

Direction

- In a large bowl, combine the cereal, all-purpose flour, sugar, baking soda, and salt. Add the eggs, buttermilk, and oil, stirring just until thoroughly mixed.
- Heat the oven to 400. Grease the bottom of 18 muffin cups (or line them with cupcake papers) and fill them with batter. Bake for 15-20 minutes, until done.

Nutrition Information

- Calories: 216.6
- Protein: 4.4
- Total Fat: 7.3
- Saturated Fat: 1.2
- Cholesterol: 24.6
- Total Carbohydrate: 34.8
- Sodium: 306.2
- Fiber: 1.9
- Sugar: 16.3

470. Ree's Herbed Cornbread

Serving: 8-10 serving(s) | Prep: 20mins | Ready in:

Ingredients

- 1 cup yellow cornmeal
- 1/2 cup all-purpose flour
- 1 tablespoon baking powder
- 1 teaspoon salt
- 1/2 teaspoon dried basil
- 1/4-1/2 teaspoon dried thyme
- 1/2 teaspoon dried sage
- 1 cup buttermilk
- 1/2 cup whole milk
- 1 large egg
- 1/2 teaspoon baking soda
- 1/4 cup plus 2 tablespoons shortening

Direction

- Preheat the oven to 450 degrees. Combine the cornmeal, flour, baking powder, salt and dried herbs in a large bowl and stir together.
- Combine the buttermilk, milk and egg in a small bowl and stir together with a fork.
- Add the baking soda and stir. Pour the milk mixture into the dry ingredients and stir with a fork until just combined. Do not overmix.
- In a small bowl, melt 1/4 cup shortening in the microwave in 30-second intervals.
- Melt the remaining 2 tablespoons shortening in a 9-inch cast-iron skillet over high heat.
- Pour the batter into the hot skillet and spread to even out the surface.
- Cook 1 minute on the stovetop, then transfer to the oven and bake 20 to 25 minutes, until the cornbread is golden brown with crispy edges.
- Let cool 15 minutes in the skillet, then turn out onto a rack to cool completely.

Nutrition Information

- Calories: 172
- Protein: 4.3
- Total Fat: 8.4
- Sugar: 2.4
- Sodium: 558.6
- Fiber: 1.4
- Total Carbohydrate: 20.4
- Cholesterol: 26
- Saturated Fat: 2.3

471. Sage Cornbread

Serving: 16 serving(s) | Prep: 20mins | Ready in:

Ingredients

- 1 cup flour
- 3⁄4 cup cornmeal
- 1 1⁄2 teaspoons baking powder
- 1⁄2 teaspoon baking soda
- 2 tablespoons fresh sage (chopped) or 1 teaspoon dried sage (chopped)
- 1 cup buttermilk
- 2 tablespoons honey
- 2 eggs
- 3 tablespoons butter or 3 tablespoons margarine (melted)

Direction

- Sift the first four ingredients together and then add sage.
- In another bowl beat buttermilk, honey, eggs, and the butter together.
- Add to dry ingredients and stir only enough to moisten.
- Pour batter into 9 x 9 greased pan.
- Bake at 425 degrees for 25 to 30 minutes or until top is golden.

Nutrition Information

- Calories: 92.5
- Total Fat: 3.2
- Sodium: 115.8
- Total Carbohydrate: 13.6
- Protein: 2.6
- Saturated Fat: 1.7
- Fiber: 0.7
- Sugar: 3
- Cholesterol: 32.8

472. Scottish Scones

Serving: 8 serving(s) | Prep: 25mins | Ready in:

Ingredients

- 1 1⁄2 cups flour
- 3⁄4 cup rolled oats
- 1⁄4 cup brown sugar, firmly packed
- 2 teaspoons baking powder
- 1⁄2 teaspoon salt
- 1⁄2 teaspoon cinnamon
- 1⁄2 cup butter or 1⁄2 cup margarine
- 1⁄2 cup milk
- Topping
- 1 tablespoon butter or 1 tablespoon margarine, melted
- 1 tablespoon sugar
- 1⁄4 teaspoon cinnamon

Direction

- Heat oven to 375 degrees.
- Lightly grease cookie sheet. In med. bowl, combine flour, oats, brown sugar, baking powder, salt and cinnamon; mix well.
- With pastry blender or fork, cut in butter until mixture is crumbly.
- Add milk all at once; stir just until dry ingredients are moistened.
- On floured surface, gently knead dough 5 or 6 times.
- Place on greased cookie sheet; press into a 6" round, about 1" thick.
- Brush top with melted butter.
- In small bowl, combine sugar and cinnamon; mix well.
- Sprinkle over top.
- Cut into 8 wedges; separate slightly.
- Bake for 20-30 minute or until golden brown.
- Serve warm.

Nutrition Information

- Calories: 271.7
- Sodium: 360.4
- Total Fat: 14.2

- Fiber: 1.5
- Sugar: 8.4
- Total Carbohydrate: 32.5
- Cholesterol: 36.5
- Protein: 4.1
- Saturated Fat: 8.7

473. Snitch Biscuits

Serving: 30 cookies - approx | Prep: 10mins | Ready in:

Ingredients

- 200 g butter
- 1 cup brown sugar
- 1/2 cup sugar
- 1 egg
- 2 tablespoons milk
- 1 teaspoon vanilla essence
- 2/3 cup flour
- 1/2 teaspoon baking soda (bicarb soda)
- 3 cups rolled oats
- 1 cup chocolate chips
- 1 1/2 cups raisins (or replace some or all with coconut)

Direction

- Cream the butter and sugars.
- Add egg, milk and vanilla and mix.
- Add sifted dry ingredients.
- Roll into balls and cook at 175C (350F) for 10-15mins.

Nutrition Information

- Calories: 181.3
- Sugar: 17.9
- Total Carbohydrate: 27.4
- Protein: 2.3
- Total Fat: 7.8
- Saturated Fat: 4.6
- Fiber: 1.5
- Sodium: 66.6
- Cholesterol: 21.4

474. Sour Cream Peach Muffins

Serving: 9-12 large muffins, 4-6 serving(s) | Prep: 20mins | Ready in:

Ingredients

- Almond Crunch Topping
- 3/4 cup toasted almond, finely chopped
- 2 tablespoons brown sugar
- 1/2 teaspoon cinnamon
- 2 tablespoons unsalted butter, melted
- Batter
- 5 tablespoons unsalted butter, melted
- 1 cup light brown sugar
- 5 tablespoons oil
- 2 eggs
- 1 teaspoon pure vanilla extract
- 1 cup sour cream (low-fat is fine)
- 1 1/4 cups all-purpose flour
- 3/4 cup quick-cooking oatmeal
- 1 teaspoon baking powder
- 1/2 teaspoon baking soda
- 1/4 teaspoon salt
- 1 cup coarsely chopped peach, pitted, skins removed

Direction

- Preheat oven to 375°F Line 12 muffin cups. Prepare topping by mixing almonds, sugar, cinnamon and butter in a small bowl until crumbly. Set aside.
- In a large bowl, stir together melted butter, oil and brown sugar. Stir in eggs, vanilla and sour cream. Fold in flour, oatmeal, baking powder, baking soda, and salt. Fold in chopped peaches.
- Using an ice cream scoop, deposit equal portions of batter into muffin cups. Distribute topping on muffins.

- Bake until muffins test done by springing back when lightly touched with fingertips, 25 - 30 minutes. Cool well, then remove from pan to finish cooling on wire cake rack.
- 9 - 12 large muffins.

Nutrition Information

- Calories: 1097.5
- Fiber: 6.4
- Sugar: 65.2
- Total Carbohydrate: 112.6
- Total Fat: 66.8
- Sodium: 487.6
- Cholesterol: 184.5
- Protein: 17.8
- Saturated Fat: 24.5

475. Southern Sausage Onion Cornbread

Serving: 6-8 serving(s) | Prep: 10mins | Ready in:

Ingredients

- 1 lb sausage (use top quality)
- 1 medium onion, finely chopped
- 2 eggs, beaten
- 1/2 teaspoon sugar
- 3/4 cup milk
- 1/4 cup vegetable oil
- 1 (17 ounce) cream-style corn
- 2 cups cheddar cheese, shredded
- 1 1/2 cups self-rising cornmeal mix

Direction

- Brown sausage and onion. Drain well.
- In medium size bowl combine eggs, sugar, milk, oil, corn and cheese. Stir in cornmeal mix.
- Pour one-half of mixture into a greased 9 x 9 inch baking dish. Sprinkle sausage and onions over mixture. Pour remaining mixture over top.
- Bake in a 350 degree oven for 35 to 40 minutes. May sprinkle small amount of cheese over top during last 3-5 minutes of baking.

Nutrition Information

- Calories: 686.8
- Total Fat: 47.5
- Sodium: 1570.9
- Fiber: 3.3
- Total Carbohydrate: 42.1
- Protein: 25.6
- Saturated Fat: 17.9
- Sugar: 4.1
- Cholesterol: 158.2

476. Spicy Corn Muffins With Irish Cheddar Cheese

Serving: 12 muffins, 12 serving(s) | Prep: 10mins | Ready in:

Ingredients

- 1 1/4 cups yellow cornmeal
- 3/4 cup all-purpose flour
- 2 tablespoons sugar
- 1 teaspoon baking powder
- 1/2 teaspoon baking soda
- 1 teaspoon salt
- 1/2 teaspoon cayenne pepper
- 1 cup buttermilk
- 1 egg
- 6 tablespoons unsalted butter, melted
- 1 cup aged irish cheddar cheese, grated
- 1 cup fresh corn kernels or 1 cup thawed frozen corn kernels
- 1/2 cup aged irish cheddar cheese, grated (for sprinkling on top of muffins)

Direction

- Preheat oven to 425 degrees F. Butter 12 standard muffin cups.
- Combine cornmeal, flour, sugar, baking powder, baking soda, salt and cayenne pepper in a bowl.
- In a separate bowl, whisk together buttermilk, egg and butter.
- Add buttermilk mixture to the cornmeal mixture and stir just until combined.
- Gently fold in 1 cup cheese and corn kernels.
- Divide batter evenly among the muffin cups.
- Sprinkle tops with the remaining 1/2 cup cheese.
- Bake 15-17 minutes, until golden and a wooden toothpick inserted into the center comes out clean.
- Remove muffins from the tins and cool at least 5 minutes before serving.

Nutrition Information

- Calories: 215.3
- Total Fat: 11.7
- Sodium: 398.8
- Sugar: 4
- Total Carbohydrate: 21.4
- Cholesterol: 46.4
- Saturated Fat: 7
- Fiber: 1.4
- Protein: 7

477. Spinach Cornbread

Serving: 8 serving(s) | Prep: 10mins | Ready in:

Ingredients

- 1 (8 1/2 ounce) box Jiffy cornbread mix
- 1 (10 ounce) package frozen spinach (thaw and squeeze out juice)
- 4 eggs
- 6 ounces cottage cheese
- 1 onion (finely chopped)
- 1⁄4 cup melted margarine (I use 1/4)
- 1⁄2 teaspoon salt

Direction

- Mix all ingredients together.
- Pour into greased baking 9x9" baking pan, or any other pan to a depth of no more than 1 1/2".
- (I cook this in a greased 9" cast-iron skillet).
- Bake at 375 degrees F for 30-50 min, until a knife stuck into the center comes out cleanly.

Nutrition Information

- Calories: 226.5
- Total Fat: 10.1
- Sodium: 662.1
- Total Carbohydrate: 24.9
- Protein: 9.4
- Saturated Fat: 2.7
- Fiber: 3.3
- Sugar: 1.5
- Cholesterol: 97.5

478. Stevia Whole Wheat Banana Bread

Serving: 1 loaf, 12 serving(s) | Prep: 20mins | Ready in:

Ingredients

- 1⁄4 cup melted butter or 1⁄4 cup vegetable oil
- 1 cup ripe banana, smooshed or mashed
- 1 teaspoon vanilla
- 2 eggs
- 1⁄3 cup milk
- 1 1⁄2 cups whole wheat flour
- 1 teaspoon baking soda
- 1 teaspoon stevia powder
- 1⁄2 teaspoon salt
- 1⁄2 cup nuts, chopped

Direction

- Preheat oven to 350F and grease a 9x5 loaf pan.
- In a large bowl, mix together butter/oil, bananas, vanilla, eggs, and milk.
- In a medium bowl, combine the dry ingredients (flour, soda, stevia, and salt).
- Mix the dry ingredients with the wet ingredients until just combined.
- Fold in the nuts.
- Pour into pan and bake for about 1 hour, or until a toothpick inserted in the center comes out clean.
- Let cool in the pan for a couple minutes to set, then remove from the pan and cool completely on a rack.

Nutrition Information

- Calories: 147.2
- Cholesterol: 42.1
- Fiber: 2.4
- Sugar: 1.9
- Total Carbohydrate: 15.5
- Sodium: 289.3
- Protein: 4.4
- Total Fat: 8.2
- Saturated Fat: 3.3

479. Stove Top Biscuits

Serving: 12 biscuits, 12 serving(s) | Prep: 5mins | Ready in:

Ingredients

- 2 cups all-purpose flour
- 4 teaspoons baking powder
- 1 teaspoon salt
- 1/4 cup margarine
- 1 cup milk
- 1/4 cup margarine (for frying)

Direction

- Combine dry ingredients.
- Cut in margarine with a fork, pastry cutter, or your fingers.
- Stir in milk.
- Form dough into 12 biscuits.
- Melt 2 tablespoons margarine in an iron skillet over medium/low heat.
- Fry half of the biscuits for about 6 minutes on each side, and drain on paper towels.
- Repeat with 2 more tablespoons of margarine and remaining dough.

Nutrition Information

- Calories: 123.5
- Saturated Fat: 1.3
- Sodium: 369.6
- Cholesterol: 2.9
- Fiber: 0.6
- Sugar: 0.1
- Total Carbohydrate: 17.3
- Protein: 2.9
- Total Fat: 4.7

480. Strawberry Oat Mini Muffins

Serving: 24 muffins. | Prep: 15mins | Ready in:

Ingredients

- 1 cup all-purpose flour
- 3/4 cup uncooked oat bran
- 2 1/2 teaspoons baking powder
- 1/2 teaspoon baking soda
- 1/8 teaspoon salt
- 3/4 cup buttermilk
- 1/3 cup frozen apple juice concentrate, thawed
- 1/3 cup unsweetened applesauce
- 1/2 teaspoon vanilla
- 3/4 cup diced strawberry
- 1/4 cup chopped pecans

Direction

- Preheat oven to 400 degrees.
- Spray 24 miniature muffin cs. with nonstick cooking spray.
- Combine flour, oat bran, baking powder, baking soda and salt in a medium bowl.
- Whisk together buttermilk, apple juice concentrate, applesauce and vanilla in a small bowl.
- Stir buttermilk mixture into flour mixture until dry ingredients are almost moistened.
- Fold strawberries and pecans into batter just until dry ingredients are moistened.
- Do not overmix.
- Spoon batter into muffin cs.
- Bake 17 to 18 minutes or until lightly browned and tester comes out clean.
- Let cool in pan for 5 minutes; remove to racks.
- Serve warm or cool completely.

Nutrition Information

- Calories: 47
- Sodium: 85.5
- Fiber: 0.8
- Sugar: 2.2
- Total Carbohydrate: 8.9
- Protein: 1.5
- Saturated Fat: 0.2
- Cholesterol: 0.3
- Total Fat: 1.2

481. Sugar Free, Gluten Free, Low Fat Peanut Butter Banana Bread

Serving: 1 Loaf, 6 serving(s) | Prep: 10mins | Ready in:

Ingredients

- 3 very ripe bananas
- 2 teaspoons vanilla
- 1 cup egg white
- 3 tablespoons unsweetened applesauce
- 3 tablespoons peanut butter
- 2 cups oats, blended to make it like a flour
- 3/4 cup Splenda sugar substitute
- 1 teaspoon baking soda
- 1/2 teaspoon baking powder

Direction

- Mash bananas in a bowl.
- Add next 4 ingredients - mix well.
- Add remaining ingredients - mix well.
- Pour into a greased loaf pan.
- Bake at 350 for 50-60 minutes.
- Let cool completely before cutting.

Nutrition Information

- Calories: 330.4
- Total Fat: 7.9
- Sodium: 345.9
- Protein: 15.9
- Saturated Fat: 1.5
- Fiber: 7.6
- Sugar: 8.4
- Total Carbohydrate: 50.9
- Cholesterol: 0

482. Swedish Scones

Serving: 6 scones, 6 serving(s) | Prep: 5mins | Ready in:

Ingredients

- 200 ml whole wheat flour
- 200 ml oatmeal (or 100 ml oatmeal and 100 rye meal if you have some)
- 45 ml sunflower seeds
- 45 ml pumpkin seeds
- 45 ml flax seeds (whole or grounded)
- 20 ml baking powder
- 200 ml low-fat Quark cheese (lattkesella in swedish)
- 2 eggs

Direction

- Mix everything with a fork (no mechanical device). The batter should be lumpy and not too processed.
- Make 6 flattish buns and pop them in the oven (200 Celsius) for about 15 minutes. Done.

Nutrition Information

- Calories: 202.9
- Total Fat: 9.1
- Cholesterol: 70.5
- Protein: 9.2
- Sugar: 0.6
- Total Carbohydrate: 23.7
- Saturated Fat: 1.5
- Sodium: 269.1
- Fiber: 5.2

483. Sweet Potato Muffins (Great For After Turkey Day)

Serving: 12 muffins | Prep: 5mins | Ready in:

Ingredients

- 3 cups whole wheat pastry flour
- 1/2 cup sugar (preferably raw or turbinado)
- 1 tablespoon baking powder
- 1/2 teaspoon baking soda
- 1 teaspoon cinnamon
- 1/2 teaspoon salt
- 2 cooked sweet potatoes (about 1 cup mashed)
- 1 cup soymilk or 1 cup other non-dairy milk substitute
- 1 tablespoon vinegar
- 1 cup golden raisin
- vegetable oil cooking spray

Direction

- Preheat oven to 375 degrees.
- Combine flour, sugar, baking powder, baking soda, cinnamon, and salt. Stir to mix.
- Mash sweet potatoes (if they aren't mashed already) in a separate large bowl, then stir in non-dairy milk and vinegar. Add flour mixture and raisins. Stir together until just mixed. The batter should be moist. Add a bit more non-dairy milk or water if the batter seems stiff.
- Spoon batter into a vegetable oil sprayed muffin pan, filling almost to the top.
- Bake 25 minutes, until tops of muffins bounce back when lightly pressed and a toothpick inserted into the center of a muffin comes out clean.

Nutrition Information

- Calories: 201.5
- Total Fat: 1.1
- Saturated Fat: 0.2
- Sodium: 261.1
- Sugar: 17.1
- Total Carbohydrate: 45.6
- Cholesterol: 0
- Fiber: 5.1
- Protein: 5.8

484. Sweet Squash (Mini) Muffins

Serving: 18 serving(s) | Prep: 15mins | Ready in:

Ingredients

- 8 cups sliced yellow squash (about 2 pounds)
- 1 1/2 cups water
- 1/2 cup skim milk
- 1/3 cup margarine, melted
- 2 eggs, lightly beaten
- 3 cups all-purpose flour
- 1/2 cup sugar
- 1 tablespoon baking powder
- 3/4 teaspoon salt

- vegetable oil cooking spray

Direction

- Bring to a boil the water and the squash. Cover, reduce heat, and simmer until tender, about 30 minutes.
- Drain well.
- Mash the squash. Using a strainer, drain well. Discard liquid.
- Preheat oven to 375 degree F.
- Mix the squash, milk, margarine, and eggs well. Set aside.
- Mix flour, sugar, baking powder, and salt; and create a well in the center.
- Place squash mixture in the well, stirring until the dry ingredients are just moistened.
- Split batter evenly among muffin pans sprayed with vegetable cooking spray.
- Bake 15-20 minutes in a 375-degree F oven. Remove from pan; let cool on wire rack.
- These only last about 3-5 days max. Before spoiling (less if left out, more if stored in refrigerator). Good for freezing though! Defrost in refrigerator or microwave.

Nutrition Information

- Calories: 147.5
- Total Fat: 4.2
- Total Carbohydrate: 23.9
- Cholesterol: 23.6
- Protein: 3.8
- Saturated Fat: 0.8
- Sodium: 214.9
- Fiber: 1.2
- Sugar: 6.6

485. T's Chocolate Chip Scones

Serving: 8 serving(s) | Prep: 10mins | Ready in:

Ingredients

- 1 1/3 cups old fashioned oats
- 2/3 cup low-fat baking mix (low fat bisquick)
- 1 teaspoon baking powder
- 1 tablespoon Splenda brown sugar blend
- 4 teaspoons Splenda brown sugar blend
- 4 teaspoons light butter, melted
- 2/3 cup nonfat vanilla soymilk
- 1/2 cup mini chocolate chip

Direction

- Preheat the oven to 400 degrees. Spray 2 cookie sheets with nonstick spray.
- Mix together in one bowl all the ingredients but the chocolate chips. Then fold in the chocolate chips.
- Mound the scones on the baking sheets leaving some space in between. Bake for 10-12 minutes or until starting to brown.

Nutrition Information

- Calories: 129.7
- Sodium: 58.6
- Total Fat: 5.5
- Saturated Fat: 2.9
- Fiber: 2
- Sugar: 7.7
- Total Carbohydrate: 19.7
- Cholesterol: 2.6
- Protein: 2.3

486. The Very Best Blueberry Bran Muffins

Serving: 12-16 large muffins, 4 serving(s) | Prep: 15mins | Ready in:

Ingredients

- 1 1/2 cups all-bran cereal (or 100% bran)
- 1 1/2 cups soured milk (or buttermilk)
- 2 cups all-purpose flour
- 2 teaspoons baking powder

- 1 teaspoon ground cinnamon
- 1 teaspoon baking soda
- 1/2 teaspoon salt
- 1/3 cup packed brown sugar
- 1 egg
- 1/3 cup molasses
- 1/4 cup melted butter
- 2 cups blueberries (frozen or fresh)

Direction

- Preheat oven to 375°F Lightly spray muffin pans.
- In large bowl, combine cereal with milk, let stand 10 minutes.
- In separate bowl, combine flour, baking powder, cinnamon, baking soda and salt.
- Whisk brown sugar, egg, molasses and melted butter into cereal mixture.
- Pour over dry ingredients and sprinkle with blueberries.
- Stir just until moistened.
- Spoon into prepared muffin pan. Bake 25 to 30 mins or until tops are firm to the touch.
- Note: to sour milk, spoon 4 tsp lemon juice or white vinegar into glass measuring cup, pour in enough milk to make 1 1/2 cups. Let stand for 5 mins then stir.
- If using frozen blueberries, do not thaw before adding to the muffins.

Nutrition Information

- Calories: 659.3
- Fiber: 10.6
- Sugar: 49.2
- Cholesterol: 86.2
- Protein: 14.7
- Total Fat: 17.7
- Saturated Fat: 9.7
- Sodium: 1023.3
- Total Carbohydrate: 120.2

487. Thyme Biscuits

Serving: 8 biscuits, 8 serving(s) | Prep: 10mins | Ready in:

Ingredients

- 2 cups all-purpose flour, plus more for work surface
- 1 teaspoon baking powder
- 1/2 teaspoon kosher salt
- 1/2 teaspoon sugar
- 1/2 cup unsalted butter
- 2 tablespoons fresh thyme leaves, roughly chopped
- 1/2 cup whole milk
- 1/4 cup mayonnaise

Direction

- Preheat oven to 375.
- In a large bowl, combine flour, baking powder, salt and sugar.
- Use a pastry blender or your fingertips to add the butter until mixture resembles coarse meal.
- Add thyme and toss.
- In a measuring cup, whisk milk with mayonnaise.
- Add to flour mixture and stir until just combined.
- Turn the dough onto a lightly floured work surface and pat into a 1 inch thick rectangle.
- Cut biscuits into squares and transfer to a baking sheet.
- Bake about 25 minutes, until lightly browned.

Nutrition Information

- Calories: 255.2
- Fiber: 0.9
- Sugar: 1.6
- Total Carbohydrate: 26.9
- Protein: 3.9
- Saturated Fat: 8
- Sodium: 251.3
- Cholesterol: 33.9
- Total Fat: 14.8

488. Vegan Choco Low Fat Muffins

Serving: 12 serving(s) | Prep: 10mins | Ready in:

Ingredients

- 1 cup all-purpose flour
- 1/2 cup whole wheat flour
- 1/2 cup granulated sugar
- 1/4 cup Splenda granular
- 1/4 cup unsweetened cocoa powder
- 2 teaspoons baking powder
- 1 teaspoon baking soda
- 1/2 teaspoon salt
- 2/3 cup low-fat vanilla yogurt
- 2/3 cup soymilk
- 1/2 teaspoon vanilla extract
- 1/3 cup carob chips

Direction

- Preheat oven to 400°; line muffin cups with paper baking cups.
- In a medium bowl, stir together the flour, sugar, cocoa, baking powder, baking soda and salt. Stir in the yogurt, milk and vanilla extract and chocolate chips just until combined. Do not beat.
- Fill the muffin cups 2/3 full with batter. Bake for 15 to 20 minutes, or until a toothpick inserted in the center comes out clean.
- Cool slightly in the pans on wire racks. Remove from the pans. Serve warm.
- Cover and store at room temperature, or freeze in an airtight container for longer storage.

Nutrition Information

- Calories: 110.8
- Protein: 3.4
- Saturated Fat: 0.3
- Sodium: 279.6
- Fiber: 1.7
- Sugar: 10.4
- Total Fat: 0.9
- Total Carbohydrate: 23.6
- Cholesterol: 0.7

489. White Chocolate Chip Cranberry Banana Bread With Coconut Flour

Serving: 1 loaf, 8 serving(s) | Prep: 1hours | Ready in:

Ingredients

- 1/2 cup whole wheat flour
- 1/2 cup white flour
- 2 tablespoons white flour
- 1/3 cup coconut flour
- 1/3 cup stevia
- 1 tablespoon molasses
- 1 teaspoon baking powder
- 1/2 teaspoon baking soda
- 1/2 teaspoon salt
- 1 apple
- 3 large egg whites
- 1/4 cup Greek yogurt
- 1 teaspoon vanilla
- 2 large bananas
- 1/2 cup white chocolate chips
- 1/2 cup dried cranberries

Direction

- Grind one small apple with a Tablespoon of water. For the Stevia, I used Truvia spoon-able sweetener. You can find coconut flour from Uncle Bobs Red Mill. I also used plain Greek yogurt. Be sure to use parchment paper in the bread pan or it will most likely stick.
- In a bread maker pan, add all the wet ingredients together (Molasses, Apple, Egg Whites, Greek yogurt, Vanilla, ripe Bananas) and mix well. Add Flours and make a well in

the center of the bread pan. Put the Baking Powder, Baking Soda, and Salt in the well. Set the bread maker for dough and let mix for 15 minutes or more then open the lid and add the White Chocolate Chips and Dried Cranberries. Let dough mix for another 15 minutes. Stop the bread machine and pour batter into a 9 inch by 4 inch bread pan lined with parchment paper sprayed with no stick spray.

- Bake at 350 F for 40 minutes in an oven. Cool before cutting.

Nutrition Information

- Calories: 175.4
- Fiber: 2.8
- Total Carbohydrate: 32.2
- Cholesterol: 1.5
- Saturated Fat: 2.1
- Sodium: 301.7
- Sugar: 14.1
- Protein: 4.4
- Total Fat: 3.8

490. White Chocolate Macadamia Nut Muffins

Serving: 12 muffins | Prep: 10mins | Ready in:

Ingredients

- 2 1/2 cups biscuit and baking mix
- 1/2 cup sugar
- 3/4 cup coarsely chopped white chocolate (we tested with Bakers Premium white chocolate)
- 1/2 cup coarsely chopped macadamia nuts
- 3/4 cup half-and-half
- 3 tablespoons vegetable oil
- 2 teaspoons vanilla extract
- 1 large egg, lightly beaten

Direction

- Combine baking mix and sugar in a large bowl; stir in chocolate and nuts. Make a well in center of mixture. Combine half-and-half and remaining 3 ingredients; add to dry ingredients, stirring just until dry ingredients are moistened.
- Spoon into greased muffin pans, filling two-thirds full. Bake at 400° for 11 to 12 minutes or until a wooden pick inserted into center comes out clean. Remove from pans immediately.

Nutrition Information

- Calories: 294.5
- Saturated Fat: 5.4
- Sodium: 340.9
- Fiber: 1
- Sugar: 17.9
- Protein: 4
- Total Carbohydrate: 32
- Cholesterol: 25.2
- Total Fat: 17

491. Whole Wheat Banana Muffins

Serving: 12 muffins | Prep: 15mins | Ready in:

Ingredients

- 3 small bananas
- 1 cup sugar
- 1/2 cup unsweetened applesauce
- 1 1/4 cups whole wheat flour
- 1/2 teaspoon salt
- 1 1/2 teaspoons baking soda

Direction

- Preheat oven to 350 degrees.
- Mash bananas and mix with sugar and applesauce until blended.
- Mix flour, salt and soda together. Fold into banana mixture.

- Scoop into lined muffin tins.
- Bake or 25 minutes.

Nutrition Information

- Calories: 133.7
- Cholesterol: 0
- Protein: 2
- Sodium: 255.3
- Fiber: 2.3
- Sugar: 19.8
- Total Carbohydrate: 32.6
- Total Fat: 0.3
- Saturated Fat: 0.1

492. Whole Wheat Banana Nut Muffins

Serving: 12-18 muffins | Prep: 10mins | Ready in:

Ingredients

- 1 1/2 cups whole wheat flour
- 3/4 cup brown sugar
- 1/4 cup flax seed meal
- 1/2 teaspoon salt
- 1 teaspoon baking soda
- 3/4 teaspoon cinnamon
- 3 -5 bananas (very ripe)
- 1/4 cup buttermilk
- 2 eggs
- 2 teaspoons vanilla
- 1/4 cup plum puree or 1/2 cup applesauce
- 1 cup pecans, chopped

Direction

- Peel the bananas and add to mixer - turned on medium speed. Begin adding wet ingredients.
- In another bowl place all dry ingredients and stir together. Slowly begin adding to mixture in bowl. Once this is all mixed together spoon into greased muffin pans 3/4 of the way up.
- Bake at 350 degrees for 20 minutes.

Nutrition Information

- Calories: 220.8
- Saturated Fat: 1
- Fiber: 4.2
- Sugar: 17.7
- Total Carbohydrate: 33.5
- Total Fat: 8.8
- Sodium: 226
- Cholesterol: 35.5
- Protein: 4.9

493. Whole Wheat Pumpkin Muffins

Serving: 12 muffins, 12 serving(s) | Prep: 10mins | Ready in:

Ingredients

- 1 3/4 cups whole wheat flour
- 1/3 cup sugar
- 2 teaspoons baking powder
- 2 teaspoons cinnamon
- 1/4 teaspoon salt
- 1 egg, slightly beaten
- 3/4 cup milk
- 1/4 cup applesauce
- 1/2 cup canned pumpkin

Direction

- Combine flour, sugar, baking powder, cinnamon and salt.
- Add egg, milk, applesauce and pumpkin to the dry ingredients.
- Mix batter until moistened. Batter will be lumpy.
- Lightly spray muffin tin. Fill cups 2/3 full and bake about 20 minutes in a 400 degree oven.

Nutrition Information

- Calories: 105.6
- Saturated Fat: 0.6
- Sodium: 149.3
- Fiber: 2.7
- Sugar: 6
- Total Fat: 1.4
- Total Carbohydrate: 21.4
- Cholesterol: 19.8
- Protein: 3.6

494. Winter Squash Oatmeal Muffins

Serving: 12 muffins, 12 serving(s) | Prep: 5mins | Ready in:

Ingredients

- 2 eggs
- 1 1/3 cups winter squash, mashed
- 1/4 cup oil
- 1 teaspoon vanilla
- 2/3 cup brown sugar, packed
- 3/4 cup rolled oats
- 1 cup flour
- 1 1/2 teaspoons baking powder
- 1 teaspoon baking soda
- 1/2 salt
- 1 teaspoon cinnamon
- 1/2 cup raisins
- 1/2 cup nuts

Direction

- Whisk together sugar and wet ingredients.
- Add dry ingredients and combine.
- Fold in raisins and nuts.
- Use 1/4 C to measure evenly into muffin tin.
- Bake at 350 for 20-30 min or until toothpick tests clean.

Nutrition Information

- Calories: 213.8
- Total Fat: 8.8
- Saturated Fat: 1.3
- Cholesterol: 31
- Total Carbohydrate: 31.1
- Protein: 4.1
- Sodium: 205.5
- Fiber: 1.8
- Sugar: 16.1

495. Ww Crumb Topped Jumbo Bran Muffins

Serving: 6 jumbo muffins, 6 serving(s) | Prep: 10mins | Ready in:

Ingredients

- 2 tablespoons all-purpose flour
- 1/4 cup all-purpose flour
- 2 tablespoons brown sugar, lightly packed
- 1 tablespoon butter, cut into small pieces
- 2 tablespoons walnuts, chopped
- 1 1/2 cups natural bran
- 1 cup whole wheat flour
- 1 teaspoon baking soda
- 1/2 teaspoon baking powder
- 1/4 teaspoon salt
- 1 large egg
- 2 egg whites
- 1/2 cup sugar
- 2 tablespoons molasses
- 1 cup fat-free buttermilk
- 2/3 cup golden raisin

Direction

- Preheat the oven to 375 degrees. Spray a 6-jumbo-cup (1 cup each) nonstick muffin pan with nonstick spray (or line with paper/foil liners).
- To make the crumb topping, combine 2 tablespoons of the all-purpose flour and the brown sugar in a medium bowl. With a pastry blender, cut in the butter until the mixture is crumbly. Stir in the walnuts.

- Combine the bran, wholewheat flour, the remaining 1/2 cup all-purpose flour, the baking soda, baking powder, and salt in a large bowl. With an electric mixer on medium speed, beat the egg, egg whites, sugar, and molasses in a large bowl until blended. Gradually beat in the buttermilk. Gradually add the bran mixture, mixing on low speed until just blended. Stir in the raisins.
- Spoon the batter into the cups, filling each about half full. Sprinkle with the crumb topping. Bake until a toothpick inserted into a muffin comes out clean, about 25 minutes. Cool in the pan on a rack 5 minutes; remove from the pan and cool completely on the rack.

Nutrition Information

- Calories: 335.5
- Total Fat: 5.6
- Sodium: 424.2
- Sugar: 37
- Total Carbohydrate: 71
- Saturated Fat: 1.8
- Fiber: 7.8
- Cholesterol: 40.3
- Protein: 8.7

496. Ww Vanilla Biscuits (Cookies)

Serving: 24 serving(s) | Prep: 15mins | Ready in:

Ingredients

- 1 1/2 cups self raising flour
- 1/2 cup custard powder
- 1/2 cup caster sugar
- 120 g low-fat butter, chopped (room temperature)
- 1/4 cup skim milk
- 1 teaspoon vanilla essence
- 30 g slivered almonds

Direction

- Preheat oven to 180 degrees C (356 degrees F). Line 2 trays with baking paper.
- Into a medium bowl sift together the SR flour and custard powder. Stir in the sugar.
- Using your fingertips, rub the butter into the dry ingredients until the mixture looks like soft breadcrumbs.
- Combine the milk and vanilla essence then stir into the mix. It should form a firm dough.
- Drop 2 teaspoons of dough in heaps onto the prepared trays. They will spread so allow space between biscuit. Lightly flatten with fork then sprinkle with almonds. Press lightly to adhere.
- Bake for 10-15 minutes or until golden on the bottom.

Nutrition Information

- Calories: 53.3
- Cholesterol: 0.1
- Protein: 1.2
- Saturated Fat: 0.1
- Sodium: 1.7
- Sugar: 4.2
- Total Carbohydrate: 10.6
- Total Fat: 0.7
- Fiber: 0.4

497. Yogurt Honey Health Mini Muffins

Serving: 24 mini muffins, 8 serving(s) | Prep: 15mins | Ready in:

Ingredients

- 1 1/2 cups cake flour (may sub pastry flour)
- 1 teaspoon baking powder
- 1 teaspoon baking soda
- 3/4 teaspoon kosher salt
- 4 1/2 teaspoons sugar

- 2 tablespoons rolled oats
- 1 tablespoon diced dried cranberries
- 1 tablespoon diced dried apricot
- 1 tablespoon unsalted sunflower seeds
- 1 teaspoon grated orange zest
- 1 tablespoon toasted natural bran
- 1/2 cup nonfat yogurt
- 1/4 cup honey
- 1 teaspoon vanilla extract
- 8 tablespoons unsalted butter, melted
- 2 eggs

Direction

- Preheat oven to 350°F and grease a mini muffin pan.
- In a large mixing bowl, sift together the flour, baking powder, baking soda, salt and sugar. Add the oats, cranberries, apricots, sunflower seeds, orange zest and bran and mix to combine.
- In another bowl combine the yogurt, honey, vanilla, butter and eggs and stir until the ingredients are well blended.
- Pour the yogurt mixture into the dry ingredients and stir to mix, just until all ingredients are incorporated. Take care not to overmix.
- Fill muffin cups two-thirds of the way with batter.
- Bake for approximately 20 minutes or until golden and cooked through.

Nutrition Information

- Calories: 279.5
- Protein: 5.2
- Total Fat: 13.7
- Sodium: 398.5
- Total Carbohydrate: 34.5
- Cholesterol: 83.7
- Saturated Fat: 7.8
- Fiber: 0.9
- Sugar: 13.1

498. Yorkshire Pudding With Herbs

Serving: 12 puddings | Prep: 35mins | Ready in:

Ingredients

- 3 large eggs
- 1 cup whole milk
- 1 cup all-purpose flour
- 1 pinch salt
- 1 tablespoon chopped fresh parsley
- 1 tablespoon chopped fresh chives
- 2 teaspoons chopped fresh sage
- 2 teaspoons chopped fresh thyme
- 1/3 cup clarified butter or 1/3 cup pan dripping, from a beef roast

Direction

- In a medium bowl, whisk eggs just to blend.
- Gradually whisk in milk.
- Sift flour and salt into egg mixture and whisk until well blended and smooth.
- Whisk in all herbs.
- This is the first key to success- let the batter stand at room temperature for AT LEAST 30 minutes!
- While the batter is resting, preheat the oven to 450°F.
- This is the second key to success- the oven must be very hot!
- Re-whisk the batter before using and transfer to large measuring cup or pitcher with a spout so it will be easy to pour.
- Heat muffin tin with 12 muffin cups in oven for 10 minutes.
- This is the third key to success- the muffin tins must be very hot!
- Transfer drippings or melted butter to a measuring cup with a spout so you can easily pour it into the muffin tin.
- Pour about 1 tsp drippings or melted butter in each muffin cup.
- Return pan to oven for about 6 to 8 minutes.

- This is the last key to success- the fat must be very hot!
- Pour batter evenly into the muffin cups onto the hot fat.
- Bake until puddings are golden and puffy, about 12 to 15 minutes.
- Puddings will sink slightly in center.
- Serve immediately out of oven while still hot.

Nutrition Information

- Calories: 114
- Fiber: 0.4
- Sugar: 1.1
- Total Carbohydrate: 9.2
- Protein: 3.4
- Total Fat: 7.1
- Saturated Fat: 4
- Sodium: 40.5
- Cholesterol: 62.1

499. Yummy Banana Nut Bread

Serving: 2 loaves | Prep: 0S | Ready in:

Ingredients

- 3 1/2 cups flour
- 1 tablespoon baking powder
- 1 teaspoon baking soda
- 1 teaspoon salt
- 2 teaspoons cinnamon
- 1 teaspoon nutmeg
- 1/2 teaspoon clove
- 2 tablespoons lemon juice
- 2 cups mashed bananas
- 3/4 cup shortening
- 1 1/4 cups honey or 1 1/2 cups sugar
- 3 eggs
- 3/4 cup walnuts or 3/4 cup pecans, chopped
- 1/2 cup raisins (optional)

Direction

- Sift together first 7 ingredients. Set aside.
- Mash bananas and mix in lemon juice. Set aside.
- Beat shortening and honey or sugar together at medium speed.
- Continue beating and add eggs in one at a time. Be sure to scrape bowl.
- Add milk or water alternately with dry ingredients. Mix slowly. Fold in bananas and nuts, and raisins if used.
- Pour into 2 greased 8 1/2" x 4 1/2" loaf pans. Bake 350 for about 1 hour or till wooden toothpick inserted in center comes out clean. Cool about 10 minutes and then turn out of pans onto wire rack and continue to cool. These loaves freeze very well. (If there is any left!).
- You can also make muffins, just reduce cooking time.

Nutrition Information

- Calories: 2735.6
- Saturated Fat: 25.2
- Sodium: 2461.1
- Fiber: 17
- Sugar: 204.3
- Total Carbohydrate: 405.2
- Protein: 42
- Total Fat: 116.1
- Cholesterol: 279

500. Yummy Pumpkin And Cream Cheese Muffins

Serving: 24 yummy muffins, 24 serving(s) | Prep: 0S | Ready in:

Ingredients

- 8 ounces cream cheese
- 3 eggs

- 2 1/2 cups sugar
- 2 1/2 cups flour
- 1/4 cup pecans, roughly chopped
- 3 tablespoons butter, melted
- 2 1/2 teaspoons cinnamon
- 1/2 teaspoon salt
- 2 teaspoons baking powder
- 1/4 teaspoon baking soda
- 1 1/4 cups canned solid-pack pumpkin
- 1/3 cup vegetable oil
- 1/2 teaspoon vanilla extract

Direction

- Heat oven to 375 degrees F. Lightly coat two 12-cup standard muffin tins with oil and set aside.
- Mix the cream cheese, 1 egg, and 3 tablespoons sugar in a small bowl and set aside.
- Mix 5 tablespoons sugar, 1/2 cup flour, pecans, butter, and 1/2 teaspoon cinnamon together in a medium bowl and set aside.
- Combine the remaining sugar, flour, salt, baking powder, baking soda, and remaining cinnamon in a large bowl.
- Lightly beat the remaining eggs, pumpkin, oil, and vanilla together in a medium bowl.
- Make a well in the center of the flour mixture, pour the pumpkin mixture into the well, and mix with a fork just until moistened.
- Divide the batter into two halves. Evenly divide one half of the batter among the muffin cups. Place two teaspoonfuls of cream cheese filling in the center of each cup and fill with the remaining half of batter.
- Sprinkle some of the pecan mixture over the top of each muffin and bake until golden and a tester, inserted into the muffin center, comes out clean, 20 to 25 minutes. Cool on wire racks.
- Note:
- These are great warm!

Nutrition Information

- Calories: 222.1
- Sugar: 21.6
- Total Carbohydrate: 32.7
- Cholesterol: 37.5
- Fiber: 1
- Sodium: 175
- Protein: 3
- Total Fat: 9.3
- Saturated Fat: 3.4

Index

A

Almond 3,4,5,6,7,8,10,67,97,173,184,221,228,232,280

Apple 3,4,5,6,7,8,9,10,11,40,47,53,68,78,85,131,132,133,134,135,137,146,166,185,198,206,217,229,238,256,272,288

Apricot 3,5,6,8,20,135,230

Avocado 6,136

B

Bacon 3,6,8,18,136,231,261

Baking 3,11,16,48,113,208,256,289

Banana 3,4,5,6,7,8,9,12,14,22,25,26,27,34,40,41,56,57,60,64,68,69,71,77,79,80,82,85,93,94,95,98,99,102,109,110,112,114,117,118,122,125,126,130,137,138,149,153,154,155,169,170,172,173,175,176,177,178,179,180,181,182,183,184,187,189,190,192,195,196,199,201,202,208,213,215,221,223,225,226,232,233,234,236,242,245,249,256,274,282,284,288,289,290,294

Basil 158

Berry 3,6,10,35,41,168

Biscuits 3,4,5,6,7,8,9,11,14,15,16,17,42,48,49,50,53,55,61,62,63,74,75,86,90,98,104,106,108,113,125,130,150,173,174,203,222,231,235,238,240,250,253,254,260,263,264,266,267,275,280,283,287,292

Blueberry 3,4,5,6,7,8,9,14,15,21,22,25,36,54,66,67,75,85,115,137,139,140,149,151,168,183,191,194,205,225,228,252,256,270,286

Bran 3,4,5,6,7,8,9,13,19,22,23,27,55,59,66,72,79,91,93,105,139,141,148,149,154,164,165,171,209,211,231,233,259,260,268,269,278,286,291

Bread 1,3,4,5,6,7,8,9,10,14,20,25,26,28,29,40,56,57,60,64,66,68,71,77,85,92,102,107,109,114,122,125,126,127,130,137,142,143,153,161,162,172,173,175,177,178,181,184,185,189,190,191,192,193,195,196,197,199,200,201,202,205,209,210,213,215,216,217,218,220,221,223,224,226,227,228,235,236,242,245,250,254,256,265,274,276,282,284,288,294

Buckwheat 8,247

Buns 4,6,8,56,155,248

Butter 3,4,5,7,8,9,16,17,19,44,53,56,57,61,75,114,122,129,130,184,185,191,206,215,237,240,258,274,275,282,284

C

Cake 4,6,7,8,75,91,126,178,223,237

Caramel 3,8,41,45,237

Carob 5,94

Carrot 3,5,8,9,38,47,85,100,237,244,276

Cheddar 4,5,7,8,9,14,73,90,132,133,185,238,239,242,244,254,281

Cheese 3,4,5,6,8,9,12,33,64,70,72,77,88,90,132,135,231,235,239,240,249,251,274,275,281,294

Cherry 3,5,7,17,18,101,204

Chicken 8,231,240

Chips 289

Chocolate 3,4,5,6,7,8,9,18,42,47,52,57,61,64,68,69,85,92,93,94,95,96,97,98,99,100,101,102,103,104,105,106,107,108,109,110,111,112,113,114,115,116,117,118,119,120,121,122,123,124,125,126,127,128,129,130,140,170,173,178,185,189,190,225,241,242,247,263,286,288,289

Cinnamon

3,5,6,7,8,9,40,43,102,134,146,184,186,212,217,228,229,246,272
Coconut 3,6,7,8,9,38,119,160,170,175,181,187,211,214,262,288
Coffee 4,7,59,126,186
Cranberry 3,6,7,8,9,19,20,29,34,44,140,164,188,209,227,243,269,271,288
Cream 3,4,5,6,8,9,12,22,35,41,42,46,50,51,57,63,70,88,105,110,114,125,126,138,141,150,160,167,172,173,175,178,183,187,190,199,201,204,206,213,223,231,242,254,257,268,270,271,274,280,294
Crumble 3,30,124,261
Cumin 6,150
Curry 8,244

D

Date 3,4,6,7,8,33,86,141,162,164,184,192,200,205,209,210,224,244
Dill 8,239

E

Egg 3,5,8,18,74,75,111,116,251,273,288
English muffin 251

F

Fat 3,4,5,6,7,8,9,10,11,12,13,14,15,16,17,18,19,20,21,22,23,24,25,26,27,28,29,30,31,32,33,34,35,36,37,38,39,40,41,42,43,44,45,46,47,48,49,50,51,52,53,54,55,56,57,58,59,60,61,62,63,64,65,66,67,68,69,70,71,72,73,74,75,76,77,78,79,80,81,82,83,84,85,86,87,88,89,90,91,92,93,94,95,96,97,98,99,100,101,102,103,104,105,106,107,108,109,110,111,112,113,114,115,116,117,118,120,121,122,123,124,125,126,127,128,129,130,131,132,133,134,135,136,137,138,139,140,141,142,143,144,145,146,147,148,149,150,151,152,153,154,155,156,157,158,159,160,161,162,164,165,166,167,168,169,170,171,172,173,174,175,176,177,178,179,180,181,182,183,184,185,186,187,188,189,190,191,192,193,194,195,196,197,198,199,200,201,202,203,204,205,206,207,208,209,210,211,212,213,214,215,216,217,218,219,220,221,222,223,224,225,226,227,228,229,230,231,232,233,234,235,236,237,238,239,240,241,242,243,244,245,246,247,248,249,250,251,252,253,254,255,256,257,258,259,260,261,262,263,264,265,266,267,268,269,270,271,272,273,274,275,276,277,278,279,280,281,282,283,284,285,286,287,288,289,290,291,292,293,294,295
Fig 7,192
Flatbread 3,43
Flour 3,9,10,66,256,288
Fruit 4,5,6,66,103,130,131,142,143,144,145,146,147,148,152,153,157,161,162,165,168,169,170,171,259
Fudge 8,241

G

Gin 3,5,6,23,46,113,143,159
Grain 4,7,8,85,90,194,221,225,246
Gravy 3,8,14,253

H

Ham 8,251
Hazelnut 4,5,8,68,104,131,242
Heart 3,24
Herbs 9,293
Honey 3,4,8,9,48,73,260,292

I

Icing 91

J

Jus 51,91,130,163,176,262

L

Lemon

3,4,6,7,8,37,50,51,75,76,87,91,143,152,154,191,201,215,26
3,264
Lime 6,158,181
Lobster 8,235

M

Macadamia 4,6,7,9,53,177,189,219,289
Mango 6,7,156,193
Marmalade 9,272
Mayonnaise 8,266
Milk 5,111,254
Millet 85
Molasses 4,59,288
Muesli 8,269
Muffins
3,4,5,6,7,8,9,10,11,12,13,15,18,19,20,21,22,24,25,27,28,29,
30,31,32,33,34,35,36,37,38,40,41,42,44,45,47,50,51,52,53,
54,57,58,59,60,61,65,66,67,68,69,70,71,72,73,76,78,79,80,
81,82,83,84,85,86,88,91,92,93,94,95,96,99,100,101,103,10
5,107,108,109,110,111,112,113,115,116,117,118,120,121,1
22,123,127,128,129,130,131,132,134,135,136,137,138,139,
141,142,143,144,145,146,148,149,151,152,154,156,157,15
8,159,160,162,164,165,166,168,169,170,171,176,177,179,1
80,181,182,183,185,187,189,191,192,194,195,197,198,199,
200,201,203,204,206,208,209,211,212,213,214,215,219,22
1,222,225,227,228,229,230,231,232,233,234,236,237,238,2
40,241,242,243,244,245,246,247,248,249,251,252,255,256,
257,258,259,260,261,262,263,264,265,268,269,270,272,27
3,276,277,280,281,283,285,286,288,289,290,291,292,294
Mustard 4,73

N

Nougat 3,45
Nut
3,4,5,6,7,8,9,10,11,12,13,14,15,16,17,18,19,20,21,22,23,24,
25,26,27,28,29,30,31,32,33,34,35,36,37,38,39,40,41,42,43,
44,45,46,47,48,49,50,51,52,53,54,55,56,57,58,59,60,61,62,
63,64,65,66,67,68,69,70,71,72,73,74,75,76,77,78,79,80,81,
82,83,84,85,86,87,88,89,90,91,92,93,94,95,96,97,98,99,100
,101,102,103,104,105,106,107,108,109,110,111,112,113,11
4,115,116,117,118,120,121,122,123,124,125,126,127,128,1
29,130,131,132,133,134,135,136,137,138,139,140,141,142,
143,144,145,146,147,148,149,150,151,152,153,154,155,15
6,157,158,159,160,161,162,164,165,166,167,168,169,170,1
71,172,173,174,175,176,177,178,179,180,181,182,183,184,
185,186,187,188,189,190,191,192,193,194,195,196,197,19
8,199,200,201,202,203,204,205,206,207,208,209,210,211,2
12,213,214,215,216,217,218,219,220,221,222,223,224,225,
226,227,228,229,230,231,232,233,234,235,236,237,238,23
9,240,241,242,243,244,245,246,247,248,249,250,251,252,2
53,254,255,256,257,258,259,260,261,262,263,264,265,266,
267,268,269,270,271,272,273,274,275,276,277,278,279,28
0,281,282,283,284,285,286,287,288,289,290,291,292,293,2
94,295

O

Oatcakes 3,9,39,275
Oatmeal
4,5,7,8,9,53,78,106,110,115,120,208,229,269,270,291
Oil 70,89
Onion 4,8,9,81,238,266,281
Orange
3,4,5,6,7,8,9,20,28,29,67,121,134,150,154,171,182,184,209
,210,211,230,270,271,272,273

P

Papaya 6,156
Parmesan 6,169,235,267
Parsley 9,273
Pastry 16
Peach 4,6,7,9,78,158,211,218,280
Pear 6,8,159,165,248
Pecan
3,4,5,6,7,9,20,78,108,140,155,182,183,203,204,205,211,21

2,219,222,224,273,275
Peel 130,133,134,159,237,290
Pepper 4,81,83
Pie 4,7,52,212
Pineapple 4,6,7,9,66,160,214,276
Pistachio 4,8,57,58,257
Polenta 7,215
Pomegranate 3,5,24,123
Popcorn 4,81
Port 67,132
Potato 4,7,9,60,222,285
Praline 3,45
Pulse 104
Pumpkin
3,4,5,6,7,8,9,24,52,58,82,85,107,123,159,161,162,185,200,
210,213,215,245,276,277,290,294

Q

Quark 284

R

Raisins 6,164
Raspberry 3,4,6,32,58,83,149,154,157
Rice 42,179
Ricotta 3,33
Rosemary 4,6,84,158,165
Rum 6,175

S

Sage 9,279
Salt 289
Sausage 3,8,9,14,253,281
Savory 8,262
Seasoning 84
Seeds 146
Shortbread 3,4,49,61,63
Soda 3,8,25,250,254,289
Spelt 4,90
Spices 146
Spinach 9,282
Squash 5,8,9,100,237,258,285,291
Strawberry 3,5,6,7,9,26,36,114,151,167,196,219,283
Sugar
4,6,7,8,9,10,11,12,13,14,15,16,17,18,19,20,21,22,23,24,25,
26,27,28,29,30,31,32,33,34,35,36,37,38,39,40,41,42,43,44,
45,46,47,48,49,50,51,52,53,54,55,56,57,58,59,60,61,62,63,
64,65,66,67,68,69,70,71,72,73,74,75,76,77,78,79,80,81,82,
83,84,85,86,87,88,89,90,91,92,93,94,95,96,97,98,99,100,10
1,102,103,104,105,106,107,108,109,110,111,112,113,114,1
15,116,117,118,120,121,122,123,124,125,126,127,128,129,
130,131,132,133,134,135,136,137,138,139,140,141,142,14
3,144,145,146,147,148,149,150,151,152,153,154,155,156,1
57,158,159,160,161,162,164,165,166,167,168,169,170,171,
172,173,174,175,176,177,178,179,180,181,182,183,184,18
5,186,187,188,189,190,191,192,193,194,195,196,197,198,1
99,200,201,202,203,204,205,206,208,209,210,211,212,213,
214,215,216,217,218,219,220,221,222,223,224,225,226,22
7,228,229,230,231,232,233,234,235,236,237,238,239,240,2
41,242,243,244,245,246,247,248,249,250,251,252,253,254,
255,256,257,258,259,260,261,262,263,264,265,266,267,26
8,269,270,271,272,273,274,275,276,277,278,279,280,281,2
82,283,284,285,286,287,288,289,290,291,292,293,294,295
Sunflower seed 220
Syrup 129

T

Tabasco 80
Tahini 4,88
Tea 3,4,6,17,87,168
Thyme 7,8,9,215,264,287
Tomato 6,75,158,169
Turkey 9,285

V

Vegan 5,9,62,72,128,129,131,288

W

Walnut 3,4,6,7,8,31,53,64,137,188,192,269

Wine 3,49

Yeast 7,8,204,263

Yoghurt 4,50

Z

Zest 4,66

Conclusion

Thank you again for downloading this book!

I hope you enjoyed reading about my book!

If you enjoyed this book, please take the time to share your thoughts and post a review on Amazon. It'd be greatly appreciated!

Write me an honest review about the book – I truly value your opinion and thoughts and I will incorporate them into my next book, which is already underway.

Thank you!

If you have any questions, **feel free to contact at:** *author@hugecookbook.com*

Valeria Tyler

hugecookbook.com

Made in the USA
Monee, IL
03 February 2024